THE TRAPPERS PROMISE

Book One

Bronwyn Trotter

This novel is a work of fiction - Character's names and places, events and incidents mentioned for the purpose of setting the story, are either from the authors imagination or are used fictitiously. Any resemblance to persons, living or dead, is purely coincidental.

Publisher: Inspiring Publishers,
P.O. Box 159, Calwell, ACT Australia 2905
Email: publishaspg@gmail.com
http://www.inspiringpublishers.com

A catalogue record for this book is available from the National Library of Australia

National Library of Australia The Prepublication Data Service

Author: Bronwyn Trotter
Title: The Trappers Promise
Genre: Fiction
ISBN: 978-0-6484592-9-3

Forward

During the year 1832, the Black Hawk Indian Wars began in the United States. Benjamin Bonneville lead the first wagon train across the Rocky Mountains. Andrew Jackson was re-elected president, and two men, Calahan Cole and Joseph Beauford Jones, made their way to the mountains to hunt wolf. Soon after arriving, more men came to join them in the hunt for valuable fur the men call skins. Some years later, Calahan is married, and Sarah Cole is born.

This is a story of Courage, Survival, Secrets and Love…

This is Sarah's story…

Chapter One

It was early morning, the mountain itself seemed to be still asleep when a grey wolf loped out of the forest and stood on a boulder looking over the mountains and valleys stretching out before it. Its gaze became fixed on a spot further down the ridge where it could see smoke billowing from the chimney of a cabin. It opened its mouth, ran its tongue hungrily around the outside, then yawned. A loud rifle report reverberated over the mountain and faded away as it echoed down the ridge. The wolf bucked when whatever it was struck it in its side, causing it to turn its head sharply, but that was just a natural reflex, the wolf was dead before it fell from the boulder. "Good shot Fergus, that's a good skin …now hurry it up, will you? …we have to get down to the cabin." Joe Jones grinned at James Fergus as he watched him draw out his hunting knife from its sheath, then waited while Fergus rushed up the incline to skin his kill. Fergus though wasn't too pleased. He wished he shot the wolf in the head, because now, the skin wouldn't fetch nearly as much money with a bloody hole in it as it would if it were a clean skin.

Trappers had been gathering at the cabin for days to wait for news of the baby's birth. Although Joe's group of four only waited one day. Some of the men were sitting, others standing, when a loud cheer went up after hearing Calahan Cole's news. Calahan stood on the porch and proudly announced, "I have a daughter." He gazed out over the wild looking bunch of men crowded around in the clearing down from his cabin. Light from the men's campfire and burning torches created a surreal glow over the crowd. The men laughed and hugged each other as they patted each other on the back. Elizabeth had only been with Calahan a year, their female baby was the first baby born on the mountain, and the men were happy for Calahan and Elizabeth. Some men were overly excited, before the birth, bets were taken as to what sex the baby would be. For the baby's parents, the wait was over. But for the trappers that won the bet! they would have to wait until they returned to Cedar Creek to collect their winnings, there was no use for money on the mountain. Tomorrow would be soon enough for most of them to get back to trapping, tonight they would celebrate. Calahan peered into the darkness, smiled at the men, then, after watching them for a moment longer, turned and went back inside.

Joe was standing by the open fire when Calahan came in. "Congratulations Cal." Joe smiled warmly at his friend and they shook hands. Calahan thanked Joe, then letting go of Joe's hand went to the bedroom to see his wife and baby. Joe remained staring into the fire, his smile fading while pondering about this moment he thought should have been his.

When Calahan came back into the bedroom, Doctor Ronald Harris and his wife Gerda were still in the room tending to Elizabeth. Doc Harris was cleaning up, Gerda was making Elizabeth comfortable. Calahan sat on the side of the bed and looked lovingly at his wife. Elizabeth looked tired but happy, relieved too, that her ordeal was over. "I love you," Calahan whispered. Elizabeth looked lovingly up at him, "I love you too Cal." Calahan bent down and kissed her.

Outside, the trappers broke out bottles of whiskey and drank to the baby's health. Noise from the men grew louder as someone played a concertina, singing could be heard from inside the cabin. Calahan and Elizabeth smiled at each other. "What shall we call her?" Elizabeth asked while cradling her baby in her arms. "How about we call her …Sarah?" Calahan reached out and gently stroked his daughter on the side of her face. "I like Sarah very much, it is a beautiful name," Elizabeth agreed.

Two days later, after Doc Harris was satisfied Elizabeth was well enough to take care of her daughter and herself, and to avoid being attacked by wolves, six men escorted Doc and his wife down the mountain and back to the small township of Cedar Creek. The men returned to the mountain to resume trapping and hunting. It was summer and they wouldn't return to town again until winter snow forced them off the mountain.

After trapping started the small, picturesque township of Cedar Creek sprang up on the banks of the Red Cedar River. Boasting a population of just twenty-five to begin with, but not long after trapping started to pay, the population swelled on close to a hundred. The United Fur Trading Company set up a Trading Post, families started to arrive, people needed clothing and food, horses needed to be shod, sold and bought. They had a doctor and a dentist. A teacher came to town and a school was set up. The saloon always did a roaring trade. A Lumber Yard was started, timber for housing was required. The Ferguson Boarding House was built for those that didn't have a place of their own to stay. Cedar Creek grew to a reasonable size, several streets were created, homes were built and a Sheriff was appointed to keep the peace. When the Trapper's came off the mountain for winter, the township swelled by twenty and business soared. Calahan and Joe made their home in the Ferguson Boarding House and drank together at the saloon. When spring came around, they travelled back to the mountain and did it all over again.

That first year, when Calahan and Joe were the only men on the mountain, having come straight from serving in the cavalry, they claimed it for themselves. Later, when other men started arriving, Calahan and Joe divided the mountain into areas and set down rules. Both Calahan and Joe fought with men that came to trap after them. Men who thought they would change how things were done. Using nothing more than their fists, Calahan and Joe took it upon themselves to set them straight.

The winter that followed the hot summer was brutal, both men almost froze after a sudden blizzard closed in on them. Waiting too long before deciding to leave, the pass leading to and from the mountain became buried under mounds of snow and they found they couldn't get through. Blizzards brought freezing temperatures with them, so the two men set up camp. Almost being forced to give up, they stuck it out and when the snow was gone, they built a rough timber cabin with a dirt floor. A large open stone fireplace was built for warmth and cooking. The cabin was built to ensure both men never got caught out with early snowfalls again. This first cabin became Calahan's, and Joe, with Calahan's help, built his cabin further up on the High Ridge so he could trap a wider area.

The following winter when the snow came, neither man waited too long before they left their cabins and travelled down the mountain to the town of Cedar Creek.

After spending all winter in Cedar Creek, the trappers are eager to return to the mountain. Taking three full days to reach it, their first night is spent camped on the open prairie. Pulling along their packhorses loaded with supplies the whole of the next day before making their second nights camp in a place beside the river the men christened 'The Wells.' Deep, bottomless pools of water looking like wells form part of the river that flows from high up in the mountain.

The area surrounding the wells is open and grassed, with stands of tall trees surrounding both sides of the riverbank, creating a sheltered haven. The men's third days travel, see them moving away from the river and heading for the base of the mountain where they never fail to come under attack from wolves. This being the trappers first kill of the new season.

A day's ride, heading away from the trail taking the men up to the pass and on to their hunting grounds, is the South Side Camp, once used when wolves were plentiful on that side of the mountain. Here, Calahan and Joe built a fort like structure backing on to the rock face. High timber walls on three sides keep wolves out. Over the years, wolves became scarce around there, so the men stay away from the South Side Camp, preferring to hunt higher up on the mountain.

Heading on to their hunting grounds, the men make their way to three large caves where they camp inside with their horses, protecting themselves and their horses from further attack from marauding wolves. The caves came into their own as shelter, having been set up by the men with loads of firewood, food, pots and pans for cooking and blankets. The caves are the last camp when travelling back to the mountain and a godsend for the men when coming down at the start of winter.

A short ride after leaving the caves, they reach the pass. A long passage of rough terrain leading through sparse trees and boulders. Once across the pass, the men are well and truly alone. Spring, when the snow has thawed, makes it a much easier ride up to the Low Ridge where Calahan has built another cabin a short distance from his old one. His new cabin is more solid than the first, with a wooden floor, hewn from the many tall trees that grow on the mountain and along the edge of the river. As the river wends its way down the mountain, it flows across open flat land the men call 'The River Flats,' and on past the Low Ridge, making its way to the floor of the valley. Flowing on past high cliffs, it makes its way south to the township of Cedar Creek, then continues on its way beyond the town. The River Flats are one of the better areas on the Rocky Mountains for hunting, a mere three hours walk along the same Low Ridge as Calahan's two cabins. The rest of the trappers have chosen to make their camp on the ridge where Joe has his cabin. The High Ridge Camp as it is known is four full days solid trek further up the mountain. Rough timber cabins have been erected at this camp to keep the trappers out of inclement weather. Trapping is good around there, most of the time.

Further up, on the very top of the mountain where the air is colder and wolves are plentiful, is the High Country. Trapping up there is dangerous, and no man dare venture there on his own. Whenever trapping is done in the High Country, men travel in large groups and every man carries one spare bullet in his pocket. This bullet though is not for killing wolves. If a man were unlucky to become separated from the rest of the men and found himself surrounded by wolves, then he would use his bullet, on himself. A man would gladly put his gun to his head to avoid being eaten alive. Twenty men live almost nine months of the year on the mountain. Most of the twenty, have been trapping for more than ten years, each man watching out for the other. So far, no one has ever had to use their bullet.

It is much harder for the trappers when leaving the mountain in the winter. All twenty men and their packhorses loaded with skins and a few meagre supplies have to traverse the pass first before making it safely back down to the caves. Deep drifts of snow and blizzards almost always hamper their journey. Leaving Calahan's Low Ridge Camp at first light, they push themselves and their horses to make it to their first camp by nightfall. After leaving the caves, the men, once again, run the gauntlet of wolf packs at the bottom of the trail. Stopping only briefly to skin their kill, they race for the wells to camp for another night. The trappers then move out onto the open prairie to spend their last night before heading into Cedar Creek to get paid. More than ten uneventful years passed by, where men hunted and trapped, with skins being taken by the thousands.

Another man from Calahan and Joe's army days came to Cedar Creek but didn't join the trappers on the mountain. Major Jefferson Hardy claimed twenty thousand acres of land a few miles outside Cedar Creek so he could breed cattle and horses. There was money to be had in cattle and horse trading and over the years Major Hardy became a very rich man.

Major Hardy was engaged to Elizabeth when he arrived in Cedar Creek. Elizabeth was an elegant city woman from Philadelphia, and not wanting her to be inconvenienced while his ranch-house was being built, he left her behind when he came out west. When the ranch-house was finished, Major Hardy travelled back to Philadelphia to do two things. One, to secure buyers for his cattle and two, to bring his fiance' out to Cedar Creek. Elizabeth was young and sophisticated, and he was very much in love with her at the time and hoped they would be married while he was in Philadelphia this trip.

It was a well-known fact, before Major Hardy met and fell in love with Elizabeth, he had a son to a woman he had an affair with. But he wasn't concerned. He wasn't in love with the boy's mother. He was in love with Elizabeth. Major Hardy's son Frank, was two years old when his ranch was completed.

When both Major Hardy and Calahan travelled to Philadelphia at the same time, Calahan's only business was to find himself a wife. Except for Joe, the year Calahan went back to Philadelphia he had been trapping on the mountain longer than any of the other trappers. It was a lonely life living on the mountain, and he wanted company, female company.

While in Philadelphia, Major Hardy and Elizabeth found themselves attending the same function as Calahan, and so out of politeness, Major Hardy introduced Calahan to Elizabeth. The moment Calahan met Elizabeth he fell in love with her. At the same time, Elizabeth fell deeply in love with Calahan, so with some trepidation, she broke off her engagement to the Major. When

Calahan returned to the mountain he brought Elizabeth back with him as his wife. Major Hardy was furious with both Elizabeth and Calahan for their deceit. He developed a deep-seated hatred for Calahan Cole for stealing the woman he was in love with, and over the years his hatred continued to fester.

Elizabeth was a beautiful woman, and angelic, her long brown hair and pale skin made her appear delicate. She was kind natured and friendly to everyone she met, and every man on the mountain fell in love with her.

Elizabeth though, hated the mountain, but loved Calahan, so for a while she persevered with the rough living conditions. Calahan showed her how beautiful the mountain could be, but Elizabeth was adamant she wasn't going to keep on living in a one room dirt floor cabin. She begged Calahan to build her a new cabin with a wooden floor, a decent kitchen to cook in, a washroom for bathing because she was a lady, she wasn't going to bathe out in the open in the river where someone might see her. There were two separate bedrooms, one for them and one for the family they planned to have.

When they left the mountain for winter that year, Elizabeth was pregnant. Arriving in Cedar Creek for the first time, Elizabeth had to endure living with the trappers in the Ferguson House. She cried a lot her first winter, so to appease her and with help from the trappers, Calahan built their winter home in Cedar Creek.

The men fashioned Elizabeth a large cedar dining table, spending many hours painstakingly polishing the table until it gleamed. Elizabeth sent to Philadelphia for furnishings to furnish their new home. By the time the house was finished the following winter, the furniture had arrived, taking six months by wagons, but the wait was worth it. Twelve high back tapestry covered dining chairs were placed around the table in the formal dining room. A four-poster bed with a red velvet canopy adorned their bedroom. A green velvet high back winged chair stood in pride of place in front of the open fire. It was the ugliest chair Calahan had ever seen. He laughed when it was brought in and placed in front of the fire. But it proved to be a comfortable chair. He soon came to enjoy relaxing sitting in it. 'Mountain View Lodge' became the grandest house in town next to The Ferguson Boarding House. It was built from the same Cedar trees growing plentiful on the mountain and along the river. Elizabeth was happy and so was Calahan.

Calahan's first winter in Cedar Creek without Elizabeth was the hardest, and the loneliest. When Elizabeth caught a fever and passed away, their daughter was two years old and this was Calahan's first year as a lone father. He put his daughter to bed then sat in front of the fire where he wept for the woman he once loved and lost. The painting hanging over the mantle reminded him of her whenever he looked at it. Elizabeth's beautiful angelic face smiled down at him, causing his heart to ache for her.

Even though their time together was short, Calahan and Elizabeth had been deeply in love and he hoped when his daughter grew up, she would find the kind of love he experienced with Elizabeth. Trapping on the mountain took him away from Elizabeth so many times and he regretted not having spent more time with her. That first winter alone was when he decided to ask four men to make him a promise. But they had to make their promise on the mountain so it couldn't be broken.

Chapter Two

Five men huddled together around a blazing campfire trying to keep warm. This particular night was freezing, winter was fast approaching, and snow could be felt in the air. Each man had his fur coat pulled tightly around his body in a desperate bid to try and keep out the cold. The logs the men placed on the fire burnt fiercely, flames and sparks rose high into the sky, but the heat was still not enough to keep them warm. Calahan was talking and the other four were listening carefully to what he had to say. They didn't dare interrupt while he asked them to make him a promise.

"Goddamn it! …I can't do this on my own," he said sounding angry. "Even now she is independent and head strong, ...and I have no doubt she will call on you at times …she is going to cause you so much pain in your heart you won't be able to bear it ...I love her and I don't want anything to happen to her!" He stopped talking and put his head down, giving a lot of thought to what he wanted to ask the men sitting with him, but now he was thinking how he might make it clearer as to what he wanted them to promise.

"I need her to be taken care of ...I want you to promise me you will take care of her if anything should happen to me ...keep her safe and make sure she is happy ...teach her to shoot well and ride fast ...teach her how to hunt and how to trap ...she will no doubt make mistakes …a hell of a lot of mistakes, believe me … but don't interfere, let her learn from them." Calahan paused for thought. "There will be times when I know she will surely get hurt ...see she doesn't get hurt bad ...I need you four to promise me you will always be there for her." Keeping their heads bowed, the men listened without saying a word. "Promise me you will love her as you would your own …remember though ...she is not yours ...none of you can make her your own." He looked into the faces of each man, letting his eyes dwell a little too long on Joe. The four men kept their heads down, only lifting their eyes every now and then to look at Calahan. His next words became more serious. "Promise to take care of her until such time as she finds the one who can break your promise ...you can't choose him for her ...he has to be of her own choosing, it is the only way your promise can be broken." His gaze rested on each man when he spoke his last words. "But! ...he can't be someone from the mountain ...I know and you know all of the men here ....and we all know what they are like ...I don't want any of them for her ... promise me you will keep those animals away from her."

The men thought about making such a promise. A promise made on the mountain between trappers was a lifelong agreement they could never break. If the promise were to be broken by any one of the four, that man would be outcast from the rest of the men. He would be stripped of his weapons and forced to survive the mountain with nothing to defend himself with. That was the law set down by Calahan Cole and Joseph Beauford Jones when they first came to trap wolves. It was Calahan and Joe's mountain and no promise ever made on their mountain had ever been broken.

Having come straight from the cavalry, all five men sitting around the campfire that night became friends. It was while in the army Calahan heard about trapping. He heard the Fur Trading Company paid good money for wolf fur, and he and his friend Joe had no families to go home too, so they decided to make their way to the mountain to hunt. They were young and adventurous and had nothing to lose. "What the hell Cole, ain't nothin' going to happen to you ...unless of course there's something you ain't tellin' us!" Will Sloan was the first to speak. The youngest of the four men, having come to the mountain a year before this night to seek adventure, and instead found friendship with these men.

When he arrived in Cedar Creek along with Brent Garrett, both men had served as foot soldiers and both, having been forced to join the cavalry, hated being in the service. They reckoned killing Indians wasn't what they were cut out for, hunting wolf was more their style. When they heard Calahan and Joe were doing well out of trapping, they decided to try their own hand at it.

Calahan looked off into the darkness before answering, his face drawn with worry. "You never know what lies ahead Will, anything can happen, a day, a week, even a year from now, you know that better than most."

"Aye ...an' what if she chooses one of the men off the mountain herself an' all?" James Fergus was thinking about what Calahan said. Fergus is the same age as Calahan and Joe, an irishman who heard about the Indian Wars in America and travelled all the way from Ireland to join the fight. He proved himself on the battlefield and forged a lifelong friendship with the men he now sat alongside of. Fergus is a fatherly type, having taken Will and Garrett under his wing when they first came to the mountain. Teaching the two young men all there was to know about trapping and over the years Will and Garrett have become like sons to him. Calahan knows if anything were to happen to him, his daughter would be able to go to Fergus.

Calahan thought about what Fergus said before answering him. "She won't choose one of them Fergus, I'm sure she already knows what all the men are like." Calahan reflected on the men he knew from the mountain. Not caring how they looked, they became unkempt and dirty, they didn't see the need to wash when they were trapping. They used foul language when they spoke, and fought amongst themselves. They became wild, most forgetting almost everything they ever learnt to be civilized, Calahan didn't want that for her.

Garrett didn't speak, preferring instead to sit quietly to digest what Calahan asked of him. He is the quietest of the four, an affable man, his sense of humour keeps everyone sane during difficult times. Calahan knows Garrett will make her laugh and make her happy. Garrett is one man that hasn't yet lost all he learnt to be a decent man. He is a good shot with a rifle and knows how to fight. Garrett will be able to teach her how to protect herself.

Out of all the trappers that hunt on the mountain these four men sitting in front of him are the best of them. That is why he chose them to make his promise. Calahan loves being on the mountain, he loves the freedom it brings and the beauty that surrounds him. He wants his daughter to love it like he does. If anything should happen to him Sarah could not be in better hands. He knows these four men will promise him they will take care of her.

Calahan looked across at Joe. Joseph Beauford Jones is the wisest of the four and his best friend. Calahan was already an Indian guide for the cavalry when Joe joined up and he liked Joe the moment they met. Joe is smart and quickly rose through the ranks to become captain. Joe, he reckons, knows the mountain better than him. Joe is the best at trapping and he trusts Joe's judgement, he will teach her everything there is to know. Joe will be the self-appointed leader of Will, Garrett and Fergus. Joe, Calahan knows for sure, will keep his daughter level headed.

The men looked over at the little girl lying sound asleep wrapped in a thick wolf fur and blanket, her long brown hair spread out behind her.

The four men didn't hesitate. They made their promise that night on the mountain. Each man saying to Calahan, they promised to take care of the little girl if anything should happen to him. Each man in turn shook hands with him sealing their promise. The night they made their promise, Sarah Cole was three years old.

Life became easier for Calahan once the promise was made, allowing him to become more relaxed. If something bad were to happen to him now, he could die with the knowledge Sarah would be well taken care of.

Years went by with little or no trouble. Calahan's four friends, Joe, Fergus, Garrett and Will, have already taken on some responsibility for looking after Sarah, even though trapping further up the mountain takes them away from the Low Ridge most of the time.

Sarah, having turned seven, was at the clearing down from their cabin, using a stick to scratch in the dirt. While Calahan was at the wood pile chopping wood for their fire, he looked over at her and stopped swinging the axe. Sarah continued twisting and turning this way and that as she kept scratching her stick in the dirt. Calahan smiled and laughed at her as he leant on the axe handle. "What are you doing Sarah?" he called. Sarah didn't look up, she was concentrating hard on her scratching's. "I'm drawing Pa." Calahan looked puzzled. "Drawing!" he didn't know where she learnt to draw, she couldn't read and she couldn't write. That was something none of the men promised, or took the time to teach her. Still holding the axe in his hand, he went over to the clearing. "What are you drawing?" he asked, studying Sarah's scratching's. "I'm drawing the mountain ...see!" Sarah pointed her stick at a crooked upside-down shape she scratched in the dirt that went up in a rough peak to form what Calahan figured, looked like a mountain. "See Pa, there's the sun coming up over the mountain, and here...!" she pointed to another round shape with four crooked lines coming out from the bottom. A long, equally crooked line jutted out the back to form what looked like a tail. The head was long with pointy ears and jagged teeth. "*....Is a wolf!*" she announced proudly, then stood back so her Pa could admire her work.

Calahan watched on as Sarah bent down with her stick and scratched a crooked line underneath the wolf and the mountain. "And what is that?"

Sarah looked up at him questioning. "Don't you see Pa ...that's the river!" Calahan could see what Sarah tried to draw. They were both engrossed in her scratching's and didn't see the four men approaching.

"Hey Calahan!" Joe called when he was nearly past the cabin. Both Calahan and Sarah turned when they heard Joe call out. Sarah squealed with delight at seeing the men. Throwing away her stick, she ran, arms outstretched, straight for Joe. "*Uncle Joe!*" she squealed.

Calahan smiled when he saw the men and laughed at Sarah as she raced toward them giggling and calling to each man. Joe held his arms out wide as Sarah raced toward him. Her long curly hair bounced as her small legs carried her quickly to Joe. She held her arms out and Joe, bending down laughing, quickly scooped her into his arms. Sarah threw her arms around Joe's neck and hugged him. Smiling, Joe carried her back to Calahan. Putting her down when he got to the clearing, he let her show him her scratching's. Will, Garrett and Fergus came along and stopped in the clearing. All four men shook hands with Calahan.

Sarah hugged Will and Garrett and Fergus in turn and said hello to them. "Now where are we going to camp with this masterpiece of art here in our spot?" Joe winked at Calahan while Sarah explained to the men what her scratching's were.

"Uncle Joe you can still camp here." She quickly scuffed her drawings out with her feet and the men took their rucksacks off their back's and put them down in the clearing. Sarah much preferred having her uncles camp near their cabin than she did her scratching's. Her four uncles were far more important to her than some silly lines scratched in the dirt.

Trapping on the mountain is paying off. There are an abundance of wolves to hunt for their valuable skins. Sarah is always there alongside her father and is keen to help. When small the men took turns carrying her on their shoulders. They played games with her and taught her how to hold a rifle and throw a knife. At ten years of age she started carrying her own rifle. She has a keen eye and is a good shot. Sarah is happiest when she is with the men. The men make her laugh and have taught her how to hunt. They have taught her to shoot well.

Off hunting with her father and the four men, Sarah spotted a snake coiled around a branch above Garrett's head. Firing her rifle, she hit the snake, taking its head off. The bullet, travelled through the snake and into the branch sending splinters of wood all over Garrett. He ducked as the snake fell off the branch close behind him, causing him to call out to Sarah. "God-damn, Sarah Cole! ... you darn near shot me!" then smiling he added. "How come you missed?"

Sarah laughed as she approached Garrett. "I never miss what I'm aiming at uncle Garrett!" and kicked the dead snake with her boot to show him what she shot.

At night, as Sarah's eyes adjusted to the dark, her vision became sharper, enabling her to see the smallest of animals scurrying around in the underbrush close by. Sarah is always aware of her surroundings, she can hear a trapper sneaking through the trees and tell who it is before they appear. She knows the sound of their voices and reckons each man has his own scent, she has taken to sniffing the air and can tell who is near.

As the years slipped quickly by, Sarah, now fifteen, has been taught how to ride fast and can dismount from her horse just like the cavalry men that taught her. She can fire her rifle while on the run and not miss anything. None of the four men have ever made fun of her whenever she makes a mistake. Over time Sarah learnt how to trap and hunt better than most of the men.

Winter came too soon for Sarah, she hated having to leave the mountain to go to Cedar Creek, the town itself just doesn't interest her. The only thing about the town she does love is Mountain View Lodge. She is proud of how her Ma talked her Pa into building the two storey house and how she got all the trappers involved in building it. Her Ma, she was told, wasn't going to live with all the men in the Ferguson House, nor was she going to camp on the riverbank, not if she had her way. Sarah wasn't told everything about her Ma, particularly her relationship with Major Hardy. All she was told, was how kind she was, and Sarah has tried her best to emulate her mother by being kind to everyone too, but then not everyone is kind in return. She doesn't understand when someone in town says something about her being a stinking trapper.

It was cold outside that fateful night, snow had fallen on the mountain and wasn't far off falling in Cedar Creek. Calahan and Sarah sat in front of their fire keeping warm and talking. Her Pa sat in the green winged chair, she was seated on a foot stool at his feet wearing one of her pretty dresses.

Sarah stared at the painting above the mantle and saw how beautiful her Ma was. It had been Elizabeth that named the house Mountain View Lodge. Upstairs from the window in Calahan and Elizabeth's bedroom. 'Their Mountain,' Elizabeth once said, could be seen far off in the distance. To everyone else, the house is simply called, 'The Lodge.'

Sarah hates wearing the frilly dresses her Pa likes her to wear whilst they are in town, much preferring to wear her trousers, she can run and ride easier in them than a frilly dress. When she wears her pretty dresses, she can only walk around town visiting friends and sit like a lady all day. Sarah hates it, she becomes bored easily. She also hates how her body seems to have changed overnight from that of a girl into that of a woman.

Calahan didn't want to go to the saloon, his hands were aching badly, his fingers were twisted and gnarled, the pain when it came was excruciating. His hands ached worse when the weather turned cold. He no longer had the strength in them to open the steel traps for trapping. Once almost losing a finger when a trap snapped shut on him, only just managing to pull his hand back in time.

It came around to him having to ask Sarah to help him undo his buttons on his shirt and trousers so he could undress for bed. When he got dressed, she would button him up. He even had to get her to unbutton him so he could use the outhouse. Sarah would stand outside and wait for him to be done, and when he came out, she helped do him up again. Calahan hated getting his daughter to do this chore. Sarah should not have to be subjected to this humiliation, nor he felt, should he.

Having taken over doing most of everything now, as well as cooking and the cleaning of their cabin, Sarah sets traps, skins wolves and has learnt how to prepare the skins to get them ready for taking to the Trading Post. When they camp out, Calahan tells her what he needs her to do, and, without hesitation, she does what her father asks of her, set the trap here, make camp there, build a big fire, load the rifles. He can still pull the trigger if Sarah sets it up for him. She has become adept at her new-found responsibilities and because she loves her father, doesn't mind taking on the new role.

This night, at The Lodge, Sarah told her father he should go to the saloon, even if it was only for an hour, she said she didn't mind if he wanted to spend time with his friends. She poured him a glass of whiskey and Calahan drank it. The whiskey sent warm blood coursing through his body and down his arms to his fingertips. His hands didn't seem to hurt as much when he drank the whiskey. Sarah poured him another and told him once more to go, she would be alright on her own. Calahan kissed her on the forehead and said he wouldn't be long.

After her father left, Sarah made her way upstairs to her room and got ready for bed. The house was warm so she dressed herself in a light cotton night dress, brushed her waist long hair, blew out the lamp and got into bed. It wasn't long before she was fast asleep.

Chapter Three

Calahan came into the saloon to have a quiet drink with the four trappers. Joe, Fergus, Will and Garrett were seated at a table with a group of men playing Poker. Benjamin Crawley, the owner of the General Store where everyone bought their supplies is one of those men. The town only has one store and Crawley thinks he is the most important man in town. Crawley, a heavy drinker and gambling man, is also the lone father of a daughter just like Calahan. His daughter Millicent, is the same age as Sarah. However, Crawley is jealous of Calahan over what he owns. Calahan owns the grandest house in Cedar Creek and everyone, especially all the trappers, fuss over his daughter Sarah. Calahan stood back and waited until the game the men were playing ended, then sat down in the vacated chair opposite Crawley. Four other men joined in for a new game that didn't take long to weed out the lesser risk takers.

Calahan and Crawley sat facing each other across the table, surrounded by men who had already folded and those that were just curious to see how the game would end. The saloon is crowded, it is bitterly cold outside and everyone has come in to get warm and fill their bellies with whiskey or beer. The barkeep has been kept busy all night. A piano player is belting out a tune in the far corner of the bar room. Scantily dressed saloon girls mingle with trappers and ranch hands.

Ten thousand dollars sits heaped in the middle of the card table. Two yellowing parchments are perched on top of the pile of money. Playing cards lay face down in front of the two men. Calahan's fingers feel stiff, they ache badly and he is struggling to lift his cards to turn them over.

Joe, standing behind Crawley watches his every move. Fergus and Will are amongst other trappers and struggling to see what is going on. Garrett is standing behind Calahan, shaking his head slightly from side to side, while looking across the table at Joe. Neither Joe nor Garrett are smiling.

Benjamin Crawley watches Calahan closely. A bead of sweat broke out on Calahan's forehead, he is worried Crawley is going to win and take everything. Crawley reckons he has the game won, he is sitting on a potential royal flush. His cards, all Diamonds, lay face up on the table for everyone to see. All he needs is for Calahan to get a low card and he to get a Jack of Diamonds and everything on the table will be his. The crowd around the table has grown bigger as more drinkers gather around to watch the final outcome.

Crawley scowled at Calahan from the other side of the table. "Hurry it up Cole, I ain't got all night!" Calahan flexed his fingers and reached for his card. His fingers hurt when trying to pick them up, so he slid them over the back of the face down card, and using both hands, flicked his card over. The Nine of Clubs lay face up in front of him. Calahan's heart skipped a beat, the card was no use to him. Shocked gasps could be heard around the table. The game was now up to Crawley. 'Easy!' Crawley thought to himself, it was now or never. Flexing his fingers, Crawley flipped his card over and held his breath. Everyone standing behind the two players around the table stared open mouthed at the upturned card. A Jack of Diamonds lay face up in front of Crawley. Crawley won everything on the table.

After the initial loud gasps of shock coming from the crowd standing behind the two men ceased, the onlookers remained silent. Joe and the other three trappers didn't like what happened either. Calahan just lost Mountain View Lodge and all his money. The four men never expected Calahan would risk losing The Lodge they helped him build, and him working hard all year to get his skins, even enlisting the help of his young daughter Sarah to skin the wolves. Theirs was a partnership, her name was on the board along with her fathers as being the winners of The Pot for this year.

The Pot, set up by the trappers, to give them something to work for meant extra money. The winner of The Pot was the trapper who trapped or shot the most wolves over the course of the year and got their skins. The lucky winner had a thousand dollars cash on top of what they got paid for their skins to do what they liked with. Calahan lost everything he earnt from his skins and what he saved in the bank from years before. He and Sarah had nothing left.

Calahan was distraught, he reached for his yellowing parchment and staggering to his feet, pushed his way through the crowd of men and went to the bar. The men stepped back to let him through. Calahan was disgusted with himself for what he had done. He couldn't get the fact he lost all the money he ever made from trapping and lost Mountain View Lodge out of his mind. He and his daughter no longer had anywhere to live when they came to Cedar Creek for the winter. 'What have I done? How could I do this to Sarah?' Calahan's mind reeled as he staggered to the bar. There was his daughter, asleep in her bed at The Lodge, not knowing he had just lost her grand home. The home he lovingly built for her mother Elizabeth, the woman he loved with all his heart. He leant on the end of the bar and unfolded the parchment, his eyes brimmed with tears, the barkeep handed him the bottle of ink and a quill.

Crawley scooped the money and his deed for his store off the table and into his hat. He laughed out loud and yelled above the noise. "Drinks are on me!" The bar room erupted, hats were thrown in the air, chairs were pushed back, some falling over, every man in the saloon rushed to the bar, they didn't care who was buying, so long as they were getting their drinks for free.

Joe checked the cards for any possible signs of tampering, but couldn't find the Nine of Clubs. Thinking the card must be somewhere there on the table, he didn't give it another thought. Everything else looked above board. Crawley hadn't cheated, he just had a lucky break.

Calahan's hands were hurting badly. He gripped the quill in his crippled fingers as best as he could, put pen to paper and trying to stop his hands from shaking and so everyone could hear, read out aloud the words as he wrote them.

"I ...Calahan Cole, on this day 1st December 1859, do sign over the ownership of the above property known as Mountain View Lodge, to one..." Calahan paused and swallowed the lump rising in his throat. A tear ran down his cheek and he swiped it away before going on, "...to one ...Benjamin Crawley."

Calahan signed the document, gave the parchment a blow to dry the ink, then carefully folded it back up. Crawley walked over to Calahan at the bar with a huge smile spread across his face. He was now the proud owner of the grandest house in Cedar Creek. He stuck out his hand to take the document. Calahan reached past Crawley's outstretched hand and opening Crawley's coat, stuffed the parchment into Crawley's inside coat pocket and patted it down.

There was a lot of noise in the saloon, the bar was crowded to overflowing, some men were forced to stand outside on the boardwalk to drink. Men reached over each other to get their free booze. Spillage was evident on men's backs as drinks were passed over the top of drinkers. The four trappers stood back and watched what was happening between Calahan and Crawley. They were just close enough to Calahan to hear him read what he wrote on the parchment.

Joe watched with interest the moment Calahan carefully placed the document in Crawley's inside coat pocket. Crawley didn't get a chance to read the writing, the ink was barely dry when Calahan stuffed it in his jacket. Joe and the other three men watched Calahan pat Crawley's pocket down. They heard Calahan ask Crawley if he and Sarah could have time to get their belongings and move out. They even heard what Crawley said in answer to Calahan's request. Joe cringed when he heard it. "You can get the fuck out of my house now Cole, I don't want you or that whore girl of yours staying in my house another minute!" Crawley laughed in Calahan's face. Calahan was furious, he clenched his fists tight, even though his hands hurt to do so, it didn't matter, no-one was going to call his daughter a whore.

Calahan raised his right arm and struck out, throwing a punch straight at Crawley's face. Calahan's fist and Crawley's face didn't connect, his arm swung through the air past Crawley's head. Crawley saw the fist coming and ducked to avoid it. Calahan felt himself begin to fall as his arm carried on through the air. He tried moving his feet to gain some sort of balance but only managed to move his right foot because his left foot seemed to be stuck fast. A heavy weight bore down on top of his foot, holding it flat against the floor. Calahan frowned, then toppled forward. Unable to save himself from falling he went down between the drinkers standing at the bar. The side of his head struck the steel footrail at the bottom of the bar where drinkers put their feet. Calahan didn't feel the blow to his head, or the crack that opened his skull. He lay motionless on the floor, his head between the men's feet. They kicked him and tried to shove him out of their way so they could get to the bar to get their free drink.

Joe and a group of men saw the attempted punch. They saw Crawley duck and they saw Calahan fall. What they didn't see was Calahan's head hitting the footrail when he fell between the legs of the men standing at the bar. Joe frowned and studied his friend lying prone on the floor. All four men waited for Calahan to get up, but he didn't seem to be attempting to get up. "Looks like he's passed out from the drink!" Garrett said to Joe above the noise of the bar room. "Let's get him up!" Fergus yelled above the din. Joe was concerned with Calahan still lying face down on the floor. As he made his way to where Calahan lay he could see a pool of liquid he thought was spilt drink from the many men crowding around the bar under Calahan's head. Joe shoved his way through the throng of drinkers and knelt down beside Calahan. He turned him over and saw his hair saturated with blood.

Joe got down on both knees and put his head on Calahan's chest to listen for a heartbeat. He looked up in dismay at the three men standing around him and Calahan. "He's dead! ...Calahan ...he's dead!" Joe repeated as he stood up, disbelief evident on his face when he looked at his hand covered in blood. Men standing closest to Joe stopped talking and looked down at Calahan, then stepped back to give Joe room. The noise in the bar slowly died away and ceased altogether when word that Calahan was dead travelled around the room. The piano player stopped playing and the barkeep stopped pouring drinks.

Crawley, standing off to one side of the bar, heard what Joe said but couldn't care less about what happened to Calahan. "The fool fell over when he tried to hit me ...you saw it ...you all saw him try to hit me!" Crawley handed his hat with the money he won from the poker game to the barkeep. "Keep this safe for me ...I've got a house to go look at." He pushed past Joe and the crowd that had fallen silent and walked out, taking Calahan's hand of cards with him. Joe knelt back down beside his friend's body on the bar room floor.

As a crowd followed Crawley through the batwing doors and into the street, and before making their way to The Lodge, a Nine of Clubs card was dropped furtively on the dusty ground outside the saloon.

Chapter Four

Sarah was woken abruptly when her blankets were pulled swiftly back. Feeling her hair being pulled violently and being dragged out of bed caused her to become instantly awake. Her body hit the floor hard and she started to scream in protest. A man's gruff voice yelled. "Come on you stinkin' mountain bitch! get up! ...you don't belong in this house!"

Sarah tried to look at the man dragging her by her hair towards the staircase. He kept pulling her along as she screamed for her father. Stumbling as she was being pulled down the stairs, she quickly grabbed the railing to stop herself tumbling all the way down. She knew the man who was dragging her, she called him Mister Crawley out of respect.

Mister Crawley kept hold of her hair as he pulled her outside the front door. Sarah's head hurt, she felt her hair was going to be pulled right out of her head. The night air was freezing, her flimsy nightdress didn't allow her any warmth, she was barefoot and shivered from the cold. "Get out you bitch, this ain't your house no more!" Crawley let go of Sarah's hair as he thrust her down the front steps. She stumbled, then lay sprawled on her stomach. Dust and dirt flew up and covered her face, her nightdress tore along the bottom and the skin was torn off her hands and knees where she scraped along the ground.

Crouching on her scraped knees, Sarah looked up at Mister Crawley standing on her front porch. Benjamin Crawley stood with his hands on his hips while glaring down at her. Sarah knew Mister Crawley well, he was a nasty man when she and her Pa had to deal with him at his store, and she knew all about his liking for drinking and gambling.

"Where is Pa?" she screamed up at him as tears began to flow. "What have you done to Pa Mister Crawley?" Sarah screamed for her father, but he wasn't anywhere she could see.

"Your drunken' Pa is dead ...bitch! and now I own this house!" Crawley spat the words at Sarah. A crowd gathered to watch what was happening. The four trappers stood amongst a group of men who came from the saloon. They couldn't stop Crawley, he won the house fair and square. Sarah's eyes searched the crowd, singling out Joe as he pushed his way to the front.

"Joe ...what does Mister Crawley mean?" she asked as hot tears dripped off her chin. "What does he mean Pa is dead? he isn't dead Joe, he can't be dead." Great sobs escaped Sarah as she begged Joe for answers. "Pa was just going to go for a little while, he'll be back soon ...won't he Joe?" Sarah was confused and babbled. "It isn't true ...is it Joe?" Sarah's eyes pleaded with Joe as he came closer.

Joe was angry, he took off his thick fur coat and wrapped Sarah in it, then picked her up off the ground. "You son-of-a-bitch Crawley, you could have left her alone until morning!" Joe's anger could be heard in his voice as he glared up at Crawley.

"Why wait?" Crawley held his arms out wide and laughed down at them. "I won it fair and square, you all saw it, you were all there, I wanted that bitch out of my house, and now she's out!" he laughed again.

Sarah collapsed in Joe's arms. "Joe, tell me it isn't true," she begged, as her tears mixed with the dust on her cheeks. "I'm sorry Sarah," was all Joe could muster as he lifted her up in his arms, and carried her off to the Ferguson House. The rest of the trappers crowded around Joe and followed him.

Joe carried Sarah inside and took her to one of the rooms used by two of the trappers. He ordered the men to clear out their belongings and the men hurriedly collected their gear and two other men made room for them in their rooms. "This room," Joe told them, "will be Sarah's for however long she needs it." Joe lay Sarah on the bed and sat with her while she cried. He ordered one of the men to get warm water to wash Sarah's hands and knees. After he cleaned Sarah up, he put her under the blankets where she curled up in a ball and cried herself to sleep.

It was the middle of the night when an ear-piercing scream shattered the silence of the house. Sarah woke up screaming for her father and the men came rushing out of their rooms to see if they could help. Sarah wouldn't stop screaming so Joe sent Fergus to fetch Doctor Harris. Doc Harris came hurrying over to the house and gave Sarah a sleeping draught in warm milk. She refused to drink it until he told her it was only warm milk to help her relax. She drank it down and slept the rest of the night.

The next morning, when she came out of her room, she stepped into a room full of men busily eating breakfast and talking. They stopped eating when they saw Sarah. A silence descended over the room as the men stared at her. Sarah stood in the doorway in her flimsy night dress, her long hair matted all over her head and searched for Joe.

"Joe! …Sarah's up!" Garrett's eyes remained on Sarah when he yelled loudly to Joe's back. Joe was standing at the fire just about ready to pour himself a mug of coffee. The men sitting around the table kept staring at Sarah. "Joe," Sarah said tearfully. When Joe saw her, he quickly slammed the coffee pot down and went to her, pulling her back into the room so fast her feet barely touched the floor, then taking a blanket off the bed wrapped it around her shoulders. "Stay her for a moment Sarah, I'll be right back." Joe left the room and confronted the men.

"None of you men get any ideas about what you just saw, if any of you ever lay a hand on Sarah you will answer to me ...understood? …she is just a child who has lost her Pa, now move over and make a place at the table for her." The men scrambled to grab their plates and mugs, and moved out of the way. A few of the men, already finished eating, got up from the table, grabbed their hats and went outside. They had work to be done and were ready to ride to Major Hardy's to begin branding his cattle. None of the men discussed what they saw with each other, not right then. They could see Sarah wasn't a child, she was a young girl in a woman's body, they had all seen through her flimsy nightdress, there was no mistaking what they saw. Sarah was unaware of the effect she had on the men that day in that house.

Joe went back to Sarah's room and brought her out to the table. Sarah sat at the table with the blanket wrapped tightly around her.

Then, glancing around at all the men watching as a plate of food was placed in front of her, she burst into tears, and hurrying back to her room, stayed there for the rest of the day and all that night.

Garrett and Fergus were told to stay with Sarah while Joe took Will to Crawley's General Store. He had to get Sarah something to wear and Crawley's store was the only store he could go to. It was a huge building that sold everything from tin pots to lady's makeup. Crawley was alone and standing behind the counter when the men walked in. Joe and Will didn't speak to Crawley, instead they made their way straight around to the men's and boy's clothing section. Joe picked out a small pair of cream coloured trousers that he thought might fit Sarah. Will selected a pale blue shirt and a pair of brown boots. They didn't know about women's underwear so they didn't bother with it.

Taking the items they selected to the counter, Crawley added up the cost. "These for that bitch you got sleepin' in your house?" he sniggered. "Whose bed she in?" Crawley began to laugh. "I bet that's real sweet for you men!" He thought he was being funny, but Joe didn't.

Joe reached over the counter, grabbed Crawley by the front of his shirt, pulled his arm back quickly and drove his fist into Crawley's face. When he let Crawley go Crawley fell backwards, crashing into the shelves behind the counter. Tins of fruit and coffee fell off the shelves and crashed around him, one clipped him on the shoulder on its way to the floor, Crawley's nose exploded in a fountain of blood.

"You son-of-a-bitch Crawley!" Will had to hold Joe back. "It isn't bad enough you threw her out in the cold, you left her with no goddamn clothes, I've got a good mind to go over there right now and get her things!" Crawley held his hand over his bloody nose as blood oozed between his fingers. "You step one foot in my house and I'll get Sheriff Clementine to arrest you for trespass, see how you like that!" Joe decided Crawley wasn't worth getting arrested for. He threw some coins on the counter, grabbed the clothes and stormed out, slamming the screen door so hard it almost fell off its hinges.

Joe couldn't understand why Crawley spoke the way he did about Sarah. Crawley's daughter Millicent was the same age as

Sarah, and Joe wondered if Crawley would like it if the men said things about her, Joe didn't think he would.

When Joe and Will got back to the house with the clothes, Garrett and Fergus were anxiously waiting for them. They had been pacing the floor and were glad to see Joe and Will come back.

"Geezers Joe," Fergus drawled in his thick Irish accent. "The undertaker was just here an' all." Joe looked at the men, Fergus and Garrett both appeared to be upset, worried looks furrowed their brows. "Crawley took some of Calahan's belongings to him last night and told him to bury them with Calahan, but the undertaker brought them here just now and gave them to Sarah." Joe listened to what Fergus was saying. "Where is Sarah now?" he asked.

"She's in her room, she's cryin' again Joe, she's got her father's things and she's cryin'." Fergus pointed to her door. "We didn't know what to do Joe, so we thought it best to wait for you." Garrett added as Joe went to Sarah's bedroom door. Joe held his hand on the doorknob and looked back at the men. As he looked at the worried faces of his three friends, he wondered just how they were going to manage to keep the promise they made to Calahan all those years ago.

Joe stepped through the door into Sarah's room. Sarah was lying on the bed, curled up under an oversized fur coat clutching her father's hat. Joe saw Calahan's rifle leaning against the foot of the bed and the sheath holding Calahan's hunting knife hanging on the bedpost. He sat on the edge of the bed and put his hand on Sarah's shoulder as he had done the night before.

"Sarah, darlin, it's Joe," he soothed. Sarah didn't open her eyes but answered him. "Go away Joe ...leave me alone." Keeping his hand resting on her shoulder, Joe glanced over at the bedroom window, seeing it pushed up a few inches, letting cold air blow in, making the room cold. "I'm not going away Sarah, if you need me, I'll be right outside." He stood up to go. "I don't need you Joe ...I need my Pa!" she sobbed again. Joe went to the window and closed it, then sat back on the bed. "If I could bring him back Sarah, I would, but I can't ...we all miss him too." There was no answer, just the sound of sobbing. Joe left the room.

Chapter Five

"When are they burying Calahan?" Joe wanted to know when he stepped up to the fire. He picked up his mug and the coffee pot and started to pour himself some coffee. He felt like something much stronger but settled for the hot liquid. Joe held the pot in the air where it hovered over his mug as Fergus answered him. "Tomorrow Joe ...will Sarah be at the burial do you think?" Fergus asked.

"Of course she will be there, chri'sake Fergus, Calahan's her father, she'll be there alright!" Joe snapped back at Fergus's seemingly stupid question. "And we will be there with her …all of us!" he poured his coffee and slammed the pot back on the stove in disgust at Fergus and the very thought of Sarah not attending her father's burial.

"I guess this means we are responsible for her now Joe?" Will stepped up beside Joe and took the pot off the stove. Shaking the pot vigorously, he could tell it was empty. It had fallen to him again to refill the pot so he could make more coffee for those men who hadn't had any yet. It seemed to him, making coffee was all he was any good for these days.

Joe glanced sideways at Will when he thought his question was as stupid as Fergus's, but he didn't curse Will. "That's right Will, the four of us are responsible for her now, just like we promised." Joe didn't know how the hell the four of them were going to handle the responsibility of taking care of Sarah now she was fifteen years old and almost certainly a young woman.

Nineteen trappers stood around the hole in the ground, the mound of dirt keeping some of them from being able to see the wooden coffin sitting beside the hole. It was pouring with rain and everyone was soaked through to their skin and shivering with cold. The only one that didn't seem to notice the rain and cold was Sarah.

Almost all of the folk from town attended the burial, a few had been close friends of Calahan's. The Livery and Stable owner Archibald Hammond and his wife Patrice were there with their daughter Sissy. Ham as he liked everyone to call him was the towns Blacksmith. He took care of the trapper's horses, as well as everyone else's and was well respected in town. When Sarah was born Ham and Patrice didn't have children of their own, being friends with Elizabeth, Sarah's mother, they came to adore Sarah. When their own daughter Sissy came along two years after Sarah, they still made time for her. Patrice was expecting her second baby and was due any day but she still felt she should attend the burial for Sarah's sake.

Doctor Ronald Harris and his wife Gerda were there too. Gerda was of German descent and Sarah when she was a little girl liked the way Gerda sounded when she spoke. 'Doc' the trappers and everyone else in the county called him, met Gerda at the Sorbonne in Germany where they were both studying to become doctors. They married before Gerda finished her studies and he brought her back to America. Later on, when they found she was unable to conceive, they resigned themselves to never having children of their own.

Fifteen years before this day, when Calahan and Elizabeth left Cedar Creek that spring to go back to their cabin to have their baby, Doc and Gerda travelled all the way to the mountain. Calahan paid Doc well to go with them. It meant leaving Cedar Creek without a doctor, but still he went. It was the only time Doc ever set foot on the mountain. When Doc delivered Sarah into the world, Gerda was thrilled. Sarah became the daughter she could never have. When Elizabeth passed away from fever she was at the cabin and Doc had not been sent for. Although it would have taken four days for someone to come for him and another four for him to get to the cabin, he would have gone, if he had been asked. Elizabeth didn't survive two weeks with the fever, she was buried on the mountain in a clearing not far from the cabin she grew to love. Doc always regretted never being asked to go, even so, Doc and Calahan had remained firm friends.

Dave and Martha Henderson were there too. They were new to the town only having arrived there a few months before the trappers came to town for the winter. The Henderson's had been travelling the country looking for a quaint little town to raise a family and finally, settled on Cedar Creek. Although they were yet to have any children, they went to the burial out of respect for the young girl.

Major Hardy attended, having served in the cavalry alongside Calahan and Joe and many of the trappers. He had many angry clashes with Calahan over the years, none more so than when he and Calahan had gone to Philadelphia on business all those years ago, when Calahan stole his fiance' from him. He has never gotten over what Calahan did. Major Hardy was thinking about Calahan's daughter being left alone on the mountain with nineteen trappers. He thought Calahan Cole had paid the ultimate price for his betrayal and now his daughter would pay as well. Both Major Hardy and Calahan had never been friendly toward each other, but he went to the burial out of respect for a man he served in the cavalry with just the same.

Some of Major Hardy's men were there too, most having known Calahan as well as anyone. Foley and Brady Andrews were two young men who came out west as greenhorns and found work straight away with Major Hardy. They not long arrived in Cedar Creek and while walking down the street, neither of them looking where they were going, Foley was staring across the street at the saloon where he and Brady were headed, and Sarah was heading for the corrals to watch the men break in some horses. Sarah came running around the corner from the direction of The Lodge and barrelled straight into Foley. Sarah fell on her backside on the street, Foley got knocked backwards but stayed upright. Sarah was looking at Foley's feet when she spoke angrily at him. "Why don't you look where you are going? you stupid goddamn..." Sarah stopped herself short of cussing when her gaze went up to his face and seeing he was new in town. Foley stared down at her for a moment. "You were the one running blindly up the street ...so why don't you look where you are going?" he said down to her, then held out his hand to help her up. Sarah didn't know him, so took one look at his outstretched hand, ignored it and got herself up off the ground. She quickly brushed the dirt off her trousers and pushed past him. Foley turned to watch her run up the street. Brady, unable to speak, stared at Sarah then over at Foley. Foley was smiling when he looked back at Brady. They didn't know Sarah was Calahan Cole's daughter at the time. Both young men liked Calahan, thinking him a fair man when they worked with him branding cattle and breaking horses for Major Hardy. Foley was twenty years old at the time of the burial, Brady seventeen, and wherever Foley went, Brady wasn't far behind. Foley took full responsibility for his younger brother. Because Brady couldn't speak, he liked to keep Brady close to him at all times.

There was someone else at the burial that day too, someone Sarah had never met.

Sarah stood beside the coffin, Joe and Fergus stood either side of her, Will and Garrett stood behind her. To the other attendees it looked as though the four men were protecting her. Sarah wore the clothes Joe and Will bought from Crawley's store. On her head, she wore her father's hat, it was big and sat down over her head, almost covering her eyes and ears, her eyes were red rimmed from crying.

Rising early, Sarah found the clothes on the chair beside her bed. She got dressed and pulled the boots on, everything fitted perfectly, if not a little too snug. The shirt accentuated her womanly breasts, the trousers pulled slightly over her hips. She picked up her father's hat and sat it on her head, then got the sheath holding her father's hunting knife and did the strap up around her waist. The strap wound around her waist three times and the knife was heavy. Sarah didn't care how she looked, these things belonged to her Pa and she was determined she was going to wear her Pa's things. She looked at herself in the full length mirror the men had taken from the washroom and put in her room for her. Her face was pale and drawn, she looked tired, her eyes had dark circles under them. The hat was much too big for her, the knife was far too large and heavy for her to carry, hanging well below her knees. All the things she wore made her look frail and small.

Sarah stepped out of the bedroom that morning and walked across to the table where the men were having breakfast. The men stopped eating and stared at her, they said nothing, quickly putting their heads down and commenced eating again lest Joe had something to say to them for looking too long at her. Sarah sat down at the table and Joe put a plate of food in front of her. There was one egg, a piece of bacon and a piece of bread on the plate. Sarah stared at the food, she hadn't eaten since earlier the night her father went to the saloon and hadn't come home, she pushed the plate away.

"You eat something Sarah, it won't do you no good not eating." Joe stood behind her chair, he reached over and pulled the plate back in front of her, Sarah pushed it away again. Joe pulled it back while the men watched from the corner of their eyes at what was happening. Sarah's face crumpled and she began to cry, she sat quietly while tears ran down her cheeks. "Eat something Sarah," Joe pleaded softly. "I don't want to eat anything!" She said through her tears. Joe didn't want to get into an argument with her so she ate nothing.

Now they were at the cemetery standing in the pouring rain. Preacher Barnes, said a few words and the coffin was lowered into the hole, Sarah didn't stop crying the whole time. The grave diggers began to fill the hole in and everyone started to leave. Joe took Sarah's hand and she reluctantly left the cemetery with the trappers.

Everyone attending the burial went back to the Ferguson House. The women folk of those men that attended prepared a supper for everyone. There were drinks for the men and tea and coffee for anyone who wanted it. The table was set with an assortment of cakes and cookies, and an abundance of hot food supplied by the town.

Sarah went straight to her room without stopping to eat. Her room, Joe told her, was hers for how-ever long she needed it. She closed the door and sat on the edge of the bed, dripping wet and feeling miserable. After a moment of feeling sorry for herself she took off her father's hat and hung it to dry on the bedpost. She unwound the sheath from around her waist that held her father's knife and lay it on the bed.

Pushing open her bedroom window facing out onto the side of the house, Sarah climbed out, then slid to the ground. No-one saw her or heard her go, they were too busy talking about Calahan and eating all the food in the other room. They didn't see her run down the trail to the river flowing below the town. She ran along the riverbank until she came to the track leading up through the trees to the back of Ham's Livery and Stable. She crept along the wall of the Livery and came out near the corrals. The horses saw her and ran around inside the corrals to get out of her way. Sarah darted along the fence, past the corrals shelter and ducked through the gate to the cemetery. She ran up to the rain sodden mound of dirt now covering her father's coffin and sat down beside it.

After sitting down on the soggy ground, Sarah pulled her knees up in front of her and wrapped her arms around her legs. She was there for an hour before she was missed back at the house. Joe took a plate of cakes and a cup of tea and knocked on the bedroom door. Sarah didn't answer, he knocked again and listened. Thinking maybe she was asleep he opened the door and went in.

He saw the wet hat on the bedpost and the knife lying on the empty bed, the bedroom window was wide open and rain poured in wetting the floor. Joe pulled the window shut and storming out of the room, threw the cup and plate on the table.

"She's gone damn it ...Sarah's gone!" Joe thought they were off to a bad start if they were going to take care of Sarah. Everyone stopped what they were doing and stared at Joe.

"Where Joe? ...where would she go in this weather?" one of the women wanted to know.

"I think I have a pretty good idea where she is, Will, Fergus, come with me, Garrett you come too." The four men grabbed their hats and rushed out of the room.

A few of the other men deciding they would go too, hurriedly put on their hats and coats and followed. The large group of men walked up the main street through the pouring rain with Joe leading the way. When they got to the cemetery gate, they could see a small figure sitting next to the mound of freshly turned earth. Sarah, soaking wet and shivering, saw the men coming and held up her hand to stop them before they could get all the way through the gate. On seeing her holding up her hand the men stopped abruptly and stayed where they were.

"Sarah, you're just going to catch fever if you stay there!" Joe was standing in front of the other men with his hand on the gate.

"Good!" she cried back at him. "Then you can bury me with my Pa!" Joe looked horrified at her. "Don't be stupid Sarah ...come on!" he begged her.

"Leave me alone, I'm not leaving ...you try to make me leave, I'll just keep coming back, so go away." Rain soaked her clothes and she tried to blink the rain out of her eyes. As she looked at the group of men standing outside the gate, she pulled her legs up closer until her knees were against her chest and wrapped her arms more tightly around her legs.

"What are we going to do Joe?" Will was worried Sarah would catch fever. If that wasn't bad enough the men all felt cold and were soaking wet. Joe kept his gaze on Sarah, he felt sorry for the lonely figure of a young girl mourning the loss of her father.

"Leave her there for just a bit, let her be with her Pa, she'll get cold and hungry then she'll come away." Joe turned and headed to the corral for shelter. The other men followed, and standing huddled under the shelter to keep dry, watched Sarah sitting by her father's grave. Joe felt helpless, Sarah looked so small and alone, he felt a lump rise in his throat and swallowed hard. He wouldn't allow himself to cry, this wasn't the time, he could wait. If this was how it was going to be, he reckoned it was going to be damn hard for him to fulfill the promise he made to his friend Calahan.

Sarah sat looking at the mound of dirt, she talked to it, she asked it why? she wanted to know how this could happen, she blamed herself, she said she was sorry she was the one that made him go to the saloon that night, it was all her fault and now he was gone. "I'm so sorry Pa." Her sobs were loud and pitiful. She remained in the pouring rain beside her father's grave for what seemed to the men like hours, getting more than soaked to her skin, her bones started to ache, she was frozen but she wasn't going to leave.

Joe and the men kept watching. "Fuck it Joe! we have got to do something before she catches her death!" Garrett very rarely cursed but he was feeling the cold too and wanted to go back to the warmth of the house. He may have trapped the mountain but he was no fool and got himself in out of the weather, a man could die from fever if he wasn't careful. "We can't leave her there, she's not going to come in." Will's teeth chattered as he spoke to Joe. "I'll go get her," Will shivered as he was about to head out into the pouring rain. Joe grabbed Will by the arm to stop him while he kept watching Sarah. "Just a bit longer, then I'll go get her."

Chapter Six

Frank stood huddled amongst the men in the corral shelter, watching Sarah sitting beside the mound of wet soggy earth, getting wetter and looking freezing and his heart went out to her. He knew what it was like to lose someone you loved. Frank thought back to when he lost his mother a few months before he turned sixteen. His mother had been good to him and he loved her dearly. He had been just like Sarah Cole, unable to be consoled.

He knew it would take time for Sarah to get over her father's death. Frank didn't know anything about Sarah, having left Cedar Creek with his mother when he was three years old and Sarah hadn't been born yet. Now that he was back living with his father Major Hardy, he attended the burial of a man he didn't know simply because his father made him go out of respect for a cavalry man. Frank didn't want to go to a burial for someone he didn't know, but now he was glad he had. He watched Sarah for a little longer and decided he couldn't stand by and let her catch her death, he had to do something.

Suddenly pushing past the men, Frank darted out into the rain. He jumped the low picket fence bordering the cemetery and running over to where Sarah was sitting, sat down opposite her in the mud and crossed his legs. Sarah saw him but kept crying. Although Frank couldn't see her tears for the rain wetting her face, he could hear her sorrowful cry. Frank decided Sarah was pretty even when she was crying and soaking wet. Sarah shivered all over, her body shook violently. She peered through her rain-soaked tears at a boy who plonked himself down in front of her at her Pa's grave. A boy who seemed to think he had a right to make fun of her.

Joe and the other men watched as Frank jumped the fence. "What the fuck is he doing?" Fergus asked Joe. Joe stopped Will from going to Sarah but hadn't been standing close enough to Frank to stop him from going. "I don't know, just watch." Joe was a patient man, he had all the time in the world and felt there was no need to hurry Sarah. Even if he himself was feeling miserable, he was happy to give Sarah time to mourn her Pa. The men pulled their coats tighter around their bodies and stood in the shelter watching as Frank and Sarah sat facing each other.

Sarah glared at Frank, water ran in her eyes and down her face and she tried to blink the water away. 'Who does he think he is?' she thought, wanting him to go away and leave her alone, but it looked to her like he wasn't going to go anywhere.

"Hello Sarah Cole, my name is Frank Mason, I'm really sorry about your Pa." He kept his voice low so as not to frighten her into thinking he was a mad man. Water streamed off Frank's head and ran into his eyes, he blinked as he focused on Sarah's face. Sarah continued to sob. "Go away!" she yelled at him. "I don't want to go away, I am going to sit here until you go too." Frank was drenched, his curly hair had gone straight and was plastered to the sides of his face, he spat water out of his mouth. The rain seemed to get heavier after he sat down. He pulled his jacket tightly around himself to try and keep out the cold.

Sarah studied this boy who called himself Frank Mason. She didn't know anyone by the name Mason in Cedar Creek. His hair was dark, almost black and it hung over his ears and over his collar. He had dark blue eyes like hers and a thin nose, his mouth was closed tight while he tried to keep from swallowing water pouring down his face. Frank could see Sarah studying him.

"I'm not going," Sarah said and kept crying. She just wanted to be left alone with her Pa, couldn't he see that, she thought through her heartache.

"Well, if you are not going, I'm not either," Frank said quietly. He studied Sarah when everyone was standing around the grave during the burial service. Noticing how pretty she was, even with her hat sitting right down over her eyes and ears, he felt a thrill run through his body, and was convinced it wasn't from being wet or cold.

Sarah's long brown hair, he reckoned would be curly when it wasn't wet, now it hung limply down her back and over her shoulders, her eyes were red from crying but he was sitting close enough to her that he could see they were dark blue like his. Her nose was small and her mouth was too. He reckoned her lips would be pink if she weren't so cold, they looked soft and inviting.

Now that he was sitting in front of Sarah, he didn't know what to say except maybe try and get her to go in out of the rain. Neither of them said anything for a long time, the sound of the rain and Sarah's sobs the only thing that could be heard. Frank began to shiver, Sarah cried some more.

Sarah finally broke the silence. "You don't know me Frank Mason and you didn't know my Pa ...so why would you want to sit here and get all wet?"

Frank shrugged his shoulders and tried smiling. "No, I don't know you, but I thought it was the proper thing to do and well…" Frank paused to try and come up with some brilliant excuse for sitting in the pouring rain looking stupid, but instead, came up with the stupidest most lame thing anyone could say at a time when sympathy was called for. "It looked like it could be a lot of fun sitting in the pouring rain and getting soaking wet." He shrugged his shoulders again but knew it was the most stupid thing he could have said. Sarah glared at him. "You are a fool Frank Mason if you think this is meant to be fun!" Sarah spat water out of her mouth, looked over at the mound of dirt next to her, and sobbed.

"Well what does that make you? You are sitting here looking like a fool too." Frank tried to make light of what he already said but realized it sounded like he was just being nasty. He went on digging himself into a bigger hole than the one that housed Sarah's father's coffin. "Why do you want to sit here and get soaking wet when your Pa is lying there, under the ground, all nice and dry?" he moaned, regretting saying his last comment the moment he said it. Everything he was saying was coming out all wrong. It wasn't how he wanted his introduction to Sarah to go. He looked sadly over at her.

Sarah's eyes widened. "You son-of-a-bitch …Frank Mason!" Sarah cursed for the first time ever, her Pa would never have liked her to curse. "Go away, you stupid boy …or I'll hit you!" she held up a fist and bellowed.

"Boy! ...I'm not a boy!" Frank laughed at her insinuation that he was a boy. He was eighteen and regarded himself a grown man. "I'm a man!" Sarah looked at Frank and clenched her fists tighter, she didn't care if he was a man, she didn't want him sitting there, it was her Pa buried here, not his.

Joe and the men couldn't hear what Frank and Sarah were saying to each other. They continued to watch the exchange between the two now drenched couple. They looked like they were talking, at least to Joe and the other men something seemed to be happening. Joe hoped Frank might be able to get Sarah to come in out of the rain. The group of men kept watching and waiting.

Frank noticed Sarah clenching her fists. "Go ahead, why don't you hit me?" He was sorry for what he said but still tried to make her angry, thinking if he could make her angry, she would be over her loss sooner and sitting in the rain might end.

It worked for him. After days of feeling miserable and then angry when his mother died and left him all alone, he let his anger go by putting on a pair of boxing gloves and punching his fists into the punching bag hanging in the gymnasium at school. He kept punching the bag until he could hardly stand up. Finally leaning against it exhausted, he cried until he could no longer cry. When he stopped crying, he began to feel better. After that he found as each day passed, getting over his loss became easier.

Frank didn't know his father at all when he returned to Cedar Creek but was welcomed back to the ranch with open arms. By the time the trappers came back to town, he had settled in to life on a cattle and horse ranch. The day Sarah buried her father was a sad day for her but one of happiness for Frank. Frank was aware his life changed forever the day he met Sarah.

Sarah stared at Frank in anger, squeezed her lips tightly together, scowled at him and clenched her hands into tight fists. "Go on Sarah Cole, you want to hit me ...so go ahead ...hit me!" Even though Sarah felt her anger growing and her chest rose and fell as her breathing became more rapid, she didn't budge. Frank's eyes softened, his voice quietened. "Why don't you hit me?" he asked, looking at Sarah sadly.

"What!" Sarah had been studying Frank and was no longer listening to what he was saying. Frank said he was a man but to her he didn't look like a man, he looked more her age. Sarah was confused by this boy/man sitting in front of her, she blinked back her tears, feeling she just wanted her father.

"Hit me, you know you want to ...you're mad at your Pa for leaving you …aren't you? He shouldn't have left you, should he? ...your Pa is dead and he isn't coming back!" While Frank went on goading Sarah, Sarah grew angrier. Suddenly springing forward on her knees, she caught Frank off guard. "You stupid, goddamn...!" for a split second she was going to call him a man, but changed her mind "*...boy!*" she bellowed and struck out with her fist.

Frank didn't see it coming, Sarah punched him on the face, blood spurted from his mouth when his tooth cut the inside of his lip. He spat blood while Sarah continued hitting him around the head with her fists. Both sides of his head were getting a pummeling, causing him to put his hands up to ward off the blows as she opened her hands and started slapping him. Sarah kept slapping and crying. Frank let her keep going until she started to weaken and her sobs became quieter. Losing her balance and starting to fall, landing hard against Frank, her arms went over his shoulders. She clung to him with her arms around his neck. Frank wrapped her in his arms and held her.

Sarah leant against him with her head on his shoulder while she sobbed uncontrollably. Frank kept his arms around her, holding her tight, soothing her while she continued to cry. Even though his body shivered from being soaked to the bone and his face stung from her slaps, he waited for her to quieten. He didn't want to leave her, not yet.

"Are you ready to go in now?" Frank asked when she had quietened. Sarah pushed herself away from Frank and sat back on her heels. Frank couldn't help noticing how her shirt clung to her body. Sarah's breasts stood out from the cold and they were right there in front of him. Sarah didn't seem to notice Frank looking at her.

"I'm ready to go in," she said. Even though she felt her heart was breaking for her Pa, she had to go, she was freezing. Frank got to his feet and held out his hand. Sarah took Frank's hand and he pulled her to her feet. He took off his wet jacket, put it around her shoulders then pulled it across in front of her, doing up a button to hold it in place.

"It might keep you a little warmer," he said trying not to draw attention to Sarah's wet shirt. Frank's jacket was drenched and didn't make Sarah feel any better, but she liked the fact he gave it to her so didn't mind. Right then Sarah was sorry she punched and slapped him, his lip was cut and his cheeks were pink where her slaps landed. Sarah looked sadly into Frank's eyes. Frank reached for Sarah's hand again and took her hand in his. Holding hands, they walked together through the cemetery gate and across to the shelter where the men were waiting. The men stood silent, watching as Sarah belted into Frank, their mouths hanging open in disbelief, but instead of interfering, they stayed where they were.

"Sarah's ready to go now." Frank's teeth chattered as he handed her over to Joe. Joe took her hand and without saying another word the group walked back to the Ferguson House.

Frank stood alone in the pouring rain and watched them walking along the street. He felt a lump rise in his throat, Sarah looked small and vulnerable against the group of big men. When they were out of sight, he went to the Livery where his horse was being kept and headed back to his father's ranch.

Frank was feverish by the time he got back to the ranch. He had given his coat to Sarah, his shirt was drenched and his body frozen. The fever hit him on the long ride home, his body started to shake violently and he thought he might fall off his horse somewhere along the trail. Barely managing to hold on, he was slumped over his horse when it carried him through the gate and came to a stop in front of his father's ranch-house.

Major Hardy's hired gun, Foley Andrews, was on guard duty, having come back from the burial with Major Hardy. He called for help as he got Frank off his horse and half carried half dragged him inside. Doc Harris was sent for but there was little he could do, he could only stand by and let the fever run its course. When word got back to the trappers that Frank had been struck down with fever, Joe worried the boy would die and all because he let Sarah stay out in the rain at the cemetery. Joe felt the blame would be all his if Major Hardy's only son died. Frank remained ill with fever for the next three weeks.

The trappers got Sarah back to the Ferguson house and took her inside, then busied themselves heating water so she could have a hot bath. Supper was over and everyone had left. The only people at the house now were the trappers. Joe sent one of the men to Doc Harris's to get Doc but he had already gone to Major Hardy's to tend to Frank. Sarah wasn't told Frank had come down with fever, Joe made the men swear not to tell her. Gerda, Doc's wife came to the house and brought with her a nightdress, a robe and a pair of slippers for Sarah to change into.

After warm water had been poured into the tub, Sarah sunk down into it and let it warm her body. Gerda sat on a chair beside the tub and lathered Sarah's hair. When her hair was rinsed Gerda held up a large bath sheet. Sarah stood up and stepped out of the tub. Gerda wrapped the warm sheet around her and rubbed her arms and legs vigorously to get her circulation going. Then helped Sarah get into the nightdress and robe. Sarah slipped her feet into the slippers and her feet stayed warm.

"Thank you Gerda," Sarah said, her eyes red rimmed from crying. She hugged Gerda and Gerda hugged her back. "You are most welcome, my dear sweet girl," Gerda soothed in her heavy German accent. It was five years before Sarah's father married Elizabeth that Doc set up his practice in Cedar Creek. The year Elizabeth came to town she brought an air of sophistication with her, and Gerda and Elizabeth soon became friends. When Sarah was two years old and Elizabeth had died, the town was never the same. Gerda lost a dear friend and she and Doc could not love Sarah any more than if she were their own child. Sarah loved them both just as equally.

Sarah and Gerda stepped into the large living area to find the table had been set for one. Gerda said her goodbyes to the men and hugged Sarah one more time. Joe asked Garrett to escort her back to her house.

Food from the wake had been consumed by those that had remained behind when Joe and the group of men went to get Sarah from the cemetery. Bacon, eggs, beans and toasted bread were being piled on a plate, coffee was being poured for the men, warm milk was poured for Sarah. “Sarah, you sit here,” Will said as he pulled a chair out for her. The men saw what Sarah was wearing and approved of it, she was covered from head to foot and had a pair of warm slippers on her feet, her long hair was still damp but it would soon dry in the warmth of the room.

Sarah sat down and looked at the table. She had a china plate, a silver knife and fork to eat with and her warm milk was poured into a china cup, the plate of food was placed in front of her. “Eat something please Sarah,” Garrett said to her softly. Sarah picked up the knife and fork and cut into the egg, she ate everything on her plate and drank her warm milk while the men sat by watching on. She ran her tongue around the outside of her mouth to lick the milk off her lips. She hadn’t realized how hungry she had been and the men were pleased when she finished all of the food.

Sarah looked across at Fergus who was sitting opposite her at the table watching her eat. “How did Pa die Fergus?” She wanted details of her father’s death, and her eyes swum with tears when she looked at him. Fergus wasn’t expecting Sarah to ask him such a thing and was taken by surprise. He sat back in his chair and looked over at Joe for support. Fergus didn’t want to be the one to tell Sarah how her Pa died, he thought Joe, being their leader, should be the one to tell her.

“He got into a fight with Crawley.” It was Joe, indicating for the men to leave, who answered. The men got up from their seats and each man said goodnight to Sarah. Sarah said good night and watched them go to their rooms. Joe and Sarah were the last two people left in the big room.

“Come and sit over here near the fire Sarah.” Joe pulled an old arm chair toward the fire and Sarah sank down into it.

“Tell me Joe ...I need to know what happened.” Sarah tried to keep her voice from wavering. Joe told Sarah what happened, leaving nothing out.

"There was a game of poker, a lot of men already pulled out, leaving your Pa and Crawley the last two at the table, Crawley and your Pa were locked in a stand-off, there was a lot of money riding on what was going to happen …Calahan ran out of money to cover his hand so he put the deed to The Lodge on the table ...we had no idea he had the deed with him, he just pulled it out of his pocket …the bet was if Crawley won he would take all the money and your Pa would sign over The Lodge to him …and if your Pa won, he would take Crawley's store and the money ...there was at least ten thousand dollars on that table." Joe paused for thought. Sarah couldn't comprehend that amount of money "Is that a lot of money Joe?" she asked sadly while looking at him. "It sure is, and if your Pa had won, he was going to take you on a trip, maybe to see the ocean." Joe couldn't help remembering Calahan telling him he wanted to take Sarah to see the ocean. Sarah had never been away from the mountain, or Cedar Creek, and a trip to the ocean would let her see that the world was a big place and her Pa was planning on taking her there for her sixteenth birthday.

Sarah didn't care to see the ocean, she just wanted her Pa. "But he lost, didn't he?" her eyes welled as she looked at Joe. "Pa lost our house." As fresh tears rolled down her cheeks, she swiped them away with her hands. Joe bowed his head. "Yes …he lost."

"What happened for Pa to have died Joe? ...what did Crawley do to Pa?" Sarah's voice cracked, her sobs became audible. At that moment Sarah stopped calling Crawley Mister Crawley, deciding he was no longer worthy of her respect. Joe kept his head down, unable to look at Sarah as he recounted the events of that night.

"Your Pa took the deed to the bar and someone handed him the ink, then he signed the deed over to Crawley as he said he would, he folded the deed, and I and a lot of other men saw him do it …he put that deed right into Crawley's pocket …Sarah what happened next caught everyone by surprise ...your Pa started to walk away when Crawley said something to him that made him real mad." Joe wasn't about to tell Sarah Crawley called her a whore and that was what made her father angry. Joe continued to tell her what happened. "He took a swing at Crawley, Crawley ducked and your Pa lost his balance and fell over."

Joe stopped talking and wiped his hand across his brow and through his hair. "He lost his balance Sarah ...and he just ...fell over." Joe repeated what he said, unable to believe what he was saying. He leant forward in his chair and looked at the floor. "Everyone thought he was drunk, Calahan just lay there, like he was dead drunk." Realising he said the word 'dead' he quickly continued talking, hoping Sarah hadn't heard. "He hit his head and didn't get up." At that point Joe's voice broke. "Your Pa …Calahan…" he sniffled. "My best friend ...was gone!" Tears Joe tried to hold back trickled down his face, he had controlled his emotions for as long as he could. Sarah could barely see for the tears streaming down her face. Sarah and Joe reached for each other. Holding on for a long time as they cried.

"I'm so sorry Sarah," Joe kept saying. "I'm so sorry." After crying for a good while, Sarah straightened herself up and wiped her eyes on the back of her sleeve.

"That's it then, isn't it? I have nothing left ...except the cabin on the mountain ...I still have that don't I? ...Pa didn't lose the cabin too, did he?" Sarah looked at Joe for reassurance.

"No, he didn't lose the cabin, you still have that." Joe wiped his face with the palm of his hand.

Sarah stood up. "I need to get some sleep." Joe stood up too and wiped his eyes with his sleeve. Sarah hugged him again and he held her tightly in his arms. "Are you alright Sarah?" Joe asked before letting her go.

"I'll be alright ...soon ...not yet ...but soon ...good night Joe." Joe said goodnight and sat back down in his chair. He waited until he thought Sarah would be asleep then opened her bedroom door to check on her. Sarah's room was warm from two fires burning in the living area. Joe crept over to the window. After asking one of the men to nail the window shut to stop Sarah sneaking out again, the window he could see, had been nailed up tight.

Joe moved silently over to the bed, Sarah was under the blankets, her long curls laid out on the pillow behind her. She had cried some more and Joe could see her cheeks were red. Sarah was holding her father's hat against her chest. Joe's eyes watered, a tear rolled down his cheek and disappeared into his beard. Sarah would be alright, she would get through this, he and the other men would make sure of that. He tiptoed out of the room and closed the door.

Three weeks passed since the burial. Each day Joe made sure he or one of the other three trappers stayed with Sarah when she went anywhere. If they couldn't be with her due to their breaking horses, they got one of the other men to stay with her. None of the trappers hesitated when asked to spend a day with her.

Each day when Sarah went to the cemetery, taking fresh foliage with her, or she just sat and talked to her father's grave, a trapper was with her. Sarah cried most of the day and the trappers reported back to Joe that it made them sad to see her crying so much. Sometimes she picked enough foliage to put in tins on the long table in the Ferguson House to cheer herself and the men up. Whenever she went out riding a trapper was sent out with her. The trappers made sure Sarah didn't run into Crawley anywhere in town. They kept her away from the store and Mountain View Lodge.

The days Major Hardy's men ran in horses to the corrals, the four trappers found themselves with a lot of work to do, breaking horse's ready for Major Hardy's cowhands to take to the city of Moreton for sale. Getting to Moreton, the closest city to Cedar Creek, takes a full two weeks hard ride on horseback. Supply wagons came from Moreton once every two months, carrying much needed supplies and other items town folk couldn't get from Crawley's store. When running a herd of cattle or horses to the railhead at Moreton, the men take anywhere from three weeks to a month, allowing for the herd to graze along the way.

There were times when none of the trappers could be with Sarah, so Joe took her to the corrals to keep an eye on her. One such day Sarah was sitting on top of the corral fence watching Garrett breaking in a beautiful two-year-old stallion. Garrett was hanging on for his life as the stallion bucked and tried to throw him off its back. Sarah was laughing at Garrett when she heard a voice behind her.

"Hello Sarah Cole." Sarah hung on tight to the fence and turned her head to the side to see who called her name. Frank Mason climbed up the fence, swung his legs over the top rail and sat beside her. "How are you?" he smiled widely at her, and Sarah, trying not to look at him, returned her gaze to Garrett.

"I'm fine," was all Sarah allowed herself to say. She could feel her face start to get hot and knew she was blushing, so paid careful attention to Garrett as he got the stallion to quieten down. The horse started to walk around in a circle inside the corral under Garretts control.

Garrett glanced over at Sarah watching him and saw Frank sitting next to her on the fence. Joe and Will standing a little further away along the fence line both looked over to see Frank sitting beside her. Fergus was on the other side of the corral, standing on one of the railings, leaning over to see Garrett working the horse. He spotted Frank too and climbed down from where he was and walked around to where Joe and Will were.

"What do you suppose that's all about Joe?" Fergus nodded his head in Sarah and Frank's direction. Since her father's burial the men became protective of her and were curious as to what Frank Mason's interest in her was. "I don't know, let's wait and see." Joe didn't think Frank posed a problem for Sarah, he was just being friendly. After all, it was Frank who coaxed her out of the cemetery that awful day a little over three weeks ago and Joe felt grateful to the lad. After hearing Frank had come down with a fever because of what he did to help Sarah, he couldn't see the harm in letting Sarah and Frank be friends.

As soon as Frank recovered from his fever, he wanted to ride to town to see Sarah, to see how she was coping after her father's death. While recuperating he found himself with plenty of time to think about her, letting his feelings for her grow. "You might ask me how I am …Sarah Cole." Frank kept his eyes on the stallion Garrett was riding. Sarah tried her best to sound disinterested in Frank as much as possible when she answered him.

"Well, how are you? ...Frank Mason!" She replied, forcing his name between her lips. Frank was about to tell Sarah he had come down with a fever because of her, but after hearing how she addressed him just now, changed his mind. He didn't want to fight with her, not after the beating he took from her at the cemetery, besides, he liked her. Whenever he was near her his heartbeat quickened, like it did that day at the cemetery and again right now, he was sure Sarah could hear his heart beating loudly in his chest. "I'm fine," was all he said as he watched Garrett working the horse. Sarah glanced sideways at him, then looked quickly away when Frank turned his head and looked at her. Frank smiled when she turned her head away.

Sarah climbed off the fence and Frank climbed down after her. As she went to walk away, Frank blocked her passage. "Want to go for a walk? …Sarah Cole," he asked, repeating her name with a broad smile across his face. Sarah pushed him out of her way and walked in the opposite direction. Joe, Will and Fergus were watching what was happening. Sarah walked quickly towards the three men, hoping they could save her from Frank. Frank walked quickly beside her.

"Hello Frank," Joe said amicably to Frank as he approached. "I'm glad to see you are on your feet, how are you feeling?" Frank nodded to the three men. "Hello Joe, I'm fine …thank you for asking." Frank kept smiling as Sarah stopped walking. She folded her arms in defiance to Frank and stood beside the three men as if to say, there Frank Mason, see, I'm with my protectors, don't try anything stupid.

"Why don't you take a walk with Frank Sarah, I'm sure you could use some other company rather than us to talk to," Joe smiled at Frank. Fergus and Will were shocked at Joe for suggesting Sarah go with Frank. They couldn't believe Joe was letting her go for a walk without one of the trappers being with her, they both glared at him. Sarah unfolded her arms and glared up at Joe too.

"Fine!" she said in obvious disappointment, then started to walk away from the men and the corrals and headed straight towards the cemetery. When she realized the direction she was going in, she stopped abruptly and Frank bumped into her back. Sarah stepped around Frank who was still grinning and headed in the opposite direction, Frank followed. As they passed Joe and the other two men Frank shrugged his shoulders, raised his eyebrows and grinned at the men, Joe laughed quietly.

Sarah walked quickly and Frank practically had to run to keep up with her. "Hold up Sarah Cole," he puffed. He only just got over his fever and his lungs were still struggling.

"If you can't keep up Mason you better turn around and go back!" Sarah walked briskly down the alley beside the Livery, then scurried down the track through the trees to the riverbank. She walked with a determined stride south, away from the corrals and Livery.

Frank stumbled along trying to keep up while his breathing came in gasps. "Geez Sarah Cole, I didn't say did you want to go for a run!" he wheezed.

"Keep up Mason or like I said ...go back!" Sarah kept walking quickly ahead. When she came to a grassed area along the riverbank below the Ferguson House she stopped. Frank was out of breath and glad when he caught up to her, but he wasn't going to admit he couldn't keep up, he wouldn't let Sarah think he was weak. He took a deep breath and broke out in a fit of coughing. Sarah looked at him, she hadn't realized Frank was ill.

Sarah sat down on the grass and pulling her knees up in front of her, wrapped her arms around her legs and gazed across the water to where three small row boats were tied up at a pier. Frank sat down next to her and did the same, then asked her how she was coping. Sarah could see Frank was struggling to breathe, she didn't answer his question, instead, asked him what Joe meant by him being a lot better.

"I came down with a fever after sitting in the pouring rain at the cemetery, I guess I wasn't as tough as you." Sarah asked Frank why he did what he did that day. He shrugged his shoulders not knowing whether he should tell her the real reason he sat with her. He was brought up never to lie so after a moment of thought decided to be truthful. "Because I like you …I didn't want you to sit in the cemetery by yourself." They studied each other's faces, Frank smiled, Sarah blushed and thought Frank had a nice smile, to her, it seemed, he was always smiling. She liked how Frank's black hair was thick with a mass of curls and how the light danced off it when the sun hit it.

They sat for a long time and talked. Frank told Sarah he was Major Hardy's son. Sarah didn't think anything of that, she didn't have much to do with Major Hardy, all she knew was, her father and Major Hardy didn't like each other, she was never told the reason for their dislike. She asked why his name was Mason and not the same as his fathers. Frank told her he had been taken away by his mother when he was three years old. He told Sarah his mother changed his name to her maiden name of Mason after she divorced his father and when she passed away, he didn't see any reason to change his name back, wanting to keep his mother's name, because it was something he had to remember her by.

Frank had never been told the truth about his mother and father never marrying. His mother never saw any reason to burden her son with such stigma as to him being illegitimate. He told Sarah about growing up in Philadelphia where his mother's parents lived and when they both passed away, he and his mother continued to live in the family home on their own until his mother became ill and passed away too.

"At least you still have a Pa, I don't have anyone." Sarah looked over the river, past where the small row boats were moored and off into the distance. Her eyes threatened to flood with tears at the thought of being without a family. "You have all those trappers caring for you Sarah Cole, I reckon you have more than anyone I know." Frank studied Sarah and could see just how pretty she was. Sarah stood up suddenly and brushed grass off the back of her pants. "I better get back now Mason." She looked down at Frank, their eyes met as Frank stood up in front of her. He was a little taller than Sarah first thought, she had to tilt her head to look at his face.

As they walked back along the riverbank side by side, Frank's hand accidently brushed against Sarah's. Sarah felt a flutter in the pit of her stomach. Frank felt the same rush he felt at the cemetery course through his body. He really did like Sarah and he wanted to hold her hand as they walked back to the corrals, but he didn't get a chance.

"Come on Mason ...let's go!" Sarah started to run up the track leading between the trees to the Livery. Frank came along behind her and caught up at the end of the alleyway. Sarah stopped and waited for him to catch his breath. Walking back to the corrals together, Sarah started to climb up on the fence and Frank stood watching her, trying to decide what he should do. "I'm heading back to my father's ranch, I'll see you again, sometime ...maybe we could go on a picnic ...Sarah Cole." He smiled up at Sarah when saying her name. Sarah liked the lilting sound of her name when he spoke it. As she balanced on one of the railings she looked back over her shoulder. "Maybe ...Frank Mason," she said, trying to make herself sound disinterested while continuing to climb to the top of the fence. Frank smiled, the sound of his name when Sarah said it, sounded soft and seductive. He unhitched his horse and climbed into the saddle, then tipped his hat to Sarah before riding away.

Sarah sat on the fence and watched Frank until he disappeared out of sight. She tried not to make him feel too welcome but had to admit she liked him. Joe saw the two of them come back to the corrals and couldn't help noticing Sarah had a pink hue to her cheeks. It was obvious to Joe, Frank and Sarah had had a nice walk.

Chapter Seven

Sarah didn't know it was Christmas day, none of the trappers were aware of it either. Joe, Fergus, Will and Garret had all been too busy since the death of their friend Calahan and what with breaking horses taking up much of their time, they were oblivious to the special day having arrived. With so much happening in the first few weeks since arriving in Cedar Creek the rest of the trappers all forgot the festive season was upon them too. It snowed overnight and the ground was frozen, a thin layer of snow settled on everything and the town was quiet.

Another day dawned in the Ferguson House. The noise around the table was deafening with everyone talking at once, even Sarah got involved in the racket. Joe was the nominated cook for the day, after the men worked out a roster his turn quickly came around again. Sarah was considered their guest and hadn't been asked to cook or clean.

"Sarah Cole ...you in there?" A voice called from outside. No-one heard it above the din at first.

"Sarah Cole ...hello!" The voice called again.

Joe was standing at the stove cooking when he thought he heard something "Listen!" he said out loud, but everyone kept up their chatter. "Shut up!" Joe yelled louder and everyone was suddenly quiet as they all looked over at him.

"What's up Joe?" Fergus asked, but before Joe could answer, the voice called out again and this time they all heard it.

"Sarah Cole ...you in there?" Sarah had a piece of bread in her mouth and when she glanced at the faces around the table, all eyes were focused on her. Joe went to the window.

"Sarah you are being called, you better get outside and see who it is." Joe was looking out the window from where he could see Frank sitting on his horse with another much smaller horse standing beside him. "Who is it Joe?" Sarah wanted to know. Joe frowned when seeing Frank outside but didn't answer her.

"Sarah Cole ...come out here!" The voice was much clearer now that everyone had stopped talking.

"Goddamn it ...it's Frank Mason!" Sarah yelled. Throwing the leftover piece of bread she was eating on her plate, she pushed her chair back, jumped up from the table and headed for the door. The men sitting around the table quickly jumped from their chairs, letting them scrape back across the floor. As Sarah yanked the front door open and stepped out on the porch a dozen men scrambled to follow her. Some grabbing their hats off the stand as they went rushing out to stand on the porch.

Frank Mason was sitting on his horse at the bottom of the steps, holding tightly to the reins of a small colt. The colt, fawn in colour with a white marking on its forehead and white stockings, stomped its hooves in the snow, the saddle on its back looked brand new. The colt stood beside Frank's much taller horse with its head held high.

"What do you want Mason?" Sarah folded her arms when she saw the colt and tried to look sternly at Frank.

"I've brought you a gift." Frank held up the reins holding the colt and smiled up at Sarah. The men crowded around Sarah on the porch and tried to look at the horse Frank said was for her. "A gift ...why did you bring me a gift? it's not my birthday!" she said defiantly.

"Maybe not, but it is Christmas," Frank kept smiling. Sarah dropped her arms by her sides when suddenly realizing what day it was. "Christmas!" she stared at Frank for a moment, then wheeling around, bumped into the men crowding around. They stepped back getting out of her way as she pushed through them and raced back inside. Joe followed her back in. Sarah stopped in the middle of the room with her back to Joe. "What's wrong Sarah?" he asked her.

"It's Christmas, and I didn't know." She turned to face Joe, her eyes misty. Running her sleeve over her nose and before Joe could say anything, she charged past him and raced back out the door. "Don't you go bringing me a gift Frank Mason, I don't want it!" Sarah's voice rose at being upset at Frank. She felt upset because she hadn't known it was Christmas and she was embarrassed because Frank had embarrassed her in front of all the men by bringing her a gift.

Frank looked dejected. "I picked him out especially for you." His smile faded slightly but didn't disappear completely. Frank talked Foley and his brother Brady into helping him select the young horse for Sarah. He wanted to give Sarah something special and hoped she would like the gift he had taken time to select for her.

"I don't want it!" she said more sternly, folding her arms again in protest. "We aren't having Christmas, so go away!"

Frank had to think fast, he didn't want to go back to the ranch, not before Sarah accepted his gift. "Well, if you don't want him, I guess I'll just have to take him back to my father …so …um …he can …shoot him!" Frank didn't think it would hurt to tell a small lie, his father had no idea he had taken the colt and bought a brand-new saddle to give to Sarah. The two horses turned together when he pulled on his horse's reins, making out he was going to leave. "Shoot him! what do you mean ...shoot him?" Sarah called to Frank's back as she rushed down the steps. Frank pulled his horse back around and the colt followed. Putting her hands up to the colt's neck, the colt stood quietly letting her rub the side of his head.

"Yep! going to shoot him ...that's what my father said," Frank lied. "I thought you could have him instead of riding that old bag of bones you've been riding." Frank's face lit up with his huge smile when he thought his lie had worked.

"I've had that bag of bones as you call him a long time, he's a good horse, I can't take your horse." Sarah kept patting the colt and instantly liked him. He had a distinct shape in the middle of his forehead and she already knew the perfect name for him.

"If you don't want him just take him for a ride anyway." Frank wanted to spend a few hours out riding with Sarah, he didn't want to spend Christmas Day with his father's guests. His father invited Benjamin Crawley and his daughter Millicent to lunch, and Frank found both Benjamin Crawley and his daughter boring.

Frank desperately wanted Sarah to take his gift. He thought if Sarah took the horse for a ride, she would want to keep him and he would have an excuse to come to town and go riding with her. Sarah kept rubbing the horse's neck and the horse was liking it, he stepped closer to Sarah and put his head down so she could rub him more.

Joe was watching Sarah and Frank closely, wanting Sarah to go with Frank. He had a plan he wanted to put in place and needed Sarah to be out of the way for a couple of hours. "Go on Sarah, go for a ride," Joe piped up. Holding her coat in his hand, he threw it down to her. Sarah caught her coat and put it on, fresh snow had fallen, it was cold outside and she wasn't dressed for it. There were murmours of agreement from the other men.

"Yeah, go on lass, a ride won't hurt you," Fergus added smiling down from the porch. Looking up at the men standing on the porch, watching her and Frank, and seeing all were smiling at them, Sarah blushed then looked at Frank sitting there smiling too, waiting for her to decide. She felt she should tell Frank Mason to go home where he belonged and take his horse with him, but something was telling her to go for a ride with him. She lifted her foot up into the stirrup and swung her leg over the saddle. The saddle felt comfortable, being brand new she would be able to mould it to her own liking.

Frank smiled and handed her the reins. Sarah wondered why Frank smiled at her all the time, was he laughing at her? She took the reins, and sitting still for a moment, contemplated what to do. She leant forward, patted the colt's neck, then gripped the reins tightly in her hands. The trappers watched closely at what Sarah was doing. Sarah straightened up and suddenly gave a yell. Kicking her heels into the colt's flank, the horse jumped forward with a jolt and raced off.

Frank was left standing still as Sarah rode at break neck speed along Cedar Creek's main street. The few men and women bravely walking along the street through the snow, saw her come charging towards them and had to run to get out of her way. The men standing on the porch of the Ferguson House took off their hats and waved them in the air, whooping and hollering and cheering Sarah on as she raced up the street and disappeared out of sight.

"Get on after her Frank," Joe called from the porch. "Keep her out for a couple of hours will you? we have something we have to do in the house before Sarah gets back." Frank didn't need Joe's permission to keep Sarah out for a couple of hours, that was what he intended, but he smiled up at Joe and called "yes sir!" Then spurring his horse, took off after Sarah, who had ridden clear over the bridge and away from town before Frank made it to the bridge.

Sarah raced across the bridge, her hair flying back in the wind. The colt was fast and sure footed, a light dusting of snow covered the ground and the road was flat. A trail of snow kicked up behind them as they galloped further away from town. Sarah didn't look back to see where Frank was or even if he was following her. Feeling the cold air on her face, she let the colt have its head and it galloped on. When they reached a stand of trees, she decided they had gone far enough. Pulling back on the reins, the colt stopped running, brought its head up and stomped its hooves in the snow, its breath escaping in warm gasps in the cold air. Walking the colt to the stand of trees, Sarah swung her leg over the saddle-horn and slid to the ground, landing on both feet.

Sarah heard Frank's horse coming before she saw it. He raced on past Sarah before seeing her standing under the trees. Sarah laughed as he kept going. Frank pulled his horse up and coming back was surprised at seeing the colt had his head down munching on shrubs as if he had gone for a leisurely ride instead of the fast-paced gallop he had just been on. "You beat me!" he conceded, smiling down at Sarah, feeling glad they were alone.

"I didn't know we were racing Mason." Sarah closed one eye to the bright morning sunshine and looked up at him.

"What do you think of him?" Frank asked. Sarah looked at the colt, he was a beautiful horse, his coat was shiny and his colour perfect. Sarah wasn't going to admit to Frank the horse was the best she had ever seen.

"He's alright ...I suppose." She pulled a piece of long grass out of the ground, leant against a tree and twisted the grass in her fingers.

"Just alright! I reckon he's the best, he's pretty fast don't you think? you were way ahead of me, so...you going to keep him?" Frank swung his leg over the front of his saddle and jumping down, chose a tree close to Sarah and leant back on it.

"No ...I can't possibly keep him." Sarah tried not to look at Frank standing so close to her. She looked down at the snow covering the ground at her feet instead.

"Why not?" Frank was confused and wanted to know why Sarah wouldn't accept the gift he was offering her.

"I just don't want him." Sarah shrugged her shoulders. She did want the horse but was afraid if she accepted Frank's gift, she would be indebted to him, and she didn't want to be indebted to anyone.

"You can't refuse a Christmas gift, it's tradition, you have to accept it." Frank needed Sarah to believe accepting a gift was the proper thing to do. Sarah pushed herself off the tree and went over to the colt. The trappers taught her all they knew about horses and she watched the men intently when they were breaking horses each winter. She ran her hands over the colt's flanks then down his legs. He certainly was beautiful, he had good strong legs and he carried her easily. The horse turned his head and nuzzled her. Sarah didn't let on to Frank she was going to keep the horse, not right then. She went to put her foot up in the stirrup but Frank didn't want to go home yet, besides, Joe asked him to keep her out for a couple of hours, so he seized the opportunity to spend some time with her. He grabbed her by the arm and stopped her from mounting the horse. When Frank held her arm Sarah felt the same flutter in her stomach she felt as his hand brushed hers when they were on the riverbank in town, causing her heart to begin to race.

"Don't go yet ...can't we sit and talk awhile?" Sarah put her foot back down. "What do you want to talk about?" Frank's cheeky grin made Sarah's heart beat faster. "I don't know, anything I suppose, just so long as we don't go back yet, can we walk down to the river and sit a while?"

They walked together through the stand of snow-covered trees and shrubs to a place on the river that was sheltered. Sarah knew this place, she had bathed here many times before snow began to fall and before it was too cold to bathe out in the open.

Here was where the river made its way over flat rocks. Small waterfalls poured into shallow pools. The area was sheltered from the wind and the sun warmed the boulders lining both sides of the riverbank. The water in the rockpools stayed warm until snow melted on the mountain, sending freezing water flowing over the rocks and on its way past Cedar Creek. Sarah called this place 'The Ponds.' Everyone around Cedar Creek knew of the ponds.

She loved to come here to bathe where the water was shallow, she didn't like the swimming hole situated south of town. The waterfall cascading into the swimming hole was high, and the water fell into it in a torrent. The hole was deep and the water in it was dark and freezing. Sarah didn't like deep water besides, she had never been taught to swim.

Frank led the way through low growing shrubs until they came out on a patch of grass. Their footsteps left tracks in the virgin snow as they walked together across the grass to the boulders. Frank climbed up on a boulder and reaching his hand back tried to help Sarah climb up.

"I don't need your help Mason!" Sarah snapped. Frank quickly pulled his hand back as Sarah stepped up on the side of the boulder. Sarah's foot slipped suddenly on the icy rock, causing her to almost fall. Frank reached out and grabbed both her arms, stopping her from falling. Sarah grabbed hold of Frank and he pulled her up to stand in front of him. When their bodies bumped together, he felt his heart begin to beat faster, Sarah felt her face turn pink. As they looked into each other's eyes, she pulled her arms free of Frank's hold and tucked her coat tightly around her before sitting down on the boulder. She pulled her knees up and wrapped her arms around her legs. Frank did the same, it seemed to him Sarah always sat like this. He was feeling warm inside from Sarah's touch and smiled to himself as he looked over at the pools of water that formed the ponds.

They sat talking for ages, both forgetting the time. Frank told Sarah where he had gone to school and that he had been school boxing champion. Sarah laughed when he told her about boxing, after all, she reminded him, she hit him with her fist and made his lip bleed. Frank said it was just a lucky punch and they both laughed about it. Frank went on to talk about his mother and describe the city he grew up in.

Sarah told Frank about her mountain, she talked about hunting and trapping, she described her cabin and talked about the trappers.

She didn't talk about Cedar Creek or her house Mountain View Lodge. Now that Crawley owned it, she no longer wanted to talk about it. She didn't tell him that she couldn't read or write and that she couldn't swim. Sarah would never divulge to anyone the fact that when she was growing up on the mountain her father nor any of the trappers had bothered to teach her any of those things. She felt it just made her seem ignorant so kept it to herself. She told him she could shoot and skin wolves and set traps. Her eyes sparkled when she talked about the mountain and she told him she couldn't wait for spring to come so she could go home.

Frank was pensive for a moment when Sarah told him she couldn't wait to go back to the mountain. He didn't want Sarah to go home, he wanted her to stay in Cedar Creek, to be near him. He liked Sarah very much and thought he might be falling in love with her. He thought about her constantly when he was at the ranch, especially at night when the house was quiet, and he was alone.

Sarah leapt to her feet and jumped off the boulder, landing on both feet in the snow. "Where are you going Sarah Cole?" Frank called after her.

"Got to go back now Mason …and stop calling me Sarah Cole!" She called over her shoulder as she raced up the track to the horses. Frank was constantly calling her by her full name and it was beginning to irk her.

"That's your name, isn't it? …Sarah Cole!" Frank followed her and caught up to her.

"Yes, it is, but I don't want to be called Sarah anymore, I want everyone to call me Cole."

"Why? …Sarah sounds better than Cole." Frank stood beside his horse.

"Nope …it is too sissy, besides, most of the trappers get called by their last name and I'm a trapper, so that's what I want to be called." Sarah lifted herself into her saddle and Frank did the same, then sat on their horses facing towards town.

Frank smiled over at Sarah. "I'll race you back Sarah Cole ...I mean, Cole." Sarah giggled at the sound of her new name then smiled back at Frank. Seeing her smile made Frank's heart flutter and heat rise in his body. They kicked their horses at the same time and raced along with their horses keeping pace with each other.

They were neck and neck as they approached the bridge into town. Frank suddenly pulled back on his reins and his horse slowed, coming to a stop just before the bridge. Sarah's horse kept going and was almost over the bridge when she pulled up. She turned back and walked the colt towards Frank. "What are you doing Mason?" she asked as she came up beside him. "I'm heading back to the ranch." Frank looked across the bridge, not wanting to go. He enjoyed spending time with Sarah, and wanted to spend the rest of the day with her but knew he had to go, his father was expecting him to spend the day with him and the Crawley's.

"Well, you still have to cross the bridge to get there." Sarah kept her horse still as she looked at Frank. Frank looked over at Sarah then smiled at her. "Are you going to keep him?" he needed to know now if Sarah had decided to keep his gift, he had good reason for wanting her to keep the colt. Sarah had finally decided. "Yes, I think I will Mason." She leant forward and patted the colt on the neck. Frank's smile widened. "Well then, Cole, that means you have to give me a gift in return." Sarah sat up abruptly and looked horrified at Frank. "But I don't have a gift for you!" Sarah was disappointed, her eyes dimmed when she thought she wouldn't be able to keep the colt after all.

"Yes, you do," Frank's voice softened. "Your gift to me, is a kiss." Sarah looked shocked, her eyes widened, she had never kissed a boy before and didn't think she was ready for such an intimate moment, besides, Frank said he wasn't a boy, he was a man, how could she be ready to kiss a man. "That's all I ask, just a kiss," Frank repeated. Frank's heart was racing as he moved his horse closer to Sarah's. Sarah's face flushed pink as Frank reached over and put his hand on the back of her head, pulling her towards him. The horses started to move apart causing Sarah to rest her hand on Frank's arm to steady herself. Frank's face came up to Sarah's, his mouth gently pressed on her mouth, pushing her lips apart. Frank's kiss felt soft and warm, Sarah closed her eyes so she could feel Frank's mouth on hers. When Frank's tongue softly touched the inside of her mouth, she felt a sudden wave of emotion rush through her that she never felt before, and she returned Frank's kiss. Frank stopped kissing Sarah and letting her go, sat back in his saddle watching her. Sarah's eyes were still closed. When she opened her eyes, Frank didn't say anything and his face looked serious. Sarah kept blushing, her cheeks were bright red and Frank was staring. Sarah wanted to escape, she kicked the colt in the flanks making it carry her toward the bridge. "What are you going to call him Cole?" Frank called as he watched Sarah's long hair bounce across her back as she rode away from him. His own horse began to follow Sarah's horse toward the bridge.

"His name is STAR!" She called over her shoulder as she raced across the bridge and down the street to the Ferguson House. Frank thought that was a perfect name. The colt had a perfectly shaped star in the middle of his forehead and he would have called him that too. Sarah picked a perfect name for her gift. Frank smiled to himself, Sarah had given him a gift too, her warm kiss was still on his lips as he crossed the bridge and headed in the opposite direction.

When Sarah got back to the house, she was feeling happy about the ride with Frank and the gift he gave her, she also felt different now he had kissed her. She had never been kissed before and having Frank's mouth on hers made her body feel warm all over. Sarah pushed the door open and rushing into the house, came to a sudden standstill in the middle of the room.

All of the trappers, watching her as she came through the door, stepped aside so she could see the table.

The table had been set ready for a feast. A long white tablecloth had been put down. There were bowls of fruit and plates of small cakes in the middle, candles and holly decorated the table along with china plates. Glasses and cutlery sat in front of every chair. At the end of the room, standing in a corner near the open fireplace, was the nicest red cedar tree Sarah had ever seen, and it was decorated with paper chains and strands of popcorn. Pretty ribbons festooned it and a big shiny star sat at the very top, and underneath the tree were gifts.

As Sarah walked slowly across the room toward the tree, her eyes misted, she had just enjoyed the best time with Frank Mason and now there was a Christmas tree in the middle of their house. She looked around at the men gathered in the living area. They were all smiling at her. "Merry Christmas Sarah" they said almost in unison. Sarah burst into tears and Joe put his arm around her shoulders pulling her to him. “Joe it’s beautiful,” she said, looking through her tears at the open fire. The glow warmed the room, and hanging from the mantle was one stocking full of small gifts.

“We didn’t mean to make you cry Sarah,” Will said. “We thought you might be happy to have Christmas with us,” Fergus added.

“I am happy to have Christmas with you ...all of you.” Sarah stopped crying and wiped her face with her sleeve and smiled at the men, the smell of cooked food filled the room. “How! ...where did you get all of this?” she asked them incredulously. “You don’t have to worry about where it all came from, you just have to enjoy it.” Garrett told her.

“Yeah, it’s all for you Sarah.” Smiling sheepishly, Logan stepped in front of Sarah. Logan was the wildest of all the trappers and the vilest, he cursed at every opportunity and had no respect for women. His intent where Sarah was concerned was not good.

“No, it isn’t …it can’t be …it has to be for all of you too ...hasn’t it Joe? you have to enjoy it too ...it’s Christmas and Christmas is for everyone …isn’t it?” Sarah spoke quickly, her voice threatening to break.

“You are absolutely right Sarah, let’s all enjoy today, we can let tomorrow take care of itself,” Joe said to everyone. The men started to cheer up, talking and laughing with each other and patting each other on the back.

“Well then, let’s eat!” Fergus said as they moved to the table. Everyone agreed to that as they pulled out their chairs and sat down.

The men sat Sarah at the head of the table as their special guest and Will was nominated to say Grace. Just because the men had no religion, saying Grace was something Sarah did with her father every Sunday at dinner. This was a special day and everyone wanted Sarah to be happy. Afterwards there was mayhem around the table when all the men waited on Sarah, passing her plate after plate of food. Christmas lunch consisted of a dozen roast chickens, baked vegetables, corn, peas and gravy. For dessert, they had Christmas Pudding and cream, Sarah ate a hearty meal and joined in with the laughter and gaiety.

While Sarah had been out riding with Frank the men raced off to Crawley’s store and bought things they thought Sarah could use. They went around town asking for bits and pieces that anyone could spare and they ended up with the best Christmas the men had ever shared.

After lunch was over, they all left the table and sat around the open fire where they made Sarah sit on the floor in front of them to open her gifts, every gift under the tree she was told, was for her. First thing she did was take the stocking down from the mantle and tip it out on her lap. There was one red apple and lots of candy, a cake of pretty scented soap, some hair pins and a lace edged handkerchief. Not knowing who had given her the gifts, she thanked all of the men. Sarah felt she had overeaten from the big meal she just consumed but still managed to pop a piece of candy in her mouth. She loved the wrapped gifts the men had chosen for her too. There was a wooden handled hair brush from Will and three different coloured hair ribbons, yellow, pink and blue from Fergus. Garrett gave her a hand mirror. Logan and Reeves pooled their money together and gave her a small wooden jewel box that she was very pleased with, even though she no longer had any jewellery to put in it. Logan was especially glad she liked it, he had his eye on Sarah. Noticing her the day she came out of her room wearing just a flimsy nightdress, he could see she had the body of a woman and wanted her to like him in the hope she would let him be the first to make her a real woman. He sat quietly by and watched Sarah's every move. Sarah opened several gifts of socks to wear with her boots, a dark blue shirt and another pair of trousers.

The last gift was from Joe. When she un-wrapped the brown paper wrapped parcel, she was surprised to see the silk shawl Joe had bought her. It felt soft, had a pretty flower pattern all over it and a black fringe went all the way around the edge. Sarah hugged Joe and wrapped the silk shawl over her shoulders, looping it at the front. Joe was glad Sarah liked his gift, he hoped it brought her some sort of happiness. Sarah thanked everyone for her gifts.

Sarah enjoyed Christmas day, and that night after leftovers were consumed for dinner, when everyone retired to their rooms and she was alone, she said a prayer for her father and shed a tear for him. She thanked the lord for all of the trappers, and thought about the kiss between her and Frank Mason.

Chapter Eight

Snow began to fall heavier as Frank headed back to the ranch to spend the rest of Christmas Day with his father and their guests, Benjamin Crawley and his daughter Millicent. On the long ride back, smiling to himself, Frank thought about Sarah's kiss. Letting the thought warm him and help him forget about it snowing. Snow came off the mountain in a flurry and continued to snow on and off for the next two weeks, piling up in deep drifts around the town and the countryside. Most people stayed indoors in the warmth of their homes, only venturing out when they needed supplies from Crawley's store, business was slow and the town was quiet.

Crawley and his daughter Millicent didn't stay long for Christmas lunch. As soon as they finished eating, they said their goodbyes and headed back to town. Crawley didn't want to get stuck out at Major Hardy's ranch because of the snow. He was a greedy man, and wouldn't shut up shop for too long, it might deprive him of a dollar. Keeping his store open meant business and business meant money. Frank was relieved to see them go, he couldn't stop himself from thinking about his kiss with Sarah. All through lunch his thoughts wandered off making Major Hardy angry when his son didn't seem to be in a very welcoming mood toward their guests.

After Christmas day had been celebrated and was behind them, most of the trappers made the difficult ride out to Major Hardy's ranch for whatever work they could get. Work mainly consisted of working around the ranch doing repairs to fences or watching over Major Hardy's herd of steers. Major Hardy's horses were left to roam his land freely. When it became too difficult to get back to town, the trappers stayed at Major Hardy's ranch, bunking down with Major Hardy's men in the bunk house. Will, Garrett, Fergus and Joe stayed indoors at the Ferguson House with Sarah. The four men talked amongst themselves while playing cards and smoking cheroots, causing the house to become stuffy.

Sarah didn't have a lot to amuse herself with while the snow kept her indoors so she decided she would do some baking, she was a good cook having learnt at an early age to cook for her and her father. Whenever the four trappers came by the Low Ridge where her and her Pa had their cabin, they camped outside in the clearing and Sarah cooked large pots of stew for the men. They always complimented her on her cooking and always asked for seconds.

Sarah made several batches of cookies and made lots of loaves of bread. The loaves and the cookies were sitting on the table covered by a clean white cloth she found in one of the cupboards. The house smelt of cigar smoke and baking, and had become very warm. Sarah was feeling the heat from working at the stove for such a long time so stepped out onto the porch to get some fresh air. The town looked pretty after the snow had fallen. The streets were covered in white, snow sat on the rooves of buildings, long crystal-like icicles hung from the awnings and glistened in the sunshine.

Frank hadn't been to town since Christmas Day, the heavy snowfall was keeping him stuck at the ranch and he wasn't happy about being unable to get to town to see Sarah.

Sarah wanted to take Star and go for a ride. Star needed to be run, he had been cooped up in the Livery for too long. Sarah went back inside. "Joe, I'm going for a ride, Star needs to run," 'and so do I,' she thought to herself.

"Where will you go in the snow Sarah?" Joe looked up from his hand of cards.

"I don't know, maybe I'll go across the bridge and up as far as the ponds." Joe knew where the ponds were. Everyone in town knew where the ponds were. Joe didn't think it would be too hard a ride if Sarah wanted to go that way.

"Well dress warm, you got your coat? Will ...you go with her!" Joe turned to Will, who had given up playing cards and was sitting in front of the fire with his eyes closed. When Joe mentioned his name, Will opened his eyes and stood up. Wanting to go alone, Sarah stared at Joe, she hoped she might run into Frank if he happened to be out riding and didn't want anyone with her.

"Joe, I can go by myself, I don't need Will to go with me." Will sat back down. Joe stared back at Sarah. "Will ...go with her!" he repeated sternly without taking his eyes off her. Sarah was his responsibility and he wasn't about to let her go riding without someone being with her. Will stood back up and went to his room to get his coat and hat. Sarah went storming off to her room and came back wearing her father's fur coat and hat. The coat was far too long for her and the bottom swept the floor. Joe already trimmed the sleeves just enough to let her use a gun, but the sleeves still hung partway over her hands. Joe expected Sarah would grow some more. He also hoped when she got taller the coat would no longer drag on the floor, he spied her father's hunting knife tied around her waist.

"Why the hell are you taking that knife with you if you are only going for a ride?" Joe's deep voice resonated around the room when he questioned her.

"You never know when one might need it Joe ...you just never know!" Sarah pulled the belt tighter. Garrett and Fergus both smiled and looked away so Sarah couldn't see them smiling at her when they saw her tightening the belt around her waist.

Waiting for Will to come out of his room, no one spoke another word to her. Joe turned back to his cards.

"Don't any of you go eating those cookies or bread while I'm gone, I know how many cookies there are and how many loaves of bread too!" Sarah had no idea how many cookies or loaves there were and the men knew it, but they didn't say anything. They remembered they never made a promise to teach her to count or read or write. There were books at the cabin, and The Lodge was full of books Sarah had never learnt to read, there wasn't time to teach her when she and her Pa were on the mountain trapping, and when they came to town there was always too many other things going on.

Will appeared from his room and he and Sarah hurried through the snow to the Livery and Stable. They got their horses and rode in silence out over the bridge. They were almost at the ponds when

Sarah stopped. “Look Will ...rabbits!” she pointed to the rabbits scurrying about in the snow.

“Want to see if you can hit one?” Will pulled his rifle out of its holster. “If I hit one, I’ll need more ‘cause …we could have rabbit stew for dinner tonight.” Sarah hadn’t thought about what they might have for dinner before she saw the rabbits. Suddenly she thought rabbit stew would be good for a change from all the chicken they had been eating. Sarah took Will’s rifle when he offered it to her.

“How many you reckon you need?” Will said leaning on his saddle-horn.

Sarah looked questioning at Will. “Don’t ask me that, you know I don’t know how many I will need, we just need a whole bunch!”

Will knew Sarah couldn’t count. “Hold up your hand Sarah.” Will held his own hand up with his fingers spread out. Sarah held up her hand the same way. “You need this many I reckon, you got five fingers on your hand so you need five rabbits.” Sarah looked at her hand. “Five fingers, five rabbits!” Sarah repeated. Will got Sarah to count her fingers on both hands. Sarah had a good mind for remembering things, by the time Will and Sarah rode back to town Sarah could count to ten.

Sarah took aim at a rabbit and pulled the trigger. The rabbit cartwheeled and landed dead in the snow. “That’s one!” Will held up one finger. Sarah held the rifle against her shoulder. The second rabbit bobbed its head up and Sarah fired. The bullet hit the rabbit between the eyes. “Two!” Will held up two fingers and Sarah smiled at him. The rest of the rabbits quickly scurried away when they heard the loud reports of the gunshots.

While they waited for the rabbits to come back, Sarah and Will trudged through the snow and collected the two rabbits Sarah shot. Both rabbits had bullet wounds in their heads. Will looked at the rabbits then at Sarah, before raising his eyebrows. The trappers taught her to shoot well, ‘maybe too well’ Will thought to himself, Sarah could be a better shot than all of them.

“I reckon one more might do!” Sarah said.

“Nah! we need to get at least three more to make a good feed.” Will looked around to see if he could spot more rabbits. He peered back to where they tethered their horses. "Look Sarah, look at our horses." Will began to laugh. Sarah looked to where Will was looking.

"Goddamn!" she said. What they saw amused them both. Their horses were stepping around and over rabbits to get out of their way as the rabbits scurried about between their hooves. They laughed quietly so as not to scare the rabbits away.

"You got your handgun Will? see if we can get two more." Sarah's eyes sparkled, she was having fun and forgot all about Frank for the moment. Will got his handgun out of its holster and took aim. At the same time, Sarah took aim with the rifle.

"Don't hit the horses Will," Sarah giggled softly, knowing he wouldn't hit the horses. Will was a good shot. Along with Joe, Garret, Fergus and her Pa, Will taught her how to shoot. Sarah reckoned the men were better shots than she would ever be.

"I won't hit the horses, how bad a shot do you think I am?" Will started waving his gun around in a crazy like fashion suggesting he was a bad shot. They were both laughing so much neither of them could hold their weapons still.

"Ready Will?" Sarah said turning serious and lifting the rifle to her shoulder. She closed one eye, steadied the rifle and aimed it toward their horses.

"Ready." Will held his handgun up at eye level and kept his arm straight as he took aim.

"Now!" Sarah whispered and they both fired. The rifle shot was louder than the handgun and echoed across the river, both horses became startled and shied at the sudden noise.

"Did you shoot?" Sarah laughed out loud.

"Course I did, take a look, there's a dead rabbit over there under our horses." Will pointed his gun at their horses.

"That's the one I shot, where's yours?" Sarah put the rifle under her arm and still laughing trudged quickly through the snow toward the horses.

"Oh no you don't, that's my rabbit!" Will yelled behind her. He tried running to catch up to her as she hurried to get to the rabbit ahead of him. "It is not!" Sarah said over her shoulder as they argued jovially back and forth. Will chased Sarah, grabbing her by the back of her fur coat, pulling her back and causing them both to stumble in the snow. Will landed on top of Sarah and hanging on tight so she couldn't get away, crawled up over her. Sarah turned over on her back and squirming, tried to get him off her, both still laughing uncontrollably as they scrambled together. They stopped laughing and struggling, and for a moment looked into each other's eyes.

Will hurriedly got off Sarah and stood up. His feelings for her were strong but he was still surprised by what just happened. He remembered his promise he made to Sarah's father counted him out of ever making her his own, nor could Sarah choose him, he was from the mountain. Sarah rolled over, got to her feet, and laughing, started to run toward the horses. If she noticed the change in Wills demeanour she didn't let on. Will ran after her and they both got to the horses at the same time and stopped.

"Well I'll be, look at this!" Will exclaimed, their encounter forgotten for the moment. Two rabbits lay dead beside each other in the snow. Sarah's shot from the rifle went through one rabbit's ear and came out the other, taking the top of the rabbit's head off. The shot from the handgun hit the other rabbit in the neck and embedded itself in the rabbit's head. They now had four rabbits. Sarah handed Will his rifle and tied the rabbits to her saddle-horn. On the way back to town Will shot another rabbit. Both Sarah and Will were happy with their catch and rode along laughing and chatting, they had their five rabbits for dinner. Sarah enjoyed being out with Will, and was glad Joe suggested he go with her. She forgot her reason for going for a ride in the first place was to see if she could meet up with Frank.

That night Sarah cooked the rabbits with lots of fresh vegetables and the men sat down to a hearty meal of rabbit stew. They enjoyed the fresh bread she baked and after dinner the men had cookies with their coffee. When Sarah turned in for the night Joe gathered the men together and spoke to them. "Sarah isn't going to be our cook, not all of the time, she is starting to clean up after us too, everyone needs to do their bit to help her, we need to make sure she has fun and is happy."

Will piped up. "We had fun Joe, Sarah and I had a shooting competition with those rabbits you ate for dinner, Sarah shot three of them, I got the other two, she was laughing a lot out there today." Will smiled broadly as he recalled the enjoyable day he spent with Sarah. He put his head down in embarrassment when seeing the men looking at him. Will liked Sarah, a lot, and enjoyed being with her. Will was thirty-four years old and Sarah just fifteen, but he didn't think he was too old if Sarah happened to want more than a friendship.

The promise made on the mountain counted all the trappers out of ever having her for themselves, but still, Will held out hope that one day, Sarah would choose someone from the mountain herself, and if she did, he hoped that someone would be him. Will was also aware there were a lot of men that felt the same way he did about Sarah.

"That's good Will, but we don't want her to do all the work around here, Sarah isn't here for that." Joe looked around the room. He didn't know how Will felt about Sarah, none of the men let on to Joe they had feelings for her. All the men agreed wholeheartedly to do their share.

Sarah woke up early as usual, she couldn't hear any noises coming from the living area, no-one was up yet. 'Good' she thought and pushed the blankets back to get out of bed. 'I'll get dressed and...' she looked down at her bedsheets, jumped out of bed and pulled the blankets back further. She looked at her nightdress, it was the same as her sheets. Sarah was in a predicament, she didn't know what to do. Rushing over to the tallboy she opened the top drawer. There was a spare nightdress folded up neatly in the drawer along with her new socks, the blue shirt and pair of trousers she was given for Christmas but nothing else. She opened each drawer only to find them all empty. Sarah looked around the room. Except for her bed, the tallboy, the full-length mirror and a chair with a lamp sitting on it, the room was sparsely furnished. There was no closet to hang anything in and everything looked dull, she hated this room. Sarah pulled the blanket off the bed and wrapped it around herself. She would have to go to the washroom but could hear the men starting to come out of their rooms, some had already headed for the outhouse and washroom.

Sarah couldn't leave her room, not now, not with all the men out there, they would look at her and they would know.

Joe might be able to help but he is a man, she couldn't possibly tell him. Maybe she could talk to Will, or maybe she could get Garrett to come in and she could tell him or even Fergus, he could help her. Sarah thought of each of them but she couldn't tell any of them, they were all men and they shouldn't know about these things, they would laugh at her.

'Pa would know what to do,' she thought to herself, remembering back a couple of years to when she first started. Her Pa found her sitting curled up in a corner of the lean-to hiding. She told him she thought she was dying and he sat down on the ground next to her and asked her why she thought that. Sarah told him, because she hadn't hurt herself, but she didn't know where it was coming from. Her Pa asked her what she meant by 'it' and she told him she was hurt 'down there' and she pointed between her legs then burst into tears. Her Pa didn't laugh, he pulled her into his arms and explained to her what was happening. She told him she didn't want 'it' and she would never let 'it' happen again, that was when he laughed, he told her she had no choice, 'it' was going to happen all the time now she was a woman whether she wanted 'it' or not, so she resigned herself to the fact she had become a woman. Now here she was, living in a house full of men and there was nothing she could do, she wasn't prepared for what was happening to her body. Sarah wasn't going to come out of her room, not ever. She went and stood against her bedroom door with her nose almost pressed against it. She could hear the men talking amongst themselves. They were crowding around the stove getting themselves something to eat out there and here she was stuck in her room.

She turned and leant her back against the wall as tears began to flow down her cheeks. She hated being a woman, she didn't ask for this, 'why wasn't she born a man?' she asked herself, they didn't have to worry about such things. She slid down the wall and sat on the floor with the blanket covering her and thought she would make a mess of it too if she didn't do something soon. But what could she do? she would have to go out there and face all the men and she wasn't going to. She stayed leaning against the wall, and trying to stifle her tears, sat there for what seemed like ages. The men were getting louder, they were all up now and fighting for a spot at the table.

A knock came on her door and she looked up, maybe if she stayed real quiet whoever it was would go away. The door opened and Joe walked in, he saw the empty bed and wondered where Sarah was, thinking she might be in the outhouse, he turned and almost went out when he spied her sitting on the floor behind the door.

"Sarah?" Joe frowned when he saw her, she had a blanket around her, her legs were bent up and her head rested on her arms. It wasn't hard for Joe to tell something was wrong. "Go away Joe" Sarah said without lifting her head. Joe came all the way into the room and closed the door behind him. "Sarah, what's wrong?" he stood in front of her while waiting for her to answer. Sarah started to moan softly and sniffle. "Go away!" she repeated. Joe wasn't going to go away, clearly something was wrong or Sarah wouldn't be crying, not this early in the morning.

"Tell me what's wrong Sarah, I can't help you if you won't tell me what's wrong." Joe waited.

"I can't tell you!" she sobbed and held the blanket over her face so she couldn't see him.

Joe walked across the room and sat on the edge of Sarah's bed facing her. He wasn't leaving until she told him what was wrong. Joe had no idea what could possibly be wrong with Sarah this early in the morning, she seemed alright when she went to bed last night.

Sarah continued to keep her face hidden, and sobbing, "I can't tell ...I can't, you are a man, Fergus is a man, you are all men," kept sniffling into the blanket. Joe wondered why she pointed out the fact they were all men. He rested his hand on the bed, then glanced down at the crumpled bed clothes where Sarah had been sleeping. Lifting his hand to straighten the sheets, he saw something he wasn't expecting to see. He could plainly see what was wrong with her. Sarah looked up at Joe at the precise moment he lifted the sheet.

"Shit!" Joe cursed and jumping up from where he was sitting on the bed, quickly dropped the sheet, looked around at Sarah and their eyes met. Sarah buried her head in her hands and cried again because now Joe knew.

"Stay here Sarah, don't you move!" Joe rushed out of her room. Sarah wasn't going anywhere, she wasn't going to let the men see what was happening to her, she wasn't coming out of her room, not ever, she buried her head further into the blanket and moaned.

Joe pushed his way through the throng of men busily getting their breakfast and rushing out the front door, took the steps down the porch two at a time.

"Where's Joe going in such a hurry?" Will wanted to know while watching Joe out the window heading at a fast pace up the street.

"He just came out of Sarah's room, something going on with her again, you suppose?" Garrett said as he stopped what he was doing. Fergus put down his plate and mug and went to Sarah's room.

"Get out!" Sarah yelled and Fergus came rushing back out. "She's sitting on the floor behind the door" Fergus told the room full of men. They all stopped what they were doing and wondered why she was sitting on the floor. Will and Garrett went to Sarah's room thinking maybe they could help.

"Oh! go away!" Sarah screamed shrilly. Will and Garrett swiftly backed out of the room. "What the hell's wrong now?" Will said to the men.

"Wait 'til Joe comes back from wherever he's going, I bet he knows what's wrong with her, then we will all know." Fergus continued getting his breakfast. The three men were sure Joe knew what was going on with Sarah, he had been in there and came out in an awful hurry, now he's gone up the street somewhere. The men went back to getting themselves something to eat.

Joe half walked half ran up the street, jumped up on the boardwalk outside Doc Harris' practice and pounded on the door. Doc opened the door expecting to see someone hurt, instead he saw Joe looking flustered standing at his door. "Joe, what's wrong, you hurt?" he held the door open and Joe pushed past him and rushed into the hallway. "No, it ain't me, where's Gerda?" Joe headed down the hall, looking for Gerda in each room as he went.

"She's in the kitchen Joe, what's happened?" Doc could tell something wasn't right, Joe was agitated and seemed in an awful hurry to find Gerda. "Why Joseph, what are you doing here this early in the morning? are you hurt or sick or what?" Gerda was still in her nightdress and gown when she looked up from the breakfast table. Joe didn't know how to start to tell her what was wrong and what he needed from her.

"It's Sarah," he started to say. Gerda put down the coffee pot she was holding. "Sarah! she is sick?" Gerda always worried when there was mention of Sarah.

"Well no, not sick, not exactly." Joe looked at Doc who had come further into the room. "Then what is it Joseph?" Gerda was confused as to the reason why the big man was standing in her kitchen at daylight and no-one was sick or worse hurt.

"Sarah, she's um..." Joe put his hands on his hips and took a deep breath. "Well, hell, goddamn it ...she's a woman!" he studied Gerda's face trying to see if she could figure out what he was trying to tell her. Gerda knew Sarah was a woman, she didn't need Joe telling her that. "She's in her room and won't come out ...she can't come out ...shit! ...we're not prepared ...well ...you know ...goddamn it! ...you know what I'm trying to say!" Joe rubbed his hand over his forehead.

Gerda kept staring at him in confusion. Joe didn't want to come straight out and say it, he was embarrassed at having to deal with Sarah's predicament. He would have to try once more to make Gerda understand him, surely, he thought she would understand what he was trying to say, after-all, she was a woman.

Before Joe could continue to explain, Doc laughed at suddenly understanding what Joe was struggling to tell Gerda. He put his arm around his wife and whispering in her ear, explained what Joe was trying to say. Joe waited while Doc finished whispering. Gerda's eyes widened at being told what Joe had been trying to tell her, her face lit up in a knowing smile. "Oh Joseph, you go back, I get dressed and come ...in a little while." Joe was relieved but wondered why it took another man to figure out what he was trying to say was happening to Sarah. "Thanks Gerda," Joe breathed a sigh of relief then nodded to Doc. "Thanks Doc." Joe turned to leave then turned back. He had one more request.

"Can you not be too obvious when you come over? Sarah doesn't need all the men knowing what she's going through." Gerda patted Joe on his arm.

"Don't you worry, I come for a visit, yes?" Satisfied, Joe left them and half walked half ran all the way back to the Ferguson House. He took the steps up to the porch two at a time and rushed back through the front door. Ignored all the men busily chatting and eating and knocked on Sarah's door, then without waiting for her to say 'come in' he went in. Sarah hadn't moved from where she was when he left her.

"Gerda is on her way Sarah, she knows what to do for you." Sarah looked up into Joe's face, "you know Joe?"

"Of course I know, I know all about you women and what happens to you every little while." Joe squatted down in front of Sarah and brushed a strand of hair from her face. He rested his hand under her chin and gently lifted her face. "It's nothing to be ashamed of Sarah."

"I'm not ashamed of it Joe, it's just I've been caught out unprepared ...that's all." Joe's eyes softened, he helped Sarah to her feet and they sat on the edge of the bed together.

"After Gerda has been, I think you should stay around the house for a few days, maybe you could do some cleaning and some laundry, I could use a shirt washed and I know a few of the men could too, it would only be for those few days you need to stay here." Sarah nodded in agreement. "But I'm not washing their long-johns Joe, they aren't the cleanest of men when they go you know!" They both laughed.

"You won't tell everyone will you?" Sarah's red eyes watched Joe's face intensely. "I won't tell anyone." Joe gave her a quick hug and left her in her room to wait for Gerda.

Gerda arrived carrying a basket covered with a cloth, she announced loudly to the men, she had just come to visit with Sarah. Joe quickly ushered her into Sarah's room and Sarah and Gerda remained in her room for several hours.

Some of the men asked Joe what was going on with Sarah. Joe told them nothing was going on and that if Gerda and Sarah wanted to visit with each other it was none of the men's business.

Gerda sorted Sarah's predicament out and got her dressed, making her leave her shirt hanging out, saying the length would cover her sufficiently to give her some dignity. Sarah wondered would the men notice she wasn't wearing her shirt tucked in as usual and asked Gerda. "Won't they know something is different?" Gerda said if the men say anything, "you tell them this is a new fashion you are trying out," and they both giggled.

Gerda helped Sarah strip her bed and they sat on the side together while Gerda brushed Sarah's hair. Gerda herself had long blond hair she wore in braids pinned up on her head, she especially loved Sarah's thick light brown hair. She twisted Sarah's hair in a single braid down her back and tied a yellow ribbon that Sarah got for Christmas around the tail.

"Oh, Gerda, I hate this room." Sarah held the hair brush in her hand.

"Why do you hate it so Sarah?" Gerda sat sideways so she could see Sarah.

Sarah waved the hairbrush about the room. "Look at it, it's a man's room." Gerda glanced around at the sparse furnishings, Sarah was right, this room was a room any man would be satisfied with.

"There is nothing pretty about this room," Sarah said sadly.

Gerda agreed and said to give her a couple of hours, she would help make her room pretty.

When Gerda left, Sarah came out to the table. The four trappers were still there. The other men all managed to leave in the snow to get to Major Hardy's ranch for some much-needed work.

Joe sat Sarah down at the table and gave her a plate of beans, an egg and a slice of bread. Sarah ate hungrily, wiping her plate clean with her bread. After eating she made her way to the outhouse and was gone for a little while.

Will wanted to know why Sarah was wearing her shirt loose. "She never wears her shirt out like that Joe, she always looks neat and tidy." Joe shrugged his shoulders. "What do I know, maybe she just wants a change," he said keeping his back to Will. Both men left it at that until Sarah came back through the door. Will stared at Sarah and Sarah noticed him looking. She felt her face start to go red so turned her back on him and stepped up to Joe at the stove.

"Joe," she whispered really softly. Joe had to bend his head close to Sarah to hear her. "Does Will know?"

"No," Joe whispered back. "He asked what you were wearing your shirt out for...why are you Sarah?" Joe and Sarah kept their voices low.

"I wear trousers Joe ...they don't hide anything." It didn't matter to Sarah now Joe knew.

Sarah turned to Will and in a loud voice asked what he thought. "What do you think Will?"

"What do you mean Sarah?" Will, taken by surprise when Sarah addressed him, looked at Joe for support. "What do you think of my knew fashion, Gerda suggested it, it's comfortable out like this." Sarah turned in a circle to show off her new fashion.

"It looks alright ...I suppose ...if you like it that way." Will wasn't going to tell her he didn't like it, it looked untidy to him.

"Yes, I like it this way, I think I'll wear it like this more often." Sarah put her nose in the air in a haughty way and turned back to Joe.

Will got his hat and went outside to sit on the porch. Joe smiled to himself and poured two mugs of coffee, one for himself and one for Sarah. Sarah drank her coffee with Joe and waited for Gerda to come back.

Both Gerda and Doc returned after raiding their own cupboards and house for things they could give Sarah to brighten her room. She was given a lace quilt that hung over the sides of her bed and almost touched the floor, two lace covered cushions sat on the bed propped against the pillows. A lace doily was spread out across the top of the tallboy, a small round floor rug was placed on the floor next to the bed for Sarah to step out on. Doc carried a side table to the house and Gerda placed it under the window next to Sarah's bed. A lace doily matching the one on the tallboy was placed on top of the table and Sarah's oil lamp sat on top of the doily. The silk shawl Joe gave Sarah for Christmas was draped over the back of the chair sitting in a corner. Pretty floral curtains were hung over the window and tied back so Sarah could see out.

Sarah and Gerda stood back and looked at the room. The two women hugged each other tight. "It's beautiful Gerda ...you do so much for me." Sarah liked that Gerda was much more than a friend. Over many winters spent in Cedar Creek, Gerda had become the mother she had never known. Gerda was pleased with how the room looked too. "You are most welcome Sarah, anything you need or if you just want to talk, you come to me, yes?" Sarah felt a whole lot happier knowing she could confide in Gerda whenever she needed. "Yes Gerda, thank you." She put her arms back around Gerda and they held each other for a few minutes more.

When Gerda left, Sarah took the four men into her bedroom to see it. The four men were amazed at the transformation. They each commented that Sarah had a lovely room. Joe was especially pleased, now he thought Sarah would feel more at home and be happy.

Sarah didn't mind staying around the house as Joe suggested, she boiled her bed sheets until they were so white when she hung them on the line to dry, they almost blinded her with their brilliance. Her nightdress was boiled and smelt clean and fresh. The men gave her their shirts to wash and she hung nineteen shirts out to dry along with some personal things of her own. She washed their trousers and was worn out by the time she finished. Sarah told the men in no uncertain words that she would not be washing any of their dirty long-johns and they all agreed they would wash their own long-johns and socks.

At the end of the day the men came home to a clean house. Their beds had been made and their shirts along with their trousers were neatly folded on their beds. Some of the men however, soon figured out by the washing they saw hanging on the line why Sarah was spending all her time around the house. None of the men discussed the reason, but some of the men had not realized Sarah was a full-grown woman until then and they began to make their feelings toward her known to each other.

Chapter Nine

When the snow finally stopped falling, Frank came to town regularly to see Sarah and take her out riding. Most of the time they rode out of town together. If they didn't go riding, they sat on the grass on the riverbank opposite the pier where three little row boats were moored. Frank asked Sarah to go for a row with him in one of the little boats but she bluntly refused. She didn't like deep water but never let on to Frank she couldn't swim, she just said she didn't want to go in the boat and he didn't press her.

The sun came out and the snow began to melt, even though deep patches of snow lay on the ground in some places, Frank and Sarah still went out riding. Not long after Christmas, they took a picnic lunch that Sarah prepared and rode out to the ponds. They sat side by side on a blanket near the boulders surrounding the ponds and ate their picnic lunch of chicken legs, fresh baked bread and fruit compote. They made a fire and drank coffee to warm themselves. They ate cookies Sarah baked and they talked for a long time.

Frank talked about his mother and showed Sarah a small black book he always carried with him he said was a bible, he told her he cherished it, not because he was religious, but because it was a gift from his Ma. He took a silver timepiece out of his pocket and opened it to show Sarah the inscription engraved on the inside, 'Frank happy 16th birthday love mother.' It was a beautiful timepiece with an engraving of a tall sailing ship on the outside cover. Sarah had never seen a tall ship before and she was fascinated by it, saying how beautiful the timepiece was. Frank told Sarah what the time was as they sat leaning together looking at the watch. He let Sarah hear the chime then closed it and put it back in his pocket.

Sarah told him about the time her Pa gave her a gold locket for her tenth birthday that once belonged to her Ma and that it held a picture of her Ma and Pa. She told Frank when the locket was closed, her Ma and Pa were kissing each other because their faces were touching. Sarah blushed when she told Frank that bit of information. She cherished the locket too she said, but it was in the house Crawley had taken and she couldn't get it. Sarah reflected on that and grew silent. Frank put his arm around her shoulders and told her he was sorry. As Sarah leant against him, he felt his body grow warm and his heart begin to race. Sarah felt comforted with his arm around her.

After finishing lunch, they lay on the blanket beside each other looking up at the sky. Frank showed Sarah how to see shapes formed in the clouds. She felt pleased when she picked out a rabbit and a bird. While Sarah was studying the clouds, Frank propped himself up on one elbow, leant over her and brushed aside a wisp of hair that fell over her face, then moved his hand down to rest on her waist. As Sarah lay quietly letting Frank lean over her, she turned her gaze up into his eyes. Frank leant down suddenly and put his mouth over hers.

It was a gentle kiss, the same as on Christmas Day. As his tongue gently touched the inside of her mouth, Sarah opened her mouth a little more and kissed him back. They held their kiss for a moment, until Frank lay back down on his back. He smiled up at the sky before closing his eyes. His heart was pounding and an ache coursed through him. It started in low and moved up through his stomach to his chest. He wanted to hold Sarah, to show her how much he loved her, but at the same time didn't want to go too far, not yet, it was too soon after her father's passing and he wanted to give her more time.

Sarah looked up at Frank leaning over her, she couldn't see the sky, or the clouds anymore, he was blocking them out. His dark curly hair fell over his forehead as he leant toward her. She looked deeply into his eyes and could feel herself becoming lost in the dark pools of blue. As Frank leant closer, Sarah felt her heart start to beat rapidly, his arm went around her waist and she could feel his body resting against hers. When he put his mouth on hers, Sarah shut her eyes and opened her mouth. Frank's tongue slipped inside and touched her teeth and her tongue. Sarah opened her mouth further and holding his warm touch against her, kissed him back. Then he was gone, Frank lay back down suddenly. Sarah lay quietly looking up at the sky, her body in turmoil. She wanted Frank to keep his body against hers, to keep kissing her. It felt wonderful when he kissed her, he made her body tingle with excitement.

Sarah sat up suddenly and started to pack up their picnic things. Frank sat up too when he saw her start to pack up. "What are you doing Cole?" Frank asked as he watched her throwing things into the rucksack.

"I've got to get back to town!" she hurriedly gathered up the rucksack and rushed to Star where she lifted the rucksack up and tied it to her saddle-horn.

"Why do you have to get back to town?" Frank followed her to her horse and grabbing her by her arm turned her around to face him, confused at Sarah suddenly wanting to end their picnic.

"I have to go, that's all." Sarah's cheeks were pink, she didn't want to tell Frank the real reason why she wanted to go back to town.

"Did I do something wrong?" Frank worried he may have frightened Sarah when he kissed her and that she may not have liked him kissing her. But she responded and kissed him back, so he thought that couldn't possibly be what was wrong.

"No Mason, you didn't, I just have to go." Sarah didn't want Frank to think he had done anything wrong, she was more afraid of her own feelings. She thought if she lay with him for too long, she would want him to touch her intimately and she had never been touched by a man before. She pulled her arm free from Frank's grasp and put her foot up in the stirrup, lifting herself up into the saddle. Frank ran to his horse and got up into his saddle, then pulled his horse around quickly when Sarah started to ride off. When he caught up to her, they rode side by side without speaking. Frank kept glancing over at Sarah and wondered all the way back to town what happened to make her end their picnic.

They returned to the Livery and Stable where Frank tied his horse to the hitching rail outside while Sarah left her horse with Ham.

"Bye Mason!" Sarah said hurrying out of the Livery.

"When can I see you again?" he called after her as she started to hurry down the street.

"When you come to town again ...I guess." Sarah kept walking. Frank followed her a little way then stopped. He watched her heading quickly toward the Ferguson House carrying the rucksack over her shoulder. Sarah's long hair tied back in a tail bobbed as she walked and her hips swayed a little. Frank felt a wave of emotions course through him as he watched her.

'So, it wasn't all that bad,' he thought. Sarah said he could see her when he came to town again. "So, what just happened?" Frank asked himself, confused with Sarah's behaviour.

"Enjoy your ride Frank?" Frank almost jumped out of his skin when he heard a deep voice behind him. He looked around to see Joe standing beside him. Joe was at the corrals when he saw Sarah and Frank ride back in over the bridge. He stopped looking over the horse Garrett was working and followed Frank as Sarah hurried back to the Ferguson House.

"Yeah Joe, I did." Frank smiled at Joe as they both stood watching Sarah until she raced up the steps and disappeared inside the house.

Joe shoved his hands inside his coat pockets. "What are your intentions with Sarah Frank?" Joe didn't see any reason not to come straight out and ask Frank what he intended where Sarah was concerned. Frank and Sarah had started to spend a lot of time together and he was responsible for Sarah's wellbeing. Joe was happy to let Sarah go riding and spend time with Frank, he wanted her to be happy, but he didn't want Frank to get the wrong idea about it. Frank thought he knew what Joe was asking him, he smiled his huge smile up at Joe.

"I intend to marry her." Frank still smiling, shoved his hands in his pants pockets and shrugged his shoulders at Joe. Joe wasn't surprised at Frank's admission, he suspected that might have been what Frank had in mind. He wouldn't discourage Frank, but he wouldn't encourage him either. "You do know she is going back to the mountain in the spring?"

"Not if I can change her mind." Frank felt confident he could get Sarah to stay in Cedar Creek to be near him.

"You won't change her mind Frank, she belongs on the mountain, that's her home and it always will be, she will be going back there come spring." Joe took his hands out of his pockets, turned, and walked back to the corrals, leaving Frank to ponder how he was going to convince Sarah to stay. "If I can't get her to stay, then I will follow her." Frank said to no-one in particular.

After spending so much time with Sarah he had fallen in love with her and was sure Sarah was in love with him, and so he believed that reason should be enough for her to want to stay with him?

Each day they spent together Frank loved Sarah more. He was pleased Sarah wasn't like any of the girls he met when he lived in Philadelphia. Sarah was full of life and they were dull. She knew how to ride and fire a rifle. The girls in Philadelphia rode around in carriages so they wouldn't ruin their pretty dresses and they talked incessantly about themselves, making him bored. Sarah and he had interesting conversations about nature, people they knew, his father's ranch and Sarah's mountain. He even kissed a girl once back in Philadelphia. That kiss when he thought about it, left him feeling cold. When he kissed Sarah, his whole body came alive. Sarah's mouth was soft, warm and inviting.

Frank had never been with a woman physically and he wanted Sarah to be his first. He hoped he would be Sarah's first. Frank was sure Sarah hadn't yet been with a man. She was fifteen, old enough to be married, but by his reckoning, she hadn't been with anyone. Frank knew from the way Sarah reacted when he kissed her on Christmas Day she had never been kissed before.

Then there was their kiss at the picnic just now. Frank came to the realization Sarah was just unsure of herself when they kissed and that was why she left in a hurry. Frank smiled to himself. He was ready for marriage and while riding back to the ranch he did a lot of thinking. Making up his mind he would ask Sarah to marry him before she could leave for the mountain. He would ask her to stay in Cedar Creek to be with him next time he saw her.

A little over a week after their picnic, Frank rode to town to ask Sarah to marry him. He slept little since the picnic, worrying about Sarah leaving and not wanting her to go. Frank was aware the trappers time in Cedar Creek was drawing to an end and he wanted to take Sarah out for a ride so they could be somewhere alone. Somewhere where he could ask her to marry him, like their favourite spot at the ponds. He had it all figured out, he would ask her, Sarah would say yes, they would get married before the trappers left to go back to the mountain so they could all join in with the festivities. Joe would give Sarah away, because ever since Sarah's father died, Joe had become like a father to her.

Frank decided as he rode past the church and the corrals, that Sarah and he could live at the ranch with his father until they got a place of their own. After all, the ranch-house was a huge house with many rooms they could make their own for the time being. He would wait to tell his father he was getting married after Sarah accepted him. It was no good telling his father he was getting married before asking her, Frank smiled to himself. His father he was sure, would give them his blessing and welcome Sarah into their family.

Frank was unaware of how much his father despised Sarah, simply because of what her father did to him in Philadelphia before Sarah was born. Frank was feeling happy as he rode in to town.

Chapter Ten

A few days after Sarah and Frank went on their picnic, Major Hardy's men ran in a herd of wild horses to the corrals. Joe and the other trappers found themselves pressed for spare time, forcing them to leave Sarah to her own devices. Sarah told Joe and the other trappers she would be alright, she hadn't cooked for a while so decided she would stay at the house and cook for the men.

When Sarah had enough of cooking, she went to the Livery and saddled Star. Since her Pa died, she hadn't a real lot of time to be alone and she wanted time to think about what she would do when she got back to the mountain and the cabin, she also wanted to think about Frank.

Sarah rode out of town without any of the men working in the corrals seeing her go. She climbed onto a boulder and sat down in the warm sunshine. She pulled her legs up in front of her as usual and wrapped her arms around them.

At first, Sarah's thoughts were all about her father and everything that happened since he died. She was positive Crawley killed him and hoped there would come a day when she could prove it. She thought about the time just a couple of months ago when Crawley threw her out of The Lodge, pulling her down the stairs by her hair making her hurt herself. Sarah vowed never to step foot in Mountain View Lodge ever again. She felt a lump rise in her throat. She had a lot of happy memories staying in The Lodge each winter, and now it no longer belonged to her.

A tear streaked her face and she brushed it away with her hand. Sarah did a lot of crying these past months and she had had enough. She resolved not to cry nearly so much, after all, she wasn't a cry baby, she was far tougher than that, besides, once she was back on the mountain she would be on her own, so she had to get used to it. Sarah told herself that from today, there would be no more crying.

She pulled her legs in closer and hugged them tighter, then thought about the day she first met Frank. He knew she was angry at her father for leaving her, letting her hit him to help her get rid of her anger, and she punched him and slapped him hard. Her body shook with cold at being soaked to the bone and her clothes clung to her. That, she remembered, was when Frank gave her his coat. It wasn't until she looked in the mirror back in her room she knew why Frank had given her his coat. Sarah blushed at the memory of him seeing her through her shirt. Frank covered her so the other men couldn't see what he saw. She liked Frank even more for doing that.

Whenever she thought about Frank, something happened to her she couldn't explain. After giving her Star for Christmas, all he asked in return was a kiss, and when their lips met, she felt emotions course through her she had never experienced before.

Again, when he kissed her at their picnic, their bodies were so close she could feel the warmth from his body as he lay against her. She still feels surprised by her own reaction to his closeness. The moment Frank's hand went around her waist and he brushed her hair off her face, she wanted to reach up and pull him down on top of her, but something made her hold back. She became confused, her body was telling her she was ready to let Frank have his way with her, but her mind was telling her she wasn't ready.

On the ride back from the picnic she felt Frank's eyes on her. Whenever he looked at her, she felt the same rush of emotions she didn't understand. After arriving back at the Livery, she just wanted to escape from his gaze and almost ran all the way back to the house, then went straight to her room to calm down. When she undressed for bed that night, she stood in front of the mirror and studied herself, becoming convinced she was ready for a man's touch, Frank's touch. So why? she kept asking herself, why did she run away from him?

Still sitting on the boulder Sarah made up her mind that if Frank kissed her again and he wanted to touch her, she would let him. She wanted to know what it would be like to have him make love to her. 'After-all,' she thought. 'I'm not a little girl anymore, I am a grown woman and I want Frank to love me.' She smiled to herself at her decision and jumped off the boulder. Landing on both feet on the grass she practically skipped up the track to where Star was tethered.

Major Hardy rode out from his ranch to check on his herd of steers that were being held at the dry gulch. His two hired guns, Foley and Brady were with him. Cowhands and trappers should be busy branding steers that hadn't already been branded. As Major Hardy got close to where the herd was, some of the men that were supposed to be watching the herd were clearly visible sitting around a fire, smoking and talking. When they saw Major Hardy approaching, they stood up quickly to greet him. Major Hardy was a tough man to work for, he wasn't called the Major for nothing. He carried a whip and wasn't afraid to use it or brandish it at men who slackened off. Major Hardy hated lay-abouts, he didn't want any of them to be wasting time, his herd was important, they meant money.

After talking with the men and making sure they were watching his herd, Major Hardy and his two gun-hands rode off along the river. He wanted to check his boundaries before riding back to the ranch-house.

They kept to Major Hardy's land until they came to a place where they could see across the river to the ponds. The view extended between tall stands of trees to the boulders on the other side. It wasn't hard for the three men to spot Sarah sitting on one of the boulders.

"There's that whore Frank has been going to town to see all the time ...I wonder if he's fucking her!" Major Hardy laughed out loud, thinking Foley and Brady, being the tough men he knew them to be, thought his remarks about Sarah might impress them. Both Foley and Brady cringed at the Major's crude remarks. His remarks especially got Foley thinking. "Well he can fuck her all he wants, but he won't be marrying her ...not if I have anything to do with it ...let's go ...I've got to talk to her!" Major Hardy spurred his horse and rode off ahead of his men.

Foley liked Sarah a whole lot more than he let on he should. He liked her the very first day he met her, when he and Brady first arrived in Cedar Creek. The day he was walking down the street one way and Sarah came rushing up the other, heading to the corrals to watch the men breaking horses. Having collided with each other, Sarah ended up sitting on the ground. Foley stared down at the girl that bumped into him and immediately knew she was the girl he wanted to marry. He asked about the girl running around town wearing boy's trousers and soon found out she was Calahan Cole's daughter. The fact her father and the trappers kept everyone away from her didn't faze Foley, but still, he didn't have much to do with her over the following two winters. Work on Major Hardy's ranch kept him and Brady busy, neither of them had much free time for themselves. It wasn't until her father died when he watched her crying at her father's burial that he wanted to put his arms around her and comfort her, but he couldn't, not with all the trappers crowded around her. Now seeing Sarah sitting on the boulders at the ponds he worried Major Hardy might be going to do something to hurt her. Foley wanted Sarah to like him and would never hurt her. He tried hard to hide the feelings he had for Sarah from everyone. Except for telling Brady how he felt no-one else knew. He didn't like the way Major Hardy spoke about her just now, still, he needed this job. Keen to marry and settle down, he was saving to buy his own ranch. He wanted to have children and the woman he hoped to marry and settle down with was sitting on a boulder over at the ponds, and right then, Major Hardy was about to do something Foley had no control over. He wouldn't disobey his boss, but that didn't stop him worrying about what he might have in mind for Sarah.

Sarah headed back toward town, she was happy with the decision she made concerning Frank. It was getting on toward dusk when she rounded a bend on the trail close to the river. Three men came riding out of the trees ahead of her and blocked her path. She recognized Foley and Brady riding with Major Hardy. She didn't have much to do with Foley, or Brady when they worked with her father branding steers. She thought them too quiet men that minded their own business, neither man got into trouble around town, no trouble that she knew of anyway. Frank's father looked sternly at her. Sarah thought Foley and Brady didn't seem at all surprised to see her.

"Well! Well! Sarah Cole!" Major Hardy sneered at her. "What are you doing out here all alone Cole?" Sarah shrugged her shoulders as if what she was doing out riding was no concern of the Major's. "I'm just out riding Major." She held Stars reins tight while her eyes darted from Major Hardy to Foley then to Brady and back to Major Hardy. "Just riding my ass!" Major Hardy suddenly barked, causing Sarah to pull hard on Star's reins and startling him. Trying to get away, Star stomped his hooves causing Sarah to pull back on the reins harder to get him to stop moving around so much. "You came out here looking for my son …well you can stop looking …my son doesn't need a no-good stinking trapper whore hanging about, so you stay away from him!" He pointed his finger at her. "You are no good Cole, you might whore around with all those men up there on that mountain, but you won't be having anything to do with my son …I've got plans for Frank and they don't involve a goddamn stinkin' trapper!" Major Hardy knew Sarah wasn't a whore, she was a young woman who had been protected from men by her father, and four trappers in particular helped him. But now her father was gone, making Sarah prey to any man. Major Hardy wanted to implant the idea of her being a whore into every man's mind that he could so they would think her the worst kind of woman and she would stay away from Frank.

Foley and Brady felt embarrassed for Sarah. Watching Sarah closely, they listened as Major Hardy went on calling her names making the two men cringe. Major Hardy turned his attention to Sarah's horse. "Is that one of my goddamn horses? …Foley, take a look at it!" Bringing his horse up beside Star, Foley reached over his horse and grabbed Star by the bridle. "I don't think so Major." Foley glanced fleetingly at Sarah while trying to make out the horse wasn't one of the Majors, knowing full well the colt was from the Major's herd.

"Get off that horse Cole!" Major Hardy ordered. Sarah didn't hesitate, she got down quickly and moved away from Star. "He was a gift …Frank gave him to me for Christmas …he said you were going to shoot him!" Sarah was frightened, her eyes brimmed with tears and she blurted out what Frank told her, thinking if the Major remembered telling Frank he was going to shoot Star, he would realize Frank saved the colt from certain death and that Star was a gift she couldn't refuse, and he would let her go. Because Frank's kiss from her had been his ulterior motive for wanting her to take his gift, Sarah didn't know Frank lied about his father threatening to shoot the horse. "Shoot him! I don't shoot my horses, not unless they are sick or injured, Frank had no right to take him ...is there a brand on it Foley?" Major Hardy could see the colt was one of the best horses to ever come from his stock. Foley got down from his horse and walked around Star making out he was looking for a brand.

Sarah didn't know what these men had in mind for her. She didn't have her Pa's knife or his rifle with her and had no way of defending herself against these men. If they were going to try something she would fight with her bare hands if she needed too, she would fight as hard as she could.

"There's no brand Major." Foley already knew there wouldn't be a brand, he and Brady helped Frank choose the horse, knowing it was going to be a gift for Sarah. Foley didn't see any harm in giving Sarah the colt if it was to make her happy. The horse hadn't been branded when Frank gave it to her and it still didn't have a brand.

"Goddamn it! If Frank gave it to her it has to be one of mine ...I tell you what Cole ...you can keep the horse …on one condition...if Frank goes to town to see you ...you tell him to stay away from you ...you tell him you don't want anything to do with him!" Major Hardy got off his horse and reached for the whip looped around his saddle-horn. He stretched the whip along the ground and held it by the stock.

"I'll show you what's going to happen to you if you don't stay away from Frank ...I'll make you so goddamn ugly …no man will ever want you!" Major Hardy made his voice threatening. He wasn't going to whip Sarah, just scare her a little. Sarah was beginning to get frightened and made to move toward Star. Major Hardy saw her move and yelled at his men. "Get hold of her Foley, you too Brady!" The two men, obeying his order, grabbed Sarah by her arms and held onto her so she couldn't get away. Sarah began to cry, tears slid down her cheeks, so much for not ever crying she thought.

"Major Hardy please ...let me go ...I won't see Frank ...please ...don't hurt me!" Sarah sobbed as she begged him not to hurt her. She tried to free herself from the hold Foley and Brady had on her but they held her so tight she thought they might break her arms.

"Don't you ever let me hear you speak Frank's name!" Major Hardy yelled, swinging the whip around his head and bringing it down quickly. The whip made a loud crack that reverberated through the air. Foley cursed out loud when he heard the whip-crack. Brady cursed silently. Major Hardy swung the whip again, this time as it whipped out it caught the tip of Sarah's hat. Sarah felt the wind caused by the whip as it sliced through the hat near her face, cutting the hat across the brim. Foley and Brady held Sarah up as her knees buckled. Major Hardy wound up his whip. "That's just a warning of what could happen to you if you keep seeing Frank, you stay the hell away from my son …and I'm also warning you ...stay the hell off my land!" Major Hardy draped the whip back over his saddle-horn. "Goddamn stinking trapper whore!" he muttered loud enough for Sarah to hear. "Let her go!" he ordered the men.

Foley and Brady let Sarah go. When her arms were free, she ran to Star, grabbed the reins and almost fell when she missed putting her foot in the stirrup. Her legs felt numb as she pulled herself up into the saddle. Kicking Star hard with her heel, Star bolted. Her heart was pounding so hard she thought it would burst out of her chest. Gasping, she tried to choke back tears streaming down her face. Major Hardy laughed as Sarah and Star raced back toward town. Foley and Brady watched on silently as Sarah's horse carried her away to safety. "You aren't worried about her telling the trappers what just happened?" Foley asked the Major. Foley was worried all three of them could be in serious trouble with the trappers once they found out what they had done to Sarah. Right then he felt contempt for Major Hardy but managed to hide his contempt in his voice.

"Why should I be worried? those men work for me while they are here and if they want to keep working for me, they will do nothing!" Major Hardy wanted to scare Sarah and he had succeeded. He wouldn't actually whip her, not on the face anyway, not where the whiplash could be seen. Foley looked along the road where Sarah had gone. He glanced over at Brady with disgust evident on his face. Brady looked just as disgusted back at Foley.

As Major Hardy rode back to his ranch, he thought about the business trip he took to Philadelphia. What a fool he had been that night to have introduced Elizabeth to Calahan Cole. After returning to Cedar Creek to build his empire, he thought he left Elizabeth safely with her parents. Hearing rumours that he and Elizabeth were no longer engaged, he raced to Elizabeth's side to find out if the rumours were true. Elizabeth confessed saying she thought it unfair she should keep him believing she was in love with him when all along she had fallen in love with Calahan. Having broken off their engagement, she straight away accepted Calahan's proposal of marriage, leaving him feeling embarrassed when word spread that he had been jilted, and furious when he learnt who the man was he had been jilted for. Angry too, when having to cover up his embarrassment by bringing Victoria, a woman he had known from his childhood and had an affair with, to Cedar Creek. Although Victoria gave him a son in Frank, he didn't love her. To him, Frank was the only good thing to have come of his relationship with Victoria.

Major Hardy remembered Cole trying to apologize to him for stealing his fiancé. He remembered him saying he tried his hardest to keep his feelings for Elizabeth hidden, thinking it was wrong for him to be in love with someone else's fiance' but adding he couldn't help how he felt about Elizabeth. But he refused to accept Cole's apology, instead he became furious with his deceit, thinking there was no excuse for a man to steal another man's woman.

Cole came back to Cedar Creek with Elizabeth as his new bride and after only a year together they had their daughter Sarah. Major Hardy resented the fact Cole married the woman he was deeply in love with and planned to marry. He refused to marry Frank's mother and when Victoria learnt he was still in love with Elizabeth she walked out on him, taking their three-year old son Frank back to Philadelphia with her. Major Hardy never forgave Cole, nor would he ever forgive Cole's daughter Sarah for her mother and father's infidelity.

He would never let his son and Cole's daughter be together, he had much bigger plans for Frank. If he had anything to do with it, his son would marry Millicent Crawley. Millicent's father now owned Mountain View Lodge. Major Hardy smiled to himself when thinking about The Lodge. Frank and Millicent would make The Lodge their main place of residence and would travel regularly between Cedar Creek and Philadelphia where Millicent is friends with daughters of railway-men, cattlemen and men who owned shipping companies that would buy his cattle and horses for transporting overseas. With Millicent's contacts, Major Hardy could see Frank becoming an important man in cattle and horse trading. He thought too, it rather ironic that The Lodge would soon end up belonging in his family. The Lodge is the grandest house in town, if not the county, so why shouldn't his son have a grand place to live. Major Hardy, as he rode along, was feeling pleased at being able to take something of value away from Calahan Cole.

His thoughts turned to Millicent, being the same age as Sarah. Admitting to himself she is nowhere near as pretty as Sarah. But he is sure, being as plain as Millicent is, she would be faithful to his son. Sarah Cole, on the other hand, was far too pretty, there was no way she would ever be faithful to Frank, just like her mother hadn't been faithful to him. He often heard his men talking about Sarah and knew from their talk a lot of men were in love with her. 'No,' he thought. 'Even if nothing came of a business career for Frank in Philadelphia. Millicent Crawley would be the woman his son was going to marry.'

Star raced over the bridge, Sarah turned him into the Livery where she jumped down and left him in the stall with his saddle on. After crying all the way back to town, she was left feeling breathless. Ham, busily working at his forge, saw her come tearing in, her face red and tear stained.

"Sarah, whatever is the matter?" He put down his hammer and came around to Sarah just as she bolted past him and out the door. He followed her outside and standing in the street, scratched his head while watching her as she ran crying to the Ferguson house. "Goddamn it, what has happened to that child now?" he said to himself. But he couldn't do anything, it was up to the trappers to sort whatever happened to Sarah out, she was their responsibility. He went back inside and unsaddled Star.

Sarah ran onto the porch and couldn't get inside quick enough. She flew through the door slamming it shut behind her. Feeling relieved at finding the house empty of men, she raced to her room, threw her hat on the floor and threw herself on the bed. Her mind was racing, she sobbed loudly. Major Hardy scared the hell out of her, he didn't want Frank to have anything to do with her, he wanted her to stay away from Frank. He called her a ...a ...what was that word? 'Whore'...that was the word. "What is a whore?" she asked herself, she didn't know what a whore was, she had never heard the men or her father use that word before, at least ways not in front of her. She would ask Joe, Joe would know, he would tell her what a whore is.

Sarah wondered what would have happened to her if Major Hardy's whip had hit her on her face. She jumped off the bed, grabbed her hat and held it up in front of her. The hat had a cut in it, going right across from the outside edge of the brim to where the hat sat on her head. The hat had been her Pa's and now it was ruined, she would have to show Joe just what Major Hardy had done. Sarah was shaking, she had another fright, just like the night her Pa died when Crawley pulled her down the stairs and threw her out into the dirt. Sarah lay back down and cried some more, unable to understand why they treated her like they did. What had she done to Crawley? It was him who had taken her house and killed her Pa, that's what Crawley did to her. And what about Major Hardy? what had she done to him except like his son? She lay down and sobbed until she heard the men coming in.

Joe and a dozen trappers came back from the corrals to the house just on dark expecting their dinner to be ready. Sarah said she would cook tonight so when they walked in, they were shocked to see the fire was out and the house was cold and dark. The table hadn't been set, Sarah always set the table for dinner.

"Sarah said this morning she was going to cook today, what happened?" Fergus stepped through the door behind Joe. "Cole's probably off with Frank Mason again!" Logan's comment when he spoke was sarcastic. Joe glared at him and went to Sarah's door. The men gathered together in the room to watch as Joe knocked. Sarah opened the door quickly, causing the men to step back when she came out. It was obvious Sarah had been crying again. The men huddled together in a group and looked at Sarah's tear stained face.

"What's happened Sarah?" Joe was tired from the days hard work but came alert when he saw the state Sarah was in. Fergus, Will and Garret moved to stand near her.

"What is a whore Joe?" Sarah blurted out. The men gasped in shock at hearing what Sarah said. They glanced quickly at each other. Some of the men turned their backs while they swore quietly, others quickly disappeared into the washroom, all trying not to look too intently at Sarah. Joe didn't answer her question right then, he was too shocked Sarah had even said the word.

"Major Hardy called me a stinking trapper whore, what is a whore?" Sarah's eyes misted as she looked into Joe's eyes for answers. Joe pulled Sarah into his arms and she pressed her face against his huge chest and cried. Sarah told herself at the ponds she wasn't going to cry anymore but this was just too much and Major Hardy had frightened her.

"It's nothing you need worry about." Some of the men could be heard making threatening comments about the Major. All of the men that worked out at the Major's ranch and at the corrals were fully aware none of them could carry out their threats.

"Goddamn ...that son-of-a-bitch!" Logan didn't like Major Hardy. He didn't like a lot of people, but he liked Sarah to the point he thought he might be in love with her, all he knew was he wanted her badly, but Joe was making it difficult for him or any other man to get near her.

"Why did he call Sarah that?" Fergus, looking at Joe for the answer, put his hand on Sarah's shoulder while she kept her head on Joe's chest.

"Just where did you see the Major Sarah?" Joe asked, gently pushing Sarah back and holding her by her arms.

"I went for a ride, I got tired of being here cooking, I just wanted to be by myself to..." she didn't finish explaining before Joe interrupted her.

"You were already by yourself ...here in this house!" he scowled, pointing his finger at Sarah as he admonished her. "You don't go anywhere on your goddamn own ...you hear me?" Joe's voice rose slightly. He was tired and felt angry that something else happened to Sarah that he was unaware of.

"Don't you go yelling at me Joseph Beauford Jones ...I don't need you yelling at me ...I almost got myself whipped!" Sarah sadly said back to Joe, while pulling her arms free. Rushing back to her room, she stopped just inside the doorway and holding on to the door, looked back out at the men. "*...And I'm a whore!*" she yelled before slamming the door shut behind her. Joe was taken aback at Sarah accusing him of yelling at her, he wasn't yelling at her, he just wanted her to understand she couldn't go off by herself.

"Did she just say she nearly got whipped Joe?" Garrett and Logan both ignored that Sarah had called herself a whore when they spoke almost at the same time.

Reeves, Logan's just as nasty partner, stepped toward the men before speaking. "She did say she almost got whipped and the only person I know who has a whip around here is the Major." Logan hit Reeves on the arm to warn him not to say too much. He didn't want to be reprimanded by the Major if he found out they said anything against him. Reeves took the hint when he looked at Logan and stepped back away from the rest of the men.

Joe told the men to get the fire going and heat up the pot of food that was sitting cold on the stove. At least, Joe could see, Sarah had prepared dinner before she went out and got herself in a whole mess of trouble. The men could dish up their own food tonight, he had to sort this mess out with Sarah. Joe opened the door to Sarah's room and followed her in.

When Joe had gone to Sarah's room, and while they heated up their evening meal, the men got talking. "Goddamn it! what the hell are we supposed to do with her?" Doyle said to Garrett. "We can't tie her up or lock her in!" Baker said.

"Every time she's left alone something happens," Garret said in answer to the two men.

"Yeah! why would he call Sarah a whore, she ain't a whore, she ain't ever been with one man let alone a whole bunch of men!" Doyle and all the other men suddenly realized what he just said. The men's murmurings went quiet when it dawned on them that maybe Sarah, being there in the house with all of them was why she was being called a whore.

"What did the Major do besides call you names Sarah?" Joe sat on the side of Sarah's bed next to her. Sarah held her Pa's hat in her hand and looked at the floor.

"He told me to stay away from Frank, he called me a whore, he doesn't want Frank to have anything to do with me, he said he would make me so ugly no-one would want me and he ruined Pa's hat with his whip, see!" Sarah held the hat up for Joe to see.

"It was on my head Joe, I felt the whip come close to my face ...I was so scared." Joe was angry at the Major for scaring Sarah, he put his arm around her and she leant against him.

"Whore means something bad, doesn't it Joe?"

Joe had to tell her what the word meant, it was no use keeping it from her, he tried to make it sound like it wasn't so bad. "It's a woman who likes being with a lot of men." Joe realized he explained it the wrong way the moment he said it, Sarah lived in a house full of men. Sarah pushed herself away from Joe and stood up "Major Hardy was right, I am a whore, because I like being with all of you men." Sarah looked horrified at Joe and Joe seeing her look, tried to explain it plainer without going in to too much detail.

"A whore is not a bad woman, she is a woman that lets a man touch her in a certain way, making that man feel good about himself, different men have different needs and well, a certain type of woman can satisfy those needs ...you are not one of those women Sarah, Major Hardy just wanted to scare you." Joe's explanation satisfied Sarah. She sat back down next to Joe and thought about Frank and those needs.

"I've never let anyone touch me Joe." Sarah thought she knew where on a woman a man may like to touch her, she felt like letting Frank touch her there but was too scared to take that step.

"I will never let a man touch me ...not ever," she added quietly. Joe thought about Frank and what Frank said about him wanting to marry Sarah. Joe liked Frank, as Frank spent more time with Sarah Joe thought he would be good for her, but they would never marry, not if Sarah didn't want anyone to touch her.

Joe explained to Sarah that loving one man didn't make a woman a whore, it meant she found someone she wanted to spend the rest of her life with. Joe hoped this would make Sarah understand more about Frank.

Joe coaxed Sarah out to the meal room to eat dinner with the men. There was a lot of talk around the table but no-one brought up

Major Hardy or mentioned the word Sarah uttered. The talk came around to leaving Cedar Creek and returning to the mountain. It was only three more weeks until they could load up their packhorses and head back up the trail. Sarah was happy when she realized their time in Cedar Creek was drawing to an end. She wanted desperately to go home, to get away from Major Hardy and Cedar Creek. Going home would make it easier for her to stay away from Frank too. It also meant she would be leaving her Pa behind for the very first time.

Chapter Eleven

After riding past the corrals and turning down the main street, Frank called at the Ferguson House for Sarah. He felt nervous but excited about asking her to marry him. He patted his pocket once more to make sure his mother's Sapphire and Diamond ring was still there, hoping to put it on Sarah's finger when she accepted his proposal.

It was early morning and Sarah was inside having breakfast with the trappers. Frank was getting used to having all the men hearing him calling out from his horse for Sarah. This time however, he decided to get off his horse and walk to the door and knock. Frank was unaware of the confrontation Sarah had with his father a few days earlier. The sound of voices inside the house stopped when they heard Frank's knock. Samuels yanked open the door at the interruption to their breakfast and stood there glaring at Frank.

"Is Sarah here? I thought she might like to go riding." Frank smiled at Samuels. Sarah came to the door when she heard Frank's voice. "Go away Mason, I don't want to go riding with you, stay away from me!" Pushing Samuels out of her way, Sarah stepped back, and slammed the door closed, leaving Frank standing on the porch. Frank was shocked at Sarah's sudden outburst, she always went riding with him. He didn't know whether he should knock again or just go away like she wanted him too. He took a chance and knocked again.

"Go away Mason!" Sarah yelled from inside the house. Frank was mystified at Sarah, he was puzzled to know what he had done to deserve her yelling at him and suddenly telling him to go away. They had enjoyed their picnic and their many rides together. The trappers watched Sarah sit back at the table and continue to eat, her face betraying what she was feeling. Sarah hated herself for telling Frank to go away, but she was more afraid if she didn't tell him to go Frank's father would come and whip her and she didn't want that. Frank hadn't been able to ask Sarah to marry him, feeling rejected, he returned to his father's ranch.

Frank wouldn't give up, he rode back to town several more times over the next week and the same thing happened. Sarah kept refusing to go out riding with him or even talk to him.

"I don't want anything to do with you Mason, so go away!" Sarah continued to rebuff Frank, but he kept asking her to go riding and each time she got angrier.

"Are you stupid Mason? I told you to stay away from me ...damn son-of-a-bitch!" she muttered. Frank was shocked that Sarah would talk to him that way, she had only ever spoken to him like that once before and that was at the cemetery when they were sitting in the rain beside her Pa's grave. He knew she was upset at the time and he brushed off her bad language. She had never spoken to him like it since, not until now. He couldn't understand her sudden change toward him. He felt wretched as once again he rode back to his father's ranch.

The last week couldn't come around quick enough for Sarah. The trappers were getting ready to leave. They gathered their supplies and made sure their horses were in top condition for the trip back to the mountain. Frank tried once more to see Sarah. Sarah was in the Livery with Star when Frank walked in. She turned quickly when she heard Frank's voice behind her.

"Why don't you want to come riding with me?" Frank hadn't slept much since Sarah's attitude toward him changed, tossing and turning and lying awake. He even cried into his pillow. He felt stupid for crying, he was a man not a boy. He asked himself why it upset him so much that Sarah refused to go riding with him. Then answered his question for himself. 'Because he was deeply in love with her' that was why.

"What's wrong Cole? What did I do to make you angry with me?" he asked her, his face furrowing with worry. Sarah ducked around Frank and ran toward the door. "Stay away from me Mason,

I'm going back to the mountain." When Sarah stepped outside into the sunshine, her long brown hair glistened in the sunlight, making her look radiant. Frank could see Sarah was happy to be going back to the mountain, which made him feel worse. He wanted to take her in his arms and shake some sense into her, couldn't she see he loved her.

"I'll follow you Sarah Cole, I'll follow you to the mountain ...because ...because well ...I love you!" he wasn't smiling when he admitted how he felt, but was glad his feelings for her were finally out in the open. At least he wouldn't let her leave without her knowing how he felt about her. Sarah's eyes widened when she heard Frank's admission and she hesitated before answering.

"You ...you can't come to the mountain, you don't know anything about the mountain, besides ...I ...I don't love you!" Sarah lied. She did love Frank, so much so she thought her heart would stop beating when she lied to him. Major Hardy scared her when he cut her Pa's hat with his whip. She took his threat seriously, not wanting him to whip her. Sarah was convinced Frank wouldn't love her if she was whipped, no one would love her if she was made ugly. She ran back to the house to escape before Frank could tell she lied. Frank stood outside the Livery and watched the trappers getting their horses loaded. They all heard Frank's admission and were watching him.

"I will follow you Sarah Cole," he said almost to himself after she had gone. Frank didn't believe Sarah didn't love him and he wanted to know why she suddenly changed her attitude toward him. Someone must know what happened to make her hate him. He decided he would ask Joe.

Frank found Joe at the corrals, checking to see if his horses were ready for the long journey back to the mountain. When Frank asked Joe why Sarah was avoiding him, Joe knew why but didn't want to tell Frank it was because his father threatened her, he didn't want to cause trouble for Frank at his home, besides, he should not interfere. The promise he made was never far from his thoughts, sometimes though he wished he never made it.

Joe would never break his promise to Calahan, but now he questioned why his good friend would make him make such a promise. Joe thought if Calahan had known what the promise was doing to Sarah he wouldn't have made him or the other three men make it. Joe had his own good reason to take care of his best friend's daughter, regardless of making any such promise.

"All I can say Frank, is, maybe you should look closer to home for the answer." Joe hoped by saying that it didn't interfere with what he promised. He looked around to see if the other men heard what he said and hoped Frank was smart enough to figure out what had changed Sarah's attitude toward him for himself.

Nineteen trappers including Sarah and their packhorses left Cedar Creek at daylight the next day. Sarah rode along behind Joe, her two packhorses tethered behind each other as she held the reins leading them in a line. The horses were loaded with a whole lot of things Joe and the men insisted she would need when she got back to the cabin. Garrett rode behind her, Will and Fergus rode behind the three of them. A long line of trappers travelled away from Cedar Creek.

The trappers didn't bother camping out on the prairie for their first night, the days were stretching out longer now spring had come. They set up their first night's camp closer to the wells, making it just before nightfall. Joe kept his eye on Sarah to see if she regretted the way she spoke to Frank. Sarah did appear quieter than usual but still mingled with the men. He understood Sarah was scared of Frank's father, but felt she shouldn't have taken her fear out on Frank.

Each day Sarah rode along deep in thought, not talking as much to the men like she used to when her father was with them. She was sad when she thought about her father and how this was the first time he wasn't coming back to the mountain. She thought about what it would be like on her own once she got back to the cabin she once shared with him.

Sarah thought of Frank and his father too. She hoped that by going back to the mountain it would give her some breathing space, she would see Frank next winter when she returned to Cedar Creek. By then she hoped Major Hardy may have had a change of heart regarding her and maybe she and Frank could become friends again. Although she didn't think Major Hardy would change his mind. For some reason he hated her and his threat's sounded final. Sarah thought about her trip home. They still had a long way to go.

They encountered a huge wolf pack lying in wait for them at the base of the mountain. This was the first time Sarah had to fend for herself against the wolves. Her father always kept her beside him so he could dispatch any wolves threatening to attack them. Sarah didn't hold back, using her father's rifle, her bullets found their mark when two wolves came running alongside Star. Star was fast, keeping up his pace as he raced beside the trappers heading for the mountain and the trail leading up to the pass. Joe glanced over at Sarah and Sarah looked back at Joe. They laughed at each other as their horses kept racing along. After the wolves went skulking back into the woods, the men along with Sarah, skinned their kill. Sarah had two wolf skins to start her collection off for the year. When the trappers got to the trail, snow still lay in patches on the ground.

They travelled slowly, being careful of the horses so they wouldn't slip on the icy trail. Before attempting to cross the pass, they made camp in the caves for their last night. Nineteen men split into groups and huddled around roaring fires in each cave. Sarah made her camp along with Joe, Fergus, Will and Garrett. They ate a hearty meal and slept soundly, then early the next morning as the sun rose over the mountains Joe led the trappers across the pass. The snow lying on the ground through the pass wasn't nearly as deep as it had been during winter. Sarah led her two packhorses and crossed safely behind Joe. They waited on the other side until all the men came across, then all of them made their way to the Low Ridge Camp and Sarah's cabin.

Getting to Sarah's cabin, the four trappers set up camp in the clearing. The rest of the trappers said their goodbyes and continued on their way up the mountain to the High Ridge Camp.

Will, Fergus and Garrett each helped unload Sarah's supplies and carried them inside. Sarah stood in the middle of the cabin, her father's belongings evident all around her. Joe stood beside her and watched her looking at everything.

"You going to be alright here on your own Sarah?" Joe put his arm around Sarah's shoulders. Sarah wiped a tear away that ran down her cheek.

"I'll be fine Joe, I've got to be, this is my home," she sniffled. Fergus and Garrett walked around Joe and Sarah and went back outside to bring in more supplies. Will carried two large bags of flour across his shoulders and pushed past them.

That night Sarah ate dinner outside with the men, then retired to her cabin to sleep. Even though the men were camped just outside Sarah spent her first night back in the cabin feeling lonelier than she had ever felt before. She slept in her own bed and tried to cry softly so the men sleeping outside couldn't hear. At daylight, she got up and dressed, then went outside to have breakfast with the men before they left for the High Ridge Camp. All four men heard her sobs during the night and tried their best not to listen, but her eyes were puffy and red and they could see by her face she had cried most of the night.

The men decided then to stay a couple more days to help Sarah with her chores. Garrett chopped enough wood to last her a month when the men would come back and chop her some more. Will and Fergus made sure her cabin was secure. Joe checked the area around the outhouse, the old cabin and the lean-to to make sure things were as they should be before he left Sarah to fend for herself.

The men packed up their camp ready to head to their own camp and hunting grounds, planning to spend most of their time hunting and trapping around the High Ridge and along the middle of the mountain. Joe asked Sarah again if she was fine staying there on her own, he thought he might stay longer with her, if only she would ask him. "Don't worry about me Joe, I just need time." Sarah reassured the men, then hugged each man and said goodbye to them.

The men were about to leave when they spotted someone coming up the trail from the direction of the pass. They stared at the man approaching on foot and leading one horse.

"Frank Mason!" Sarah couldn't believe her eyes as Frank looked up and waved his arm. "Goddamn, it is Frank!" Joe sung out to Frank and waved his arm in acknowledgement. "Where are you going Frank?" he laughed. Joe was pleased to see Frank, now he hoped Sarah and Frank would get to spend time together without Frank's father interfering.

"Where be your goddamn horse Frank?" Fergus yelled. They all laughed excitedly and rushed toward Frank to greet him, all except Sarah, her heart began to beat faster at the sight of him. Sarah stared at Frank until he got within hearing distance. Frank grinned back at the men as the four men crowded around him and patted him on the back, but he didn't get much of a chance to speak with any of them before Sarah started to berate him.

"You get back where you came from Mason, the mountain ain't no place for the likes of you, you don't belong here!" Sarah shocked even herself when she spoke, her voice sounded angry and threatening, just like Major Hardy's when he threatened her. Frank let go of his packhorse and coming closer to Sarah, looked directly at her without wavering.

"You don't own the mountain Cole, I can go anywhere I want to, if I've a mind too!" his face looked drawn, having endured four days travelling to get to the mountain. Wolves attacked him and killed one of his horses, then he lost his way. It was the thought of seeing Sarah that kept him going. All he wanted to do was wrap his arms around her and hug her and here she was talking to him the same as she had back in Cedar Creek. He was glad to see her and thought she may have felt the same way about him, but he was disappointed at the greeting he got from her.

"You think you're going to hang around here, well you're wrong, don't you go thinking you are welcome here …cause you are not!" Sarah snapped angrily. Frank wasn't going to give Sarah the satisfaction she thought she was going to get by berating him.

"I came here to learn to trap, not to hang about with you, what makes you think you're so special ...because …you are not!" he added, copying Sarah's retort. "Let's go Joe." Frank was dead on his feet and couldn't take much more traipsing up mountains, but he would keep moving if it meant Sarah would think he wasn't there for her. Sarah was shocked by Frank's retort, she turned and walked angrily into her cabin, slamming the door closed behind her.

Joe listened to the exchange between the young couple facing off in front of each other. 'Goddamn it if she wasn't a pain in the arse' Joe thought when Sarah disappeared inside. 'Frank came all this way to be with her and she treats him like he's nothin, that girl needs to learn about men, and she isn't going to learn about them this way.'

Sarah waited a few minutes until she regained her composure, then opened her cabin door and came back outside carrying a bucket. Joe told her they would wait another day, giving Frank time to rest before they started up the trail, while secretly hoping the two of them might sort out their anger toward each other. Frank watched Sarah walk past him, defiantly swinging the bucket back and forth as she walked down the incline toward the river. Joe watched Frank watching Sarah, able to tell just from the way Frank looked at Sarah that he was in love with her.

Joe remembered Frank told him at the Livery he was going to marry Sarah and Joe believed him. Joe thought Sarah was being unfair to Frank but was aware Sarah had to make her own choices when it came to choosing the man she would spend the rest of her life with. If it had been up to Joe to choose for her, he would choose Frank, but his hands were tied, he only hoped over time Sarah and Frank would sort out their differences, if only Major Hardy would stay out of it.

Coming back up the incline with her bucket of water, she struggled to carry it as water slopped over the top. Her Pa used to fetch all their water for them, filling the barrel they kept outside the front door, and the one inside the washroom, but now both barrels stood empty. Sarah refused to let Will or Garrett fill her water barrels, she wanted that job herself to get her mind off being alone. Sarah decided she wasn't going to fill both barrels up completely until the men had gone.

Frank rushed over to help her, grabbing the handle of the bucket, all the while Sarah gripped the handle tight as they both struggled with it.

"Let me help you with that," Frank insisted. When Frank's hand covered Sarah's he felt a sudden rush at touching her.

"Let go Mason ...I can do it myself." As they pulled against each other's grip more water slopped out of the bucket wetting their trousers.

"Let go!" Sarah yelled through gritted teeth. Frank let go and at the same time so did Sarah. The bucket fell to the ground and

tipped on its side. The rest of the water spilled out wetting their boots before soaking into the ground.

"Goddamn it! now look what you've done!" Sarah snapped angrily, picking up the bucket and heading back to the river.

"I'm sorry Sarah," Frank said softly. "I was only trying to help." Sarah got down the trail a little way and yelled back at Frank.

"I don't need your help Mason ...and stop calling me Sarah!" The men heard her loud angry reply, and feeling sorry for Frank, averted their eyes away from him. Frank went back to the men.

"Let her do it Frank," Joe said to him.

"I was only trying to help her Joe." Frank sounded tired and upset.

"You best leave her alone for now, being back here is probably making her a bit edgy, Sarah and her Pa lived in that cabin and now she has to get used to doing things on her own." Frank sat to one side of Joe and the other men while they set up a temporary camp.

Frank glanced up at Sarah as she came struggling back with another bucket of water. This time he didn't get up from where he was sitting, instead turned away so he couldn't see her struggling with the heavy bucket. Joe was probably right he thought, Sarah just needs time. He watched her carry the bucket of water inside and close the door.

Night came around quickly, the men sat around their campfire to eat and before too long settled down to sleep. They had an early start in the morning if they wanted to get on their way to the High Ridge Camp. Frank lay awake, his mind on Sarah alone in her cabin. She would be in her bed so near to him and still he couldn't go to her.

Getting undressed, Sarah lay her clothes on the chair beside her bed where she could get at them if she needed them and climbed into bed. She didn't bother with nightclothes now she was back at the cabin, hating the restriction on her body when they became twisted in the night. She had to wear a nightdress when living with her Pa and she didn't mind wearing a nightdress when she was living with all the trappers in the Ferguson House, but now she didn't have to, not now she was alone. She pulled the blankets over her body, then lay awake unable to fall asleep, her mind on Frank sleeping not far from her. 'Why had Frank come to the mountain? I told him to stay away from me, I stayed away from him, that was what Major Hardy wanted me to do, so why wouldn't Frank do as I asked? Why was he putting me in danger? I love Frank …but I can't be with him …he has to stay away from me like his father wanted.' Sarah found it hard to go to sleep knowing Frank was just outside.

Frank finally fell asleep and didn't wake up until he felt someone shaking him. He opened his eyes to find Joe standing over him.

"Frank, we got to start heading off if we want to make up some ground, the High Ridge Camp is still several days walk from here, and we want to be closer to it before nightfall." Frank got up and rolled up his bedroll then finished off the coffee the men left for him. Joe knocked on the cabin door and Sarah came out. Frank glanced up at her and could see she was already dressed ready for the day.

"We're leaving Sarah." Joe put his arms around Sarah and gave her a hug. "We'll be back in about a month, unless you want us to come back sooner." Sarah clung to Joe with her arms stretched around his solid belly, not wanting him to go.

"See you in a month Joe," she said almost too softly. Will, Fergus and Garret all hugged her and said their goodbyes. Frank hung back and waited until they were ready to go. He didn't know what he should do where Sarah was concerned. He would like to hold her and say goodbye to her too, but knew she wouldn't let him, he didn't know whether he should say anything to her or not.

The four trappers walked their horses along the trail between tall trees. Sarah stood at the side of the cabin and watched them go. Frank looked back at Sarah as he walked past her. When he got a safe distance away, he raised his arm and waved. Sarah folded her arms and didn't wave back.

Frank was hurting inside, he wanted Sarah to acknowledge him. But Frank had no choice, he had to go with the men. He followed the trappers along the trail leading to the High Ridge Camp. Sarah waited until the men disappeared into the woods, then went back inside her cabin.

Sarah hated herself for being so mean to Frank, she wanted desperately to be friends with him, but was afraid if she was friendly to him, because he awakened something inside her with his kiss, she wouldn't be able to stop herself from wanting him. She also dreaded the fact she would have to face Major Hardy when she went back to Cedar Creek next winter. She closed the door to her cabin, leant back on it and wept.

Chapter Twelve

It took Joe and the men four full days of trudging up the steep incline to get to the High Ridge Camp. They could hear wolves howling not too far away as they travelled up the trail. Each man carried their rifle at the ready for impending attacks. When several wolves got too close, they were soon shot and killed. The men getting the skins before they arrived back at their camp.

When the men arrived at the camp night had almost fallen. Frank was shocked by the makeshift cabins and rough timber structures that were built for shelter in and around a large clearing. A firepit full of wood was burning in the centre of the camp and several trappers were huddled around it. When they saw it was Joe's group approaching, they shouted their greetings and rushed toward the men.

Trappers came out of their shacks when they heard the men's shouts. They shook hands and patted Frank on the back, surprised to see him. Frank wondered if he hadn't made a terrible mistake coming to the mountain.

The men found Frank a space to camp in one of the makeshift cabins. The floor was dirt and the walls had gaps in them letting the heat of the day and cold night air in. He stowed his gear in a corner of the shack and settled in.

By the end of the first week he hadn't done much trapping but had blocked most of the gaps in the walls and built a stone fireplace to warm the cabin against inclement weather. He ate outside around the huge fire with the trappers and joined in with their banter. He spent the rest of his days following Joe around. He was already a good shot with a rifle but Joe had to show him how to set traps.

Joe gave Frank several of his traps to start him off. "You can buy some of your own when you get back to Cedar Creek next winter," Joe told him. Frank wasn't sure if he would last until next winter or whether he would come back to the mountain the following spring, his only reason for being here was to be near Sarah.

When Frank got his first wolf Joe taught him how to skin it. Frank's skins were slowly piling up. Not wanting any of the trappers claiming them for themselves, he kept them stored in his makeshift cabin where he could keep an eye on them. Frank was slowly becoming adept at skinning. At first the men made wisecracks at him and he felt like he didn't belong, but once he started to get skins, they stopped tormenting him and at the end of the first month Frank started to fit in.

He let his beard grow and his hair became unruly, he didn't bother to bathe because the other men didn't bother. After having shot several wolves instead of trapping them, Joe helped him make a coat out of the poorer quality skins. Garret made him a fur hat. When Frank put the furs on, he looked like he always belonged on the mountain. Frank was pleased with himself and took to trapping like he was born to it, gradually beginning to like the men. He especially came to like Joe, Fergus, Will and Garrett. The four men seemed to take him under their wing, and taught him all about the mountain.

The men still at the camp were sitting around the camp fire talking about trapping. Some were skiting about the quality of the skins they got when the talk came around to the High Country. "Lots of wolves up there," Fergus was telling Frank. "Why aren't you up there then Fergus?" Frank asked him. Frank was feeling at ease with the men, his face broke out in his usual big smile. "Can't go up there on your own Frank," Garrett interjected. The men sitting around the fire nodded in agreement. "Why not?" Frank wanted to know all about the High Country, maybe that's where he should be, getting lots of skins so Sarah would be impressed, maybe then she would accept him.

"A man on his own is dead if he goes up there, you can't go up there unless you're with a lot of men for protection, more men means more guns!" Fergus went on.

"More men means more chances of survival against the wolves, too many wolves up there, got to wait 'til they come down here." Joe had been quiet while listening to the men. "There are a lot of wolves on the mountain, we let them breed up in the High Country so we can keep on hunting them." He reached inside his coat and took a bullet out of his shirt pocket, then held it up for Frank to see. "If you go up there you better be carrying one of these."

"Why only one bullet Joe?" Frank laughed. "Wouldn't you need more than one?"

"This bullet is not for shooting wolves." Joe looked seriously at Frank. Frank stopped laughing and stared at Joe.

"You get surrounded by wolves and run out of bullets, you better be carrying this spare bullet in your pocket 'cause you ain't goin' to get out alive ...one bullet to the head and you won't know a thing when those wolves start gnawin' on you." Joe put the bullet back in his pocket.

"No man wants to be eaten alive Frank," Fergus finished. By the time the men stopped talking Frank's eyes were wide. He started carrying a spare bullet for his handgun in his pocket.

A month passed by in a blink of an eye, trapping wolf was becoming easy work. Frank came out of his shack to find Joe and the other three trappers packing their rucksacks. "Where you going Joe?" Frank rubbed the sleep out of his eyes.

"Heading back down to the Low Ridge, told Cole we would call back that way to check on her, see she's got enough wood to keep her going, that sort of thing." Joe watched Frank for his reaction to the news of them heading back to see Sarah. Frank hadn't talked with the men about Sarah since being at the camp and no-one talked about her to Frank. Frank suddenly wondered how Sarah had managed on her own and if she was alright, he wanted to see her too.

"I'll go with you." Frank rushed back to his shack to get his rucksack. Joe stopped packing his gear and followed him.

"I think you ought to stay here for the time being." Joe leant on the door frame as he watched Frank get his rucksack and start packing.

"Why Joe? why should I stay here?" Frank became visibly upset at Joe telling him to stay behind but kept putting things in his bag.

"Frank, you go down to Cole's camp and before you know it the both of you start fighting, it isn't good for anyone, so stay here." Joe was hoping that if Sarah didn't see Frank, she would feel something for him. "I'm coming with you goddamn it!" Frank quickly packed his rucksack. Joe gave up trying to argue with him. He wasn't supposed to interfere where Sarah was concerned, but he didn't promise he wouldn't interfere where Frank was concerned.

Joe could see Frank wasn't going to give in. He had no choice but to let him go with them. "Alright come on."

They came up on Sarah's camp toward the afternoon of their third days hike, everything looked like it should. The cabin looked sound and smoke was billowing out of the chimney. Joe knocked, then when there was no answer, he opened the cabin door and looked inside, only to find the cabin empty. The men searched around the camp, Sarah was nowhere to be found.

"She can't be far away, the fires going and a pot of food is warming on the side." Joe informed the men as they looked around. Will walked around to the lean-to where Sarah's horses were housed. Star and the two packhorses inside had fresh water and feed.

"I guess we better set up our..." Joe started to tell the men to set up camp when he spied Sarah walking through the trees from the direction of the River Flats. She had her rifle slung over her shoulder, she wore her father's hat and the hunting knife was tied around her waist, several skins were visible tied to her rucksack on her back.

Frank saw her coming towards them, she appeared to have been walking for a while, her face was flushed, she looked well, but he knew she couldn't have gone far when her fire was going and food was cooking, the wolves she killed and skinned must have been close by. Frank felt a lump forming in his throat, he had been too busy to think much about her while he was learning to trap. Walking all over the mountain took its toll on him and every night he collapsed onto his furs and slept like a dead person. Now seeing her all his emotions came rushing back. 'Maybe,' he was thinking. 'I should have taken Joe's advice and stayed at the High Ridge Camp after all.' Sarah saw the men standing in the clearing. "Hey Joe!" she called and waved. "Hey Sarah!" Joe returned. Joe walked over to her and they hugged. Joe put his mouth close to Sarah's ear and whispered, "Frank is with us."

Sarah nodded, acknowledging what Joe said, then walked over to the clearing where the other four men were. Frank stood back and watched her with Joe. When he saw her coming toward the clearing his heart began to race. He was nervous and wasn't sure what sort of greeting he would get. Sarah stood her rifle against a log, took her rucksack off her back and sat it on the ground, then said hello to Fergus and gave him a hug. She walked over to where Will was preparing the campfire and greeted him happily. Garrett stepped up and received a greeting and a warm hug too. Then she looked at Frank, seeing he had begun to grow a beard and his hair looked wild, curls hung over his collar. Sarah thought he looked strong and handsome at the same time. She felt a sudden rush course through her body at the sight of him, not having felt that way since coming back from Cedar Creek. "Hello Mason," Sarah stood away from him and didn't attempt to hug him. "Hello Cole," Frank managed to say without giving his feelings away.

While Joe and the other men took turns chopping wood and checking Sarah's cabin, Frank went to the river with the bucket and filled the water barrel that stood on the porch. Sarah stayed inside away from the men while they worked. The men stayed for two days making sure Sarah had enough firewood, her horses were exercised, fed and watered, her cabin roof was checked for leaks and they ate food Sarah cooked. Frank kept out of Sarah's way as much as possible but occasionally they couldn't help being in close contact with each other.

Sarah told Frank about the second water barrel in her washroom. "You care to fill that Mason?" she smirked. Without saying a word, Frank carried the bucket back and forth from the river and filled the second barrel. As he tipped water into the barrel, he took the opportunity to look around the washroom. A huge cast iron bathtub stood on legs in the middle of the room making him wonder how it was brought up the mountain. There was a wooden stand with a pretty floral dish and matching china jug near the inside doorway leading into the cabin. A tall mirror stood to one side and a large copper bowl with a stone fireplace under it for heating water was built near the door that led to the outside. Frank smiled to himself when imagining Sarah bathing in the big tub. Feeling his face start to burn at the sudden thought of Sarah being naked in the washroom, he quickly emptied the bucket and hurried outside and back to the men.

That night after dinner, Sarah took a large pot of coffee to the men camped in the clearing. She filled each of the four trapper's mugs with steaming hot liquid, then approached Frank gingerly. "You want some coffee Mason?" she said, trying to act nonchalantly. "Yes please." Frank held up his mug and Sarah filled it.

"Thank you Sarah." Frank glanced quickly up at Sarah when unexpectedly saying her name, and Sarah just as quickly looked into his face. Frank felt a pang in his stomach when he looked into her eyes, thinking he saw something that reminded him of the old Sarah, the Sarah he knew before she changed her attitude toward him. Sarah smiled faintly and walked back to her cabin. Frank wanted to follow her and ask her why she was treating him the way she was.

Frank didn't get a chance to follow her, Garrett came over and started talking. "We leave tomorrow Frank, heading back up to the High Ridge Camp, you coming with us or going to the River Flats?" Frank was still looking at Sarah's cabin. "Back to camp I expect," he said without looking at Garrett. Garrett looked in the direction Frank was looking. "Best you forget about her Frank." Garrett walked back to the other men and the fire. Frank was never going to forget about Sarah, he was still very much in love with her and was determined he would get her to love him.

The months went by and the men continued to hunt and trap along the High Ridge. Their collection of wolf skins were beginning to mount up. Frank wanted to try trapping and hunting on his own and Joe suggested the best place for him to trap was the River Flats. It was open land and grassed, bordering on the edge of dense forest. Frank would have no trouble hunting along the river.

Frank took Joe's advice and made his way to the River Flats where he built himself a shelter. Cutting down trees and building a rough cabin, he lined the walls on the inside with canvas he used to cover his supplies, this would do to keep the cold wind out. On the outside, he layered the shelter with tree branches covered in foliage to make it blend in with the surrounding forest. His firepit was built just outside the entrance. When the fire was lit, heat warmed the inside and at night Frank slept comfortably on furs and blankets with the warmth keeping him from getting cold. Frank's body bulked up from the physical work of chopping trees and building his shelter, his arms and legs became more muscled, his hair and beard grew longer. Frank felt fitter than he had ever felt before. He trapped along the river for four months until he got lonely for company, then he left his camp and his skins he collected and went back to the men at the High Ridge Camp.

Frank managed to last out the year. Winter crept around again, snow began to fall on the mountain, the ground soon became covered and snow drifts piled up around the walls of the shacks. "Looks like time to get packing," Joe said to the men. "Better get your skins together Frank, we head out of here tomorrow." That night Frank slept fitfully, thinking about Sarah and Cedar Creek. He hated the idea of having to return to his father's ranch, there was only trouble for him and Sarah in Cedar Creek. 'Why?' He asked himself. 'Why couldn't he and Sarah stay on the mountain? Maybe then they could be together forever.'

Chapter Thirteen

After collecting his skins from the River Flats, Frank made his way to Sarah's cabin where he was to meet up with Joe and the rest of the trappers. He had a good load of skins to take back to Cedar Creek and felt good about himself. Instead of relying on his father to give him an allowance he had earnt his own money. He was proud of the fact he could live rough like the trappers and not a city man.

Up at the High Ridge Camp, before the snow could settle in deep drifts, the trappers packed their things. Loading their skins onto their packhorses they made their way down the mountain to the Low Ridge where they stopped to collect Sarah on their way through to the pass. Frank came riding in to the Low Ridge Camp from the direction of the River Flats and met up with the trappers coming down the trail from the High Ridge.

Frank hadn't seen Sarah for more than four months, Joe and he agreed he would stay away from her for a while and Frank thought it best to do what Joe asked of him, immersing himself in learning the business of trapping.

The men arrived at Sarah's camp as more snow began to fall heavily. Her packhorse was already packed by the time they came riding in single file down the trail to her cabin. Sarah was dressed warmly, her father's long fur coat was tied with a piece of rope around her waist to keep it closed against the cold, a thick scarf was wrapped around her head and tucked into the front of the coat keeping her head warm, her hat with the split brim was pulled down on her head over the top of the scarf.

Joe pulled his horses to one side and stopping, climbed down and went over to where Sarah had her horses tethered at the bottom of the cabin steps. Fergus pulled his packhorse past Sarah and Joe and kept going down the trail, tipping his hat to Sarah as he went by. Will followed on behind Fergus, Sarah and Joe watched the men as they filed past.

Garrett smiled down at Sarah and said "howdy Cole," as he and his horses passed her. "Howdy Garrett," Sarah smiled up at him. Sarah looked up, nodded and smiled at the trappers coming behind Garrett. When she saw Frank in the line, she stopped smiling. Frank looked down at Sarah, his face sombre. His hair and beard Sarah noticed were longer than when she had seen him months before. He looked like he belonged on the mountain and his borrowed packhorse was loaded with skins. Frank didn't acknowledge Sarah, instead kept his horses moving on down the trail behind other trappers.

Sarah and Joe checked her cabin was securely locked up and Joe helped her get up on her horse then, mounting up himself, took the reins of his packhorse and took off after the lead men. The trappers made room for Sarah to file in behind them. Two trappers and their packhorses rode along between her and Frank.

The pass wasn't easy to get through this year. Even though they were leaving the mountain well before the pass became cut off, a blizzard blew up making it difficult for Joe to see the trail. Years before, he left red markers high up in the trees that lined the trail for the few stragglers that stayed behind to find their way easily through the pass to the caves. The group Joe led arrived at the caves near dark, filing in one by one into the largest cave and bringing their horses in out of the blizzard.

Several fires were lit inside the huge cave to ward off the cold, groups of men crowded around to keep warm. Wind howled in through the opening of the cave but everyone was sheltered well out of its cold draught, the horses were fed and watered. Joe, Will, Garrett and Fergus shared their fire with Sarah. Three other men, Logan, Reeves and Frank joined them. They cooked and ate their meals and settled down for the long night.

Sarah spread her bedroll out on the opposite side of the fire near Garrett and Will, as far away from Frank as she could get. When they finished their meal's, Sarah reached for the coffee pot and the men held up their mugs as she walked around the fire and poured each of them coffee. When she got to Logan, he gave her a sly look while she filled his mug. Ever since Sarah moved into the Ferguson House to live with the men, Logan had a desire to be the first man to bed her. Sarah didn't seem to notice the look he gave her. When she came around the fire to where Frank was sitting, she stopped. While he held his mug up for her to pour him coffee, they glanced into each other's eyes. Sarah felt a pang in her stomach. Frank didn't register any emotion on his face. Sarah couldn't tell what Frank was feeling or thinking right then. She poured him his coffee then went back to her bedroll on the opposite side of the fire.

The next morning they packed up in silence and headed for the trail, it was to be a long day's journey to their next camp at the wells. When the trappers reached the bottom of the mountain, they bunched up for protection against an attack from hungry wolves that made their way down the mountain to hunt. Sarah and Frank rode in the middle of the group so Joe could keep Sarah as safe as possible, deciding Frank could ride beside her.

The wolves came charging from the forest. 'About twenty of them,' Joe thought. When he opened fire, the other men joined in. The wolves ran in close, Sarah spurred her horse on and Frank kept up with her. One wolf, getting past the trappers, came between the horses, snapping its teeth at the heels of Sarah's packhorse. As Sarah raced along, she quickly twisted the reins of her packhorse around her saddle-horn, getting it tied just before the wolf rushed past her packhorse and went for Star's hooves. Frank pulled his rifle out of its holster and made to shoot. Sarah had her rifle ready too. Star kicked out with his hooves as the wolf kept coming. Sarah fired first, the wolf rolled and fell under Frank's horse, causing him to hold on tight as his horse trampled the wolf and kept going. Joe and the group of trappers were kept busy, shooting a lot of wolves before the rest of the pack decided they'd had enough and disappeared back into the forest.

Several men in the group stopped to skin the wolves they shot. They worked fast while Joe, Fergus and Will kept guard against another attack. Garrett skinned his kill, leaving a bloody mess staining the snow-covered ground. Sarah and Frank leapt off their horses and staying close to the group, walked around together to stretch their legs.

"Good shooting Cole," Frank said as he smiled at Sarah. His heart was racing but not from the sudden rush he felt when they were running from wolves, but because he and Sarah were standing together and seeming to be friendly.

Sarah blushed when she saw Frank's familiar smile, admitting to herself she missed his smile, it made her feel warm inside and she had to force herself to keep calm. "Thanks Mason," was all she could manage to say to him. Joe came over to where Sarah and Frank were standing with their horses. "You two alright?" He didn't wait for a reply. "That was pretty close, we won't be hanging about here too long, we need to make it to the wells before nightfall." Joe looked from Sarah to Frank and back again, he could see they seemed to be getting along. Joe's eyes twinkled when he saw how Sarah's face appeared flushed, it could have been from the ride or it could be she was happy to be talking to Frank. Joe wasn't sure which but he didn't care, so long as the two of them were getting along, that was all that mattered.

As the group rode toward the wells, Sarah and Frank rode alongside each other, talking about the wolves and their time on the mountain. Without thinking, Sarah asked Frank what he was going to do when he got back to Cedar Creek.

"I'm going back to my father's ranch." Frank looked over at Sarah and frowned when he told her what he planned on doing. Sarah had gone quiet because she knew Frank going back to his father meant she would have to stay away from him. Neither of them spoke the rest of the way to the wells.

Once the trappers made it to the wells, their camp was set up in a clearing on the banks of the river. Frank placed his bedroll next to Garrett and Fergus, Sarah didn't have anywhere to put her bedroll as the men bunched up around the fire. The only place she could find to sleep was a gap between Frank and Garrett.

That night when everyone settled down to sleep, Frank lay on his side facing Sarah. Sarah was under her blanket, lying on her side facing Frank, her fur coat wrapped tightly around her for warmth.

They looked at each other across the small gap between them. Frank didn't speak to Sarah and Sarah didn't speak to Frank. Sarah closed her eyes and wished the morning would come quickly, she didn't want to be so close to Frank when she hadn't seen him for many months, now here they were thrown together on the trail. 'One more night camping out,' she told herself. 'Then we will be back in Cedar Creek, Frank will go back to his father and I will have to stay away from him.' Sarah rolled over and turned her back on Frank. She felt a sadness she hadn't felt since watching Frank walk away from her after he arrived unexpectedly on the mountain.

Frank watched Sarah sleeping. He wouldn't give up on trying to win her over, he loved her now as much as he ever did. Frank told himself he would see Sarah when they returned to Cedar Creek. He watched Sarah turn her back on him, then rolled over and turned his back on her. Joe watched the two of them ignoring each other from under his hat.

When they made their camp out on the open prairie, the last day's ride from Cedar Creek, they were well away from the area where wolves hunted. Occasionally a lone wolf did venture out onto the prairie. If the wolf was lucky, a rabbit or prairie dog would be its main meal. The camp was open to the weather and a cold wind blew across the prairie. Everyone kept their coats wrapped tightly around them for warmth. The fires that night, were built from wood the men carted on their packhorses from the wells. Frank spread out his bedroll in the open, keeping well away from the fire and nearer to a group of men. He didn't want to be too close to Sarah when they were so close to Cedar Creek. He was to go home to his father and knew for some reason he didn't understand, Sarah wouldn't want to see him. Joe made Sarah sleep closer to the fire for warmth, he also wanted to keep an eye on her now they were getting closer to town.

The trappers arrived in Cedar Creek well into the afternoon of their fourth day's journey, they were tired and all of them were in bad moods from the long journey and lack of sleep. A lot of town folk came out to greet them with cheers and waves, the town would come alive now the trappers had come back. Cedar Creek became a sleepy town once the trappers returned to the mountain, not much money was spent and businesses found trading slow. Cattle and horses were left to roam and feed out on the open prairie. But when the trappers returned each winter, the men eagerly spent their earnings from their trapping and when they worked for Major Hardy, they spent up big around town. The saloon made a lot of money for its owner Kathleen, and when the men weren't eating at the Ferguson House, they ate at the eatery next door to the saloon before going back to the house to sleep. The Livery always made money. Doc Harris was kept busy checking everyone for ailments and the dentist got busy with teeth pulling and cleaning, business was good for everyone.

The first stop for the trappers was the Trading Post to unload their skins and get paid, they had to find out who got the most skins and who would win The Pot.

Each year, every trapper put a portion of their earnings from their trapping into a Pot. The Pot being a good thousand-dollar cash prize for the trapper who collected the most skins. After seeing there were a lot of men trapping on the mountain, The Pot was set up by Calahan Cole and Joe Jones with the idea to find out who was the best trapper. They reckoned a little competition made for an interesting time. Arthur Morley, the owner of the bank kept the money for The Pot in his safe and whoever won got the cash to do what they wanted, besides being paid for their skins by the Fur Trading Company, the trapper with the most skins almost always doubled their money with The Pot.

After tallying up the skins, Fess who ran the Trading Post wrote the trapper's names on a board out the front of the Trading Post for all to see. Joe was written up at the top again, winning The Pot with a hundred skins. Frank was written up in the middle of the board which was no shame, he got patted on the back and some of the men even shook his hand. He was pleased with himself for not being near the bottom of the list.

Sarah didn't fare so well, her name was written on the very bottom. She looked at the list of names that she couldn't read, then fell into deep thought while staring at the board. When Sarah and her Pa trapped, almost every year since Sarah was twelve and he made her his partner, they were written up at the very top. They won The Pot last winter, then lost it all the night she sent her Pa to the saloon where he got into a game of Poker with Crawley, the night her father died. Sarah still blamed herself for causing her father's death and she still firmly believed Crawley killed him. There was nothing anyone could say to sway her against believing Crawley did it. Sarah felt disappointed she was on the bottom of the list.

"Don't worry Sarah, this is your first year on your own so that wasn't so bad, you'll do better next time," Joe reassured her. Sarah didn't hang around to wait for the men to follow her. She got her chit and headed for the bank.

Getting to Morley's bank, she found she didn't have an account. Her father's book had been emptied out and closed the night of the Poker game. Morley opened her a new book and it took time. Joe and some of the men came into the bank while Morley and Sarah were putting her account in order. Joe stood back and listened carefully as Sarah and Morley discussed her new account. Sarah felt embarrassed that Joe and the men were there to see her having to open a new book. She put her head down and not looking at any of the men, left the bank quickly. After leaving the bank she made her way straight to the Ferguson House.

Frank looked for Sarah at the Trading Post but couldn't find her anywhere amongst the crowd of men. He wanted to say he would see her around town and tell her he would be going back up the mountain next spring. He made more money than he expected he would so made up his mind there and then he would go back to the mountain to try to better himself and prove to Sarah he could trap as well as any of the other trappers. Frank left the men and after coming from the bank headed out of town to his father's ranch. Sarah stood at the window inside the Ferguson House and watched as Frank rode away.

Joe stepped up to Morley ahead of the other men. He spoke quietly with Morley for a few minutes keeping the men waiting. They were beginning to get edgy until Joe told them what he proposed. The men were all in agreement with what Joe proposed and got on with putting their chits in.

Chapter Fourteen

When Frank arrived back at the ranch, his father greeted him pleasantly. Although he showed his disappointment in Frank for having defied him, mentioning he wasn't happy about him following, 'that stinking trapper Cole' as he called Sarah. While Frank was away Major Hardy vented his anger on his cowhands, keeping them on their toes until he finally admitted to himself he couldn't do anything to bring Frank back home. He would just have to wait until Frank himself returned. Major Hardy thought Frank was just feeling his spurs and would be over Sarah Cole when he came back. He was relieved when Frank returned safely. He hoped, now Frank had gotten trapping and chasing after Sarah Cole out of his system, Frank would settle down.

Major Hardy's thoughts about Sarah hadn't changed, having found out Frank followed her to the mountain, he was furious, vowing he would see Sarah punished for taking his son away from him. He lost Frank once before and was determined he would not lose him again, not to a stinking trapper, not to the likes of Calahan Cole's daughter. He planned to invite Millicent Crawley to the ranch to reacquaint her and Frank.

Foley and Brady, when seeing Frank was back, went to the barn to help him unload his packhorse. "How was it on the mountain Frank?" Foley asked as he sat some of Frank's belongings on the floor.

"I did alright." Frank unpacked his things without paying much attention to the two men.

"Did you get with Cole?" Foley pressed, unable to forget the fact before Frank left to go to the mountain, he had the audacity to ask him, to help get his supplies and packhorse ready. Foley was well aware Frank went to the mountain so he could be with Sarah. If Frank slept with Sarah he would be devastated, because two years before Frank fell in love with Sarah, he fell in love with her himself, only he had been too shy to do anything about it. He hoped at that moment, Frank never got to be with Sarah. He thought his question reasonable. "That, is none of your business Foley!" Frank wasn't about to admit to Foley Sarah rejected him, he thought himself a man and was embarrassed when Sarah told him to stay away from her. Foley could see he wasn't going to get the answer he wanted and had to let it go for now.

Brady knew Foley was in love with Sarah. His brother constantly annoyed him when all he talked about was Sarah, saying he would like to buy a farm, marry Sarah and settle down to have children with her. Of course, he wanted Foley to marry, and he didn't care whom he married. He wanted to have a home too, instead of living at Major Hardy's ranch in a bunkhouse full of angry, smelly men. He hated being Major Hardy's gun-hand, all he ever wanted was to be a farmer.

Frank had been home a week when his father called him into the study to tell him about the Dinner Party he was organizing. "Son ...seeing how you have returned safely from the mountain and to welcome you back home, I'm inviting a few people for a Dinner Party on Saturday night." Major Hardy smiled happily and patted Frank on the shoulder. "Who will you be inviting?" Frank wasn't against having a Dinner Party but had no doubt who his father would invite. No doubt Millicent Crawley would be on top of the list. "Just a few people I thought you might like to catch up with." Major Hardy smiled at his son while continuing to pat him on the shoulder. "Will you invite Sarah Cole?" Frank asked. Guessing his father's dislike for Calahan Cole, he had a feeling he wouldn't invite Sarah. Major Hardy was stunned at Frank's question and dropped his hand off Frank's shoulder. "No, I will not be inviting that ...that!" He hesitated, not wanting to antagonize Frank when he had only just returned home. "...I will not be inviting that girl to this house!" Major Hardy's face went red with anger.

"Then don't bother with a party, because I will not be there, and Sarah is not a girl, she is a woman!" Frank never thought of Sarah as a mere girl, to him she was a beautiful woman, he was deeply in love with her and couldn't help the way he felt about her.

Major Hardy snapped at Frank. "You will attend this party Frank, you need to get acquainted with important people, not some stinking trapper." Frank interrupted his father. "You mean get acquainted with Millicent Crawley don't you father?"

"Millicent Crawley has standing, both here and in Philadelphia, Sarah Cole has none, she's just another trapper …you want to fuck her, then by all means go ahead and fuck her, but Millicent Crawley is the woman that will get you places, you need to get to know her Frank." Major Hardy's face reflected his anger, his blood boiled, he went on. "You don't have to love Millicent, but marry her and you can have your whore on the side." Frank gasped, his eyes widened in shock when his father suggested he should marry someone else and make Sarah his mistress. Right then he hated his father for the way he talked about Sarah, it only served to make him dislike him even more than he already did.

"Sarah is not a whore!" Frank yelled. "I will not marry Millicent Crawley …where on earth do you get such notions? I will never marry Millicent …and another thing, I have never slept with Sarah, and I will not …not until we are married!" Frank clenched his fists, angry at his father's insinuation that he slept with Sarah out of wedlock and she with him.

"You will never marry that female trapper, not if I have anything to do about it!" Major Hardy was just as angry as Frank after Frank's outburst. Frank stormed out of the house without retaliating, saddled his horse quickly and rode to town, wanting desperately to see Sarah. There was no way he would do what his father wanted. Frank knew his father could be manipulative, he ran the ranch with an iron fist and wielded his whip to remind his men who was in charge.

Frank's mind was in turmoil as he raced away from the ranch. He wouldn't marry Millicent Crawley, not ever. It was madness that his father would even contemplate him marrying Millicent. He didn't hate Millicent, but he didn't love her. Millicent was an innocent pawn in his father's plan for him to marry. He loved Sarah and he kept telling himself over and over as he rode to town that

Sarah was not a whore. He was as sure as he could be that she hadn't been with any of the trappers, admitting to himself he couldn't keep track of all the men while on the mountain. A lot of men went their separate ways, not seeing each other for months. There was no way for him to know if any of them visited Sarah at her cabin, he had to trust they hadn't. He was sure Sarah was still pure, but his mind kept racing with thought's that didn't bare thinking about. Could Sarah have been with any of the men? she seemed very friendly with Will and Garrett, too friendly perhaps. Frank hated the way he was thinking but couldn't stop himself from thinking the worst.

Sarah's sixteenth birthday passed while she was on the mountain. Frank's nineteenth birthday came and went while he was there too. Both he and Sarah were old enough to marry without anyone's permission. Frank would marry for love before he would ever marry for money or standing. What did he care about his standing in the community, he was one of those his father called 'stinking trappers.' He had proven that on the mountain.

By the time Frank rode in to town, his horse was lathered with sweat. He rode past the corrals where men were busy breaking in his father's horses. He looked for Sarah as he rode by and couldn't see her sitting on the fence as she usually was and she wasn't standing anywhere amongst the men.

With his heart racing, Frank went to the Ferguson House and walked up to the door. He still felt angry with his father for what he said about Sarah. He banged his fist on the door and waited, but the house remained quiet, it was obvious no one was home. Frank leant his head on the door. "Sarah," he whispered. He wondered why he thought Sarah would be at the house, it was a beautiful day, even though it was winter the sun was shining and the sky was clear. He thought maybe Sarah was out riding. He knew her favourite place was the ponds, so he took a ride out there to look for her.

Her horse wasn't there either, there was no sign of her. Frank was disappointed at not being able to find Sarah so continued riding the trail leading along the river toward the cliffs, crossing the river back onto his father's land and passing by a small shack. After becoming interested in taking a look inside the shack, he pulled up his horse and tethered it to the rail of the small stoop.

The shack was made up of one room, the timber floor and walls were solid, the room was empty of any furnishings, a stone fireplace took up most of one wall. Frank liked the look of the shack and thought it would be a good place to be alone with Sarah. They could sit on a blanket on the floor in front of a blazing fire and talk. Thinking there was no harm in dreaming, he imagined Sarah letting him make love to her. Frank left the shack and rode over the rolling hills that formed a gully near the cliffs and headed back to the ranch.

Saturday night came around far too quickly. Frank hadn't had many occasions to dress for dinner since his mother passed away. He dressed in black trousers, then teamed it with a white cotton shirt and a black jacket, a cravat was neatly tied around his neck. He wished Sarah was coming to the Dinner Party so he could see her in a dress. Sarah, he imagined, would look beautiful, her long brown hair would drape over her bare shoulders, her breasts would sit where they would be noticeable in a well fitted dress, enticing him when he looked at them. He felt disappointed that he hadn't seen Sarah in town so he could have talked to her, now tonight, he had to content himself with Millicent Crawley.

Major Hardy's dinner guests consisted of Benjamin Crawley and Millicent. Doctor Ronald Harris, his wife Gerda, Sheriff George Clementine and his wife Maisie. Harold and Mary Finch and Roy and Felicity Connell were there too. These last two couples considered themselves very close friends of Major Hardy's. Frank sat beside Millicent. The talk around the table was amiable and when the meal was over Major Hardy suggested Frank take Millicent for a walk.

"Frank, why don't you take Millicent out to the garden, a walk in the night air would do you both good." Major Hardy planned to get Frank and Millicent to spend as much time together as possible. Frank glared down to the end of the table where his father sat, but to Millicent he smiled sweetly. "Of course, Millicent, would you take a walk with me?" he pushed his chair back and held out his hand to Millicent.

Millicent giggled shrilly and put her hand in Frank's. Frank felt the cold thin hand Millicent placed in his and felt a shudder run through him, her hand was so unlike Sarah's. When he held Sarah's hand at their picnic, her hand was warm and soft and he felt a sudden tingle of desire rush through his body.

Doc Harris, watching Millicent and Frank go to the garden, thought of Sarah and what she told him when she came back to town from the mountain. Sarah visited him for her checkup to make sure she was keeping healthy as she always did from an early age. Doc and Sarah talked at length about her year on the mountain, how she missed having her father there with her, and about Frank. Sarah told him and Gerda about her feelings for Frank and how Major Hardy had warned her to stay away from him. Watching Frank with Millicent tonight, Doc Harris thought perhaps Major Hardy was right, Sarah should not get herself involved with Frank Mason.

Frank let Millicent's hand go and he and Millicent walked beside each other along the path winding between tall shade trees and low growing shrubs. Paper lanterns swung gently in the breeze. As they walked, Frank took in Millicent's appearance.

The dress Millicent wore was a pretty soft yellow evening dress, lace adorned the edges of the tiny puffed sleeves, pulled high to cover her shoulders. Her sallow skin paled against the pale yellow of the dress. Her undergarments bunched up noticeably underneath it and the dress hung limply from Millicent's thin frame. Her breasts were non-existent and her dark hair was pulled back in a tight bun.

Millicent liked Frank very much and hoped he liked her. Her father told her Frank was interested in her and wanted to become friends. Noticing Frank looking at her in her new dress made her feel beautiful. She hoped Frank would ask her to marry him, even though she would never let him touch her. That didn't matter, she would never let any man touch her, it was simply too disgusting. Millicent shivered at the very thought. She heard her father say Frank touched Sarah Cole in a particular way. As far as she was concerned, Sarah Cole was a whore and didn't mind letting any man touch her.

Frank tried to make conversation with Millicent, 'after all' he thought, 'it wasn't her fault their fathers were pushing them together.'

"Tell me Millicent." He stopped walking and turned to face her. "What have you been doing to pass the time this past year?"

Millicent giggled her shrill girlish laugh. "Well," she started. "I spent most of my time at finishing school for ladies in Philadelphia, daddy paid for me to attend, it cost him a lot of money." Millicent felt special because her father spent a lot of money for her to become a lady. Frank didn't comment.

"Daddy bought me my dress, do you like it?" As Millicent twirled, the dress seemed to move loosely on her thin frame. "It cost a lot too!" Frank switched himself off when Millicent started to talk, wishing he hadn't asked her to tell him about herself. Millicent went on without drawing breath.

"I learnt how to dance, daddy said I'm a good dancer, when I showed him what I learnt of course, I learnt how to walk properly too," she giggled again. "I had to walk with a book balanced on my head." Millicent giggled even more, and it began to get on Frank's nerves. Frank became bored and disinterested as Millicent prattled on. He looked at Millicent but didn't see her, instead, he imagined Sarah wearing Millicent's dress. Sarah's skin was like silk and her breasts would sit up high in the bodice showing off their fullness. Sarah wouldn't need to wear undergarments to hide her figure. Letting the soft material brush against her skin she would be a picture of beauty. Frank heard Millicent snort as she giggled and couldn't wait for the evening to end so he could get away from her.

"You must be feeling cold Millicent, perhaps we should go back inside where it is warm." He escorted her back inside. When it came time for the Crawley's to leave, Frank said goodbye to Millicent, kissed her on the hand and quickly went upstairs to his room, relieved the Dinner Party was over.

Over the course of winter Frank spent more time with Millicent at the behest of his father, attending dinners at the Crawley's and accompanying Millicent to Dinner Parties around the county. Not wanting to argue with his father, he thought by doing this, it was much easier to keep the peace between them, but he was adamant, when the trappers went back to the mountain in the spring, he would be going back with them.

Christmas came and went. Sarah didn't see Frank on Christmas day, not like she had her first Christmas without her Pa. Frank gave Star to her that day and it made her feel special. Sarah reckoned

Frank didn't come to see her because he was enjoying spending all of his time with Millicent Crawley.

Frank hated that he was having to spend so much time with Millicent, he wanted desperately to spend time with Sarah. He had a gift for her for Christmas that he hoped she would accept, but his father had other ideas. Frank was forced to spend Christmas day entertaining Millicent and her father when they turned up at the ranch early. Frank was of the opinion his father organized for them to arrive early for lunch just so he wouldn't be rude and leave their guests.

Sarah spent most of her time with the trappers. The men tried their best to make Christmas joyful for her, but she disappeared into her room straight after dinner and stayed there until the next day. Over the course of winter, some of her days she filled with visiting the few people she considered her friends. Her first visit was with Esther Morley, the bank manager's wife. Esther showed Sarah her many pieces of embroidery she made and gave Sarah a small doily for her room. She then spent some time with Gerda, sitting on her back porch drinking coffee and talking about the mountain and goings on in town. Gerda was a wealth of information, but never discussed anything private about Doc's patients. Sarah avoided talking about Frank as much as possible.

Sarah heard talk Frank was spending most of his time with Millicent and knowing this didn't make it easier for her, she tried avoiding him as much as possible, but Cedar Creek was a small town and Sarah couldn't help bumping into him on several occasions.

As Frank headed toward the saloon with a group of Major Hardy's men, Foley and Brady amongst them, Sarah was on her way to Crawley's store. As usual, Sarah wasn't watching where she was going, so she and Frank bumped into each other outside the store. They stared at each other for a moment, neither knowing what to say to the other. Frank got up the courage to speak first. "How are you Cole?" Sarah's face burnt bright red, she wasn't about to let him know how she felt, because she felt horrible at seeing him up close and so unexpectedly. Her eyes narrowed, her answer to Frank didn't take him at all by surprise, he knew she would know about him spending time with Millicent.

"None of your goddamn business Mason!" Sarah pushed past Frank and rushed inside Crawley's store. Frank was left feeling a little put out. Foley smirked, he got the distinct impression Sarah didn't like Frank.

Sarah was riled up before she got into Crawley's store and an argument broke out between her and Crawley. They spat venomous words at each other. Sarah took hold of a stand of fresh vegetables just inside the door and pushed it over, spilling the contents all over Crawley's floor. He cursed her and called her vile names before she went rushing out the door and slamming it shut behind her. Sarah came away knowing Crawley killed her father. When she informed Joe what Crawley said, he didn't believe her. She tried to tell Garrett and Fergus, but they brushed her off too. Will didn't believe Crawley could do what Sarah told him he had done, stating it just wasn't possible. Sarah didn't say another word to anyone, instead seethed and vowed to herself she would not let Crawley get away with it.

Frank stood at the bar with the men, but he didn't feel like drinking now he had seen Sarah. He wanted to talk to her, to explain there was nothing going on between him and Millicent, that he was only seeing her to keep his father happy, but he didn't get the chance. After he and the men went back to the ranch, the men set about getting their gear ready for the next day. Frank would be joining the men too, on a long cattle drive.

For the next month Major Hardy's men drove a herd to Moreton where they were herded onto rail cars to go to Fort Jefferson for transport to the east. A thousand head of cattle left Major Hardy's ranch and Frank went with them.

Sarah heard Frank joined the cattle drive and would be gone for a month. Winter would almost certainly be over by the time he came back and spring would be here. At least, she thought, he wouldn't be spending any more time with Millicent, and she wouldn't have to stay around the Ferguson House trying to avoid running into him. She saddled Star and went out riding to clear her head. Her ride took her out over the bridge and along the river to the ponds. She loved going to the ponds where she could sit on the boulders in the warm sun and be alone to think.

After sitting on the boulders for a good while, she went riding further along the river toward the cliffs. Crossing the river, she rode up a small rise, pushed her way through the trees and came to the small shack. Sarah got off Star and went inside to look around. The one room shack with its large fireplace looked inviting. Leaning her back against the fireplace, she folded her arms, then thinking this would be a nice place for two people to be alone, she thought of her and Frank. They could lay on a blanket in front of a blazing fire and Frank could make love to her. She closed her eyes and pictured her and Frank lying naked in each other's arms.

Sarah shocked herself by thinking about Frank making love to her, even though there was no one to see her she felt her face start to burn. She ran out of the shack and jumped on Star. 'I can't be thinking this way about Frank, not now he is seeing Millicent Crawley, I have to stay away from him.' Sarah's mind and body was in turmoil as she rode away from the shack.

She rode out of the trees not thinking clearly and didn't realize she had ridden further onto Major Hardy's land. Star followed the river along its banks until they came to the opposite side of the ponds. It wasn't until Star began to fidget, Sarah realized where she was. She pulled Star hard by his reins and quickly continued on while scanning the area around her. Suddenly spotting three men, Major Hardy, his two gun-hands Foley and Brady, coming toward her at a gallop. Her heart leapt in her chest at being caught on the Major's land. She spurred Star on and tried to outrace them across the river, but they came on her fast and cut her off. Foley grabbed Star by the bridle, pulling him to a stop.

"What are you doing on my land Cole? I thought I warned you to stay off my land!" Major Hardy barked as he brought his horse up beside Star.

"I'm just out riding Major, please, let me go." Sarah was frightened, this was what she hoped would never happen.

Major Hardy narrowed his eyes when he saw an opportunity to put his plan for Frank and Millicent into action. "Cole, I got some news you might be interested in …my son and Millicent Crawley are engaged and will be married in the spring when you trappers have gone back to that mountain of yours, so you needn't bother coming out here thinking you might see him, he isn't the least bit interested in you."

Foley looked stunned, this was the first he heard about Frank being engaged to Millicent. He looked at Sarah and thought this news could be good for him, now he might have a chance with her, Foley's heart beat quickened. Sarah took Major Hardy's news badly, her eyes filled with tears, her lip quivered, she pulled hard on Stars reins forcing Foley to let her horse go. She raced over the shallow river and up the rise on the other side. "You want me to go after her Major?" Foley watched Sarah ride away, he saw her tears and once again felt he lost any chance he may have had with her. He thought he must have been mistaken when thinking Sarah hated Frank, it was obvious by the look on Sarah's face she was in love with him. "No, let her go, she got the message." Major Hardy was satisfied Sarah would no longer pose a problem to him, his plans for Frank were coming to fruition, now all he had to do was get Frank to propose to Millicent.

Chapter Fifteen

Before Frank left on the cattle drive, he informed his father that when he returned, he was going back to the mountain to be with Sarah and that he was going to marry her. Major Hardy became angry with Frank and father and son had a furious argument. Frank decided, if he went on the cattle drive, he wouldn't have to spend any more time with Millicent Crawley, or fight with his father. Nor would he see Sarah, but he had to do something to stop his father's crazy notion of getting him and Millicent together.

He figured he would get back to Cedar Creek from the cattle drive in plenty of time to travel back to the mountain with the trappers. It would be safer if he travelled with them and not later on. Not like after they all left Cedar Creek the first time he went to the mountain. Clearly there was safety in numbers when arriving at the base of the mountain where wolves were lying in wait.

Major Hardy had other plans for Frank. He ordered his men to make the cattle drive take longer so there would be no way Frank could get back before the trappers left town. Major Hardy hoped if the trappers were gone, Frank would realize it was futile to contemplate going back to the mountain and he would resign himself to staying at the ranch. Major Hardy formulated another plan just in case his first plan failed.

He was in luck the day he and his men Foley and Brady were out riding the range to check on his cattle and saw Sarah riding near the ponds. The three of them chased her down and he put his second plan into action. He lied when telling Sarah Frank was engaged to Millicent. He knew from the look on her face she believed his lie, she was crying before she left them on the trail and rode back to town. He was satisfied his plan was working, Sarah Cole he was sure, would leave Frank alone.

Frank was angry, the cattle drive was taking far too long, they spent too many days letting the cattle feed along the trail, the men seemed to be deliberately taking their time, stopping every few hours to rest and let the cattle graze. When they finally arrived at Moreton, he had to wait at the railhead until all the cattle were loaded and the train had departed before he could head back to Cedar Creek. He had been gone four weeks already and now it would take him another two weeks hard riding to get back.

When Frank made it back to the ranch Foley told him the trappers had left three weeks before. Frank missed his chance to ride back to the mountain with the trappers. But still, he rode to town and made arrangements with Ham at the Livery to get his packhorse ready for the trek up the mountain, he would head back alone in a day's time.

Dinner that night was strained. Frank argued with his father over how long the cattle drive took, accusing his father of deliberately stalling him from going back to the mountain with the trappers. Major Hardy cursed Sarah, telling Frank he was a fool to think his life would amount to anything if he got together with her, insisting Frank marry Millicent Crawley. Frank couldn't wait to leave his father's presence and retired to his room, only to get up again at midnight and sneak out. He hightailed it to town and rode out before daybreak making good progress the first day. He kept going all day and into the night until it got too dark to know where he was. He came to the wells unexpectedly and was relieved when he spotted the old camp site from their trip down the mountain at the start of winter.

He made his camp in the very same clearing knowing it was a safe camp, then rode hard all the next day, hoping he wouldn't have the same bad luck as he did the year before when he got attacked by wolves and lost his horse. When he got as far as the trail up into the mountain, he pulled his rifle out of its holster and held it in preparation of an attack. He rode on cautiously through the trees and on up the trail, furrowing his brow with concern when he didn't meet with any resistance.

Frank made camp when it got too dark for him to follow the trail. He was well aware the trappers never camped out on the trail, instead opting to push on until they made it to the caves. But then his journey started on the wrong foot from the outset. He made a huge fire, heated some food, drank coffee and listened for the sounds of wolves, becoming increasingly worried when he couldn't hear them howling. Frank didn't sleep, fearful he might come under attack sometime in the night. Remembering what the trappers told him about being caught out alone by the wolves and having to use a single bullet to end your life so they wouldn't eat you alive, he took a bullet from his gun-belt and put it in his shirt pocket, hoping he wouldn't have to use it. Frank wasn't aware the wolves had moved to higher ground around the caves. Early the next morning Frank rode up the mountain trail heading for the caves and straight into a pack of hungry wolves.

His ride up the mountain was taking forever. The trail was steep in places and he had to be careful his horse didn't trip on loose stones and undergrowth. Midday came and went, it was now mid-afternoon and he felt tired from lack of sleep. He kept going until he could see the caves ahead of him. He planned to make his last camp there for the night and head up to the Low Ridge Camp and Sarah the next day.

Frank was thinking about Sarah when he heard rustling in the forest behind him, his two horses were becoming agitated. Frank pulled his horses reins in closer and checked his rifle for bullets. He gripped his rifle in his hands with his finger on the trigger in readiness. When the wolves came out of the forest, he let go of his packhorse to fire his rifle. His rifle shots echoed down the mountain as wolves surrounded him. He fought for ground, the wolves going for his horse's legs trying to bring them down. His packhorse ran kicking wildly through the trees. Frank jumped off his horse and took cover, enabling him to get clear shots at the wolves. His horse bolted through the trees in the same direction as his packhorse and disappeared with wolves right behind it. Frank's only thought then was, 'now I have lost both my horses.'

Hiding behind fallen trees and logs Frank opened fire. Each time he reloaded his rifle, he felt he was losing the battle. His heart was pounding, he was in trouble, wolves came at him from all directions. He took aim at a wolf charging straight towards him, its teeth bared. Before he got off a shot, he heard another shot coming from somewhere amongst the trees. He watched as the wolf charging toward him barrelled head over heels and dropped dead in front of the log he was hiding behind.

Another hail of shots rang out and Frank wondered who the shooters were. Wolves started running back into the forest, trying to escape the onslaught of bullets raining down on them. One wolf though, raced in close behind Frank. He turned swiftly and fired, his bullet ripped into the wolf's neck and travelled up through its head coming out between the wolf's ears, turning the wolf's brain to mush and killing it instantly. Frank saw two trappers running through the trees. He recognized Logan and Reeves as they fired off more shots at receding wolves as they came racing toward him. When the wolves were gone, Logan and Reeves stopped running and walked over to Frank.

Logan grinned at Frank. "Well Mason, you almost got your chance to use your bullet."

"What the hell Logan, where did you come from? why aren't you up at the High Ridge Camp?" Frank was relieved at seeing the two men, their presence saved him from certain death, the three men shook hands.

"We came to try our hand down low, we're not trappin', just huntin', what are you doing here Mason?" Reeves asked him as they shook hands. Reeves knew exactly why Frank had come back to the mountain, and it wasn't trapping that brought him here, a wide grin spread across his craggy face.

"I'm here to trap, how the hell did all these wolves come to be here? Why aren't they at the bottom of the mountain?" Frank wasn't about to tell Reeves or Logan he was here to be close to Sarah. The two men looked around at the dead wolves. "Sometimes the wolves move their huntin' grounds and you got to follow 'em." Logan kept grinning slyly at Frank. Logan wasn't just here to improve his skin tally either, he also hoped to run into Sarah somewhere when she was out trapping, but so far, he had no luck. The four trappers taught her how to hide her tracks. She knew the mountain better than most of the men and could hide her trail so no-one could find her, she was so good at it, he was unable to track her down, and he didn't want to chance getting her at her cabin where Joe and his partners could find out and take their revenge out on him.

Reeves didn't believe Frank had come to the mountain just to trap, Frank was here for Cole. Reeves knew how keen his partner Logan was on Cole. Logan talked incessantly about her, saying how he would like to get her into bed and be the first man to break her in. He cringed every time Logan described certain parts of Cole's body. He liked Cole too, but knew he didn't stand a chance with her and let his feelings slide. Every trapper had been warned by Joe and his three friends to keep away from Cole or they would answer to them. The four men would punish any man severely who thought he had a right to touch Cole without her permission. Reeves reckoned Logan would rue the day if he thought he would ever get to bed her. He turned his attention back to Frank and Logan.

"They live here Mason," Logan was saying, he looked around at the wolves they killed. "This is good," Logan said pulling out his hunting knife. "We'll be right back, you want to get a fire going and maybe get some coffee brewin'." Reeves pulled out his knife and the two men proceeded to skin the wolves.

"Hey, some of those are mine!" Frank reminded the men he killed most of the wolves and that he wanted their skins. He set about making a fire and brewing coffee, then while waiting for the pot to boil he skinned his kill.

Frank and the two men sat around his fire drinking coffee and talking. After some time, Reeves went for a walk to relieve himself in the forest. It wasn't long before he came walking back with Frank's packhorse in tow. He grinned at Frank, "found your horse feedin' over yonder, the wolves must have cleared out when they got wind of us." Frank's other horse came walking out of the forest behind his packhorse. All three men camped that night in the caves. Next morning Logan and Reeves went with Frank through the pass and took him along to Sarah's camp.

Sarah wasn't at her cabin when they got there. Frank thought she would be out trapping, and in a way, he was glad she wasn't there, he didn't want her to know he was back, not right then, not when Logan and Reeves were with him. He watched Logan and Reeves making their way back down the trail that led to the caves.

"Aren't you going up to the High Ridge Camp?" Frank said to Logan as he walked off. "Hell no, doin' more huntin' down around the caves, we only brought you here to be with your woman." Logan sneered at Frank. "Cole's not my woman!" Frank snapped angrily. Logan was relieved when Frank said Sarah wasn't his woman, thinking he was still in with a chance to be the first to bed her. Frank packed up his packhorse and headed off. Riding up the trail to the High Ridge Camp would take him at least another three days to get to the other trappers.

Frank thought if he had been alone, he would have liked it if Sarah had been at her cabin so he could have seen her and said hello, but he wasn't going to admit it to Logan and Reeves. Another thing he thought as he made for the trail was, it was true, Sarah wasn't his woman, at least not yet.

Logan and Reeves hunted around the caves for a few more days and having taken a lot of skins, stood a good chance at winning The Pot. On their way to the High Ridge Camp they made their way back past Sarah's cabin. Sarah was at her cabin when they got there and not wanting them to hang about told the two men to keep going, they could make their camp further up the ridge away from her cabin. Sarah didn't trust Logan, he looked at her strangely and said things she wasn't sure what he meant, she didn't like his attitude toward her. Sarah kept her rifle handy and her knife strapped to her waist until she was sure the two men were gone. She was comforted by the fact that if anything happened, she could tell Joe and the men would be punished. Sarah warned Logan by telling him Joe would be by any day soon and she would be sure to tell him they had stopped by. Logan took the hint, he didn't want trouble from Joe. Neither Logan or Reeves thought to tell Sarah Frank was back on the mountain.

After three more grueling days of riding uphill, Frank made it to the high Ridge Camp. He killed two more wolves on his way but didn't meet with any further resistance. When he made it into camp, he found all the men were either off checking their traps or hunting. Horses were tethered to a rope hitching line and no-one was guarding them. Frank decided, when the men came back to the camp, he would bring that to Joe's attention He unpacked his supplies and stowed them in the shack he made his stone fireplace in the year before. It looked like no-one had been camped in the shack, so he made it his again for this year.

Joe and the men made it back to camp just on dark, carrying their fresh trapped skins on their backs. When they saw Frank sitting at the firepit with a pot of stew, they waved to him and gathered around to help themselves to the food Frank had prepared. Frank managed to get himself a plate of stew before it was all gone. Joe wasn't sure if he should welcome Frank back after spending all his time with Millicent Crawley. Joe knew without a doubt Sarah was in love with Frank and had watched her pining for Frank all winter. Several times Sarah saw Frank with Millicent and so stayed in her room and not come out until a day later, her eyes red rimmed and Joe knew she had been crying.

When Frank informed Joe no-one was watching their horses, Joe got mad after learning the guard had gone off chasing after a lone wolf and had left the camp for several hours. The trapper didn't appreciate the blow to his jaw that felled him, and didn't appreciate Frank telling Joe he went missing.

Frank stayed at the High Ridge Camp for a month. He wasn't getting the amount of wolf skins he wanted in his traps and his hunting wasn't fairing much better. He was tired of the men ribbing him about his trapping and hunting and wanted to be on his own to prove himself so made a decision to head back down the mountain to the River Flats. When Frank let Joe know he was leaving the High Ridge Camp and going back to hunt along the river, saying he wanted to get back to his own camp, Joe wished him luck and they shook hands. Joe was of the opinion Frank wanted to be closer to Sarah but didn't say anything.

The River Flats weren't far from Sarah's cabin and Frank knew it would only take him three hours walk to get to Sarah if he wanted to see her. He could hide amongst the trees and watch her, but he didn't want to spy on her. Not only would it not be right, Sarah would know he was there. She had keen eyesight and her sense of smell was unlike anything he had ever seen before. He chose to stay away from her, and to build up his amount of skins for his chance at The Pot, he planned to hunt in the opposite direction to Sarah's cabin and trap in the forest around his camp.

Chapter Sixteen

Sarah moved quietly through the trees and undergrowth, carrying her rucksack on her back and her rifle slung over her shoulder. As she walked stealthily along, she spotted a wolf standing in the trees not too far away. Quietly removing her rucksack off her back, she sat it on the ground at her feet, then cocking her rifle, lifted it to her shoulder and took aim.

The wolf turned its head and looked toward Sarah. Its piercing blue eyes stared straight at her. Sarah had a good clear shot. The wolf's thick fur was worth a lot of money and it was taking her a long time to get her pile of skins together. Time moved on, weeks drew into months and now it was the end of summer, autumn was here and the trees were beginning to lose their leaves. The nights were beginning to get cold, soon it would be winter.

There were only a few months left to get enough skins to make the trip to Cedar Creek worth her while. She needed to build up her skins to enable her to survive the winter and restock her supplies for next year. Sarah's traps were set a little higher up on the mountain behind her cabin, making it an easy walk to her traps and back to the cabin in one day.

But trapping was slow, she decided hunting over at the River Flats would give her a better chance of catching wolves as they hunted along the river. The River Flats were only a few hours walk from her cabin, this meant she could get some skins and head back well before dark.

She and her Pa always set traps that took them two days away from their cabin, those times they camped out under the stars for the night. Sarah stayed close to her Pa during those nights, as the dark worried her. Her vision was sharp, she could see in the dark but couldn't see quite far enough into deeper shadows to make out what was out there. She was always relieved when they made it safely back to the cabin before nightfall.

This wasn't the first time she had been hunting at the River Flats since coming back from Cedar Creek. She had been across there several times before and had walked along the edge of the river looking for signs of wolves. Spotting several places where wolves had been, she went to the Flats to look around. Walking along the rocky riverbank she was about to kneel down to take a drink when she saw what looked like a shelter. It had been built well away from the river near the edge of the forest. When she went to take a look, it surprised her how well built it was.

The walls of the shelter were built out of tree trunks, the outside covered by branches, the inside lined with canvas to keep the cold out and it stood high enough for her to walk inside without bending over. A firepit of stones had been built at the entrance. Sarah could tell the heat from the fire would warm the inside of the shelter. Inside in one corner was a pile of skins. The floor of the shelter was layered with more skins and blankets.

Taking a look around, Sarah found two items she recognized. A small black book she had been told was a bible and a silver timepiece on a chain that was carried in a pocket.

"Frank Mason!" she remarked out loud while wondering just when did Frank come back to the mountain, she hadn't seen him or heard that he had returned. She looked up and down the river, there was no sign of him. She didn't want to be there when he came back so walked away as quickly as she could across the rough stones covering the riverbank and headed back the way she came, making her way quickly back to her cabin.

Sarah couldn't get the fact Frank was living and hunting on the River Flats out of her mind. Was he there alone? she wondered, and if he was, why was he hunting alone? why wasn't he with Joe and the other trappers? had he been anywhere near her cabin? she didn't think so, she would have known if he had, her instinct would have told her he was close by.

Sarah was back there now, hunting above the River Flats. She had no choice but to come back here. Her traps netted her a few skins but she needed a lot more if she was to take part in The Pot. She wanted her name off the bottom of the list at the Trading Post. Sarah kept away from the area where Frank had his camp. She didn't want to run into him, not if she could help it. But she was curious to know how he looked and if he was well. Maybe she thought, she could see him if she hid amongst the trees. Deciding, doing that wouldn't be fair on Frank, he didn't need her spying on him. Even though the River Flats were only a short three hour walk from her cabin, he hadn't been near her cabin to spy on her, at least she hadn't sensed he had.

The wolf was in her sights, Sarah took careful aim. When the wolf turned its head, Sarah stared down the length of her rifle straight into the wolf's eyes, becoming mesmerized by it as they stared at each other. The wolf turned suddenly and loped off in the opposite direction. Sarah cursed herself for not shooting and made to follow.

Taking only a couple of steps in the direction the wolf had taken, she felt herself falling. Too late, the undergrowth wasn't hard ground, it was a tangle of vines and brush. Tumbling through the undergrowth, tearing her shirt as she fell, she tried desperately to hold onto her rifle as she went crashing down but had to let it go to save herself. Her rifle flew up in the air, crashed against the vine covered rock wall and went off.

At the same time as hearing the loud report, a searing pain hit Sarah's left shoulder. Still tumbling over and over then landing on the hard ground on her side with the wind knocked out of her, she lay dazed for a moment trying to fathom out what just happened.

When she rolled onto her back she was looking up at a canopy of trees and a high rock wall. Taking a look around at her surroundings and finding herself lying at the bottom of a small ravine, she tried to sit up. A sharp pain shot through her left shoulder and down her arm, causing her to scream in pain. She looked at her arm, saw a gaping blood-soaked hole in her shoulder, her shirt was saturated with blood oozing out of the hole and running down her arm. She reached over her shoulder with her right hand and felt along her shoulder blade, feeling for an exit wound. There was none, the bullet hadn't gone through.

Sarah sat where she was for a moment and tried to think, she felt faint, she couldn't stay there and bleed for too long, she had to get help. Help wasn't far away, all she had to do was get to the River Flats and Frank's camp. If he was there, he would have to get the bullet out of her, if he wasn't, she would have to dig it out herself. Blood now dripped off her hand onto the ground, she needed help and she needed it fast. Sarah wondered where the wolf had gone, she hoped it had left but doubted it, she couldn't see her rifle anywhere either and she didn't have time to look for it. At least she still had her knife, she put her hand on the handle to reassure herself. Taking the knife out of its sheath, she cut the bottom off her shirt, scrunched the rag up in a ball, then quickly stuffed it inside her shirt and pressed it hard against the wound. It hurt like hell but helped to stem the flow of blood. She began to walk along the edge of the rocks back through the trees. If she could get down to the river, she would be alright.

Sarah held her left arm close to her body as she walked up the side of a small rise. The noise of the river grew louder as it rushed along, telling her she was getting closer. She tried to hurry, and slipping on loose stones, put her arm down to stop herself from hitting the ground hard. Her stomach churned, the pain was so bad she thought she was going to pass out. She felt like crying but this wasn't the time for being weak, her life depended on being strong. Sarah pushed her way through the trees, staggered into a clearing and stopped in her tracks.

Standing in the clearing, she found herself on a ridge high above the river. Stumbling several times over loose stones, she made her way to the edge and looked down. The river below flowed between stone covered riverbanks and off into the distance. The camp she had to get to was a long way over near the trees behind her. There was no way down to the River Flats from where she stood, she would have to go back the way she came and walk through the forest, that would take her longer to get help, much longer. "Goddamn it," she muttered through clenched teeth. "I don't have time." Sarah said feeling light headed.

Turning to head back into the forest, she pulled up in shock when she saw the wolf she had been hunting come out of the trees and was now blocking her path. The wolf smelt fresh blood and followed her scent, thinking she was easy prey. Sarah was just another wounded animal, she was food. The wolf bared its teeth and made a low guttural growl. 'Now there really is no way off the ridge' she thought to herself, her heart racing. 'Calm down,' she told herself. Blood dripped off her fingers as her arm hung by her side, the rag covering her wound was saturated.

She remembered her father saying if she ever got hurt and was bleeding not to panic or she would bleed faster, and she could die quicker. Her father told her during his time in the cavalry, battle wounded men would panic, their hearts would beat fast with fear and they bled faster, dying from loss of blood. Sarah took a deep breath and slowed her breathing.

Looking behind her at where she was standing, she had to make a quick decision. There was only one way down and that was to go off the ridge and into the river. If she was lucky, she would float to the edge and be able to get out, but if she wasn't lucky, because she couldn't swim, she was going to die and it wouldn't be from a bullet or a wolf, it would be from drowning. 'However,' she thought as she tried to stare down the wolf. 'I'm not going to go alone.' Reaching down ever so slowly so as not to startle the wolf, she drew her knife out of its sheath. Holding the knife in front of her, Sarah waited. She felt oddly calm, her heart beat slowed, the blood stopped dripping off her fingers.

Taking a furtive step backwards, Sarah's foot suddenly twisted sideways on loose rocks, causing her to stumble. The wolf made its move, it snarled and raced toward her. Sarah acted fast, forgetting the pain in her arm she put her bloodied arm up to protect her face as the wolf, its teeth bared, leapt high. She crouched low, the wolf was above her, its underbelly exposed. Sarah stood up quickly, yelled loudly and plunged her knife deep into the wolf's gut behind its rib cage. The sudden searing pain in her left arm returned, almost causing her to black out. While screaming loudly she pulled her knife back hard, tearing the wolf open. Her sharp knife sliced along its body, coming out between its back legs. The wolf crashed violently into her, its jaws wrapped around Sarah's arm, its black eyes stared blankly as the knife cut into its gut. Both Sarah and the wolf stumbled backwards. The wolfs innards spilled out covering Sarah's body as they plummeted off the ridge and into the river below. The wolf was long dead before it hit the water. Sarah hit the water on her back and blacked out.

Frank walked slowly along the edge of the river, heading back toward his camp, he didn't hurry, there was no need, there wasn't anything at his camp to hurry back for. He had a good days hunting, carrying four skins tied to his rucksack on his back. He left camp at daylight that morning and walked for several hours searching for wolves. His luck was in when he shot a grey wolf as soon as he rounded the bend in the river. He skinned it there beside the river and rolled up the fur, the other three wolves he killed on his way back to camp. Feeling worn from the many days of waking up at dawn and hunting until dark, then being unable to sleep for thinking about Sarah and his father's outrage at him for wanting to marry her, he was glad for the time alone to think about everything. But he hadn't solved his problem of Sarah not wanting anything to do with him. He was glad to be heading back to camp to eat, he would try to get some sleep so he could head out again at first light. His skins were building up steadily and he wanted to take as many as he could back to Cedar Creek to show not only the trappers but his father he could survive on his own.

He was stepping over the rocky shore of the riverbank, his eyes scanning his surroundings for wolves as he approached his camp when something on the ridge caught his eye. A blinding flash of light shone in his eyes causing him to squint. He stared up at the ridge and it happened again. Almost sure someone was up there standing on the ridge, Frank walked faster. As he got closer, he kept his eyes on the ridge where he could see a figure standing near the edge, and whatever it was the figure was holding was shining brightly in the sun.

Standing by the side of the river directly across from his camp, he recognized who it was on the ridge. "Sarah?" he said to himself in amazement, his heart skipping a beat. 'What is she doing here? and what is she doing up on that ridge?' he asked himself. "SARAAAH!" he yelled loudly and waved his arms in the air trying to attract her attention, but she didn't see him or hear him. He could see it was Sarah's knife the sun reflected off, causing it to shine in his eyes, and could see how close she was standing to the edge and wondered why she was holding her knife in front of her while looking back toward the forest. He frowned and moved his line of sight to the trees but couldn't see what it was she was looking at from where he was standing. "What the hell does she wear that is red?" he had never seen Sarah wear anything that was red before.

He watched in horror at Sarah suddenly crouching down, her arm shooting up in front of her and at a huge grey wolf leaping towards her. Frank's eyes widened, his heart went to his throat as he watched Sarah and the wolf plummet off the ridge. He dropped his rifle, tore his rucksack off his back and ran. As he ran, he watched Sarah and the wolf hit the water together. Frank ran as fast as he could across the stony riverbank towards them. When he got to where the ridge rose up, he couldn't go any further, huge boulders bared his way. He stopped at the edge and watched as the gutted carcass of the wolf floated to the surface, then waited for Sarah to come up for air.

When Sarah didn't come up, Frank tore off his boots, hurriedly discarded his fur coat, dived in without hesitation and swam to the spot where he had seen her enter the water. He took a deep breath, dived down and looked around. Unable to find her he swam back to the surface. When he couldn't see her there, he dived again, swam toward the bottom and spotted her long hair floating in the water. Feeling sickened when he saw Sarah lying on the riverbed, Frank grabbed hold of her long braid and pulled her up as he swam back to the surface. He came up quickly, gasping for air, and brought Sarah out of the water with him. Sarah came up quickly but didn't take a breath. Frank put his arm around her waist and swam with her to the riverbank where he lifted her out of the water and lay her on the rocks, then bending over her put his ear to her mouth and listened. Sarah wasn't breathing, Frank's heart was in his mouth with the thought she could be dead. Laying his head on her chest he was thankful when he heard a faint heartbeat. Sarah was still alive, so Frank got to work.

When at school in Philadelphia, he took part in many swimming carnivals and learnt how to save someone from drowning. He never before had to use his life saving skills and hoped it would work now. He lifted Sarah's head back and opening her mouth, covered her mouth with his and proceeded to blow air into her lungs, breathing again and again, each time stopping to listen for Sarah's breath.

"Come on Sarah, breathe!" Frank looked at Sarah's shirt, how it was torn, almost exposing one of her breasts, the bottom of one side was torn away and there was blood oozing from a hole in her shoulder. He lifted her shirt aside and looked at the wound, then realized the red shirt he thought Sarah was wearing must be her blood soaking her clothing. Frank wondered how Sarah had come to be shot. Had another trapper shot her mistaking her for a wolf? he would have to wait for Sarah to wake up to find out. He was breathing air into Sarah's lungs when she suddenly gurgled and coughed up water. Frank wanted to kiss her with relief but rolled her onto her side instead and let her breathe in air and bring up more water. Rolling her onto her back, Sarah opened her eyes and gasped as she tried to focus on Frank. "Frank ...help me!" she whispered before passing out.

Frank almost cried, Sarah hadn't called him by his first name since meeting him at her father's burial. He picked her up in his arms and carried her over the rocks to his shelter. Before anything, he had to get Sarah out of her wet clothes so she wouldn't catch a fever. He lay her next to his firepit so he could spread out a blanket, then glancing at his fire, saw the fire was out. He would have to relight it but not until he got Sarah sorted. Pulling off her boots, he threw them near the firepit, undid the buttons on her shirt and suddenly sat back on his heels. Before he went any further, he looked at Sarah lying there in front of him. He was about to undress her, Sarah would be naked, and vulnerable. Frank wasn't thinking about anything other than helping her, he would never touch her before they were married. Sarah was badly hurt and needed his help, he had to try not to focus too much on what he was about to see.

Frank took a deep breath, swallowed, then pushed the front of her shirt open exposing her. He couldn't help but look at her firm breasts, or her delicate pink nipples. He stopped looking long enough to sit her up and remove her shirt completely. When Sarah's head flopped against his chest, he slid the shirt down her arms and over her hands then gently laid her back down before removing the sheath from around her waist. He undid the buttons on the front of her trousers. Working quickly, he pulled her trousers down until he had them over her knees. He had a quick look at her body, taking in the thick matt of dark hair between her legs before pulling her trousers all the way off. Frank had never seen a naked woman before now, and here was Sarah, the woman he wanted to marry, lying completely exposed in front of him. He forced himself to stop thinking about her nakedness and picked her up in his arms, then holding her close, carried her into his shelter where he lay her on the blanket and wrapped it around her. He quickly covered her with several skins to keep her warm. 'Now,' he wondered. 'What do I do about the wound in her shoulder?'

The wound in Sarah's shoulder looked bad. Frank had never had to deal with a bullet wound before. He got a wad of bandages and pressed them hard against the wound. Sarah screamed and came around. Frank sat back when Sarah looked at him through pained eyes. "Goddamn Sarah," Frank said. "What happened?" Sarah kept looking at Frank but didn't seem to see him. "Sarah what happened?" he repeated.

"Get ...out," Sarah said softly and closed her eyes. Frank couldn't quite make out what she was saying. Thinking she was telling him to get out of his shelter, he put his head down close to her face so she could hear him. "This is my shelter Cole, I don't have to get out," he said reverting to using her last name in anger. Here he was trying to help her and she was telling him to get out, no way was he taking that from her, even if she was badly hurt.

Sarah opened her eyes and lifted her head a little to look at Frank. "No, that's not what ...get it out Frank ...get ...bullet ...out." Sarah's head flopped back on the blanket. Frank was sorry he felt angry with her when he misunderstood what she said. "Hell Sarah, I don't know how." Sarah kept her eyes closed against the pain while she tried to tell Frank what to do to help her.

"Get a knife and dig it out." Sarah watched her father dig a bullet out of one of the trapper's legs when he had been accidently shot while out hunting. Another trapper mistook him for a wolf creeping through the underbrush and fired at him, luckily for him he only got shot in the leg. The trapper's wound healed and he was fine. "You have to get it out or I'm going to die, dig it out ...pour gunpowder in ...light it." Frank looked horrified at Sarah. "Jesus Cole!"

Sarah felt she was going to pass out again, she looked desperately at Frank, and through gritted teeth, repeated what she wanted him to do. "Get a goddamn knife and dig around until you find the goddamn bullet ...stick something in the goddamn hole to soak up the blood, then put the goddamn powder in the hole and light it!" Sarah felt like she was in a nightmare. "It will seal the wound and stop the bleeding." She kept her head turned toward Frank, her eyes pleading with his. "You can do it Frank ...but you got to do it now." She closed her eyes. Frank had to do what Sarah asked, he didn't want her to die.

Frank hurriedly lit the fire and got his knife. After shoving the blade into the red-hot coals, he cut off one end of two cartridges for his rifle to get the gunpowder, then grabbed a wad of bandages to put in Sarah's wound. He took his knife, the wad of bandages and the gunpowder and sat next to Sarah, then held the knife up to show her he was ready. Sarah looked at him and saw the knife. "Let the knife cool and get me a stick." Frank felt sick, he wasn't too keen on digging the bullet out of Sarah. "A stick?" he was confused at Sarah's sudden request for a stick. "I need a small stick to put in my mouth, I don't want to bite my tongue when you stick that knife in me." Frank hurried out to the fire and finding a small twig, broke it to shorten it and brought it back to Sarah. He put it in her mouth and she held it between her teeth. "Ok Cole?" he looked at her and she nodded.

As Frank pushed the knife into the wound Sarah screamed and bit down hard on the stick. Tears rolled down the side of her face as she felt him digging around inside her shoulder. She tried to stay awake but the pain was unbearable and she couldn't stop herself from passing out. Frank was glad Sarah passed out, that meant she wouldn't feel it when he poked his fingers in the wound.

He held a piece of metal up to the lamp light. What appeared to be a flattened bullet came out of Sarah's shoulder. The wound quickly began filling with blood, Frank pushed the wadding into the hole and got the gunpowder. He went to the fire, brought back a thin twig burning on one end. Pulling the wadding out of Sarah's wound, he quickly poured the gunpowder in, stuck the lighted stick to it and watched the gunpowder burst into flames. Frank jumped back in horror at smelling Sarah's flesh burning. Sarah woke from the searing pain the burning gunpowder caused and screamed while clenching her teeth harder, causing the stick to break between her teeth. Relief washed over her at the bullet being removed, but blacked out from the burning sensation in her shoulder. Frank sat back against the side of the shelter, unable to believe what he just did to the woman he loved. His eyes welled, tears flowed down his cheeks as he watched until the gunpowder stopped burning and the bleeding stopped. While Sarah lay passed out, he poured water from his canteen over his bloodied hands to clean them before carefully removing the stick from her mouth. He covered the now blackened wound with bandages, tucked Sarah's arms under the blanket, covered her back over with furs to keep her warm, then leant over. "I love you …Sarah Cole," he whispered, tears still wetting his face as he bent down and kissed her.

Frank didn't have any other weapon and he could hear wolves howling in the distance. He needed to retrieve his rifle and skins from where he dropped them. He put one end of a long thick branch in the fire and waited until it caught, then taking the branch out of the fire he held it up. The flame threw off just enough light for him to see where he was going. He hadn't bothered to get out of his own wet clothes and his body shivered from the cold as he walked back towards the river.

Walking across the stones took time in daylight, now it seemed to take forever in the dark. He came upon the river and turning south, walked along until he tripped over his rucksack and pile of wolf skins, almost jumping out of his own skin when he stumbled over them. Thinking he had stumbled onto a live wolf, he cursed loudly and picked up his rifle. While slinging it over his shoulder he picked up his rucksack, then gingerly made his way back to his camp in the dull light of the burning torch.

Frank knew he had to get out of his wet clothes, he would be no good to Sarah if he was lying next to her with a fever. He stripped off in front of the blazing fire, gathered up his and Sarah's wet clothes and hung them over a rope line to dry. He hadn't brought any other clothes to change into so put on his fur coat and wrapped a fur around his hips tying it with a length of rope to keep it in place. The fur barely covered the top of his legs. He went into the warm shelter and lay down beside Sarah and watched her steady breathing until he fell asleep.

Frank woke when he heard Sarah stirring in the middle of the night. Sitting up he bent over her. "It's alright Cole, you're safe now," he reassured her.

Remembering what happened, Sarah tried to sit up but her shoulder hurt, making her fall back in pain.

"Did you get the bullet out?" she managed to ask.

"Yes, I got it out, do you want to see it?"

"No, I don't want to see it!" Sarah said almost angrily.

"It was flattened."

"Flattened?"

Frank reached behind him and took the flattened bullet out of his supply box where he put it next to his bible and timepiece so he could show Sarah when she was well enough to see it. He held the bullet up in front of her. Sarah looked at the bullet Frank held in front of her face. "Goddamn ...it must have bounced off the rocks ...so that's why it didn't go right through." Frank put the bullet back in his supply box. "What happened, can you tell me?"

"I shot myself."

"Shot yourself? how?" Frank's voice sounded incredulous when he questioned as to how Sarah came to shoot herself.

"I was following a wolf ...stepped into some undergrowth ...bushes gave way and I fell ...had to let go of my rifle, I don't know where my rifle ended up ...couldn't look for it ...no time." Sarah moaned, her shoulder was throbbing. "I was heading for your camp when I came out on the ridge ...goddamn wolf followed me ...I think you know what happened then." Sarah's voice cracked when she related what happened. Frank knew what happened but wanted to know how she knew he was camped here at the River Flats. He never ventured over near Sarah's cabin so she wouldn't have seen him anywhere.

"How did you know I was here?" He whispered as he lay back down beside her.

Sarah closed her eyes while she struggled to stay awake. "I ...I came this way a few weeks ago ...saw the camp ...you weren't here."

"How did you know it was my camp?"

"I saw your book …in a box …over there ...in the corner." Sarah's voice trailed off.

He knew the book Sarah referred to. When he was ten years old his mother gave him a bible as a christening gift. Frank remembered showing it to Sarah when they went out riding in Cedar Creek, he remembered telling her he cherished his bible. Frank wished they could go back to that time when they went riding to the ponds. They were happy back then.

Sarah went quiet, her eyes were still closed. "Cole," Frank leant over her. "Cole" he said again, but Sarah had given in to her ordeal and had gone back to sleep.

Frank woke at daylight and made himself hotcakes and coffee. While sitting at the fire, he went over what Sarah said happened to her. She told him she didn't know where her rifle was. That rifle Frank knew, belonged to her father and he decided he would go take a look to see if he could find it.

Before he did that though, he wanted to see if he could retrieve Sarah's knife from the river, he wanted to find her rucksack too, wanting to have them back for when she went back to her cabin, that way he thought, she might be grateful for his help and she wouldn't be so mad at him all the time. Frank expected Sarah would be at his camp for a week while she got strong enough to walk back to her cabin. At least he hoped she would stay for the full week, that way he would get to spend some time with her.

His clothes were still damp so he decided not to put them on, he would only have to take them off again to swim in the river to look for Sarah's knife. He walked along the riverbank until he came to the ridge where Sarah had fallen in. He removed his coat and the fur from around his legs and stepped into the cold water.

When Frank dived under his body shuddered from the sudden impact the cold water had on him. He swam down and came up several times before seeing the knife resting on the riverbed. He held his breath and swam back down, bringing the knife up to the surface. Without glancing around, he climbed out of the river and stood on the bank shivering. Only then did he see Sarah standing on the riverbank, a blanket wrapped tightly around her.

Frank was holding the knife in his hand and was startled to see Sarah standing there staring at him. He reached down quickly, grabbed the fur and tried to hold it in front of him before she saw anything. "Goddamn it, Cole! what the hell, you were asleep when I came down here!"

"Well I woke up Mason …didn't I?" Sarah sounded just like she used to, her voice had an angry tone to it. Thankfully, the wound on her shoulder was still covered by his makeshift bandage. "I saw you coming here dressed like ...like …I don't know what!" she looked at her knife in his hand. Frank was too late if he thought she hadn't seen anything.

"I came to get this." He held up her knife while holding the fur in front of his crotch. Frank watched as Sarah's face started to turn pale, she turned quickly and stumbled her way back toward the shelter. Frank picked up his coat and followed her.

"You should have stayed in the shelter, you're not ready to get up and walk about."

"I need to head back to my cabin," Sarah said over her shoulder as she lay back down, her face had gone white and she was sweating. Frank stopped at the fire and quickly pulled on his trousers. "Come on Cole get under the skins and rest." Frank covered her back over with the skins he had trapped.

"I'll just stay for a little while longer, then I'm heading back." Sarah had a vivid picture in her mind of Frank standing on the riverbank naked, his body toned and muscled. Sarah knew his body must have bulked up from the physical effort it took to make his shelter and hunting on the mountain. When she woke up and found herself alone in his shelter she looked about and saw him heading off toward the river. Then when she tried to stand the blanket fell away, making it obvious Frank had undressed her and undoubtedly saw her naked too. Sarah felt embarrassed that he would have seen her breasts and the hair that grew between her legs. Well, he had hair on his crotch too, thick black hair, she closed her eyes trying to forget what she had seen.

"Yeah right! you do that, I wouldn't want you to stay here any longer than necessary." Frank said while he covered her. Sarah didn't hear him, she had already passed out. Frank couldn't understand why Sarah's attitude had changed again, he saved her life and now she wanted to get up and go before she was ready. While Sarah slept, Frank went out looking for her rucksack and rifle. Following the trail back to the forest and heading due east to the ridge above the river, he came across Sarah's rucksack still sitting where she put it to shoot at the wolf. Carrying the rucksack on his back, he took a few careful steps over to an area where he saw bushes had been trampled. He climbed down into the small ravine and saw dried blood on the stones at the bottom. He looked back up to where he climbed down. It was a long way down through dense trees and shrubs, and he was surprised Sarah hadn't broken any bones as well as shooting herself.

Frank searched the bushes and found the rifle wedged between the branches of shrubs and the rock wall. He was gone most of the day and when he got back to his camp, he put both Sarah's rucksack and rifle at the entrance to the shelter where she could see he had retrieved them. He put his head into the shelter, Sarah was still sleeping. 'Good,' he thought. 'She won't be going anywhere just yet.' Sarah slept on and off for the next two days. Frank caught a rabbit in a snare and cut it up to make a stew. Between Sarah's sleeping and wakefulness, he fed her the broth and gave her water.

When Sarah finally woke, Frank was sitting by the fire. She felt much better, even though her shoulder hurt like hell and burned with pain. Sarah was hungry, she sat up and gripped the blanket across her chest.

"Where are my clothes?" she called loudly so he could hear her.

Frank looked startled when he heard her yell at him, he didn't like the tone of her voice, if Sarah was going to be angry, he decided, he would treat her the same.

"Your clothes are here!" he pointed to where they were hanging over the rope line. "You want 'em ...you come and get 'em." He put his mug to his mouth, drank his coffee and tried his best to ignore her. Sarah frowned, she couldn't understand Frank's sudden angry tone, all she did was ask him where her clothes were.

Sarah stood up on shaky legs, then holding the blanket tightly around her made her way out of the shelter. Trying to get her clothes off the line, she found she couldn't lift her left arm because of her wound and had to hold the blanket with her right hand, putting her in a predicament. If she were to let go of the blanket it would fall to the ground and she would be standing naked in front of Frank.

Frank came out of the river naked and she had seen enough of him to know he was right when he said he wasn't a boy.

"I need my clothes Mason," she said trying to keep her voice lowered so he wouldn't think she was angry at him.

Frank kept his tin mug near his mouth. "What do you want me to do about that Cole?" He knew once she got dressed she would leave, and he didn't want her to go, not yet. He kept drinking his coffee.

"Can you take them to the shelter for me?"

"Why? can't you get them? you have two hands!"

"I can't, I have to hold on to the blanket."

"You afraid I might see something I haven't already seen?" Frank put his mug to his mouth and took a mouthful of the hot liquid.

Sarah didn't say anything, now she knew for sure Frank had seen her when he undressed her, no-one, not even her Pa ever saw her naked, her Pa wouldn't dare go into the washroom while she was in there bathing, Frank had seen her whole body. She went back into the shelter and sat down, her face red with embarrassment, and felt like crying at the indignity of the situation she found herself in. Frank got up and getting her clothes, carried them to the shelter entrance and threw them at her, making Sarah flinch when the clothes landed on her.

"Go ahead, go back to your cabin, you've been here long enough!" Frank grabbed his rifle and walked away from the camp. Sarah didn't understand why Frank was angry with her. What had she done except be hurt and ask him for help? Sarah waited until Frank disappeared from sight, then trying not to cry, let the blanket go and hurriedly pulled on her torn shirt. The wound in her shoulder gave her trouble when she moved her arm. She found it easier to pull her trousers on if she sat down, then stand up to get them over her hips and do up the buttons. She came out of the shelter and found her boots sitting side by side near the fire. After pushing her feet into them, she was ready to head back to her cabin. She looked around for Frank but couldn't see him anywhere.

Sarah found her rifle and rucksack propped up beside the entrance to the shelter, her knife was in its sheath sitting on top of her rucksack. She felt grateful Frank found them for her but she wouldn't thank him, he was mad at her for some reason she didn't understand, so she wasn't going to speak to him at all. Sarah was headstrong and if Frank was going to be angry with her then she would be angry right back at him. She just wanted to get back to her cabin. The sheath holding her knife, she gingerly tied around her waist, her rucksack she put over her right shoulder, she picked up her rifle and held it with her right hand. Everything felt heavy, she would have to carry the rucksack and her rifle on her right side for the whole three hours if she wanted to get back to her cabin.

"To make sure you get to your cabin, I'll take you back on my horse." Sarah swung round to find Frank standing behind her. After walking a little way along the riverbank Frank stopped. He wasn't mad at Sarah, he was mad at himself for his angry outburst. He couldn't let her go like this, he wouldn't walk away from her, not when she was hurt, so he turned back to his shelter and found her ready to go.

"It's alright, I don't need your horse …I can find my own way back." Sarah spoke softly and turned her back on him so he couldn't see her eyes fill with tears, determined she wouldn't cry in front of him.

"I know you can, alright ...no horse …but I'm going with you anyway." Frank was sorry for the way he spoke to her.

Sarah didn't argue with him, she didn't have the strength. He collected some things together and put them in his rucksack then put the rucksack on his back. He planned to be back later that day so his packhorse was left tethered to the tree beside his shelter.

"Let's go." He headed along the riverbank ahead of her until they got to the trail in the forest, then Sarah took the lead.

Sarah walked for about an hour until she stopped and put down her rucksack. Frank followed closely behind and saw her stagger. She held on to the trunk of a tree to stop herself from collapsing then sat down under the tree to rest. Frank didn't need to sit down, he stood a little way away from her, opened his canteen and took a drink. Sarah pulled her legs up in front of her and put her right arm across her knees, then put her head down and rested it on her arm.

'I can't do this,' she thought. 'I feel so dizzy, I should have stayed at Frank's camp.'

"You need to move if you want to get back to your cabin before dark." Frank put the lid back on his canteen and hung it over his shoulder.

Sarah lifted her head and looked at Frank. "Don't worry Mason, I'll get there." She was determined she wouldn't give in, not in front of Frank, she didn't want him to think her weak. Frank could see the dark circles under Sarah's eyes and could see she was struggling to make it back to her cabin and thought she should have stayed at his camp until she was feeling better. Sarah pulled herself up off the ground and they kept moving. They stopped once more when Sarah broke out in a sweat, her feet felt heavy and her rucksack felt like it was full of rocks, she staggered several more times but pushed on.

Sarah was struggling to keep going, Frank thought maybe he should help her. He could at least carry her rucksack for her, but he didn't offer, he wanted her to suffer a little, maybe then staying with him wouldn't have been such a bad thing.

They weren't far from Sarah's cabin when she suddenly leant against a tree to rest. 'Thank god,' she said to herself when she spied her cabin through the trees. 'I don't have the strength to go any further.' Frank walked out of the forest and stopped. "Well Cole … you are home." Without answering, Sarah staggered past him and on up to her cabin.

Chapter Seventeen

"I'll get going then." Frank stood near the trees facing the way he had to go to get back to his camp. His horse was tethered to a tree outside his shelter and he wanted to get back before wolves discovered it.

Sarah dropped her rucksack on the porch and leaning her rifle against the wall, turned to see Frank heading back toward the trail.

"When did you stop loving me Frank Mason?" She called after him as she put her hand on the wall to steady herself. Frank stopped dead in his tracks and kept his back to her. He frowned and wondered why Sarah would be asking him such a thing. She had to know he never stopped loving her. It was Sarah who didn't love him, it was Sarah who treated him like a nobody, it was Sarah who didn't care about him, she had been the one that pushed him away, not the other way around.

"I never stopped loving you, what about you? did you ever love me? what about the way you have been treating me?" He said, keeping his back to her when he answered.

"I can't love you, you're engaged to Millicent Crawley, you're getting married ...or have you forgotten?" Sarah felt she was going to pass out if she didn't lay down soon. To hold herself up, she moved to the door and leant against it.

Frank was even more confused when he heard what Sarah said. He turned back from the trail and went up onto the porch where she was leaning against the door. "Who told you I was engaged to Millicent Sarah?" he waited for her to answer, but already guessed the answer. Right then it dawned on him why Sarah had stopped seeing him. Sarah didn't answer, she looked sorrowfully into Frank's eyes. Frank wanted to take her in his arms and kiss some sense into her. “My father told you that didn’t he? he told you I was going to marry Millicent Crawley?”

Tears ran down Sarah’s face. “Your father told me you got engaged to Millicent on Christmas Day, that’s why you didn’t come by the house, isn’t it? you were celebrating your engagement, your father said you would be married come spring ...so why did you come back to the mountain Frank? why?” Sarah cried, her head felt fuzzy, everything around her suddenly felt so out of focus.

“I am not engaged to Millicent Crawley, my father lied to you, he has been pushing Millicent at me ever since I came back to Cedar Creek ...I came here because I love you Sarah, I have loved you ever since I saw you that day you were soaking wet at your father’s burial, I want to be with you ...you are all I have ever wanted!” Frank was almost yelling at Sarah.

Did Sarah hear Frank correctly? She suddenly felt a wave of dizziness wash over her, why did she feel so hot? Frank looked deeply into Sarah’s eyes. He rested his hand on the back of Sarah’s head and pulled her up to him. His kiss was gentle but Sarah didn’t respond, her legs went out from under her. Frank caught her before she could fall and lifting her into his arms, kicked open the cabin door and carried her inside.

Frank rushed into the closest bedroom and lay Sarah down on a huge iron framed bed, then felt her skin. Perspiration had broken out on her forehead, but her skin felt cold, Sarah was burning with fever. Frank got busy, he lit a fire and soon had the cabin warm. He undressed Sarah for the second time and put her under the blankets. He wiped her body with a warm damp cloth and sat with her through the night. When she became delirious, he held her in his arms as she relived the night her father died and she was thrown out of her house. He held her when she said something about being whipped that he couldn’t understand, and she relived fighting off the wolf on the ridge. He held her and comforted her when she cried.

While Sarah slept on and off most of the next two days, he cleaned her wound and gave her water and broth to keep her hydrated. Frank took the time to shave off his beard and make himself a bath in Sarah's big bathtub, soaking in the tub until his fingers became shrivelled. He managed to get outside to get some fresh air and more water on the third day. Sarah slept but wasn't getting any better. Frank worried, Sarah's shoulder turned black and the wound, even though he cleaned it, was starting to fester.

He was coming back to the cabin carrying a bucket of water up from the river when he saw the four trappers. Joe was walking ahead of Garrett. Will and Fergus were further back along the trail. Frank was relieved to see the four men coming toward the cabin with their rucksacks and rifles over their shoulders.

"Joe, Garrett, hey!" Frank waved, put down the bucket and hurried over to the men.

"What are you doing here Frank?" Joe asked while eyeing Frank suspiciously.

"I'm here with Cole, she's inside ...she's ill Joe." When Joe heard Frank say Sarah was ill, he pushed Frank aside and rushing inside went straight to where Sarah was sleeping. After taking a quick look at her Joe flew back outside in a rage. He grabbed Frank by his shirt front and lifted him off the ground, pulling him up against him.

"What the fucking hell have you done to Sarah Frank? you son-of-a ...goddamn it ...if you've hurt her, so help me I'll kill you!" Joe was livid. He wouldn't abide anyone hurting Sarah.

Will, Garrett and Fergus all stared at Joe as he lifted Frank off his feet. Fergus rushed inside to take a look at Sarah for himself. When he came back his face was ashen. "Jesus Christ Joe ...Sarah's got a goddamn infected wound in her shoulder!"

Still holding onto Frank, Joe shook him. "How did Sarah get that fucking wound Frank?"

"I didn't do anything Joe, she shot herself and..." Joe didn't wait for him to finish.

"*Shot*! Sarah's fucking *shot*! Christ almighty!" Joe let Frank go with a savage push and raced back inside. He lifted the blankets away from Sarah's shoulder and saw for himself the black festering wound. Joe cursed loudly, knowing straight away Sarah's body was being poisoned by the infection.

"What did you fucking do to her? you son-of-a-bitch ...*get in here Frank!*" Joe yelled at the top of his lungs. Will and Garret pushed Frank ahead of them through the cabin. They gathered around the side of the bed and looked down at Sarah. All three men sucked in their breath in disgust at the sight of the wound and Sarah lying ill with fever.

"Well Frank! what did you do?" Feeling wild with anger, Joe pointed to the wound. He was meant to protect Sarah, as far as he was concerned, the promise they made when Sarah was three years old had been broken, the four of them had failed to keep her from being hurt bad.

"I did what Sarah told me to do, I got the bullet out, put gunpowder in the wound and sealed it to stop the bleeding."

"Well you didn't do it right, goddamn it ...she was still bleeding under this goddamn awful mess." Frank looked horrified at Joe, he could see what he had done had poisoned Sarah.

"Get out Frank!" Joe looked at Fergus "*Get him out of my fucking sight!*" Joe yelled furiously at the men.

Frank was beside himself. The men were blaming him for what happened to Sarah, he had no choice but to walk to the door with Fergus and Will as they forced him out of the cabin. Before they could push him all the way out, he stopped at the door and turned to Joe. "I'm sorry Joe, I would never hurt Sarah ...you must know that" his voice breaking. "I love her," he added almost inaudibly.

"*Get out!*" Joe bellowed. When he sat down on the side of the bed, he didn't look at Frank. Holding Sarah's hand in his, he brushed her damp hair off her face. Will and Fergus thought if they didn't get Frank out of the cabin Joe would kill him. They took him down to the clearing where they quickly set up camp.

"What are we going to do Joe?" Garret asked when Joe pulled the blanket back up over Sarah's shoulders.

"We are going to open the wound and clean it out, we have got to let the rotten blood out." Joe was furious with Frank, now he had to fix what Frank had done and Sarah was going to suffer some more. So long as Joe did it right, Sarah would come out of it alright, but if he made a mistake, Sarah could die. But he had little choice, if he didn't do something, Sarah was going to die anyway. Joe was mortified, he hadn't seen something like this since being in the cavalry, and that was a very long time ago, and even then, he had only watched the cavalry medic perform what he was about to do.

Will and Fergus got Frank to help them set up their camp while Joe and Garrett stayed inside with Sarah. Frank just wanted to escape, he didn't like the way the men were looking at him, neither man spoke a word to him. Frank didn't care if they weren't going to talk to him. He tried explaining to Will and Fergus how Sarah shot herself and was attacked by the wolf and how he pulled her out of the river. He told them it was Sarah herself who told him how to get the bullet out, but from the looks on their faces he didn't think they cared when he explained fully what he had done.

Frank, Will and Fergus all heard Sarah's agonizing scream. Sarah's scream frightened Frank and he made to run toward the cabin, wanting to see for himself what Joe and Garrett were doing to her, but Will and Fergus grabbed hold of him and held him back. "What are they doing to Sarah?" Frank cried as both men held his arms firmly.

"They will be opening the wound!" Fergus said sadly. Fergus was worried. Worried the four of them may have broken the promise they made to Sarah's father. He remembered the exact words they promised. 'See she doesn't get hurt bad,' and here it seems, she was dying from an infected wound. Fergus worried they weren't doing a very good job of taking care of her. If Sarah died the four of them would be forced to leave the mountain by the other trappers, they would go back to living a civilized life and he more than likely would have to go back to Ireland, and he was in no way ready for that. He loved it here on the mountain. His life as a trapper would be over.

Will took Frank back to the fire, all three men sat quietly and waited. Frank sat with his head down praying that Sarah would be alright. It wasn't his fault, he only did what Sarah asked of him and now she was worse off because of it, he kept glancing over at the cabin. When it became dark Frank watched a lamp light burning in one of the windows and shadowy figures moving about behind the glass. He couldn't help wondering what was happening inside. It was getting on toward midnight when Will gave Frank Garrett's bedroll and told him Garrett would be sleeping in the cabin along with Joe. Frank lay down on the bedroll and pulled the blanket almost over his head. He didn't want to look at the men, he thought he knew what they were thinking. Even though he explained what happened he reasoned the men had every right to hate him. 'Don't they know I love Sarah and that I would never hurt her' he said to himself. He had not meant for any of this to happen.

Will settled down on his bedroll, it was going to be a long night. His thoughts were of Sarah too. He hoped she would pull through, she was tough but this was something even a man would have trouble surviving. What Frank had done to her wasn't his fault if what Frank told them was true. Frank did his best, it was all any of them would have done. Will worried that the four of them had broken the promise to keep Sarah safe, but how could they keep her safe when they were off trapping the mountain? they couldn't watch Sarah all of the time, no one could. She had to be her own woman, she was a trapper just like they were, and had managed to survive her first year back on the mountain alone. Will knew Frank was in love with Sarah. He felt strongly about her too but conceded defeat when Sarah showed more interest in Frank than him. He hoped Sarah and Frank would sort out their differences and get together. If Sarah and Frank were to marry, Sarah would become Frank's responsibility, then he, Garrett, Fergus and Joe would be free of their promise. Will didn't hold any grudges against Frank, he was a greenhorn trapper and a man that was very much in love. But as he lay quietly on his bedroll he thought if Sarah didn't survive the night, they would be made to leave the mountain because the promise would have been broken. Will said a silent prayer for Sarah.

Frank kept his head covered and thought about his father, asking himself just exactly when did his father tell Sarah the lie about him being engaged to Millicent Crawley. They had the Crawley's as their guests at the ranch for Christmas lunch and he wasn't able to leave to see Sarah and give her the gift he had for her. The small box was still safely tucked away in his saddle-bag. He planned to slip the ring on her finger as a Christmas gift, then ask her to marry him, but as it happened, he never got the chance. He went on the cattle drive to Moreton a few days after Christmas. Frank worked out his father told Sarah he and Millicent Crawley got engaged on

Christmas Day and that they would be married in the spring while he was away on the cattle drive. 'Goddamn that son-of-a-bitch!' Frank swore under his breath. Sarah thought he had fallen 'out' of love with her. So, Sarah had believed him when he told her that he loved her. His father, he realized, was turning Sarah against him. Frank vowed he would have it out with his father when he returned to the ranch this winter. He would tell his father in no uncertain words that he was going to marry Sarah. He told his father before he was going to marry Sarah, and he would keep on telling him again and again until his father accepted it. That, he concluded, was if Sarah would agree to marry him. But first Sarah had to survive this nightmare they were both now in.

Joe sat on a chair beside Sarah lying in what used to be her fathers' bed. Joe wondered just why she was sleeping there and not in her own bed. 'Frank must have put her in this bed and undressed her, what else did he fucking do?' he wondered. Joe slept fitfully, waking every so often to check on Sarah. Garrett was getting some sleep on the couch in the living area. There were two bedrooms in the cabin, one was Sarah's the other her father's. Joe got up and going to Sarah's room, opened the door and looked in. Her room had been stripped, the bed and dresser were still there but the blankets and patchwork quilt and all of Sarah's belongings were gone. Joe went back to Sarah. Her quilt was folded neatly on the foot of the big iron bed. He opened the top two drawers in the tallboy and found her belongings were folded neatly in the drawers. Frank hadn't moved her, Sarah moved herself into her father's room.

Sitting down on the side of the bed, Joe lifted Sarah up gently, held a mug to her lips and gave her a drink of water. Sarah drank a little. The four men took turns watching Sarah over the next few days and nights while she continued to pass from sleeping to wakefulness. Frank wasn't asked to watch over her. He felt the men hated having him around, so made up his mind to get away from where he wasn't wanted. He planned to head back to his camp on the River Flats the next day.

Joe and Garrett took turns watching Sarah through the night. The sun was high when Joe went outside to get some much-needed fresh air. Frank hadn't left yet and was over at the clearing. Joe looked fleetingly in his direction before going back inside. He asked

Garrett to go fetch Fergus to take over watching Sarah so he could get something to eat. Garrett did as Joe told him. Fergus came in to take his turn and asked Joe how Sarah was doing.

"She's sleeping right now, fevers broke, I think she will be alright." Joe reached over and gently brushed Sarah's hair off her face while she slept.

Fergus was relieved at the news that Sarah was going to be alright. "You going to tell Frank Sarah will be alright?"

"Not yet, let him stew for a while longer."

Fergus felt sorry for Frank, he knew Frank wasn't to blame for what happened to Sarah. Frank told him what happened and he believed him. Frank wasn't the type to tell lies, he was just inexperienced when it came to things that happened on the mountain. Fergus thought Frank should be given a second chance. He could tell how deeply Frank loved Sarah, he could see it every time he looked at Frank.

"He's been stewin' Joe, he's really sorry for what happened." Fergus tried to defend Frank.

"Yeah well, so he should be!" When it came to Sarah, Joe had no sympathy for anyone that tried to hurt her.

When Sarah started to wake up, Joe and Fergus hurried over to the bed. Sarah opened her eyes. "Frank," she said softly. Joe grunted, "so now she gets better, we sit with her for three nights and all she can do is ask for Mason." He wasn't at all surprised, he knew from the very first day Sarah and Frank met at the cemetery what was happening between them.

"It's Joe Sarah." Joe sat down on the side of the bed and took her hand in his. Sarah focused on Joe's face. "Hey Joe ...Frank …he did good ...he got the bullet out."

"Yeah …and he did it all wrong, we had to open you up again, goddamn it."

Sarah frowned and thought about what Joe was saying. She thought she had been hallucinating when she felt the recurring pain in her shoulder. Sarah didn't want to blame Frank, not now when he had taken care of her and come to her cabin with her. "Don't be mad at him Joe, I'll be alright."

"How are you feeling right now?" Joe kept hold of her hand.

"I'm feeling ...hungry." Sarah didn't know how long it had been since she had eaten anything.

Right then Joe knew Sarah was going to be alright, he told Fergus to go get her a plate of food. Fergus raced out to the clearing and dished up a plate of hot stew Will had prepared for the men. He ran past Will and Garrett who scratched their heads in wonderment at what the hell Fergus was doing. Fergus didn't enlighten any of them that Sarah was asking for food. Balancing the plate of hot food in both hands, he raced back inside. On his way through to the bedroom he grabbed a spoon. By the time he got back to the bedroom Sarah was sitting up leaning against pillows that Joe gathered from the other bed.

When Fergus left the room to get the plate of food, Joe asked Sarah if she had something she could put on to cover herself, he didn't want her lying there naked with the men wandering in and out of her cabin. Sarah told Joe to get one of her father's shirts out of the tallboy. Joe thought all the things in the tallboy were hers. He pulled open a drawer and lifted out a shirt that had been washed and ironed. Sarah would have done that he noted, she was a good housekeeper, even though her father was no longer there she was still looking after his washing and ironing as well as cooking and keeping the cabin clean.

Joe carried the shirt over to Sarah and helped her sit up. Sarah held the blanket tightly in front of her when he put his arm around her bare back. While helping her get the shirt on, he asked her to tell him what happened. She told him in detail about how she shot herself after trying to follow a wolf, then being attacked by the same wolf and falling off the ridge into the river. She told him how Frank pulled her out of the river and helped bring her back by breathing air into her. By the time Fergus came in with the plate of hot food, Sarah was sitting up with the shirt on and Joe knew the full story.

Joe fussed over Sarah, fluffing up the pillows behind her, making her lean back on them and making sure she was comfortable. Fergus handed Joe the plate and Joe put the plate on a pillow on Sarah's lap. Sarah ate hungrily, the food wasn't nearly as good as what she could cook but it was hot and it filled her empty stomach. Sarah told

Joe and Fergus they didn't have to stay to watch her eat. Both men could see she would be fine, so, while she ate, they went out to the campfire to get themselves some food.

Sarah's horses were in need of exercise. Joe and Fergus were still inside seeing to Sarah when Frank went over to the horses and took Star out of the lean-to. Frank knew Sarah let Star swim in the river when the weather was good. He walked Star down the incline where he took off his boots and rolled up his trousers, he led Star into the river then let him go. Star walked out into deep water while Frank, sitting on a large rock with his legs bent up in front of him watched him swimming back and forth across the river. Frank was unaware Sarah was awake.

Joe came out of the cabin and went over to where Will and Garrett were standing at the fire. Both men were busily tucking into a plate of stew. They both let out an audible sigh of relief when he let them know Sarah was going to be fine. Will's prayer had been answered, they wouldn't have to leave the mountain after all. Joe asked if either one of them didn't mind going in to sit with Sarah. Will said he would go, he took his plate and walked quickly up to the cabin and disappeared inside. Joe looked around for Frank but couldn't see him anywhere "Where is Frank?" he asked Garrett. "He's down at the river, with Star." Garrett pointed over the incline to the river.

Joe headed down the incline at a fast pace, wanting to let Frank know Sarah was going to be alright. After talking with Sarah, he felt maybe he shouldn't have been so quick at blaming Frank for her predicament. He hadn't believed Frank when he told him what happened. Sarah would always be his responsibility and he felt relieved that she had pulled through.

When Joe walked down to the river, he found Frank perched up on a large boulder, sitting in the sun. Star came out of the river and rolled around in the dirt, kicking his legs in the air while Frank watched him. Joe smiled, that horse was just like a kid, give 'em a bath and what do they do? they go straight out and play in the dirt. "Frank!" Joe called as he came strolling down the incline. Frank looked around and saw Joe striding towards him. He jumped down from where he was sitting and stood facing Joe, unable to tell from Joe's face if he was mad at him or not. Frank avoided Joe whenever he came out of the cabin, but if Joe wanted a fight Frank was ready to defend himself. Star stopped rolling in the dirt and stood up. As Joe approached Frank the horse shook himself and flicked his tail to free himself of dust and dirt.

"Sarah is going to be alright, she is sitting up eating some of Garrett's stew. She told me what happened, you can go up to the cabin and see her if you want." Frank felt a lump rise in his throat and thought he might cry when Joe told him the good news, but he didn't want to show weakness in front of Joe. Instead of answering, Frank turned and walked over to Star who was still shaking his head from side to side. Joe could see Frank was upset and leaving him alone, hurried back up the hill to the clearing, he was hungry and the stew smelt good.

Frank stood where he was for a moment letting Star put his head over his shoulder. He leant on Star and put his hand around his neck, there was no way he could go up and see Sarah, not yet, not while he was upset. Joe said Sarah was going to be alright and Joe didn't hit him, but he didn't apologize to him either. He didn't want the men to see him crying so he stayed down at the river for a long time. The men put their heads down when they could hear Frank's sobs from where they were at the clearing.

After taking Star back to the lean-to, Frank made his way over to the clearing. Joe had finished eating and gone back inside. Frank wasn't quite ready to barge in on Sarah, he had to compose himself first. He helped himself to some food, then sat cross-legged on Garrett's bedroll to eat his meal. After finishing eating, he felt he was ready to go to the cabin. Fergus was at the stove making coffee when Frank came in. "You want some coffee Frank, its fresh?" The men seemed in better spirits now Sarah was going to be alright.

"Not yet, I might later." He said going to the bedroom door. Joe and Sarah were talking softly to each other but he couldn't make out what they were saying, except for one thing, he heard them mention Millicent Crawley's name.

Joe was sitting on the chair beside Sarah's bed. Sarah was holding a mug of coffee in both hands, she had slid down a little in the blankets and so pulled her knees up to stop herself from sliding down any further.

"Do you love him Sarah?" Joe asked her softly.

"I can't love him Joe, he is engaged to Millicent Crawley."

"He is not engaged to Millicent, who the hell told you that?" Joe had a good idea who told Sarah Frank was engaged to Millicent. Major Hardy wanted to cause trouble from the very day Sarah met his son. Joe knew Frank spent a lot of time with Millicent but only because his father made him.

"Major Hardy told me to stay away from Frank because he was engaged to Millicent." Sarah hadn't seen Frank come into the room.

"And you believe him?" Joe was leaning forward on his chair talking to Sarah quietly.

"Why should he lie?" Sarah had been looking at Joe when she answered, her gaze went over Joe's shoulder when out the corner of her eye she noticed Frank standing in the doorway.

"Joe!" Frank interrupted Joe before he could answer Sarah's question and came all the way into the room. Looking over Joe's shoulder, Sarah's heart skipped a beat when she saw how Frank looked tired and haggard. Joe turned to see Frank standing behind him. "Come in Frank," Joe said as he stood up and moved to the door. "I'll be right outside if you need me." Joe gave a half smile to Sarah and left them alone.

Frank and Sarah looked at each other. "You want to sit down Frank?" Sarah said as she patted the bed next to her. Frank sat down in the chair Joe vacated.

"You alright?" Frank asked her.

"Yeah …I'm alright, Joe cleaned the wound." Sarah sounded proud that Joe had taken care of her.

"Did you know I was doing the wrong thing when I dug the bullet out of your shoulder?" Frank looked into Sarah's eyes and felt like running from the room, feeling unable to sit with her knowing instead of the bullet nearly killing her he almost killed her by what he had done.

"No, I didn't, I saw my Pa dig a bullet out of one of the trappers legs when he got shot and he did what I told you to do." She waited for a moment before going on. "Only Joe said after you light the gunpowder you're supposed to clean the mess out of the wound and sew the wound up." Sarah screwed up her nose. "I didn't remember that part, Joe reminded me I was about seven at the time." Sarah smiled and tried to make light of what happened. Frank kept his eyes on Sarah's face as she told him what he should have done, she didn't apologize to him for getting him in trouble with the four men. "That's why I got infected, Joe sewed me up ...see!" Sarah pulled the shirt off her shoulder so Frank could see where Joe had stitched her up. A piece of black thread stuck out of Sarah's skin from under the new bandage covering her wound. Frank glanced at part of her exposed breast as she held the shirt open for him to see. "Cole, we have to talk." Frank had something on his mind and it wasn't good.

"We are talking ...aren't we Frank?" Sarah pulled her shirt back over her wound and smiled at Frank.

Frank wasn't smiling, he didn't feel much like smiling these days, he felt like he had lost the friendships he worked hard at making with the trappers when he came to the mountain for the first time. "The men blamed me for what happened to you," he said sternly.

"Do they still blame you?" Sarah stopped smiling and became serious.

"I don't know, I haven't spoken to them and they haven't spoken to me." He started to sound angry, their conversation wasn't going the way he wanted it to go, he paused for thought then told Sarah he was leaving. "I'm going back to my camp and then when I go back to Cedar Creek this winter, I'm not going to come back."

Sarah leant back on her pillows and remained quiet while Frank continued. "I'm not going to fight with you anymore Cole, I obviously don't belong here." Frank looked down at his hands. "Maybe my father was right, maybe I should be marrying Millicent Crawley." Frank finished talking suddenly and standing up, turned abruptly and knocked over the chair. "And my names Mason!" he called over his shoulder as he rushed out of the room.

Sarah was confused, she thought she was wrong about Frank and Millicent. That he was going to marry Millicent wasn't what Frank said to her outside the cabin when they came back from his camp on the River Flats. Frank kissed her and told her he loved her, or had she been delirious at the time and imagined it? Sarah covered her face with her hands. Her mind was in turmoil. 'So Frank doesn't love me, Joe said he loved me, he said Frank wasn't marrying Millicent, how could Joe be so wrong?' Sarah tried to hold back her tears but they flowed down her cheeks and dripped off her chin.

Sarah threw the blankets back and tried to stand. She wanted to talk to Frank, to ask him about what he said to her on her porch. After being in bed for so long Sarah's head swam at suddenly standing up. She grabbed the side of the bed and sat back down. Her father's shirt rode up causing her legs to become totally uncovered. She tugged at the shirt pulling it over her knees and sat there unable to walk without becoming dizzy. She remained where she was and cried, the thought of having lost Frank spinning in her head after he said he was leaving the mountain for good.

Joe was outside telling the men to pack up, now Sarah was over her fever and was on the mend, they would be leaving first thing in the morning. Will, Garrett and Fergus packed their gear ready to head out for their camp on the High Ridge. Will and Garrett cut Sarah a pile of wood and stacked it near the front porch. Sarah had only to step down from the porch to get the wood. Fergus walked back and forth to the river carrying two buckets of water at a time and filled Sarah's two water barrels.

Joe felt satisfied Sarah and Frank's dilemma was over when he left Frank talking to Sarah. He couldn't hear any loud voices so imagined they were getting along. When Frank came rushing out of the cabin Joe was stunned by the look on Frank's face. Something had happened and Joe wasn't happy, what had Sarah said to Frank now? he wondered.

Frank picked up his rucksack and rifle and threw them over his shoulder. Joe hurried over but before Joe could say anything Frank spoke first. "I'm heading back to my camp at the River Flats and then I'm leaving." Joe studied Frank's face, in confusion. Did he and Sarah have an argument? What the hell happened for Frank to be leaving? "Why are you leaving Frank?" Joe asked confused. Frank looked toward the trees and the trail that led to the River Flats. He just wanted to get out of there, he had enough of the men questioning him about everything he did with Sarah. He knew they hated him for what happened, he wasn't about to stay where he wasn't wanted. "I asked you why you are leaving?" Joe repeated sternly, pushing his coat open and putting his hands on his hips in a defiant manner, which wasn't unusual for Joe. His handgun and hunting knife looked menacing and Frank didn't like the accusing way Joe was looking at him, making him even more determined to leave.

"I don't belong here Joe, come winter I'm leaving the mountain." Frank began to walk away.

"We all leave the mountain in the winter Frank." Joe laughed half-heartedly. Frank stopped. "Yes …but I'm not coming back, Sarah doesn't need me, she has all of you to take care of her." Joe was stunned at Frank's decision to leave and not come back.

"For Christ sake Frank, you follow Sarah for two years and now you're giving up?" Joe wasn't going to interfere, but he was going to say his piece.

"Sarah doesn't love me, she never has." Frank made to walk off. Joe grabbed his arm and stopped him. "That's shit Frank, you leave now and you will never know if Sarah loves you or not …stay here!" Joe stormed back into the cabin. Frank didn't wait for Joe to come back out, he headed toward the trail and disappeared amongst the trees.

Sarah was sitting on the side of the bed weeping when Joe went back to her. He sat beside her and pulled her into his arms. "He's leaving Joe, he doesn't love me, he said he's going back to marry Millicent Crawley."

"I told you, he isn't going to marry Millicent, it's you he loves, it's as plain as that pretty nose on your goddamn pretty face." Joe touched his finger to the tip of Sarah's nose. "You can stop him leaving, you know what you have to do." Joe thought maybe he was interfering but he had to stop this nonsense, both Frank and Sarah had to realize they loved each other and Frank's father had to stay out of it. Joe was sure the four of them could deal with the Major if necessary. Sarah didn't make to go after Frank to stop him leaving. "Why would he say he was marrying Millicent if he isn't, let him go, if he doesn't want to stay here to be near me…I will just have to bear it." Joe looked at Sarah, he knew she was making a mistake about Frank, but it was her decision. "Are you sure this is what you want Sarah?"

"Yes Joe ...it's what I want." It wasn't what she wanted at all, but she had no choice, she had to let Frank go. Sarah got back into bed, pulled the blankets up to cover her, then turned her face to the wall. Joe listened to Sarah for a moment, she was crying softly but had made up her mind. Maybe this is what is meant to happen Joe told himself. Sarah made her choice so they would have to abide by it. Joe left the room. When he stepped outside, Frank had gone.

Chapter Eighteen

Having told Frank to wait while he went back inside the cabin to talk to Sarah, Frank, sure Sarah didn't love him, didn't hang around. He returned to his camp on the River Flats to find his horse was gone. The tether was still tied to the tree, the rope frayed where it had broken from his horse straining against it as it kicked and bucked, trying to escape the wolves that came along the river to hunt. Sensing the horse nearby, they attacked and once loose, chased it down until they caught it. Frank continued to spend the next few weeks trapping and hunting along the river and in the forest around his camp. His collection of skins grew each day and Frank felt pleased with himself.

The storm hit late in the afternoon, it was violent in its destruction, trees were uprooted and hail lashed the ground, tearing leaves and branches from the trees and blowing them violently around. Frank's shelter was taking a beating, he cowered inside trying to escape the downpour and violent winds that howled across the river. Streaks of lightning lit up the sky, coming dangerously close to the ground near his camp. Frank's skins were getting a drenching. The shelter began to leak, part of the roof and side wall came down as a tree crashed into it. Frank hastily shoved some things into his rucksack and dived outside with just enough time to save himself then ran for shelter in the dense forest. Strong, howling wind with the force of a small tornado twisted trees violently around as he ran through the trees. Hail was replaced with pouring rain, the heavy downpour didn't help Frank, he fought his way through the forest and headed for the only shelter he could think of, all he hoped was that Sarah would give him shelter. The storm was relentless, Frank struggled on for several hours while countless branches smashed into him and driving rain made it difficult for him to see where he was going.

Sarah could hear the wind howling outside, heavy rain lashed the windows, lightning lit up the sky, she was grateful for her sturdy cabin. Except for one small leak that had developed in her ceiling everything seemed to be holding up. The storm was so violent, trees were bent over and some had been uprooted not far from her cabin. The lean-to wasn't nearly as sturdy a structure as her cabin. Wanting to check on her horses to see how they were coping with the storm, she opened the door and raced outside into howling wind and torrential rain. As she reached the lean-to it shook violently against the wind, rain soaked the ground around the edges inside. The walls of the lean-to only coming half way up the sides, left Sarah's horses subjected to all types of weather. Star and her two packhorses were a little on edge but otherwise safe. She checked their tethers and while making sure the walls were secure made a mental note to herself to ask Joe and the other men to build the walls higher, closing her horses in out of the weather.

Sarah raced back to the cabin getting a further drenching on her way back. As she made her dash up onto the porch, a bolt of lightning struck a tree on the edge of the forest not far from her cabin. There was a loud explosion and sparks flew as the tree split in two and burst into flames. The ground shook making Sarah scream in fright. The lightning bolt wasn't the only thing that made Sarah scream.

When lightning lit up the porch, she saw someone standing in the shadows. Her heart went to her mouth as the figure stepped toward her. Putting her hand up to her chest to hold on to her heart, she almost fainted in fright until she recognized who it was. "Frank Mason!" she called, but her voice got whipped away in the wind. "What are you doing here Mason?" she yelled louder to get above the storm.

"The storm blew down my shelter!" Frank yelled back. Sarah thought Frank sounded different, almost angry, but of course he was different, ever since her shooting accident they had become distant, now here he was standing on her doorstep.

"You better come in." Sarah opened the door and Frank followed her inside.

Frank removed his rucksack off his back and sat it next to his rifle on the floor just inside the door. "Hang your coat there and take off your muddy boots." Sarah said pulling out a chair as she passed the table on her way to the washroom. Frank took off his coat, sat on the chair and pulled off his boots while Sarah disappeared into the washroom to take off her own boots and dry her hair. She rubbed her hair briskly to dry it then took a towel out to where Frank was standing in front of the fire getting warm.

"Tell me again…what happened?" Sarah asked while putting a pot of water on the stove to make coffee. Frank moved back to give Sarah room at the fire and watched her while he dried his hair. "A tree came down on my shelter …I had just enough time to get out …I figured the only place I could go was here." Frank finished drying his hair and ran his hands through it to straighten it, except his hair was curly and nothing he could do would stop it from curling when it dried.

"So, you thought it best to come all the way here!" Sarah was busy at the stove with her back to Frank.

"Where else was I to go? ...I can go and stay in the lean-to with the horses until the storm blows over." Sarah listened to Frank, he had never sounded this way before, he didn't sound like the Frank she knew, his voice was deep, more masculine, there was a sadness about it too. "You don't have to go to the lean-to, you can stay here, I'll make you up a bed in the other room." It didn't matter to Sarah if they didn't get along, she wouldn't put him out in the storm.

The storm caused the roof of the cabin to leak, both Garrett and Fergus checked Sarah's cabin to make sure it was sound but this storm had loosened something making water drip onto Sarah's table. She hurriedly removed the full pot of water and placed an empty pot in the middle of the table under the drip. The continual 'tang, tang' of the drips hitting the bottom of the pot echoed in the silence that followed.

Sarah heated up the left-over stew she prepared the day before, then set two places opposite each other. Frank sat facing her across the table.

"What about your skins? what will happen to them now your shelter is ruined?" Sarah was about to tuck into her stew, the spoon was almost to her mouth.

"They'll be alright, I'll go back when the storm..." Frank didn't finish what he was about to say before something fell from the ceiling and landed in the pot sending water all over the table. Sarah and Frank both jumped back as a stream of water poured from the ceiling and splashed into the pot. Frank looked at the large piece of black wood floating in the water. Sarah reached in and picked the piece of wood out. "Goddamn!" Sarah cursed as they looked up at the ceiling. A large hole had developed and the stream of water continued to pour down filling the pot in no time. Sarah took the now overflowing pot and replaced it with another much larger pot.

Frank frowned as he watched Sarah rummaging through a wooden trunk. She came back carrying a hammer and a handful of long nails.

"Where are you going with those?" Frank stayed at the table but wondered at what Sarah might be going to do. "I'm going outside to fix that goddamn leak once and for all!" She shoved the nails in her trousers pocket and opened the cabin door. A violent gust of wind howled through the opening blowing her hair back off her face.

"You are not getting up on the roof in this storm, you will fall off and break you neck!" Frank warned but remained where he was seated. Sarah held the hammer up. "Why don't you just sit there and stay dry Frank!" Her remark sounded sarcastic to Frank, he looked down at the plate of stew sitting in front of him. What did he care if she wanted to go outside in the storm and get herself killed by falling off the roof? When he looked up, she was gone.

Sarah bolted out the door, ran down the steps and out into the storm. She grabbed the ladder leaning against the wall at the bottom of the steps and struggled with carrying it around the side of the cabin against the wind. Rain pelted her and she was soaking wet all over again. Managing to lean the ladder against the side of the cabin, she grabbed a wooden slat off the pile stacked against the wall and holding the hammer in one hand and the slat in the other, clambered up the ladder. Wind and rain howled across the roof. The ladder began to slip, Sarah held on tight until the wind eased off suddenly. She kept going, pulling herself up over the roof until she found where the leak was coming from. Peering into the hole with one eye, she could see the table in the light cast by the fire, but Frank was nowhere to be seen. Sarah didn't have time to worry about where he had gone, she lay the slat over the hole and started hammering furiously against the wind that started blowing again.

Frank raced out into the rain, ran around the side of the cabin and saw the ladder leaning against the wall. He stood at the bottom of the ladder and looked up as strong wind and driving rain lashed him. Sarah had disappeared up onto the roof. He watched as the ladder started to slide sideways. Grabbing it so it wouldn't fall, he kept his face turned up to the roof watching for Sarah, unable to hear any hammering for the howling of the wind.

A long few minutes passed before Frank saw Sarah's feet come over the side of the roof searching for a foothold. He moved the ladder to position it under her feet. Sarah felt her feet touch a rung and brought her feet down slowly. Frank kept holding on tight to both sides of the ladder while Sarah climbed down. When Sarah's feet were on the ground, she found herself standing between Frank's outstretched arms. She turned and faced him as lightning flashed all around. Sarah and Frank stared into each other's eyes. The moment took Frank back to the time when they were both at the cemetery, both had been soaked to the bone then as they were now. Sarah had gone back to the Ferguson House with the trappers and he had gone back to his father's ranch with a fever, Frank kept his eyes focused on Sarah.

Sarah looked up into Frank's face, remembering the time at the cemetery too. "Frank," Sarah mouthed against the wind. Frank took his hands off the sides of the ladder and wrapped his arms around her. Their mouths came together as Sarah dropped the hammer and reaching up, put her arms around Frank's neck. This kiss was not like when Frank kissed her at Christmas when he gave her Star, nor was it like their kiss at the picnic, this kiss was much more passionate. Frank's mouth forced Sarah's lips apart, his tongue slipped between her teeth. Sarah let her tongue feel Frank 's tongue as it delved deep inside her mouth. Their kiss was heated, both of them held it for a long time. A sudden bright flash of lightning and rolling roar of thunder shook the ground around them bringing them both back to reality. Frank didn't want to let Sarah go, but they had to get back inside out of the storm. When they separated, Sarah took hold of Frank's hand and they ran hand in hand back to the porch. Sarah opened the door and ran inside where she turned to face Frank.

Standing inside the cabin both dripping wet, neither of them felt cold, their kiss warmed them and they had all but forgotten the storm. The leak had stopped, Sarah smiled at Frank. "The roof is fixed." Frank was staring, he didn't care about the leak, he wanted more of what they had just done. Sarah felt self-conscious at Frank staring at her, she spun around quickly and headed for the bedroom. A few minutes later she was back carrying a dry shirt and pair of trousers.

"I'll go to the washroom, you can get out of your wet clothes in the bedroom," Sarah called over her shoulder. "Wrap a blanket around you and I'll hang your clothes up to dry." Frank went to the bedroom where he stripped off his wet shirt, pushed his trousers down to his feet and stepped out of them. He picked his wet clothes up off the floor and glanced through the open doorway. Sarah hadn't closed the door to the washroom, his line of vision went straight to where she was undressing.

It was warm in the cabin. Inside the washroom, Sarah removed her wet clothing. She lifted her arms to undo her wet braid, then twisted her hair until water ran out of it. Shaking her hands to get the water off them, she reached toward the door handle where the towel was hanging and caught Frank looking at her through the doorway. She quickly held the towel in front of her to cover herself as best as she could but didn't move to close the door.

They stood staring at each other across the cabin. Sarah stared at Frank's body. Frank told her once before he was a man not a boy, and from the sight of him he definitely was not a boy. Sarah felt a warmth rush through her. Frank, carrying his wet clothes, walked slowly from the bedroom toward the washroom. Sarah remained still and kept watching as he came toward her.

"Sarah," Frank whispered, as he came through the door. He could see the scar on her shoulder where Joe had sown it up had healed well and didn't appear to be giving her any trouble. He dropped his wet clothes on top of Sarah's on a chair, reached out with his hand and rested it on the side of Sarah's face. Sarah closed her eyes, feeling his hand against her cool skin. Frank leant forward, brought his mouth down on hers and kissed her softly. Sarah let go of the towel, moved her hands over Frank's bare chest bringing them up around his neck. Frank slid his hands around Sarah's back, encircling her and bringing Sarah's body against his. She returned his kiss passionately, feeling all of his body as he pressed himself against her. Lifting Sarah into his arms, he carried her to the bedroom.

Frank lay Sarah on the bed, letting his eyes travel over her as he lay down beside her. He had seen her naked, twice before now, but still a thrill coursed through him when looking at her. Her breasts were full, and firm, her nipples hard pink buds, his eyes roamed over her flat stomach to the mound of hair between her legs. He looked at her firm muscled legs. She was fit, after spending years walking the mountain her body was toned. Sarah lay back against the pillows and let Frank study her.

While Sarah watched Frank studying her, she took her time to look at him. His body had changed since coming to the mountain. Walking everywhere, trapping and hunting, his body was lean and muscular, his chest had expanded, his breasts were firm and his nipples round and hard. Sarah looked at his tight stomach. Muscles flexed all the way down his legs, making them look strong. Sarah had seen his naked body before too, after coming out of the river from where he retrieved her knife. A thick mat of dark hair surrounded his manhood and Sarah desperately wanted to run her fingers through it. Sarah turned on her side to face Frank. "Frank," she whispered. Frank looked into Sarah's deep blue eyes, then, pushing her gently onto her back, moved her legs apart so he could get between them. Sarah watched as he knelt between her legs. A tingle of excitement coursed through her as his hands moved upwards, moving ever so slowly over her hips then sliding up to cover her breasts. Frank felt her nipples harden under his touch. An ache of wanting started between Sarah's legs, she couldn't wait for Frank to make love to her. Frank slowly slid one hand over her stomach. While hovering over her, rubbing his hand through the mat of hair between her legs several times, he curled his fingers under her, pushing them into the warmth of her body. Sarah watched as Frank's manhood became erect as his desire for her grew. She had never seen a naked man before Frank, and was intrigued by what was happening to him. "Is that normal Frank?" she asked as she took her eyes off his manhood and looked up into his face. Frank felt his body react this way before. An ache started in his crotch when he undressed Sarah in his shelter and again when he undressed her in her cabin when he came back with her from the River Flats. He wasn't put off by what Sarah was asking him. "It's what happens to me when I look at you," he whispered.

"Will it hurt?" Sarah asked as Frank kept exploring. Sarah felt his hand between her legs, his fingers gently probing, he was being careful, she wanted him to do more.

"I've never done this before Frank." Sarah needed him to know it was her first time. Frank looked into Sarah's eyes. He had been right when he thought now would be her first time. "I've never done this before either, I'll try not to hurt you." He bent his head and kissed her. Sarah was pleased to learn this was his first time too, she parted her legs a little further. Frank felt his manhood hardening, and lowering himself gently on top of Sarah, pushed himself forward. Sarah reached up, held her arms around the back of Frank's head and pulled him closer, bringing their mouths together as Frank pushed himself further.

"Am I hurting you?" Frank asked softly as he moved back and forth. Sarah's breasts felt smooth and hard where they pressed against his chest. Keeping their bodies locked together Frank looked at Sarah's nipples, at how they were standing up, giving him a sudden desire to push harder.

"No." Sarah could hardly speak, she was too busy concentrating on how Frank was making her feel.

Frank pushed forward, Sarah lifted her legs over the back of his as she felt him moving deeper. Frank felt Sarah beginning to respond to his thrusting. As his groin pressed against her womanhood, he continued to move back and forth, heightening the feeling he was getting from her. He began to thrust faster and reaching around Sarah lifted her against him. Sarah started to respond in kind when she felt a tightness inside her suddenly ease. Sarah's body awakened, Frank thrust deeper as their bodies locked together, slowing down just enough to let Sarah join in. They kept their bodies moving in rhythm, neither of them speaking as they watched each other intently. Frank felt himself almost ready. His body was feeling Sarah's response to his thrusting as he deflowered her. Unable to hold back, "Sarah" he moaned, as his thrusting quickened. Sarah clung to Frank, her arms tightened around him, her breathing came in gasps as she felt something beginning to happen. She liked how Frank was making the feeling between her legs build, she worked her body, keeping in time with him.

"Oh Lord, …what is …happening?" Sarah suddenly gasped as her now fully swollen womanhood went into uncontrollable spasms. She continued to gasp as her orgasm peaked. Frank came suddenly, giving in to his thrusting, holding Sarah against him while his manhood continued to throb. Frank wrapped his arms tighter around her and moaned a deep, satisfying moan.

The storm continued to rage outside but Frank and Sarah didn't notice, they had fallen asleep in each other's arms, both exhausted and happy from their first sexual experience with each other.

Sarah woke early the next morning as she always did. The first thing she needed do was head to the outhouse. She lifted Frank's arm off her chest and made to move off the bed when she saw the stain on the bedclothes. "Frank," she said shaking him trying to wake him. "Frank!" she said again. There was blood on Sarah's legs and she started to panic. She couldn't understand why she was covered in blood. *"Frank!"* she screamed as she shook him.

Frank woke with a start when he heard Sarah scream. "What! what is it?, Sarah what's wrong?" Sarah started to cry, blood covered her fingers where she touched her body and she held her hands up to show Frank.

"Frank what's happening?" Sarah was frightened, her monthly cycle wasn't due, so this wasn't good. Frank's eyes widened. "Shit!" he cursed, as he flew off the bed and raced to the washroom.

"It's alright," he reassured her, coming back with a cloth. "I know what's happened." Using the cloth, he wiped the blood off Sarah then tried wiping between her legs as she continued to cry. "Don't touch me!" she cried hysterically. Frank stopped wiping her and sat back on the bed.

"It's alright Sarah," he repeated softly, trying to allay her fears. "It's because of what we did, it's normal for your first time, you don't feel any pain, do you?" Sarah thought about what Frank was saying. "No," she sobbed. Frank pulled her into his arms, feeling her naked body, how warm and soft it felt, he moved his hands gently over her to comfort her.

"It's both our first time, I had to make way for me, next time we do it, it will be easier," he reassured her.

"How do you know that? you didn't bleed." Frank laughed, "men don't bleed Sarah, only women." Sarah lifted her head and looked at Frank. "Well that's not fair!" Sarah wiped her face on a corner of the bedsheet and they both laughed.

"Now I have to wash these sheets again ...I only did them this week." Frank lit the fire under the washstand and heated up water for Sarah and him to bathe. Frank thought it was a wonderful mess they were both in. Sarah was everything he thought she would be, he loved her more than ever now he had made love to her.

Since the night of the storm Sarah let Frank stay with her at her cabin. Over the next few days he cut wood and refilled her water barrels, helped her walk her horses and swam them in the river. Sarah told Frank he could take one of her packhorses to his camp and bring his skins to her cabin where he could store them in the old cabin next to her skins. Frank was grateful for Sarah's offer, they both rose early to pack their rucksacks with enough food for the one-day journey, planning to stop at Frank's ruined camp site for lunch before heading back to her cabin so Frank could store his skins.

Frank emptied his rucksack on Sarah's table to make room for food. She had a frown on her face when she looked at a book that fell on the table. "What is this?" She picked the book up to look at it and Frank took it back off her. "It's just a book." Sarah took it back off Frank and flicked through the pages. There were beautiful drawings of wolves along with trees and mountain scenes. Sarah looked at Frank as she turned more pages. Frank had drawn pictures of people, the four trappers Joe, Will, Garrett and Fergus all graced the pages of Frank's drawing book. Frank was studying Sarah while she looked at his drawings. When Sarah came to a drawing of her, she stopped turning pages. "Frank, this is me!" she said, amazed at the drawing's likeness to her. Frank took the book off her and closed it. "When did you draw me?" Sarah was smiling at him, she had never seen him with his drawing book. "I drew it from memory," he said shoving the book back in his rucksack, his face turning pink when Sarah continued smiling at him. Frank couldn't help it, he smiled back at her. "Will you draw more pictures?" she asked as she finished packing food into his rucksack. "Of course, I love to draw." Frank was pleased Sarah liked his drawings. They set off hand in hand for the River Flats and Frank's camp.

Sarah set out lunch on a blanket on the ground and she and Frank ate a hearty lunch while talking about their future together, after lunch they lay down beside each other to rest. They kissed and fondled each other until their petting became more serious. Frank undid the buttons on Sarah's trousers and pushed his hand between her legs. Sarah pushed her trousers down over her knees to give him better access. Frank loosened his trousers and climbed on top of her. They made love on the blanket in the sunshine. When they were done, they straightened up their clothes then lay beside each other deep in their own thoughts.

"Remember the picnic at the ponds Sarah?" Frank suddenly rolled over and leant over her, his body pressed against Sarah's breasts. Frank looked down into Sarah's eyes and Sarah looked up into his. "You remember, I was leaning over you like this and I kissed you." Sarah looked over Frank's shoulder at white fluffy clouds which were forming shapes above her, she tried to pick out shapes as she watched them roll across the sky. Sarah remembered what Frank was asking her. "I remember."

"From that day you stopped liking me, can you tell me why?" Frank's body was pressing down on her, holding her down while waiting for her to answer him.

"You kissed me and I was scared I was falling in love with you, I didn't know about love, not that kind, I rode out to the ponds a few days later to think about us and I decided that if you kissed me again I would let you touch me ...but on the way back to town ...I happened to cross paths with your father." Sarah talked fast remembering that day vividly. "He threatened to whip me if I had anything to do with you and I got scared, I didn't want to be whipped Frank, so I pretended I didn't like you ...I guess I was a ...a coward." Frank rolled off Sarah and lay back down on his back.

"My father!" Frank closed his eyes. "He wants me to marry Millicent Crawley and have standing in the community." Sarah turned her head and looked sideways at Frank.

"He told me you were engaged to be married in the spring, you spent a lot of time with Millicent last winter..." Sarah paused and looked back up at the sky. "Do you love her Frank?"

Frank sat up suddenly and looked angrily at Sarah, then got to his feet. "You shouldn't have to ask me that Sarah! ...not after what we have been doing!" he said down to her.

Sarah got up as Frank stormed over to where his shelter had collapsed and started pulling tree branches off it. "Frank?" Sarah said, standing behind him.

"Don't Sarah!" he snapped at her and kept savagely throwing tree branches to one side.

"I only..." Sarah knew Frank hadn't made love to Millicent, he told her she was his first but it didn't mean he didn't love Millicent, he spent a lot of time with her over the winter months and perhaps he did have feelings for her.

"You only what?" he turned to face her, his eyes dark with anger.

"Nothing!" Sarah didn't know what to say, she didn't want Frank to be angry with her so she said nothing. Sarah helped Frank pull branches and trees off the shelter. They didn't speak at all while Frank packed his skins onto the packhorse himself. Sarah wasn't able to help him and he had a lot of skins. If she were to help, he would be disqualified from taking part in The Pot, that was the rule. Sarah thought it a stupid rule, who would know? but she would know and so would Frank. Frank thought he could be the winner this winter and he had good reason to want the money.

While Frank loaded his skins, Sarah wandered over to the river, folded her arms and stood looking at the water rushing over rocks. This was the same place she had fallen in after shooting herself in the shoulder and fighting with a wolf. It was where Frank pulled her out and saved her from drowning. Frank came over and stood beside her and looked at the river.

"Skins are all loaded, we better start back," Frank said without looking at her. Sarah didn't answer, she had nothing to say. She turned away and went back to his ruined shelter. Frank followed her and could see she wasn't going to talk to him. They headed back to her cabin, neither of them speaking to the other for the three-hour journey.

They arrived back at the cabin in silence. Frank took the packhorse straight to the old cabin where he unloaded his skins. They would be stored alongside Sarah's skins until it was time to leave the mountain for Cedar Creek. Sarah went inside to prepare dinner while Frank remained outside unloading the packhorse.

Dinner was strained when neither of them got up the courage to speak to the other. Frank kept glancing over at Sarah while she kept looking down at the food on her plate. When dinner was over Sarah cleaned up the dishes and went into her old bedroom. She was gone for quite a while and Frank wondered what she was doing. Frank stayed sitting out by the fire, still feeling a little annoyed with Sarah asking him if he loved Millicent. Because Sarah, after their lovemaking, had to know he loved only her, he thought she had no reason to question his love for her.

Sarah came out of the spare bedroom. "I've made you up a bed, you can sleep in there." She rushed into her room and closed the door before Frank could say anything to her. Frank stood up and looking at the closed door thought now they weren't going to sleep together. "Sarah?" Frank questioned in confusion. He rushed to the door and tried to open it but found it locked. "Sarah open the door!" Frank banged his fist on the door. "Sarah don't do this ...not now ...please ...let me in!" Frank begged as he leant his head on the door. Sarah stood behind the closed door and lowered the latch over the hook to stop Frank from getting in. Weeping silently, Sarah undressed and climbed into bed and cried some more. Why couldn't Frank answer her? she asked him a simple question but instead of answering her he got angry with her for asking him if he loved Millicent. She cried most of the night, convinced Frank truly loved Millicent.

Frank continued to lean on the door. "Sarah open the door," he said softly "If it's about Millicent Crawley no, ...I don't love her, I have never loved her, it's you I love, I have always loved you, please let me in." Sarah didn't answer him or open the door. He tried once more to get her to open the door. "I only spent time with Millicent to please my father ...Sarah come on ...open the door." But Sarah didn't reply. Frank gave up begging Sarah to let him in and went to the other room. Not bothering to undress, he lay down on top of the bed to think. He was angry with Sarah for asking him if he loved Millicent, he didn't think he needed to answer that question. It should have been obvious to Sarah that he loved her, he was here on the mountain with her, he followed her for two years to be here with her. Frank wondered where their love was going to take them. Sarah would always be strong willed and stubborn. He tossed and turned all through the night.

Frank rose early. Knowing Sarah would get up at daylight as she always did, he took his rifle and went to the outhouse. When he came back, he washed his face and hands in the dish in the washroom, then went and stood at Sarah's door to wait for her to come out.

Sarah got up and dressed, she felt tired and a little queasy, not having slept well from crying most of the night and thinking about her and Frank and why she had driven a wedge between them. It was her fault they were fighting. If she hadn't asked Frank about Millicent everything would have been alright. But she wanted to know that Frank loved her and her alone, she couldn't be with him if he loved another woman, she thought her question was reasonable.

The door opened and Sarah stepped out, straight into Frank standing at her door. She quickly ducked around him, grabbed her rifle and headed out the washroom door to the outhouse. "Sarah, we need to talk!" Frank called after her. He didn't try to stop her and would never use force against her, opting to wait until she came back inside to have it out with her.

Sarah stood her rifle against the washroom wall and looked at him. Frank could see she had cried most of the night. "Oh Sarah, don't do this to us," he said softly. Sarah's eyes watered. "I think I asked you a fair question Frank, you didn't say you didn't love

Millicent when I asked you, instead you got angry with me, what was I to think?" Frank listened to Sarah's concerns. When she finished, he leant over her and pointed to her door. "I stood outside that goddamn door last night and told you I didn't love her, that I loved you and you ignored me, I am not going to fight with you over bloody Millicent Crawley!" Frank stepped closer to her, took her face in his hands and kissed her. "I love you, Sarah Cole, with all of my being." Sarah's eyes brimmed with tears as his warm hands held her face up to his. "And I love you, with all of my heart, Frank Mason." They wrapped their arms around each other and held each other tight. "Can we get some sleep now?" Frank laughed, he kissed Sarah again, he was tired from hauling trees off his shelter and not sleeping all night. "Come to bed Frank." Sarah took Frank's hand and they went back to bed.

Sarah and Frank spent the rest of the day in bed making love and sleeping some more. When they awoke from sleeping in each other's arms they made love again. Sarah got out of bed when it was dark to fix them both some food. She pulled on one of her father's shirts and walked to the stove to make hotcakes, busily going about getting the food while Frank watched her from the bedroom. Sarah had long legs that disappeared up under the shirt she was wearing. Frank felt a twinge of wanting surge through his body as he watched her. Sarah put a plate of hotcakes and two mugs of steaming coffee on a tray and carried the tray back to the bedroom. She sat leaning back on pillows at the head of the bed while Frank sat at the foot.

Frank watched Sarah while they ate and Sarah watched Frank. Sarah paid particular attention to his crotch. Frank saw her looking at him and smiled his wide grin that Sarah loved. Sarah put her mug down on the tray, and reaching up to the buttons on her shirt, slowly undid each button until the shirt hung open. Frank stopped smiling and became serious. Sarah could see his body's reaction to what she was doing. She opened her shirt, slid her hands across her breasts, slowly pushed the shirt over her shoulders and let it fall down her arms. She threw the shirt on the floor while keeping her eyes on Frank. Frank stared at Sarah's breasts, seeing her nipples standing up, he could tell she was as aroused as much as he. Frank removed the tray off the bed and crawling along the bed to Sarah, pulled her down under him and made love to her again.

As the days turned to weeks Sarah and Frank spent more time in bed than they did trapping. When they did venture out, they went for long walks along the river near Sarah's cabin. They held hands as they walked and whenever the urge came over them, they stopped where they were and made love. Frank couldn't get enough of Sarah and Sarah wanted Frank to make love to her no matter where they were.

Sarah cleaned up after dinner while Frank filled the huge bathtub in the washroom with warm water he heated in the washstand. He placed candles around the room filling it with a romantic glow, then went to Sarah and took her hand in his. "Come with me ...Sarah Cole!" he smiled then led Sarah to the washroom. "We are going to bathe together instead of one at a time." He undressed while Sarah watched, taking his shirt off quickly, then proceeded to remove his trousers slowly, letting Sarah watch his manhood bob free from its confines. Frank pushed his trousers down his legs, stepped out of them then threw them aside. He straightened up and let Sarah look at him. "Sarah," Frank whispered as he stepped up to her. Taking her hand, he placed it on him. Sarah hadn't been game to touch Frank there and the feeling she was getting from him was making her blush. Continuing to hold him while he undid the buttons on her shirt and trousers, Frank pushed her shirt open. Sarah felt Frank's response as he removed her shirt. Taking he hand away Frank knelt in front of her, pulled her trousers down her legs, then without warning, kissed her while letting his tongue slip between her legs. Sarah gasped, pushed her hands into his hair and held him to her. Frank stood up, touched her face with his hand and stepped into the bath, leaving Sarah feeling she wanted more.

Sarah stepped into the tub and sat with her back to Frank. Frank reached around in front of Sarah and taking the soap, lathered her breasts, then, sliding his hand between her legs, rubbed his fingers over her womanhood. Sarah became aroused as his fingers delved deeper. She leant back against Frank and gasping with each of his movements felt herself coming. She stopped him from going any further when she suddenly turned around to face him, bringing her body over his legs and onto his lap. Frank's arousal was complete, he took hold of her hips and pulled her down over him. They pushed against each other making water slop over the sides of the tub soaking the floor, working themselves into a frenzy until Frank lifted Sarah out of the bath and carried her to the bedroom. They were still very wet, but neither seemed to care if they were making the bed wet. Frank found it easy to slip between Sarah's wet legs. Both of them having become excited, Frank pushed deeper, Sarah wrapped her legs around him, holding him to her. Frank filled Sarah with his love as Sarah clung to him.

The days wore on, stretching into weeks. Sarah and Frank finally decided if they were going to take part in The Pot, they needed to get out and get more skins. They packed their rucksacks. Sarah put on her fur vest and secured it around her waist with a thin piece of rope. Her father's hunting knife hung at her hip. She loaded her rifle and put a box of shells in her rucksack along with enough food to allow them to camp out for one night. As the nights were getting colder a blanket was rolled up and tied to the top of her rucksack. For extra warmth, they would sleep under wolf skins when they trapped them.

Only planning to be away from the cabin for one night, Frank packed his rucksack with enough food and bullets to last them several days. Frank wasn't going to take a chance in case something happened and they couldn't get back. He packed his sketch book and some pencils. When at school, drawing was his passion next to boxing and swimming. He drew Sarah's cabin while she was recovering from her wound to her shoulder. He sketched Joe and Fergus, both Will and Garrett, along with other trappers that he found interesting when he camped with them at the High Ridge Camp. He drew mountain scenery and wolves. He sketched Sarah when they stopped to rest after hunting along the River Flats. She stood on a boulder smiling off into the distance, her rifle up at her shoulder aiming at a pretend target. Frank captured Sarah's love for him in her eyes. When he sketched a close up of her looking straight at him, her dark blue eyes held him spellbound.

It was just on daylight when they set out. They walked up the mountain beyond Sarah's cabin to check traps Sarah set before Frank had come to stay at her cabin. A wolf carcass was caught in one of her traps but it had been there far too long, what other animals didn't eat the rest had rotted away, its skin was beyond saving. Sarah was disappointed at not having checked her traps earlier. Frank and her love making kept her from venturing out. She felt she needed to be more determined to go out hunting instead of lying around all day making love to Frank. They moved on, Frank shot a wolf and skinned it while Sarah watched on, impressed at his new-found skill. Frank was a quick learner, but then he had a good teacher when he told Sarah it had been Joe that taught him how to skin his kill. As they moved further up the mountain, Sarah began feeling a little queasy, she felt her stomach rise up in her throat and the trees and ground start to swim. She fell suddenly, landing on the hard ground. Frank was standing too far away from her to catch her before she fell. He rushed over and helped her sit up. "Sarah what happened?" Squatting in front of her, he quickly opened his canteen and gave her a drink. "I don't know, it just came over me suddenly ...I ...I feel ill." Sarah drank several mouthfuls of water, then wetting her hand, wiped her face with it. Frank sat down beside her and let her rest a while. When they moved on, Sarah seemed to come good, the illness disappeared as quickly as it came. Sarah shot two wolves they spotted skulking about in the forest. Frank watched in awe as Sarah skinned the wolves, clearly, she was more adept at skinning than he was. She was quick, the knife sliced neatly along the wolfs body making the skin come away from the carcass clean. Frank was amazed at Sarah's ability.

That night, they made camp near a group of boulders. To keep wolves away and keeping their backs to the rock wall, they built a huge fire at the front of them. Sarah heated beans in a small pan and put them on slabs of freshly baked bread. They ate hungrily after the long day of walking, hot mugs of coffee warmed them. They cuddled up to each other under the blankets and talked. Frank held Sarah close, sliding his hand in under her shirt, he cupped one of her breasts and gently massaged it, making them both become aroused. They made love before loading the fire with wood and huddling together under their blanket for the night.

Next morning when they woke Sarah was ill again, she made her way from the camp to relieve herself but didn't get very far before her stomach contents came up. Frank was worried she was coming down with something. They both agreed to head back to the cabin earlier than they planned. They had six skins between them and that would have to do.

Sarah stopped several times on their way back down the trail toward the cabin, she didn't know what could be making her ill. They made it back to the cabin by midday when Sarah started to feel better, making both of them surprised and a little confused. Sarah felt well but they stayed around the cabin and the next morning when Sarah woke up before her feet touched the floor she almost threw up. She ran through the washroom and out the side door, forgetting to grab her rifle in her hast, just lucky no wolves were lurking about. Frank followed her and held her while she was sick, after which he made her go back to bed to rest. Both of them were getting worried, neither understood what could be happening to her. As the weeks went by, Sarah's body began to feel bloated and her breasts were becoming tender. They worried she had caught an unknown illness. Each morning Sarah continued to be sick then each evening she felt fine. It was one evening though, while getting dinner, Frank saw Sarah stumble and knock over a chair, he managed to catch her before she hit the floor, then sat down with her on the floor and held her until she came around. Neither Frank nor Sarah could figure out what was causing her illness.

Autumn was behind them. Winter arrived bringing freezing winds with it, snow fell for the first time making the ground icy. Frank was kept busy chopping more wood to keep the cabin warm. Sarah stayed in bed most mornings not rising until midday. As the snow got deeper Sarah knew it was time to leave for Cedar Creek. She sat with Frank at the table to discuss what they were going to do when the trappers came by.

Frank and Sarah made plans for when they returned to Cedar Creek for the winter. "You pack your skins Frank and when Joe comes by, I'll say you got here early." Frank wanted to be truthful with Joe, he didn't want the men to think he and Sarah weren't together. But Sarah didn't think she was ready to tell the men Frank was staying with her. The other trappers would be along any day now, well before the pass became blocked so Joe could get everyone and their skins off the mountain.

Sarah and Frank got busy making plans for when Frank went back to his father's ranch. They planned to meet up at the shack on Major Hardy's land so they could be together without anyone knowing. Frank told Sarah to count the days until they would meet, a week before Christmas.

"I can't count Frank." Sarah put her head down in embarrassment at having to tell Frank she didn't know how to count, but then she remembered. "I could count to ten," she held up her hands. "Will showed me how to count rabbits on my fingers." Frank laughed and kissed her. He tore a page from his drawing book and drew up boxes, then numbered the boxes with the days in each month. He drew a circle around the day he and Sarah would meet at the shack.

"Each morning when you get up the first thing you do is put a cross in a box." Frank showed Sarah what he meant. "When all the boxes are crossed out up to the circled box you head out to the shack, I'll be there waiting for you." Sarah took careful note of how Frank crossed the boxes. He handed her the small pencil and got her to cross a box. "That's today, tomorrow you cross this one, the next day you cross this one." He pointed to each box. "Keep going until all the boxes are crossed out." Sarah leant over and kissed Frank, understanding what he was showing her. He folded the paper and handed it to her along with the pencil. "Keep it safe Sarah." Sarah put the pencil and paper in her rucksack.

It was snowing heavily outside. Sarah knew Joe would be on his way from the High Ridge Camp. She took Frank by the hand and led him to the bedroom where they undressed and spent the rest of the day making love.

Sarah was fretting, she wanted to ask Frank if he would be seeing Millicent Crawley when they got back to Cedar Creek, only she wasn't sure how to broach the subject without making Frank angry.

Frank could see something was bothering Sarah, she had become quiet when she was preparing dinner. He stood behind her while she stirred the stew and wrapped his arms about her. "Tell me Sarah, what are your thinking?" Sarah stopped stirring the pot and leant back against Frank. "I don't want us to fight Frank ...not now ...not when we are ready to go back to Cedar Creek." Frank turned her around to face him. "What do you mean? ...we aren't going to fight!" He paused when he looked into her sad eyes. "We aren't going to fight ...are we Sarah?" He held her away from him and tried smiling at her.

"I want to ask you something, but I know it's going to make you angry with me ...I don't know how to say what I want to ask you without making you angry." Sarah was so worried she felt like she was going to be sick, which wasn't unusual for her these days.

"We won't fight Sarah ...what do you want to ask me?" Frank kept hold of her. Sarah took a deep breath. "Will you be seeing Millicent Crawley when you go back to your father's ranch?" She waited for Frank to get angry with her for mentioning Millicent, but he didn't get angry. Frank didn't want them to fight about Millicent Crawley, not now they were getting along so well.

"Not if I can help it, I will try to avoid her like the plague, but I may not be able to avoid her all of the time ...just you remember Sarah ...it's you I love, not her." Frank pulled Sarah into his arms and held her tight. Sarah put her arms around Frank and rested her head against him.

"What is the plague?" Sarah looked up at Frank, confused by what he said. Frank laughed out loud. "It's a deadly disease that killed a lot of people a long time ago, and I will treat Millicent Crawley like she has it!" Clinging to Frank, Sarah made a mental note to herself that when she got to town, she would ask Doc Harris to tell her more about the plague, she hoped 'the plague' was not what was making her sick.

The trappers, with Joe in the lead, arrived two days later, stopping only briefly at Sarah's cabin on their way past. Frank was sitting on the porch in the cold when the men started to ride by. Joe, Fergus, Will and Garrett pulled their packhorses up to the front steps of the cabin to collect Sarah, when they spied Frank sitting on the top step.

"What are you doing here Frank?" Joe asked him suspiciously. He got off his horse and started up the steps. The other three men followed him.

"Waiting for you Joe." Frank tried to sound nonchalant. "Where did you get the coffee?" Fergus asked, leaning over to look in the mug as he went up the steps onto the porch. Joe knocked on the cabin door and went in before he was invited.

"Cole made it for me, there's more inside, she's been expecting you lot." Frank remained where he was while the men filed inside

Sarah's cabin. Sarah hugged Joe, Fergus followed him in then Will then Garrett, Sarah hugged each man in turn.

"How long has Mason been here?" Joe looked around the cabin, nothing seemed out of place. "He arrived this morning …I gave him coffee …didn't want him freezing out there." Sarah grabbed four mugs off her cupboard and poured steaming coffee into each one. "I'm all packed, so drink up so we can get on the trail and get out of here."

The men drank their coffee while Sarah put on her fur coat and wrapped her scarf around her head. They watched as she pulled her father's old hat with the split brim down on top of her head and pulled the cord tight under her chin to keep it in place. Sarah doused the fire with water and made sure it was out before she left the cabin.

Joe thought Sarah seemed a little too anxious to get going, she had never liked leaving the mountain and always made her dislike of it known to the trappers, this time however she didn't say anything. Joe made her ride beside him so he could keep his eye on her all the way to the caves.

Frank and Sarah kept their distance from each other, only coming close when Sarah went around the camp fire to pour the men their coffee. When she got to Frank Joe watched the two of them carefully. "Want coffee Mason?" Sarah said in her sternest voice, keeping her back to Joe as she winked at Frank. Frank held up his mug and Sarah filled it. "Thanks …er …Cole," Frank replied while trying to keep a straight face. Joe thought Frank held Sarah's gaze a little too long but let it go.

The group made their way to the bottom of the mountain without any attack from wolves. "The wolves," Joe told the line of trappers. "May have stayed on the mountain this year as sometimes they did." It didn't mean they could relax, the trappers kept themselves alert, bunching up for protection, their rifles at the ready. Two wolves were encountered further away from the base of the mountain and they were quickly dispatched. As everyone rode along a lone wolf could be heard howling in the distance.

The trappers made a safe journey to the wells where they set up camp for their second night. Trappers split into groups, Frank and Sarah stayed with Joe's group. Will, Fergus and Garrett along with several other men huddled around their fire. Several fires were burning bright, lighting up the camp sites. Sarah spread her bedroll out on the same side as Joe and Fergus. Frank put his bedroll opposite them next to Will and Garrett.

Everyone soon settled down for the night. Joe lay on his back with his head resting on his saddle. He pulled his blanket up higher over his fur coat and adjusted his hat over his eyes, leaving it up just far enough so he could see everyone sleeping around the fire. He particularly wanted to be able to keep an eye on Sarah and Frank.

When the camp was quiet and everyone was asleep Frank pushed his blanket back and got up. Joe saw him get up and watched him walk away from the camp. He thought Frank was just going to relieve himself until he saw Sarah get up and head in the same direction. Joe got up and followed Sarah, keeping a good distance between them so she wouldn't know he was following her. He stood hidden behind a large tree and thick bushes from where he saw Sarah meet up with Frank. He watched as Frank put his arms around Sarah and Sarah hook her arms around Frank's neck. Joe raised his eyebrows in surprise when he watched the passionate kissing that followed. He stayed watching until both Frank and Sarah started to fondle each other. Sarah's hands were busy unbuttoning Frank's trousers inside his fur coat and Frank's hands went up under Sarah's shirt. Joe had no doubt what Frank and Sarah were feeling with their hands.

Joe pulled back quickly into the dark when Sarah suddenly looked in his direction. "Damn!" he said quietly. Did she know he was there? Sarah's sense of smell was acute and Joe reckoned she could sniff out a jack-rabbit five-miles away.

Joe went back to the campfire and lay down, he wouldn't sleep though, not until the two of them came back. Joe's mind was working overtime. 'Frank and Sarah are together, obviously they have been together before this, but why the hell are they being so secretive about it? unless it's because, when they get back to Cedar Creek, they have to stay away from each other, damn Major Hardy, he is the cause of Sarah and Frank's secretiveness.' Joe pulled his hat back down over his eyes and waited. It was a long time before Sarah came walking back to her bedroll, where she quickly lay down and pulled her blanket over her head. Joe saw Frank come back a few minutes later and lay down.

Next morning when Sarah woke up feeling ill, she dug in her pocket and found a piece of candy and popped it in her mouth. She was grateful for the candy, having found the bag in a tin in her cabin. When eating a piece, the sweet candy helped stop her stomach from rising. So, she kept the candy for when her stomach threatened to erupt.

The trappers rode hard as they headed toward Cedar Creek. Crossing the open prairie and making one final camp before riding into town at noon the next day.

The Trading Post was the first stop for everyone. It took several hours for all the skins to be carried in, tallied up and stowed away. Fess worked alone and it took him some time to get the men organized and quietened down so he could write the names up on the board. Until he wrote all the names on the board no-one knew who won The Pot.

The list of names grew. Joe was on top again followed by Garrett. Several other men's names came next then Frank was written up. Fergus and Wills names were written up under Frank's. A lot of the trappers were surprised with Frank's tally, especially Fergus and Will. Frank surprised even himself, he didn't think he had that many skins but was satisfied with where his name was written. Sarah's name was on the bottom again, disappointed, she stood off to the side while the men congratulated each other. There was a lot of bragging and goading going on and the room was noisy.

As Frank pushed past Sarah, his hand brushed hers when one of the trappers accidently shoved him. Their eyes met and they held each other's gaze for a moment. Joe was standing over at the potbelly stove and seeing Frank's hand brush Sarah's, saw the exchange of looks between the two. Joe saw the sad look that came over Sarah's face as Frank left the Trading Post. Sarah's look convinced him Sarah and Frank had been seeing each other for some time. But what did it mean now they were back in Cedar Creek? Frank was going back to his father's ranch and Sarah, Joe knew, would have to stay away from him. Joe turned away.

Sarah left the Trading Post and went to the bank, she didn't hang around there too long only spending enough time for Morley to get her money put into her account and then headed to the Ferguson house to unpack her belongings.

Chapter Nineteen

Sarah counted down the days, crossing them off her piece of paper each morning just like Frank had shown her. The paper and pencil were hidden between the folds of her spare nightdress in her top draw of her tallboy so no-one could find it. The only person that ever went into her room was Joe, and Sarah was sure he wouldn't go through her things.

Sarah worked the nails out of her window and climbed out into the dark. It was raining just like it rained the day she snuck out to the cemetery when she buried her Pa. But there was a difference. That time was a sad occasion, this time was a happy occasion, this time she was going to meet up with Frank. It was a moonless night, rain began to fall long before Sarah left the Ferguson House and she wore only a thin coat that didn't give her much protection. Her hair, face and legs were wet but she didn't care, Frank was waiting for her. She spurred Star on and rode like the wind.

Frank was already at the shack waiting, Sarah could see his horse standing in the rain tethered to the railing of the small stoop. She quickly tethered Star alongside of Frank's horse, ran up the steps and raced excitedly through the door. When she got inside, she stopped, hurriedly removed her wet coat and threw it on the floor. The fire was already alight and the warm glow lit up the room. Candles lined the mantle and the hearth in front of the fire. A blanket had been spread out. A picnic basket lay open on the blanket, sitting beside it was a bottle of wine and two glasses. Frank was standing in front of the fire when Sarah came in.

He smiled at her and held out his arms. Sarah ran across the room and threw herself into Frank's embrace. They kissed passionately and held each other for a long time before taking off their boots and sitting down on the blanket in front of the fire.

Sarah sat between Frank's legs, her back resting against his body. He put his arms around her, pressed his cheek against the side of Sarah's cheek, letting her wet hair brush his face. "I've missed you so much Sarah," he whispered in her ear. "I've missed you too Frank," Sarah said softly. After a moment of warming by the fire Frank poured them both a glass of wine. They drank a toast and ate biscuits with cheese. Sarah screwed up her nose at the bitter taste of the wine, so left her glass still full, sitting by the fire.

Then, kneeling in front of each other they looked into each other's eyes. Frank lifted his hands to the front of Sarah's shirt to undo the buttons while Sarah kept her arms down by her sides and her eyes firmly fixed on Frank's face. Sarah waited a long time for this day, filling her days with visiting her few friends, cooking for the trappers or sitting on the fence at the corrals watching the men breaking horses, only once did she go to the ponds to sit on the boulders, not staying too long for fear of running into Major Hardy or his men. To keep her out of trouble, Joe made Will or Garrett go riding with her when she said she needed to let Star run.

As Frank slowly opened the front of her shirt, Sarah's heart pounded in her chest. When he cupped her breasts in his hands, her breathing began to get faster. Frank moved closer and leant forward. Sarah got up on her knees, letting him put his mouth over her breast. Her hand went around the back of Frank's head so she could hold him against her. She closed her eyes as he gently ran his tongue over her nipple. The gentle movement of his tongue made the excitement rise in her body. Frank let her nipple slip from his mouth and sat back to look at it. Sarah's nipple had become hard and erect and Frank's body responded quickly to what he had done.

It was Sarah's turn, she unbuttoned Frank's shirt, pushing it over his shoulders and down his arms. He quickly pulled his hands free of the sleeves and Sarah dropped his shirt on top of hers beside them. She moved closer to Frank and kissed each of his breasts. Desperate to have Frank make love to her, she pushed his trousers down his legs giving his manhood the room it needed to become erect. Frank quickly undid Sarah's trousers and pulled them down her thighs. He removed Sarah's trousers over her feet, felt himself becoming fully aroused and moaned. He held Sarah against him as his desire for her gained momentum. While Frank made slow, gentle love to Sarah, he thought about the day he rode out and found the shack. This is what he wanted back then. Now he and Sarah had finally been together on the mountain he could make love to her as he thought that day.

Sarah maneuvered her body under Frank as he came against her. When Frank began to thrust, Sarah made her body keep in time with him. She dreamt of Frank and her making love in the shack but hadn't known she would be pregnant when they made plans to meet here. She was excited and scared at the same time about having a baby and couldn't wait to tell him she was going to have his child. The emotion in Frank's body was building, he couldn't get enough of Sarah and kept pressing himself hard against her soft, smooth body, letting her firm breasts move against him as he moved his manhood gently back and forth. Sarah became fully aroused from his warmth between her legs. Her womanhood swelled, making her tighten her legs around him. The feeling inside her was building as she pushed herself against Frank.

When Sarah's body reached its climax, a sudden thrill ran through her, coursing down her legs into the tips of her toes, at the same time racing up through her body and down her arms to her finger tips. Frank felt his throbbing manhood give in, he put his arms around Sarah and held her tight. They remained for some time clinging to each other. Completely satisfied from their lovemaking, they lay in each other's arms, their bodies depleted of strength.

"Sarah sit up for a moment ...please." Frank helped her sit up. She sat on her knees facing him, curious to know why Frank wanted her to sit up. Frank took a small knife out of the picnic hamper and crawled on his hands and knees to the wall beside the fire. Sarah frowned and watched him begin to carve something in the timber wall.

"Frank, what are you doing?" she tried to see what he was doing and leant sideways to see around his naked body.

"Wait and I'll show you." Frank kept his back to Sarah when he answered. Sarah watched Frank's back as he worked. His back was broad and solid, his skin smooth and without blemish. Since trapping on the mountain his arms had become strong, his legs muscled, his backside was round and smooth. Sarah felt a wave of love for him course through her body, she wanted to touch him some more. "You can look now." Frank turned to Sarah and seeing her watching him, smiled. Sarah crawled on her hands and knees and sat on her legs beside Frank where she could see he had carved something in the wall. She stared at it trying to make out what it was. "What do you think?" Frank looked at the bewildered look on Sarah's face.

"What do I think?" As well as being unable to count, Sarah hated to admit she couldn't read. "What does it say?" Frank looked confused at Sarah then looked back at what he carved. He should have realized Sarah couldn't read, he knew she couldn't count so had already taught her how to mark off the days for them to meet here at the shack. Frank moved behind Sarah and wrapped his arms around her.

"It says …Frank Mason loves Sarah Cole." Sarah looked at the words. "Frank Mason loves Sarah Cole," she repeated. "What about …Sarah Cole loves Frank Mason?" she said trying to look back at him. "That goes without saying Sarah, I know you love me or you wouldn't let me make love to you the way you do."

Sarah sat facing Frank, she was about to tell him she was pregnant. Frank looked at Sarah's body, after they made love her body glowed. Frank put the knife back in the picnic basket and lifted out a small box. He smiled at Sarah as she watched him take the small box out of the basket, then watched as a frown furrowed her brow. "Sarah, I have something I want to ask you," he began, but Sarah cut him off when she spoke at the same time. "Frank I have something I want to tell you." They laughed at each other. "You first," Frank said, keeping the smile on his face. "No, you go first Frank." Sarah studied him. When he got back from the mountain to his father's ranch his hair had been neatly cut, it still looked thick and very curly, his face was clean shaven and smooth. He was handsome and Sarah loved him.

"Sarah." Frank held up his hand and opened the little box. "Will you marry me?" This was the gift Frank had been saving to give to

Sarah last Christmas when he was unable to leave the ranch and his father's guests to give it to her. The ring belonged to his mother and he wanted Sarah to have it, but he had to wait for the perfect time to give it to her and being here together in the shack he knew was the perfect time. Sarah's eyes never left Frank's when he asked her to marry him, her eyes welled and tears flowed down her cheeks. Sarah looked at the blue Sapphire sitting between two small Diamonds sparkling in the glow of the fire. "What is the matter Sarah?" Frank was worried Sarah was going to turn him down. Had he mistaken her feelings for him? Sarah put her hands up to her face. "Sarah what's wrong?" he asked her again.

Keeping her hands covering her face, she started to sob uncontrollably as she tried to speak. "I'm …I'm ...pregnant!" Frank stared at her in disbelief. "What?" he closed the box and pulled her hands away from her face. Sarah's face was wet when she looked longingly at Frank trying to see if he understood what she was saying. "I'm going to have a baby," she sobbed through her tears.

"Are you sure?" Frank's face broke out in a huge smile.

Sarah shook her head vigorously up and down. "Doc Harris says I am ...you know how I've been sick every morning and ...and sometimes …I faint?" Frank nodded, he remembered when she began to get sick, he would never forget the worry he went through thinking she was going to die from something she may have caught. "Doc called it morning sickness," Sarah went on. "You get that when you are going to have a baby." Sarah continued to sob as she told him what Doc explained was wrong with her.

"Oh Sarah, I love you so much." Frank put his arms around her and held her as tight as he dared, now he knew she was going to have his baby he didn't want to hurt her.

"You're not disappointed?" Sarah nestled against Frank as he held her. Frank's arms comforted her, the glow from the fire warmed their bodies.

Frank held her in his arms, unable to believe it. Sarah was going to have his baby, he was going to be a father. He held onto her more tightly, not wanting to ever let her go. "I could never be disappointed with you Sarah, we are going to have a baby and ...you will marry me ...won't you?" he realized Sarah hadn't answered when he asked her to marry him. He held the ring up in front of her again and smiled at her. Sarah sat up straighter, her breasts stuck out further and Frank couldn't help glancing at them while holding up the ring. Sarah burst into tears again when she answered, "yes Frank, I will marry you." They kissed passionately and Frank slipped the ring on Sarah's finger.

They lay together wrapped in the warm blanket. Frank felt Sarah's stomach for signs of the baby. Sarah giggled, "Doc said it is about this big," she held up her little finger. Frank smiled and kissed her. They listened to the rain falling outside and made plans for the future. Sarah couldn't wait to tell Joe her news, she was sure he would be happy for her. The four men wouldn't have to keep her father's promise anymore. Frank couldn't wait to tell his father he was marrying the woman he loved and that he was going to be a father. He prayed he would be a better father than his father is to him. Sarah and Frank felt comforted listening to the rain as they fell asleep curled up in each other's arms.

Sarah was wrenched to her feet. She screamed for Frank as lightning lit up the sky followed by loud rumblings of thunder. Frank was dragged naked kicking and screaming outside into the storm. Sarah was unceremoniously dragged outside, coming wide awake after the men grabbed her by her arms. Sarah felt the cold night air on her naked body. "*Let her go you bastards!*" Frank screamed. The men let her go when Frank yelled at them, causing Sarah to stumble in the rain and fall in the mud. She got up, looked around at all the men then screamed for Frank. Foley and Brady were standing off to one side holding Frank firmly by his arms.

Major Hardy sat in his buckboard, the cover sheltering him from the storm while six of his men stood in a semi-circle holding burning torches so the torches could light up the area in front of the shack. Frank was kept to one side of the circle where he could still see everything that was happening. Major Hardy ordered his men to seal up the shack. Frank heard the hammering as the men nailed boards across the windows and doors, sealing both Frank's and Sarah's clothes inside.

Sarah was crying hysterically, she was in a circle of men and she was naked, she felt humiliated, this was worse than when Crawley threw her out of The Lodge, at least then she wore a nightdress. Sarah tried to cover herself by folding her arms across her breasts. She knelt down on the muddy rain-soaked ground making her body as small as she could to hide herself, her long hair hung over her back and shoulder's. The rain helped make her hair stick to her body, covering her back from the staring eyes of the men. "*Frank!*" she screamed.

"Well now, what have we got here? Frank and a fucking whore ...or perhaps that should be, Frank fucking a whore!" Major Hardy laughed, his voice booming out for all the men to hear. Sarah stayed crouched as low as she could, the cold rain made her shiver and she was frightened. "All you men have a good look, if any of you want a whore, here is your chance!" Major Hardy laughed harder and sneered down at Sarah crouching in the mud.

"*Don't any of you men dare think about touching her!*" Frank yelled. "*You touch Sarah the trappers will make you pay ...and goddamn it ... so will I!*" Frank didn't care that the men could see his body, but he wouldn't let them look at Sarah, she was going to be his wife, he loved her, these men were going to die if they tried to do anything to hurt her. Frank looked at each man and memorized their faces. The men turned their backs when Frank warned them about the trappers. They didn't want trouble from the trappers, there were too many of them for these few men to deal with. Four trappers in particular had their own way of dishing out punishment. They witnessed Joe Jones beating a man almost to death for a lot less than what was happening right here.

But Major Hardy warned his men too. "If you don't turn around, you won't work for me or anyone else, in this county or any other!" The men needed work, some had families to support, they wouldn't survive without Major Hardy's money and he could stop them from getting work anywhere, such was the power Major Hardy wielded. They turned back to face Sarah, their hats pulled down low over their faces shielding them from the rain, their eyes downcast on the muddy ground.

Major Hardy got out of his buckboard and walked toward Sarah. "*Don't you hurt her you bastard ...you hurt Sarah and I swear ...I will fucking kill you myself!*" Frank screamed when he saw the knife in his father's hand. He twisted and turned in Foley's and Brady's hands, wanting to get to Sarah to save her from his father. Frank's skin was getting wetter, his arms were becoming slippery. Foley and Brady struggled to hold onto Frank as he squirmed. Both men hated what they were doing, but they had orders, they had to do what their boss told them to do. Sarah knelt closer to the ground and kept crying. Strands of her long hair fell over her shoulders and hung in the mud.

"Hurt her! ...I'm not going to hurt her Frank ...I told her to stay away from you ...she needs to learn disobedience has consequences!" Major Hardy held the knife up for the men to see. Frank's eyes were wide with fear. "What are you going to do?" he had never known his father to be this cruel vicious man standing in front of Sarah. He hadn't known what his father was capable of, not until this very moment. Major Hardy bent over Sarah and pulled her hair into a bunch. Placing the knife carefully under her hair, he sliced the knife through, cutting her hair close to the back of her neck. He held up the hair he cut off in his hands and showed it around the circle of men, and laughed at what he had done. "There, you see Frank ...I didn't hurt her!" He threw Sarah's hair in the mud in front of her. Sarah cried when she saw it floating in the pool of muddy water, her sobs became louder as she kept her head down, her body shook from exposure and fear, she felt she was going to be sick or worse faint. If she fainted now, the men could do anything they wanted to her, and she wouldn't be able to defend herself, she forced herself to hang on. She held her arms tight across her chest, her back exposed to the rain and to the men now her long hair was gone.

"*Sarah it's alright ...It's only hair ...it will grow back!*" Frank called, trying to comfort Sarah with his words. "It's alright Sarah, I'm here ...I love you." Sarah heard him say it was only hair and it would grow back, but as Frank said he loved her lightning streaked across the sky as the storm grew more violent. Thunder grew louder, drowning out the rest of the words Frank had spoken. The rain continued to fall in torrents.

As Sarah held her arms around her body, Major Hardy spotted the ring on her finger. He grabbed her hand and forced her arm up where he could see the ring better. Sarah tried to pull her hand back. "What the hell Frank, you put a ring on this whore's hand!" He twisted Sarah's hand around until she was forced to lift her body up from where she crouched. He looked closely at the ring as he pulled it forcefully off Sarah's finger. "Goddamn son-of-a-bitch, this ring was one I gave your mother." He put the ring in his pocket. Sarah wrapped her arms back around her body and weeping, crouched back down in the mud.

Major Hardy went back to his buckboard and got out his whip. "You son-of-a-bitch …don't you dare!" Frank knew what his father intended, Sarah told him his father threatened to whip her if she didn't stay away from him. "Don't ...father please …don't!" Frank shook with fright, begging his father to spare Sarah as he struggled to get free from Foley and Brady's grip. "Sarah didn't do anything wrong ...please father ...don't do this!" he cried. Sarah looked up when she could hear Frank pleading with his father. Major Hardy stood near his buckboard facing her while he spread the whip along the ground. Keeping a firm grip on the stock, he swung the whip above his head. Sarah closed her eyes and braced herself for what was to come.

Foley swore and Frank heard him. "Fucking Christ!" he spat vehemently and loosened his grip on Frank. Brady found it hard to keep hanging on when Frank's arms became slippery from the rain. He cursed silently and felt his hand's slip along Frank's arms. Frank twisted and turned, trying to get out of their hold. Foley gave up holding Frank's arms and let him go. When Brady saw Foley let go of Frank, he let go too. Frank felt his arms suddenly come free. He rushed towards Sarah as his father swung the whip in a wide arc. Foley dived forward when he saw Frank run toward Sarah. He didn't like what the Major was about to do, he had to try and get both Frank and Sarah out of harm's way. Frank threw himself across Sarah's back as the whip came down. Frank's arms went around Sarah's shoulders to shield her. The whip cracked across Frank's back, his skin split apart, the cut went deep, opening Frank's back from his right shoulder down his back to his left buttock. Frank screamed an agonizing scream of terror. The men looked on in horror at what they were witnessing. Wanting no part of this horrendous scene unfolding in front of them, they cursed the Major when they heard a low guttural sound escape Frank's throat. Sarah felt Frank stiffen across her back as the whip caught him. She opened her mouth to scream but her voice caught in her throat by the sheer horror of what was happening to Frank.

Foley rushed toward Frank, almost reaching him and Sarah when the whip caught Frank. Foley looked wide eyed at Frank as the whip opened a huge gash across his back. The end of the whip suddenly flicked up and away from Frank and shot upward towards Foley's face, but he saw it too late, the tip sliced his chin, travelled up his cheek and continued over his forehead slicing through the brim of his hat. Foley screamed in agony and put his hands to his face as he fell to his knees in the mud. The men, coming out of their state of shock, jumped into action. Brady ran to Foley and lifted him up. The rain stung Foley's face, he couldn't see, blood poured from the cuts and ran through his fingers. Brady and the men helped Foley get to his horse.

Frank couldn't hold on any longer, he slid off Sarah's back into the mud where he lay beside her. He held his face up to Sarah as he struggled to speak. "I love you Sarah," he managed to say in unimaginable pain. Sarah looked into Frank's eyes, she could see the pain the whiplash caused in them. His eyes suddenly dimmed as his body went limp. Sarah's mind told her Frank was dead, she tried to scream, her mouth was wide open, but no sound escaped her lips.

Major Hardy saw what he had done and was horrified. The whip wasn't meant for his son, nor was it meant for Sarah, he was only going to bring it down alongside her to scare her, but everything had gone horribly wrong. He had to do something to save his son. He ordered his men to get Frank quickly into his buckboard where they lay Frank in the back and covered him with a blanket to keep him warm. One of the men climbed in with Frank, the rest of the men ran to their horses. Major Hardy ordered a man to ride to town fast to get Doc Harris and bring him to the ranch. Frank and Sarah's horses were taken away with them. Star pulled back on his lead trying not to go, he bucked wildly as he was dragged away. The buckboard raced back to the ranch taking Frank with it. Sarah was left in the storm, naked and alone, already in deep shock and shivering from the cold.

Sarah remained crouched in the mud as the rain continued to pour, she couldn't cry anymore and her voice was gone. Lightning continued to streak the sky, thunder rolled off into the distance. Sarah looked around and could see Major Hardy, his men and her horse were all gone. When she tried to stand her legs felt weak, she collapsed back into the mud, forced herself to stand again and headed for the shack. Her legs gave way again before she could get to the stoop, falling several times before finally staggering up the steps to the door. Seeing the boards nailed across the door, Sarah pulled on them but they wouldn't budge. She could see the windows were boarded up too. There was no way she could get inside to get her clothes. Sarah had no strength left in her and felt she could pass out at any time. She slid crying, down the wall, and crouching in the corner of the small stoop, pulled her legs up as close to her body as she could and wrapped her arms tightly around them trying to make herself warm, but her body continued to shake violently.

Frank was carried upstairs to his room where he was placed face down on his bed, his body bloodied from the deep gash to his back. Doc Harris rode quickly through the storm to get to the ranch to tend to Frank. When he was ushered to Frank's room, he pursed his lips in disgust at what he found. Frank was covered in mud, the gash in his back so deep it barely missed exposing his backbone. Frank was bathed while his bed was cleaned. He remained unconscious for several days and didn't know what happened to Sarah once he passed out.

Major Hardy was beside himself, this was not what he planned, he just wanted to scare the girl. Cutting her hair was one thing, whipping her was another, more sinister act. He wouldn't really have whipped her, he just wanted to put enough fear into her so she would stay away from Frank. He didn't care if Frank wanted to fuck her, he could have as much sex with her as he wanted. All he wanted was for Frank to marry Millicent Crawley and live in The Lodge that once belonged to Calahan Cole, a man he hated with all his being.

Major Hardy knew a woman like Millicent would never be able to satisfy Frank. He hadn't meant to hurt his son, he loved Frank, didn't Frank know that?

Chapter Twenty

While some of Major Hardy's men helped Frank upstairs to his room in the ranch-house, Brady helped Foley to the bunkhouse where the cowhands hurriedly patched up his face. Wadding and bandages were placed over the cut on his forehead, his cheek and his jaw. A bandage was wound around his head to hold it all in place. The men talked amongst themselves, swearing and cursing the Major for what he did tonight. "Mason can't be blamed for falling for a girl like Cole, she is so goddamn pretty." One of the men that had been at the shack said in dismay.

Foley tried not to speak, his face hurt like hell but he tried his best to listen to what the men were saying. "She sure has got a body though, you see those tits?" Another of the men sniggered. Foley had no trouble hearing that man's comment and snapped. He grabbed the speaker by the shirt front and lifted his feet off the floor, slamming him against the wall of the bunkhouse so hard it shook the room and through gritted teeth and excruciating pain he yelled at the man.

"You son-of-bitch! you say anything like that again about Sarah I will fucking kill you!" Foley's feelings for Sarah hadn't diminished after seeing her with Frank. He didn't like what happened to her and he didn't like what the men were saying about her, it was degrading, Sarah didn't deserve their remarks.

"Hold it Foley!" Some of the men grabbed Foley and made him let go of the man. The man straightened himself up. "I didn't mean anything by it Foley, Jesus take it easy."

The men's banter started to grate on Foley. "Just look at what the Major did to you, all because of her you got your fucking face cut up and you stick up for her …Christ!" The talk in the room continued between the men.

"Cole doesn't deserve what the Major did and neither does Mason, shit …what he did to Mason is bad, and Mason being his own son makes it far worse, Cole and Mason are in love, anyone can see that!" One of the older men said in Sarah and Frank's defence. Foley was in love with Sarah too, he hated that she was in love with Frank.

Foley lay back down to let his head clear and kept listening to the men talking. "What do you suppose is going to happen when the trappers find out what happened to Cole out there tonight?" A cowhand that hadn't been at the shack asked.

"Nothing happened to her!" One of the cowhands that had been there snapped angrily.

"Yeah? ...well the Major cut off her goddamn hair and left her fucking naked out there ...it don't take much to get the goddamn trappers riled up when it comes to Cole!" The men were starting to sound worried. They knew the trappers would take revenge on them if they touched Sarah. They weren't sure what the trappers would do about the Major once they found out it was him that cut off her hair. Foley stood up without warning, grabbed his hat and headed for the door. Brady was equally scared, knowing they were in big trouble with the trappers. He could see Foley was going to leave the bunkhouse and followed him to the door. He wasn't going to be left behind, wherever Foley was going he was going with him.

"What are you two doing? where are you going?" The men asked when they saw Foley open the door.

"I'm going back out to the shack ...we left Cole out there and she can't get back in to get out of this fucking storm!" Foley held the door open, rain was still pelting down and the wind was picking up. 'And she will be scared,' he thought to himself. "You can tell the Major if you want, but I'm not leaving her out there." Foley dived out into the rain and Brady followed him, both raced to where their horses were tethered. Foley kept his hat pulled down over his face to protect it from the rain but the split brim wasn't helping, the bandage started to get wet.

Keeping his horse in stride with Foley as Foley spurred his horse faster, Brady rode through the storm. He was scared, scared to think what kind of trouble they could be in with the trappers. He wasn't a bad person, he might ride beside the Major as his gun-hand but he still hated doing what the Major asked him to do. He had to stick with his brother, even if it meant hurting those he thought were his friends. They arrived back at the shack and couldn't see Sarah anywhere. "She has to be here somewhere," Foley said through gritted teeth. "She wouldn't try to walk back to town …not in the state she is in."

Flashes of lightning lit up the sky, and Brady, seeing something on the stoop, tapped Foley on the arm and pointed. Foley looked toward the shack and could see Sarah curled up in the corner of the stoop trying to protect herself from the rain. Foley brought his horse up to the steps and tethered it to the stoop rail. He got down and undoing his bedroll, quickly unfolded the blanket and walked up the steps holding the blanket out in front of him. Sarah lifted her head and saw someone coming toward her. She couldn't make out who it was in the dark, a flash of lightning put an eerie hue on the man's face. She could see the bandages but didn't recognize Foley. Sarah was fearful the Major's men had come back to finish what the Major had started. She started to cry and shake her head from side to side in fear "No! no! please …don't ...I can't!" she cried hysterically. Foley spoke softly so as not to frighten her. "Shush Sarah, it's me, Foley, I'm not here to hurt you ...shush now." He put the blanket over her and lifted her to her feet. Sarah stood up on shaky legs. While wrapping the blanket tightly around her, Foley kept holding her in his arms to comfort her until Brady came up on the stoop carrying another blanket and wrapped it around her. It was the first time since the whipping Sarah felt safe.

Sarah looked up into Foley's bandaged face. "What happened to you Foley?" she cried. "Never mind what happened to me, we are here to take you back to town." Foley passed Sarah to Brady who held onto her while he got back on his horse. Brady then lifted Sarah up in front of Foley. Foley put his arms around her while taking hold of the reins and held her tight. When Brady was back on his horse they rode off at a gallop, back toward town, wanting to get Sarah back to safety as fast as they could.

Foley hung on tight to Sarah as she sat sideways across his horse. Her head bounced against his chest and her body was being thrown about as they raced along. After enduring several miles of being bounced around Sarah couldn't take any more. Foley held his arms around her but it was no use.

"Foley, stop!" Sarah tried to get Foley to hear her, but he couldn't hear anything above the storm, Foley's horse galloped on.

"Foley please ...*stop!*" Sarah had to move her head away from Foley's chest and yell louder to get him to hear her. Foley pulled up his horse when he saw Sarah appear to say something. Brady brought his horse alongside when he saw Foley's horse slow down and come to a stop. "What is it Sarah?" Foley's face stung badly from being wet. "Are you alright?" he asked through gritted teeth.

"No, I'm not Foley ...I'm ...I'm pregnant!" Foley and Brady looked at each other for a moment, both thinking they heard wrong. "What did you say?" Foley asked her again to be sure he heard right.

"I'm going to have Frank's baby!" Sarah said, letting out a sob. Foley thought that was what she said, he pulled Sarah closer and wrapped his arms around her more snuggly. Glancing across at Brady he started to walk his horse to make it easier on Sarah. It was going to take them a lot longer to get to town and his face stung like hell, but he wasn't about to let Sarah be hurt any more than she already was. 'Frank's a lucky man,' he thought to himself as they rode along. 'Damn him.' Foley realized then he should have known Frank and Sarah would go all the way when they were together on the mountain. He didn't need proof they had been together in the shack. When Major Hardy got the men to rush the shack, he was disappointed to see Sarah and Frank sleeping naked in each other's arms. Before then, he held out hope for himself, but now Sarah was expecting Frank's baby, he felt he had no hope of ever having her love. He wondered as they rode along what Major Hardy would say about Frank getting Sarah pregnant. Foley imagined the disgusting language his boss would let fly with.

"Is Frank alright Foley?" Sarah didn't think she had any more tears left in her but she kept sobbing.

"I don't know Sarah, I haven't seen him, the Major sent for Doc so maybe he will be alright." Sarah didn't speak again, she rested her head against Foley's chest and closed her eyes. Foley and Brady walked their horses all the way to town.

The town was in complete darkness when they arrived, it was late and everyone was asleep. The horses moved silently down the street toward the Ferguson House. Brady hopped off his horse and Foley handed Sarah down to him. Brady held her until Foley got down, then Foley took Sarah back in his arms. The two men climbed the steps to the porch.

The house was quiet, they knew all the trappers were asleep, the trappers worked hard all day, branding cattle and breaking horses for the Major. Foley didn't care, he and Brady were going to wake them up. Foley stood back while Brady banged his fist loudly on the door. Brady kept banging until a lamp light was visible in the window. The door was suddenly wrenched open and Joe stood in the doorway in his long-johns, a rifle held up in his hands. Foley pushed past him into the room, Brady followed Foley in. Joe saw Sarah in Foley's arms and frowned in disbelief. Trappers started to come out of their rooms carrying their handguns, some held rifles in case they were needed. They wanted to see what the banging and the loud voices were. Joe closed the door behind the men.

"What the fucking hell is going on?" Joe's eyes widened as he looked at Sarah wrapped in wet soggy blankets in Foley's arms. Foley's face was a mess, both men were soaked through. Joe put his rifle down and Foley quickly handed Sarah to him. Foley held on to the edge of the table to stop himself from collapsing. Fergus and Garrett quickly grabbed him and sat him in a chair. Joe held Sarah in his arms, the blankets dripped water, Joe's long-johns were getting a drenching.

"Don't take the blanket off her she's not..." Foley tried to finish what he was going to say but gave in to his pain and passed out. It was no use the trappers asking Brady to tell them what happened to Sarah, the men were aware he couldn't speak a word.

"Joe, he whipped Frank ...Major Hardy ...he killed Frank!" Sarah sobbed loudly as Joe carried her into her room where he saw the window wide open. Wind and rain came howling through when he opened the door. Joe looked at the window, he hadn't thought Sarah would be able to get the nails out of the windowsill, but she was a determined young woman and very much in love with Frank. "Damn it Sarah, you are seventeen years old, and a goddamn woman, you don't have to go sneaking out the window every time you want to see Frank!" his voice was stern when he admonished Sarah.

"Don't you yell at me Joe, I don't think I could stand it if you yelled at me." Joe sat Sarah on a chair next to her bed. The wet blanket slipped over her bare shoulders and Joe saw her short hair. "That fucking bastard!" he swore loudly. Sarah put her hand up to her head and cried, "it's alright Joe, its only hair, it will grow back." She kept sobbing as she remembered Frank saying that to her before he got whipped. Joe could see from Sarah's bare arms the reason Foley told him not to take the blankets off her, he pulled the quilt off Sarah's bed.

"Get out of those wet blankets Sarah and wrap yourself in this, I'll come back shortly." Joe pulled the window down and left the room. Sarah shivered when she dropped the blankets and wrapped herself in the quilt. She curled up in a ball on her bed, closed her eyes tight and thought about what happened. 'Frank was dead for sure, he wouldn't have been able to take such a whipping.' She was going to have his baby and she didn't think she could go on without him.

Joe closed the door to Sarah's room and went back out to talk to Foley and Brady. "Will, go get Doc." Brady shook his head vigorously from side to side. Foley opened his eyes and managed to speak for Brady. "Doc won't be there ...he'll be out at the Major's ...tending to Frank ...if he's alive," he added.

"Will, go get Gerda ...at least she can tend to Sarah." Will didn't hang about, he hurried out the door and raced to Doc's practice. While they waited for Gerda, Joe changed into his trousers and ordered the men to build up the fire and make lots of coffee.

"Get a fire going under the washstand and heat up a bath for Sarah," he ordered. A dozen men scurried around making coffee and filling the washstand with water. They lit the fire and waited for the water to heat up so they could bale it into the bathtub. They were all anxious to know what happened to Sarah and Frank.

"What happened Foley?" Fergus, standing the closest to Foley asked. Joe waited for Foley to speak.

"Frank and Sarah were at the shack ...together," he started. Joe and the men listened as Foley recounted what had taken place. He ended with Brady and him bringing Sarah back to Joe. The men were silent after hearing Foley's account of the night, Joe was wild with anger. Foley managed to speak through his pain some more. "I like Sarah ...as much as anyone," he quickly added. "I don't want to see her get hurt ...if I had known what the Major was going to do, I would have stopped him ...there was no way I would ever let her be whipped." He cringed against the pain in his face. "Thanks for bringing her back Foley ...you too Brady." Joe nodded to Brady and shook both men by the hand.

"There is something else you need to know Joe." The pain in Foley's face was beginning to take its toll, excruciating pain shot through him every time he opened his mouth to speak. Joe could see Foley was struggling to talk.

"What is it Foley ...what else is there to know?" Joe didn't expect the next thing Foley told him, neither did any of the other trappers. "Sarah is pregnant."

Will and Gerda, who was carrying a black bag, came hurrying in. "What is going on tonight? Ronald has gone out to the Major's ranch in this awful weather, something about Frank being hurt and now here we are, what is it with you men?" Will hadn't been able to tell her anything about what happened to Sarah, he had gone to fetch her before Foley related what happened. Joe took Gerda's bag. "Gerda, can you go in to Sarah's room and help her? She is in real need of you tonight."

'If Sarah ever needed Gerda more than the night her Pa was killed, tonight was the night,' Joe thought.

"First, I look at this man, what happened to you Foley?" Gerda asked in her heavy German accent. "He got whipped by Major Hardy." Fergus told her, but he didn't elaborate on the details. Everyone, even Gerda was well aware Major Hardy carried a whip and knew how he liked to wield it to show he was in charge. "You help get him on the table and I look at him." The men helped Foley lay down on the table. "What are you going to do Gerda?" Foley asked her through his pain. "First I remove these bandages." Gerda carefully removed the bandages then studied his face. "Hold the light closer so I see." The light shone over Foley's features, the bloodied cut on his face looked deep. "Tut! Tut!" Gerda clicked her tongue in sorrow at what she was looking at. "I am going to have to sew you up." She said busying herself with her bag. "Get me some warm milk." Gerda started to order the men in the room and they jumped at her commands. While Gerda waited for the milk to heat up, she took a quick look in Sarah's room. When she came out a few minutes later, the look on her face was enough to tell the men Gerda was upset at seeing Sarah in such a state as she was in.

"Make enough for Sarah too, she will be needing it." The milk was warmed and Gerda poured some of it into a tin mug. She took a small bottle from her bag and poured liquid from it into the milk and stirred it. "You drink this Foley." She handed the mug to Foley. "When he is asleep, I sew." Brady, standing by the fire with Will, removed his wet coat and now that he was warming up, felt a little better. When one of the men handed him a hot mug of coffee and gave him a pat on the back, he was relieved to know the trappers weren't angry with them for what happened to Sarah. "How long before this stuff works?" Foley asked, the pain was getting worse, his face stung when Gerda removed the bandages. "About twenty minutes, you lay still Foley while I go see to Sarah." Gerda looked at Garrett. "You tell me when he is asleep, I come back."

The men bailed warm water from the washstand into the bathtub, half filling it. Gerda walked Sarah out of her room, taking her past all of the men standing around the table to get her to the washroom. Sarah kept her quilt wrapped tightly around her as she looked around the room at all the men standing with their backs to her. She knew Joe made them turn their backs so they couldn't see the state she was in. Joe was the only man watching. He felt at a loss for words now he knew Sarah was pregnant.

Gerda helped Sarah get into the tub. When Sarah was covered by the warm water Gerda looked at her hair. Several long uneven strands hung over her shoulders. Gerda held a strand in her hand. "I get scissors and fix." She went out and coming back with the scissors from her bag, got busy snipping the untidy strands off and neatening the ends. "There Sarah, that not too bad, your hair is quit pretty short." Sarah couldn't care less about her hair, she just wanted Frank to be alive.

Sarah stepped out of the tub and after drying her, Gerda dressed her in the long night dress she had given Sarah when she came to stay with the trappers after her father died two years previously, she then helped Sarah back to her room.

"Gerda, Foley is asleep," Garrett said, sticking his head through the door as Gerda put Sarah into bed. "I come now," she said without turning around. She tucked Sarah in, "I be back in one moment," she said, holding up one finger to Sarah before going out to the men. Getting the rest of the milk she poured a small amount of the liquid she had given Foley into it, stirred it around and took the milk in to Sarah. A few minutes later she was back. "Sarah will sleep until tomorrow, you watch after her Joseph." Gerda was a tiny woman and she craned her neck to look up at Joe.

Joe, saying he would watch out for Sarah, secretly hoped he would do a better job than what he had been doing. Gerda went to the table and started to sew Foley's face. She pulled the wound closed and with deft fingers stitched down his face finishing under his chin. By the time she finished, the wound didn't look too bad. Joe and the trappers watched her as she worked. Joe thought Gerda would have made a good doctor.

The trappers kept Foley and Brady at the Ferguson House with them until the next day, when the storm had passed. Foley was feeling much better now his face had been stitched up. Even though his face still hurt somewhat he went straight back to work with the Major, staying out at the ranch for the rest of winter. Except for taking Star back to Ham's Livery so Sarah knew her horse was safe, he stopped going to town with the cowhands like he used to at the end of their working week for a much-deserved drink. Instead, he let Doc Harris and Gerda tend to him at the same time they visited Frank to tend to Frank's wound. Feeling embarrassed about how he looked now his face was scarred, he stayed away from town so Sarah in particular couldn't see him. He would be glad when Sarah returned to the mountain, allowing his face time to heal for when she returned the following winter. He hoped by then his face would have healed sufficiently for her not to think him ugly.

Chapter Twenty-one

Sarah hadn't seen Frank since the night at the shack. The four trappers kept her with them for the rest of winter, taking her everywhere they went, to avoid any more trouble. Doc checked Sarah to make sure she and her pregnancy were going along well. Although she still took things slowly, she got over her morning sickness and felt able to ride. When winter came to an end and spring was in full bloom the trappers returned to the mountain for another year of trapping. Sarah travelled back to the mountain with the men to have her baby.

Sarah arrived back at her cabin safely and the four trappers made sure she had everything she needed before they left for the High Ridge Camp. Sarah's first night back at the cabin proved harder than the first time she returned to the mountain since her father died, and being unable to be with Frank was a more upsetting thing to have to contend with. She was happy her and Frank's baby was growing inside her but sad because Frank wasn't with her to enjoy it. While still in Cedar Creek, she learnt Frank survived the whipping from his father. Millicent Crawley was the only person allowed to visit while he recuperated and because of Major Hardy's threats, Sarah wasn't allowed anywhere near Major Hardy's land. Sarah believed Frank would marry Millicent Crawley after all and she would be forgotten. She slept little that first week back at her cabin.

Each day for the next month, Sarah went out and set her traps. She was lucky, catching several wolves. She went hunting with her rifle, shooting at anything that moved. It helped vent her anger at what happened to her and Frank. In the evenings, she took her coffee and sat on her porch and watched the stars twinkling in the clear night sky. Occasionally when she felt too tired to trap or hunt, she sat on the rocks near the river and looked across the ridge down through the trees to the valley below. It was a long way to Cedar Creek where Frank was.

The month passed by slowly, Sarah got herself into a daily routine of getting up at daylight, dressed, breakfasted and then headed out to check her traps. She was gone from her cabin most of the day, returning home by late afternoon. Her belly grew a little rounder each day, it soon became difficult to do up the top of her trousers so she tied a piece of rope around her waist and tucked her trousers over it, her shirt she left to hang loose. It felt uncomfortable but it was the best she could do.

Frank spent most of the winter lying on his stomach, unable to move because of the whiplash that split open his back. He missed Sarah terribly and pined for her, wanting desperately to see her. Besides Millicent Crawley, Doc Harris and Gerda were his only other visitors, coming to the ranch twice a week to bathe him and tend to his wound. Frank asked Doc about Sarah each time he visited. Doc told him Sarah was doing fine, she was being well taken care of by the trappers and they were keeping her with them constantly. Frank was relieved at the news and happy when Doc told him she was still carrying his baby. Frank knew his father wouldn't be happy if he found out Sarah was pregnant. He didn't think his father deserved to know he would soon be a grandfather, and he wasn't going to give his father the satisfaction of belittling Sarah. He asked both Doc and Gerda not to say anything. They kept their word and nothing was said. Millicent visited Frank on several occasions at the insistence of her father and Major Hardy. She sat with him while he lay face down on his bed, neither of them knowing what to talk about. The air in the room was strained and Millicent was glad when her visits were over. Frank felt the same. Millicent didn't want to have anything further to do with Frank now he had been scarred, she didn't like it that everyone in town would know, if her father and Major Hardy's plan worked, she would be marrying a scarred man. She would never be able to let a scarred man make love to her, it was simply too horrible and distasteful, it was bad enough she would have to let a man touch her at all. Millicent begged her father to send her to Philadelphia for a holiday and he bowed to her request. She left Cedar Creek a week after the trappers went back to the mountain. Frank was glad when Millicent left town, he didn't need her visiting him, he didn't need or want her pity, he just wanted Sarah.

Gerda didn't have to tell Frank about the night Sarah was left naked and alone in the storm at the shack, he had seen the indignation of Sarah squatting from the prying eyes of his father and his men for himself. But Gerda told him how Foley and Brady returned to the shack, all the while Foley must have been in excruciating pain from the whiplash to his face. She told Frank about Foley wrapping Sarah in blankets and taking her back to town to the safety of the trappers.

When Frank's wound healed sufficiently and he could get out of bed, he took long walks around the ranch. The first thing he did was go to the bunkhouse and thank Foley and Brady for helping Sarah. Foley told Frank even though he was doing what he was ordered to do that night, he hated doing it. Frank distinctly heard Foley curse while he held him by his arms trying to stop him from going to Sarah's aide. He was sure Foley and Brady deliberately let go of him so he could get to her. Frank apologized to Foley for being whipped along with himself. Foley spoke for Brady saying how sorry they both were about what happened and that if they had known what was going to happen, both of them would have found some excuse not to have taken part. Frank said if they hadn't been there the outcome may have been worse for both him and Sarah. Frank asked Foley if he wouldn't mind helping him one more time.

Foley conceded he would have to put his feelings for Sarah aside, it was the least he could do to help Frank after Frank suffered so much pain for being in love with her. He rode swiftly to town where he bought two horses from Hams Livery and Stable. He loaded one horse with supplies. A saddle and bedroll were put on the other horse, a rifle hung from the saddle and ammunition was stashed in the saddle bags. Foley left the two horses at the Livery and rode back to the ranch.

That evening Frank ate dinner with his father. The day's Frank spent with his father were strained, he didn't want to be in the presence of a man he no longer considered worthy to be called his father. They argued when Frank mentioned he was going back to the mountain and would be marrying Sarah, not once mentioning Sarah was pregnant. The whipping hadn't deterred him from wanting to be with her, it only served to make him want to be with her more. Frank sat quietly while his father retaliated by calling Sarah every vile name he could think of.

Frank felt bitter at his father calling Sarah names. "Did mother have to put up with this kind of talk from you? ...if she did then I'm not at all surprised she divorced you." Major Hardy's answer rocked Frank even more. "Divorce ...your mother never divorced me Frank ...your mother and I were never married!" Major Hardy was surprised by the shocked look that crossed Frank's face. "Well I'll be damned ...she never told you …you are a bastard!" Major Hardy put his head back and roared with laughter at Frank not knowing about his parent's marital arrangement.

Frank stormed out of the room with his father's words and laughter ringing in his ears and went upstairs to his room. He couldn't believe his mother and father were never married, he had never been told. Why hadn't his mother or his grandparents been honest with him? Still, Frank thought his mother had been lucky not to have married the Major, she had been spared from the vile arrogant man he would never again call his father. Frank couldn't help it, his tears flowed freely at the lie his life had become.

When the house was quiet, Frank got up and got dressed, he put his fur coat and hat in his rucksack, he loaded a canvas sack with items he bought from a catalogue Doc Harris brought him from Crawley's store. Having plenty of time on his hands while he waited for his wound to heal, he read the catalogues with interest and found some items he liked. He gave the orders to Doc and he sent them away for him. By the time the items came back on the supply wagon it was spring and the trappers had returned to the mountain.

Taking the canvas sack with him, he crept down stairs and out into the yard where he made his way to a gully that ran along the outside of the fenced corrals. Foley and Brady were in the gully waiting for him with a horse. Frank shook hands with Foley and the two men said goodbye. Foley, supposedly on guard duty, had to stay at the ranch, so Brady rode to town with Frank. At the Livery, Frank handed Brady the reins of the horse he rode to town on.

They parted company with a hand shake and Brady took the horse back to the ranch so Major Hardy wouldn't find out it was missing.

Frank went inside the Livery and found the two horses Foley bought ready and waiting for him. He hooked the canvas bag to his saddle-horn then climbed into the saddle. He rode out over the bridge and turned the horses toward the mountain. Ham stood in the shadows of the Livery and saw him go. Ham smiled to himself, he knew Frank was returning to Sarah. Every person in town knew what happened to Frank and Sarah out at the shack. Some thought they deserved what they got for being ungodly and having sex before marriage. Others thought they were just two young lovers stealing time together and didn't think what Major Hardy dealt them was fair. None of the gossipers ever heard Sarah was pregnant.

When Major Hardy came to town a few days later enquiring as to the whereabouts of his son, no-one would say where Frank had gone. Ham never liked Major Hardy's arrogant attitude, he was happy to keep Frank's whereabouts to himself. But Major Hardy didn't need telling where his son was. He already guessed Frank had returned to the mountain to be with Sarah. His hatred for Sarah for stealing his son away from him right then, was never more ardent.

The water barrel on Sarah's front porch was almost empty and needed filling, so she carried the bucket down to the river and tried filling it. She made several arduous trips back and forth to the cabin from the river and was feeling she had had enough. The barrel was still only half full, this bucket, she decided, would have to be her last for today, she would finish filling the barrel tomorrow. The barrel in the washroom was already empty and it would have to stay that way until the four trappers came by, then she would get a fresh lot of wood chopped and both her water barrels would get filled. Sarah decided when she needed water for bathing, she would use the water from her drinking barrel.

As Sarah came trudging up the small incline from the river carrying the last bucket of water, she glanced up the hill toward her cabin. It seemed so far away and she was struggling to carry the heavy water filled bucket. The front door of her cabin stood wide open, she was sure she closed it when she came outside. She stopped walking and looked around. She didn't have her rifle with her, it was leaning against the wall inside the door to the cabin.

"Who the goddamn hell...?" she looked toward the woodpile and saw two horses, one a packhorse fully laden, the other had a saddle on its back. Sarah didn't know these horses and was afraid she had an unwelcome visitor. She looked to see where she could hide when she spied someone coming out of her cabin and stand on the porch, causing her heart to leap in her chest. She dropped the bucket and water spilled out, running all over her feet and down the incline. Sarah began to run toward the cabin. "*Frank!*" she called. "*Frank!*" almost stumbling over on the loose gravel path as she cried his name. Frank heard Sarah calling out to him and saw her come running up the track from the river. He hurried down the steps and sprinted toward her. "*Sarah!*" he cried as they reached each other. Frank spun Sarah around as their bodies came together and held her against him. Sarah's arms went around Frank's neck, she pulled his face down on hers, their kisses touched each other's mouths wildly. Sarah's eyes flooded with tears. "Frank, oh! Frank" she sobbed, "I missed you so much." Frank held Sarah tight. "I missed you too ... oh Sarah!" They walked back to the cabin with their arms wrapped tightly around each other.

After sitting at the table talking about their time apart and drinking several mugs of coffee, they got busy unloading Frank's packhorse. After Frank insisted Sarah not carry anything heavy, she helped carry the lighter things inside. Frank sat a bag just inside the door of the cabin. "Don't touch that bag!" he ordered and smiled. Perusing the canvas bag Sarah could see whatever was inside stuck out in all directions, she shrugged her shoulders and continued to help unload the supplies. Frank's two horses were put in the lean-to, then fed and watered along with Sarah's horses.

That night while sitting at the table for dinner, Frank told Sarah how Foley and Brady helped him come back to her and how the wolves chased him at the bottom of the mountain. Telling her he only managing to make his escape because the two horses Foley bought were fast. He shot at the wolves killing several but kept going, making the trail up the mountain to the caves with no further trouble. He told her a little about how he spent the winter months lying flat on his stomach and when he was finally able to get up, he sat around the ranch only taking short walks to the corrals and back to the ranch house. Sarah asked him about his back. "My back is fine." He didn't look at her when answering, making Sarah believe he was still suffering because of it. Sarah wanted to see what his father had done to him, so made up her mind she would wait until they were in bed, then she would see for herself.

Before retiring, Sarah heated water and poured it into the dish in the washroom for Frank to freshen up. He spent some time in the washroom preparing for bed while Sarah sat on the side of the bed waiting for him. When he didn't come to bed she got up and went to the washroom. "Frank," she said softly as she went through the door. Frank didn't want Sarah to see his back, he thought it made him ugly and she wouldn't want to make love to him if she saw the cruel raw scar that stretched all the way to his buttocks. His whipping made him feel self-conscious, he wanted Sarah as much as ever but wasn't sure of himself anymore. He wiped his face with the wet cloth. When Sarah called to him, he turned to see her standing in the doorway, his eyes red rimmed. Sarah could see he had been crying quietly to himself. "I'm alright," he said softly. Sarah went to him and wrapped her arms around him. "It's all right Frank, come and make love to me." She kissed him softly and led him to the bedroom. Frank sat on the side of the bed and Sarah pushed herself between his legs. He reached up, undid the buttons on her shirt and slid the shirt down her arms. Sarah's breasts were as beautiful as ever, firm and full. He leant forward and taking a breast in his mouth, rubbed his tongue over her nipple. Sarah wrapped her arms around Frank's neck and held him against her. He undid her trousers and pushed them over her knees. Sarah stepped back, pushed her trousers down her legs and stepped out of them. Standing in front of Frank she let him look at her. Frank could see the change in Sarah's body, having started to swell with their child, her stomach was no longer flat. Her mound of dark hair and long legs still enticed him. Frank didn't want to remove his shirt, preferring to leave it covering his scar, but Sarah wanted to feel his body against hers so he let her help him remove it, reluctantly pulling his arms out of the sleeves. "Let me see Frank" Sarah asked him quietly.

"No Sarah, you don't want to look at it." He said keeping his back turned away from her.

"Yes I do …please let me see," Sarah pleaded, her eyes filling with tears as she looked at him. Ignoring her request, Frank stood up and undid his trousers. Sarah knelt down in front of him and pulled his trousers down his legs, then looked up at his body. He was the same strong virile man she remembered. Frank sat down on the edge of the bed to let her take his trousers off and to prevent Sarah from seeing his back. Climbing into bed, Sarah lay on her back, and Frank lay down beside her, thinking if she were to put her arms around him, she would feel his scar. He brought his body gently down on top of Sarah's and, not wanting her to hold him, took hold of both her hand's, keeping them on the pillow beside her head.

Their lovemaking was strained, Frank wasn't the same as before the whipping when they had been able to make each other's bodies seem to float on air. Sarah didn't come and Frank was quick to finish. After finishing, Frank rolled onto his back and went straight to sleep. Sarah shed a quiet tear and waited until Frank was sleeping, determined to see what Frank's father did to him. She knew it was the reason he couldn't make love to her like he had before.

Sarah waited while Frank stayed asleep on his back. After a while she thought she would just close her eyes for a moment but soon fell asleep too. Sometime during the night while Frank slept, he forgot about his scar and not remembering Sarah was a light sleeper, rolled over onto his side away from her. Sarah felt him move beside her and woke up. Now was her chance to see for herself what his father had done. She lifted the blanket carefully and pushed it away from his back then looked at the long ugly purple scar. Sarah put her hand on his back and gently ran her finger down the length of the scar and started to cry. It was her fault he was scarred and now his once perfect back was ugly, but it made no difference to her, she loved him just the same. Sarah's sudden sobbing woke Frank, he sat bolt upright when he knew she had seen what he hoped she would never see. "Goddamn it, Sarah, this is why I didn't want you to see!" He quickly got out of bed and grabbed his shirt. Sarah got out of bed with him.

"Don't Frank, don't cover it." Her tears wet her face as they dripped off her chin. She took hold of his shirt and threw it back on the chair, then held him. "Come back to bed." Frank couldn't help noticing how sorrowful her face was, he loved her so much it hurt him to see her crying. He climbed back into bed and Sarah lay back on the pillows. Letting his head rest against her breasts, he wrapped his arms around her and wept openly. Sarah wept with him. They slept comforted, in each other's arms for the rest of the night.

Sarah woke up at daylight and found Frank looking at her, his eyes still a little red from crying. "I love you so much ...Sarah Cole." Frank had been waiting for some time for Sarah to wake up so he could tell her he loved her. While looking into each other's eyes, Sarah moved her legs apart and Frank positioned himself between them. They held each other tenderly. Frank was gentle when he made love to her. Caressing each other with their bodies, letting their orgasms build. Their bodies moved in rhythm until the moment of completion came for the both of them. They remained holding on to each other, neither wanting to finish.

After both rested from their lovemaking, Frank got out of bed and walked to the door where he dropped the canvas sack. Sarah watched him walk across the room then out to the living area. The raw purple scar stood out prominently on his back. She felt the lump rise in her throat and tried to swallow it, her eyes again filling with tears. Frank had endured such pain and all because of her. He came back into the room carrying the sack with him and sat on top of the blankets at the foot of the bed. Sarah wiped the back of her hand across her eyes to dry her tears and pushed the blankets off herself, then sat on top of the blankets facing him. Frank looked at her body and they both smiled. Frank then reached into the sack and pulled out a wrapped parcel.

He handed the parcel to Sarah. "Merry Christmas Sarah," he said, leaning forward and kissing her as she took the parcel. Frank sat back and waited for her to unwrap it. Sarah studied the parcel, seeing how it was wrapped in brown paper with a yellow ribbon tied around it. She smiled at Frank and tore the ribbon and paper off. Keeping the ribbon beside her and throwing the paper on the floor, she was left holding a wooden box. "What is it Frank?" she wanted him to tell her before she opened it.

"Open it and see." Frank leant back against the steel frame of the bed and his back hurt, he winced as the steel post pressed into his scar. Sarah saw him wince and put the box aside. She grabbed a pillow from behind her, got up on her knees and crawled along the bed to Frank.

"Put this behind your back," she said leaning over him, her breasts right in his face. "Sarah!" he laughed. "What?" she said as she looked down. Franks face was almost pressed against her breasts so she pushed her breasts at him in fun. Leaning forward, Frank put his hands on her hips and held her while she slipped the pillow behind his back. The pillow felt good, cushioning his back against the bedpost. Sarah climbed onto his lap and sat down, Frank and Sarah had only ever been in this position once before, in the bath. When they started kissing and fondling each other, Sarah felt herself becoming heated. Frank moved his body under her and she felt all of him between her legs. While Frank kept holding her hips, Sarah rubbed herself against him. Their lovemaking suddenly became frenzied. Sarah felt her womanhood swelling. Frank could feel his manhood fully engrossing her. Keeping their bodies together, they kept up the momentum until both of them unexpectedly came. Frank lay on his back and looked up at the ceiling, his breathing coming in gasps. Both had completely forgotten about the wooden box for a moment. "Good God Sarah, what was that?" he looked sideways at Sarah lying beside him and smiled. "I don't know Frank, but whatever it was ...it was ...wonderful!" they both laughed. Sarah looked up at the ceiling along with Frank, her face flushed with colour, her breathing heavy, her body feeling alive. "We aren't hurting our baby by doing what we are doing …are we?" Sarah suddenly asked. Frank assured her Doc Harris said it was alright if they wanted to continue to make love, that it wouldn't hurt their baby.

Sarah thought about Frank having discussed their lovemaking with Doc Harris and knew Doc wouldn't discuss it with anyone else. She discussed having her baby with Doc herself when she thought she might be on her own. She had to be prepared for what would happen when she went into labour. Sarah reached over Frank's naked body for the wooden box. Frank propped himself up on his elbow alongside Sarah and watched her open it.

Inside the red velvet lined box was a pistol with a long silver barrel engraved with ivy, the chamber was plain silver and the grip made of ivory. Sarah looked at Frank. "Do you like it Sarah?" Frank asked as he sat up. Sarah lifted the gun out of the box and held it in both hands to look at it. "It's beautiful."

"I got it especially made for you ...look ...it has my initials on one side ...see?" Frank turned the gun over to the carving of a wolf where he pointed out his initials, "FM …Frank Mason." He turned it over to show Sarah a carving of a mountain and other initials. "SC …Sarah Cole ...that's your mountain." Frank smiled at her. Sarah held the small gun, a Paterson Colt, in her gun-hand, she spun the chamber and when it stopped spinning aimed the gun around the room. The gun was light in weight and could hold five .36 calibre bullets. "Why did you buy me this Frank?"

"I want you to be safe Sarah, I want you to be able to protect yourself from men like my father, if he ever tries to hurt you, you can shoot him with this." Sarah looked at the gun. "I have never shot a person Frank, I don't think I could."

"Supposing what happened to us at the shack that night and supposing you had a gun, wouldn't you have used it? …I know I would have, I would have killed the bastard before he had a chance to whip either of us!" Frank became angry when remembering his father calling him a bastard. Sarah didn't blame Frank for calling his father names, but Sarah didn't know what to think. 'Would she have used it? maybe! but would they be alive today if they had tried to shoot the Major? she didn't think so! the Major had too many men with him for Frank and her to have been able to defend themselves.'

"I love the gun Frank, and I am going to learn how to shoot straight with it." She rested her hand along the side of Frank's face and kissed him. "Thank you," she said, then went to get out of bed. "Not so fast Sarah, I have more gifts." Sarah sat back on the bed "Frank I didn't get..." He knew what Sarah was going to say. "Don't worry about it, you loving me and having our baby is enough for me."

Sarah unwrapped a Yager lever action .54 calibre rifle that had a wolf engraved on its wooden stock. The opposite side was blank except for two small letters. Carved down low on the stock were Frank's initials. Frank told her it would be better for her to use instead of her father's double-barreled shotgun and then he held up a really small box. He got off the bed and knelt down beside it. Sarah giggled at him kneeling naked beside her bed.

"Sarah Cole, will you marry me?" Frank opened the box and revealed a small gold band with a green Emerald surrounded by a circle of Diamonds. Sarah felt a lump rise in her throat, her eyes misted. "Oh Frank, you know I will." Frank got up off the floor, pushed Sarah down on her back, straddled her and kissed her. Sarah laughed when she looked at him hovering over her, parts of Frank were dangling and Sarah couldn't help herself, but she stopped laughing when Frank slipped the ring on her left hand. They kissed each other passionately then Sarah looked at the canvas bag.

"What is that Frank?" There was something left in the bag. "That is mine!" Frank got off Sarah and pulled another box out of the bag that was larger than the one that held the pistol. He opened the box and lifted out a Colt Walker Revolver .44 calibre six shooter, it was all black and it was heavy, weighing a whopping 4lb 9 ounces.

"This is for my own protection, I can only just hold the damn thing though, it is pretty heavy." He handed it to Sarah. It was so heavy she had to take hold of it with both hands to lift it. Frank took it back from her. Sarah looked at Frank, at his face, how he held the gun up and pointed it out the bedroom door toward the fireplace and around the room and how he held it firmly in one hand. Frank looked at Sarah, she didn't look too happy back at him. "We need to be protected when we go back to Cedar Creek each winter," he explained. There were boxes of ammunition in the bag for the pistol, the small rifle and the colt .44, Sarah didn't say anything more about the guns.

"Where will we stay in Cedar Creek?" Sarah wondered about that now they were spoken for and were going to have a baby.

"We can stay with the trappers in the Ferguson House, you have a room there, don't you?" On his way back to the mountain, Frank thought it all through, deciding he was never going back to his father's ranch. The Major called him a bastard and Sarah a whore, and as far as Frank was concerned that ended his relationship with his father. As he rode along, he made a promise to himself he would never return. Neither Frank nor Sarah could have foreseen how ironic his thoughts of not ever returning to his father's ranch were soon to become.

"Yes, I have a room there, but we would be married and have a baby, it would be cramped and a baby crying would annoy the men."

Sarah thought the trappers wouldn't mind her and Frank living with them, but with a baby, she wasn't so sure.

"We'll manage until we can get a place of our own." Frank embraced Sarah and kissed her. Frank was happier than he had ever been in the past two years, he followed Sarah all the way to the mountain and now she was his. Sarah and Frank spent many happy days together at the cabin. Whenever they took long walks hand in hand along the riverbank, they carried their rifles. Frank's heavy handgun was shoved down the front of his trousers where he could easily get at it. Sarah carried her pistol in her rucksack while she wore her hunting knife strapped to her non-existent waist, her belly had swollen enough to be seen clearly under her shirt. Frank thought she looked amazing. Frank carried his sketch book in his rucksack. After the wild storm that destroyed his shelter sent him running for cover to Sarah's cabin and into her arms, he had drawn a sketch of her standing on a boulder with her rifle aimed at an imaginary target. That sketch showed a smiling happy Sarah, now as she sat on the ground in front of him while he drew her, her hair was short and curly, her eyes were sad when she looked at him.

"What are you thinking about Sarah?" Frank asked while he leant back against a tree and sketched. "I'm thinking how much I love you …Frank Mason."

"Then why do you look so sad?" He stopped sketching and reached out to her. "I'm sad because I waited two years to have your love, we could have had so much more time together."

Frank put his sketch book aside, and reaching out for her, drew her into his lap. He leant back against the tree while Sarah sat in front of him with his arms around her. "We will have a lot more time Sarah, after our baby is born, we will become husband and wife, we will live happily together and grow old together, our children will grow up and give us grandchildren.

"Children!" Sarah sat up and turning around, looked deep into Frank's eyes. "We will have more children …or have a whole lot of fun trying." Frank smiled his wide smile that Sarah loved. Sarah hit him on the arm and jumped up. "You have to catch me first," she said as she ran from him. Frank jumped up and chased her. Sarah didn't run too fast, she wanted Frank to catch her. He grabbed her around her non-existent waist, and pulling her down on the grass, lay partly on top of her. As she squirmed and tried to get away from him, he started to become aroused. Slipping his hand inside her shirt he cupped her breast, then moved his hand over her swollen belly and pushed his hand inside her trousers. Sarah became aroused too. When his fingers curled under her and explored her, she helped him undo his shirt and the front of his trousers and they made love on the grass before walking hand in hand back to the cabin.

Sarah and Frank spent lazy days sitting on boulders down by the river near Sarah's cabin. They loved to watch Star and their packhorses frolicking in the water and rolling in the dirt. They made love on a blanket under the stars. Sarah's stomach grew and she became exhausted easily when they went out trapping.

Joe, Fergus, Will and Garrett came by the cabin two months after Frank came back to the mountain. They heard he was back and was staying with Sarah after several other trappers passed by the cabin on their way to hunt along the River Flats. The four men came to see if Sarah needed any chores done around the cabin only to find Frank had done all the work himself. When they asked if there was anything at all she needed them to do, Frank informed them firmly he could do everything Sarah needed doing. Satisfied Frank was capable of helping Sarah, the men made camp for one night, saying they would leave first thing the next day seeing how Sarah didn't need any of their help.

That night, Sarah and Frank sat outside and ate dinner with the men. Frank carried out a chair from the cabin and Sarah sat on it. Frank fussed over her, getting her a plate of rabbit stew then sat next to her while they ate. The four men watched Frank closely. Later, after everyone finished eating, he took his silver timepiece out of his pocket and announced to all that it was time Sarah went to bed to get some much-needed rest. When she said goodnight to each of them, she smiled at Frank, put her arm in his and let him lead her back inside the cabin. With that loving gesture the men were equally satisfied Frank would take good care of Sarah. They could see she was very much in love and happy. The men felt certain they would be free of their promise as soon as Sarah and Frank were married.

Chapter Twenty-two

After leaving Sarah's cabin the trappers returned to the High Ridge, allowing Sarah and Frank time to be with each other before their baby was due. Frank and Sarah were both naked as they sat facing each other on their bed. Sarah leant back against a stack of pillows at the head of the bed and Frank leant on a pillow against the iron frame at the foot. While Frank studied Sarah's belly that was swollen with their baby, Sarah stretched her legs and pressed her foot against Frank's crotch. Frank lifted Sarah's foot to his mouth and licked her toes. Sarah giggled when his tongue tickled her foot, sliding down on the pillows as Frank crawled up between her legs. He couldn't lay down on top of her now, her belly was too big so Sarah rolled over onto her side. Frank lay down behind her, put his arms around her, pushed himself between her legs and while massaging her breasts, made love to her. Sarah and Frank were exhausted after their love making, both slept deeply for the rest of the night.

Sarah rose early to make breakfast, her first chore after coming from the outhouse was washing herself. When she got down on her knees to light the fire under the washstand to heat water, she looked at the scorched floor in front of the stand and remembered back to when the fire had almost burnt down the cabin.

She was ten years old at the time, and she screamed when a piece of lit wood rolled out from under the washstand causing her father to come running. Calahan saw the fire starting to take hold, the floor in front of the washstand was already well alight. He grabbed the bucket, scooped water out of the washtub and threw it on the floor dousing the flames. Sarah stood back and watched her father put out the fire she started. "Goddamn Sarah!" Her father wasn't yelling at her, but Sarah could tell he was angry. "What were you doing lighting that fire?" he asked her sternly. "I was just going to do some washing Pa." She said, looking up at him sadly.

"You want to do washing you tell me and I will light the fire, you could have burnt down our cabin, don't you go lighting that fire again!"

"I want to do some washing Pa …would you light the fire for me …please?" Sarah smiled demurely up at her Pa. Calahan rested his arm on the washstand and looked down at her. He never quite knew what to say when she spoke so innocently to him, she always found a way to pull at his heartstrings. "Alright darlin …you clean up this mess first, then I'll relight it for you." He gave her a hug, even though she had nearly burnt down their cabin.

The fire was burning now under the washstand, her belly got in her way making it a chore to get up off the floor after lighting it. The water heated up in no time. Sarah washed her face and hands then soaped up the cloth and wiped it over her body, washing under her belly and between her legs. Sarah smiled to herself, Frank made love to her and made her wet. She was happy Frank could still find her attractive enough to be able to be satisfied. She felt ugly with her bulging belly but Frank kept telling her she was beautiful. While Sarah bathed, Frank dressed and went outside to get wood for the fire, she heard him come back in carrying his arms full of firewood.

Sarah pulled one of her father's shirts over her head. "Frank, can you help me please?" Frank heard her call him from the washroom and looking through the doorway found her sitting on a chair with her trousers on the floor at her feet.

"Could you put my trousers on me?" Sarah laughed. "I can't bend over anymore." Frank's smile spread out over his face. He knelt down in front of her and putting her feet into the legs of her trousers, pulled them up to her knees then lifted her off the chair.

"Ho! Sarah, you are getting heavy!" he laughed and Sarah hit him on the arm. She laughed then too. Frank pulled her trousers up over her knees. Her stomach got in his way when he tried to pull them over her hips.

"That will have to do, I'll tie some rope around you to keep them up." Frank's eyes crinkled at the corners, he crossed them and made a face.

"Stop laughing, it's not funny, I'm as big as a horse." Frank laughed out loud. "Did you say horse or house?" Sarah was laughing uncontrollably when she hit him harder, making them both laugh. Frank put his arms around her and kissed her. "I love you ...my big house," he added as he went back to put more wood on the fire. Sarah straightened up the oversized shirt she was wearing and waddled out of the washroom to make them breakfast.

It wasn't until they sat down to eat that Frank decided it was time to tell Sarah what he planned on doing, but he was finding it difficult to tell her, knowing she would be angry. Sarah could feel the tension in the room. When he finished eating, he sat back and appeared deep in thought. Sarah's instinct kicked in and she looked across the table at him. "What is it Frank? ...what are you thinking?" She knew straight away Frank was thinking of doing something she wouldn't agree to. Frank twisted his fork around in his hand. "I'm thinking ...we need more skins." He knew Sarah would be against what he planned, he didn't look up at her, instead kept his eyes focused on his empty plate.

Sarah put down her knife and fork and stared at him. "We have enough skins for this year," she returned.

"No, we don't! ...and I'm not going back to my father's ranch, not after what he did, I want to be able to take care of you and our baby myself, and the only way to do that is if I get more skins." Frank's eyes darkened with anger at the thought of having to go back to his father.

"Where will you go to get these skins ...the High Ridge Camp or the River Flats?" Sarah put her hands in her lap and looked at him. If Frank went to the River Flats, she would see him sooner rather than later, but if he went to the High Ridge Camp it would be weeks before she saw him again. "I want you to stay here ...with me ...I'm so close to having our baby and I don't want to be on my own."

"I'll be gone for three weeks at the most." Frank moved around the table and kneeling at her feet, rested both his hands on the top of her legs. "I'll go up to the High Ridge Camp and hunt with the men, that way I'll be back in good time for our baby to be born." He moved his hands, rubbing them over Sarah's stomach, then pushed her oversized shirt up and kissed her belly. He smiled his wide smile that he knew Sarah couldn't resist. Sarah's heart melted when she looked at him. "You'll just go to the High Ridge Camp and hunt with Joe and the other men?" she asked again, needing reassurance the High Ridge would be as far as he would go. Looking lovingly down at Frank, she held her hands on the side of his face and tried to bend toward him to kiss him, but her stomach stopped her. Frank stretched himself up and they kissed.

"Yes, I'll just go to the High Ridge Camp, I don't want to be away from you too long." He slid his hands inside her shirt, feeling how warm her breasts were, he rubbed the palm of his hands over her nipples and felt them getting bigger. He got up and pulled Sarah to her feet. "I just got dressed Frank." Frank undid some of Sarah's buttons, then lifted her shirt over her head to remove it. "I know, but now you have got me worked up I need you." They undressed each other and went back to bed, spending the entire day making love and laying about, neither of them bothering to get dressed again.

The next morning Frank packed his rucksack, dressed in his fur coat and pulled his fur hat down on his head. Sarah walked with him as far as the trees behind the cabin to where the trail led further up the mountain and on to the High Ridge. Frank kissed Sarah and held her. "I love you Sarah ...don't worry ...I'll be back in three weeks." Sarah didn't want to be alone for that long, but Frank wanted to do this for her and their baby.

"I'll see you in three weeks ...please don't go up to the High Country, stay around the High Ridge with Joe, there are plenty of wolves there for you to hunt." Frank held her tight and didn't say anything in answer to her plea. Sarah didn't know why she mentioned the High Country, Frank already knew of the dangers up there, maybe it was because she just wanted to remind him.

Sarah watched Frank walk away from her through the trees and up the trail as far as she could see. When he disappeared out of sight Sarah had an ominous feeling sweep over her, she felt dizzy and hurried back to the cabin. It was going to be a long three weeks until Frank returned.

Each day as Sarah waited, she busied herself around the cabin. She cleaned their bedroom, airing out the blankets and bedsheets.

She tried scrubbing the floorboards, but when she got down on her knees, found it too difficult to get back up so left the floor as it was. Gerda gave her all the baby clothes she needed for when her baby arrived. She washed and folded the clothes and packed them away in her tall chest of drawers. She prepared her own things for the impending birth, her night clothes were washed and folded in her draw. She couldn't trap now for the size of her belly, she had to leave getting skins to Frank.

She felt her baby kicking and each day while she waited for Frank to return, she spent time sitting out on her porch holding her belly. She talked to it and hummed a tune she made up, letting her humming soothe her as well. Each day she crossed off the day on a new calendar Frank made for her. The circle marking the day he was to return seemed so far away. Sarah walked as far as the trail leading up to the High Ridge to watch for him. She carried her rifle just in case she saw any wolves or a rabbit she could shoot for her dinner.

Frank made it to the High Ridge Camp. Men that were still in the camp came out of their shacks to greet him "Why aren't you with Sarah?" Garrett asked him. "I can't lay around every day, I'm here to get skins, I've got a family to provide for!" Frank informed Garrett proudly. Garrett thought if he had a woman like Sarah he wouldn't mind lying around every day, but kept that thought to himself. Frank was here now and he and the other men would keep an eye on him to try to keep him safe until he returned to Sarah.

That night, Frank sat around the fire with the men. Joe came back from hunting to the camp in the dark and was surprised to see Frank there. They talked about Sarah and her impending birth and Joe wasn't happy Frank left Sarah alone this late in her pregnancy. Joe was even more angry with Frank when after only hunting along the High Ridge for a week, he suggested wanting them to go to the High Country.

"You said there are a lot of wolves up there and we could get plenty of skins to get us through to next year." The men were astounded at Frank wanting to go to the High Country. "You are not going up there, laddie," Fergus said. "It means certain death to go up there, we already told you how dangerous it is."

"Yes, I know, but you also told me there was safety in numbers, so if all of you come too, we could all get lots of skins, you said yourself Joe that the wolves breed up there." Frank tried his best to convince the men to go with him. When Sarah told him not to go up to the High Country, he had already made up his mind that was where he was going.

"We have traps set along the High Ridge we need to check before we can go up to the High Country." Joe was sitting on the ground leaning back on a log at the firepit. Fergus and Garrett both looked over at him, unable to believe what he was saying. "Are you thinking about going up there, Joe?" Fergus asked him.

"Maybe! we haven't been up there for a long time, but we still have to check our other traps first." He looked at Frank who came and sat down alongside of him. "How about if you hang about here for a few days, then we can all go for a look up there." Joe wasn't in a hurry to go to the High Country but he wasn't against going up there either.

"Yeah, alright, I'll wait a few days, then we can all go." Joe and the other men were satisfied with Frank's decision to wait for them. They called it a night and turned in. They had an early start in the morning if they wanted to check all their traps before going to the High Country with Frank.

Some of the men woke early and got themselves something to eat before Garrett and Fergus came out of their cabin and went to the firepit for some hot food. Joe came lumbering out of Frank's shack, the look on his face told the group he wasn't happy.

"Anyone seen Frank this morning?" he asked as he got closer to the firepit. The men looked at each other and shook their heads, no-one had seen him. "Fuck!" Joe cursed and looked up toward the High Country. "He's gone up to the High Country on his goddamn own! goddamn! that son-of-a ...goddamn it!" Joe stopped himself short of cursing again.

"What do you mean Joe? why would he risk doin' that?" Fergus scratched his head.

"He's a goddamn ignorant greenhorn that's why! can't get through to him about nothin!" Joe was furious with Frank.

He got the men to search the whole camp just in case Frank was there and he was worrying for no reason, but when Frank couldn't be found they knew he left sometime in the night. Frank had at least eight hours head start on them.

"Get your gear, we are going after him, *now!*" Joe stormed back to his shack and got his rucksack. He checked his rifle, loaded it, then put six boxes of rifle shells in his sack. He checked his shirt pocket for a single bullet, took it out, looked at it then put it back in his pocket. He hoped Frank had the sense to put a bullet in his pocket, Joe was thinking Frank was going to need it. "Son-of-a goddamn…fucking! …goddamn it!" Joe cursed angrily to himself. An hour passed before the men gathered at the firepit and Joe began to lead them up the trail to the High Country, putting Frank nine hours ahead of them.

Frank didn't want to wait a few days, he wanted to get his skins and get back to Sarah. He checked his rifle and tramped his way up the mountain through tall stands of trees. He could hear wolves howling in the distance and knew he was getting close. He checked his rifle again. Frank checked his rifle several times already and was thinking maybe he should have waited for Joe and the other men, but it was too late now, he had come too far. He found what looked like a trail and followed it. The wolves howls sounded to be getting closer. His colt .44 was in his rucksack and he had a skinning knife tied around his waist. As Frank got higher into the High Country the air grew colder. He stopped in a clearing and while putting on his fur coat and hat, looked out across the mountain range. The mountains appeared blue the further away they got. Frank smiled to himself, Sarah would love it up here, the view was spectacular, mountains and green valleys stretched off as far as the eye could see. When he heard movement behind him, he swung around, bringing his rifle up to his shoulder. After seeing there was nothing there, he moved further on up the trail. That first night he made camp in a clearing, lighting a large fire, allowing light from the flames to spread out in a wide arc. Frank didn't sleep much, only catching snatches of sleep as he kept a watchful eye out for wolves. Although he could hear wolves howling close by, he didn't meet with any trouble that first night.

Joe and the men were forced to make camp when it got too dark for them to proceed any further. Joe remained angry at Frank and kept blaming himself for Frank's stupidity, asking himself why Frank would be so stupid as to venture up to the High Country on his own after the men told him how dangerous it was.

Frank left his camp at first light, not bothering to eat, not wanting to waste time getting to the top of the High Country where wolves were plentiful. He didn't think there would be too many wolves for him not to manage on his own, he wanted as many skins as he could carry, he would soon have his own family, he needed to provide for them. So far, he had an easy trek up the mountain, still not meeting with any resistance from wolves.

Joe got the men on their feet early, they made good time but Frank was still a good four or five hours ahead of them. By the time they came across Frank's first camp, the ash was cold in the fire, Frank was long gone, Joe cursed some more and pushed on.

Frank made his second camp when he reached a stand of trees near a rock wall and an outcrop of boulders on top of the mountain range. He gathered arm loads of deadwood and built a huge fire keeping his back to the rock wall and the fire to the front. If wolves attacked in the night, he would have protection with the wall and flames from the fire. The wolves did come in the night, they came in packs. Frank fell asleep and forgot about his fire. When he woke, he heard wolves howling nearby. He lifted his rifle and looked at the fire, seeing it was going out he put the last of his wood on it and waited. It was only a few hours until morning then he would be able to see where the wolves were, if he could hold on that long. He heard rustling in the undergrowth and fired a shot towards it, wasting a bullet when he hit nothing. He heard a wolf howl, then another and another.

Joe was still feeling angry. Once more being forced to make camp when they couldn't see to go on. They were getting close to the very top of the mountain range, much further than what Joe and Calahan had both called the High Country.

The wolves surrounded Frank just before dawn, he saw them coming in for him and fired as fast as he could, his heart pounding, aware he was in trouble. The wolves charged at him from both sides of the trail. Frank was relieved after managing to kill several wolves and the other wolves disappeared back into the dense forest. He checked his ammunition, his rifle bullets were all gone, leaving only his .44 to protect himself with. He wondered if Joe and the other men cared that he hadn't waited for them. He hoped they did and were on their way to help him, he knew he couldn't hold the wolves back much longer.

Frank knew he made a terrible mistake as he watched the sun begin to rise over the mountain range. He watched the brilliant glow as it slowly ascended into the sky. The mountains stood out against the golden rays of the sun. The tall trees and brilliant gold and yellows of the escarpments shone in the sunlight. He had a sudden ethereal feeling of being close to his mother. He knew what was coming and hated that he would leave Sarah and his unborn child this way. He loved Sarah with all his heart and soul. His eyes filled with tears as he pulled his hunting knife from its sheath.

The bullets for his .44 ran out when the sun came fully up over the mountains. He pulled the single bullet out of his pocket and put it in the chamber of his handgun, his hands were shaking and he was crying. He loved Sarah so much and wanted to grow old with her. He wanted to see their baby grow up, now he would never know if he had a son or a daughter.

He reached into his rucksack and took out his little black bible and pencil and quickly scribbled Sarah a message beneath the message his mother wrote to him when she gave him the book. He opened the book and read a passage from Psalm twenty-three, a passage he read many times while attending church as a child in Philadelphia. "Yea though I walk through the valley of the shadow of death I will fear no evil, for though art with me." The wolves attacked as Frank repeated the words over and over. Frank held his gun to his head as the wolves came for him.

The trappers were on the trail, they moved fast, wanting to make up for lost time, Frank, Joe thought, was still several hours ahead of them. Joe stopped walking when he thought he heard the echo of a gunshot in the distance. When he started off again at a cracking pace, he made the men move faster.

They came across the first of the dead wolves Frank killed before they came to the place where Frank made his camp. The men kept their rifles at the ready. A pack of wolves could be seen fighting over something. The men fired their guns, killing several wolves, sending the rest of the wolves scattering, making their escape back into the forest.

Joe, Will, Garrett and Fergus and several other trappers gathered around what the wolves had been fighting over. They looked down at what was left of Frank Mason. Joe squatted over the remains, lost for words as a tear ran down his cheek. Joe had come to like Frank and had hoped Frank would have lived with Sarah until they were both old and grey. Joe carefully went through the pockets of Frank's clothes. He found the little black bible covered in blood and his silver timepiece. Joe handed them up to Fergus.

Sarah went out early for the short walk to the trail leading up to the High Ridge Camp. She came back to the cabin and sat on her porch looking out over the clearing where the trappers camped when they came by, the trees she noticed had become very still. There was no hint of wind, not even a slight breeze. She thought it rather strange, she had never seen such a thing on the mountain before. She looked around at the trees and standing up, leant on the railing holding onto the post with one hand while resting the other on her belly. She looked around at the stillness that had come over the mountain, not a sound could be heard.

A sudden light breath of wind touched her face and lifted her hair, it swirled around her then disappeared as quickly as it had come. Sarah gasped and felt a sudden sadness come over her. "Frank," she whispered. Joe and the men buried Frank. They dug a deep hole and covering him with the rich mountain soil, stacked rocks on top to form a mound, then, Will fashioned a wooden cross. Garrett carved Frank's name in the cross and the date, they stood silent around the grave and said a prayer. They left that place as quickly as they could and hurried back down the mountain. The men huddled around their camp fire on the return trek to the High Ridge Camp, sitting with their heads bowed in solemn thought. Frank was the first man to have been lost on the mountain.

Joe gathered all of the trappers at the High Ridge Camp to tell them what happened to Frank. He blamed himself for not stopping him. The men stood silent as they listened to Joe tell them if he had been a little earlier, he would have been able to save Frank. Some of the men packed supplies for the three-day trek back down the mountain to Sarah's camp. They were going with Joe to give Sarah the news. Joe hated what was to come, he hated that he had to be the one to tell Sarah.

Sarah walked to the start of the trail, sure by her crosses on her calendar, it had been three weeks since Frank left. She spied Joe and Fergus coming toward her through the trees.

"Joe!" she called, and smiling, waved her arm. Joe didn't acknowledge her, he looked at her swollen belly and felt a sadness come over him, it was a terrible task he had to do. He came closer and stood in front of Sarah, Fergus stood solemnly alongside Joe.

Sarah looked beyond Joe and Fergus. Garrett and Will were both coming toward her and some of the other trappers too. Sarah noticed how sombre they all looked. She looked for Frank amongst the men, then at the men crowding around her. "Where is Frank Joe? is he with you?" Sarah looked up at Joe then at Fergus, the men couldn't speak. "Joe?" her eyes questioned.

"Sarah!" Joe reached out to hold her as she started to crumple. Sarah knew Frank wasn't coming back, she had known that day when she was standing on the porch when a silence descended on the mountain. Frank came to her in a breath of air and touched her for the last time. "No! ...no! ...Joe! ...he's coming back ...don't you go telling me he's not coming back ...please Joe ...don't!" Sarah's eyes overflowed.

"Frank is dead Sarah."

Joe and Fergus helped Sarah into the cabin, the other men made camp in the clearing. Joe stood inside Sarah's cabin and handed her Frank's black bible that he had cherished. Sarah told Joe it had been a gift from his mother, she tried to look at it through her tears as she held it in her hands, she could see clearly it was stained with Frank's blood.

Joe handed her his timepiece, Sarah informed Joe sadly how Frank loved to tell her the time and would pull it out of his pocket and announce in a loud voice what time of day or night it was.

Sarah's tears grew worse when Joe lay Frank's black .44 on Sarah's table. These three things and his sketch book were all Sarah had to remember Frank by, those and her unborn child. She looked through her tears and told Joe to get out. "*Get out! …get out!*" she screamed, her face crumpling as she sat on the floor holding the watch and bible in her hands.

There was nothing Joe could do, he left her to grieve and went outside to the other men. They listened to Sarah crying inside the cabin for Frank. There was nothing any of them could do to console her, all they could do was leave her alone to cry. Several hours passed before Sarah opened her door and came out of her cabin. Joe and the men were busy preparing themselves something to eat. "*I want you all to go, you goddamn stinking sons of…!*" Sarah stood on her porch and still sobbing, called out loudly to them. "*…I don't want you here!... you hear me! ...I hate you! …get away from my cabin ...get out of my sight!*" Sarah spat the words vehemently at the men. Holding her hand under her belly she fought to keep herself from crumpling to the floor. Watching her, the men stayed where they were. Joe alone, approached Sarah standing on the porch.

"*Don't you come near me Joseph Beauford Jones, you should have stopped Frank from going to the High Country, you were meant to protect him ...I hate you the most ...you made a promise …you should have taken care of Frank!*" Sarah screamed until she felt herself beginning to sway. Turning, she rushed back inside, slamming the door behind her. Joe stood stock still, he didn't think he deserved her angry words and didn't want to leave Sarah in the state she was in, but he had no choice, if she wanted him to go, he would have to go.

Joe gathered his things. The rest of the men left what they had been doing, picked up their possessions and started to walk off. Joe stood outside Sarah's cabin door. He faced the closed door and hoped when he spoke Sarah could hear him. "I'm sorry for what happened to Frank Sarah, but I didn't promise you I would look after him, no one did, he was stupid, he knew about the High Country, so don't you go blaming me." Sarah flung open the door causing Joe to step back. "Frank wasn't stupid, I loved him, I didn't love a stupid man ...you may not have made a promise to me, but you made a promise to my Pa …you promised you would take care of me, and Frank was with *me*!" Sarah pointed her finger at herself. "You said you would take care of him whenever he was with you, I don't want you here, I will never ask you for anything ever again

...never!" Sarah's eyes were red from crying and anger etched her face. She left Joe standing numb on her porch and slammed the door. Joe leant his head against the door for a moment then turned and headed after the men.

"We going to leave her like that Joe?" Garrett asked when he caught up to them. "No, we are not leaving her, she's emotional that's all, she's just lost Frank, she'll get over it ...given time." Joe walked on until they got out of sight of the cabin. He was hurt by Sarah's angry words, he loved her like he would his own child, he knew he had broken his promise since having to take care of her and he would keep on breaking it if necessary. "If we aren't leaving her, why are we leaving?" Garrett was as upset as Joe at Sarah saying she hated them, they had been good to her since her Pa died and he felt they didn't deserve her hatred.

"She's not far from dropping that kid, I don't think she knows how long she's got, we aren't going back to the High Ridge, we'll go to the River Flats, we can hunt around there for a while, that way, we won't be too far away and we can keep an eye on her." Joe was upset with Sarah telling them to go, but he wouldn't desert her. Garrett, Will and Fergus agreed. The four men moved quickly through the forest.

Chapter Twenty-three

Leaving the clearing at Sarah's cabin like she asked them to, the trappers headed for the River Flats. Sarah was left with little chopped wood for her fire, so she tried chopping the wood herself, but swinging the axe tired her and it was difficult, her now huge belly kept getting in the way of her swing. To keep her fire going she resorted to picking up deadwood dropped from the trees near her cabin. She wished Fergus and Garrett were here to help cut the wood for her. She hadn't wanted to be nasty to them, but they had let her down and she told them so, and now she couldn't go back on her word, she would have to manage the best she could.

It was almost a month since Frank died and Sarah didn't want to go on without him. She forced herself to get out of bed and pulled on one of her father's large shirts over her swollen body. His shirts were the only thing she could fit into now she was so big. Waddling over to the fire, Sarah looked in her coffee pot, becoming angry when finding it empty. Desperately needing water to make coffee, she checked the bucket, it was empty too. The water barrel kept on the porch, near the front door had a little water in it, but not enough for what she needed, besides, she couldn't reach the bottom to get it. She had no choice, she would have to go down to the river and bring up some water.

Sitting on a chair, she managed to push her feet into her boots. Frank already removed the laces months before, so she could get her feet into them without struggling to tie them up. She became used to stomping around the cabin with the boots flopping loose on her feet. After pushing her feet into her boots, she stood up and pulled her hair back in a tail. Even it had grown some over the last few months, her hair was long enough now to tie back. Opening the front door, she was about to go outside and head down the trail to the river when a sudden gush of water began pouring down her legs to form a pool on the floor. Sarah thought she wet herself but hadn't felt like she needed to go. With the water continually dribbling down her legs, she quickly waddled back to the washroom and grabbing a towel, put it between her legs. She didn't feel any pain so waited until the flow almost stopped.

Grabbing the bucket angrily, she continued to wet herself as she made her way down the track past the clearing. When she got to the edge of the river, she struggled to get down on her knees. Finding her belly hanging in her way, she spread her legs wide to accommodate it. Keeping one hand on the ground to support herself, she reached out with the bucket in her other hand and tried scooping water into it.

The bucket quickly filled and started to sink to the bottom. Sarah struggled to hold onto the handle so she wouldn't lose the bucket. Lifting the bucket as far as she could, she tried taking hold of the handle with both hands when a sudden sharp pain shot through her body, causing her to let go. Putting her hands on the ground to support herself, she watched as the bucket sank to the bottom of the river.

When the pain eased Sarah held her hand under her belly and tried to stand. Thinking she should get back to her cabin as quickly as possible, but struggling to get off her knees, another sharp stabbing pain shot across her stomach and through her back, stopping her from going anywhere. The pain seemed to be all over her body, making it hard for her to stand. Sarah began to panic, she needed to get inside where it was safe, but still, she made herself wait.

Checking the sky, Sarah could tell it wasn't morning, it looked more like late afternoon. Long shadows stretched across the ground as the sun dipped behind tall trees on the other side of the river. Soon it would be dark. Realizing, she must have slept the whole day, she tried to stand once more, getting to her feet before more pain doubled her over.

Taking a deep breath and holding her stomach, she managed to get as far as the rocky outcrop lining the riverbank. Here there was a patch of grass growing amongst the rocks where she thought she could lie down. She pulled herself in between the rocks, sat down and waited. Thinking the pain subsided enough for her to go back to the cabin, she put her hands on the rocks either side of her and tried to get up. When she looked down, she saw her legs covered in blood, the hem of the shirt she was wearing was soaked with it. The realization she was about to give birth right there on the riverbank worried her. She never had a baby before and didn't expect she would be giving birth outside her cabin, especially not on the riverbank.

Sarah lay back and contemplated what she should do. She couldn't afford to panic, she was going to have to do this by herself, no one was here to help her. She slowed her breathing to enable her to relax but the thing worrying her the most was she would be in the dark, she was afraid wolves would smell her scent, and she didn't have her rifle.

She scolded herself at how stupid she had been for not bringing her rifle with her to the river. Still distressed about losing Frank, she lost track of time, she thought it was still morning and wouldn't need her rifle just to walk a little way to get water.

The light was fading fast and she had lain between the rocks for longer than she knew. Watching the fading light and every now and then trying to suppress the pains overtaking her body, she tried to remember what Doc Harris told her. After going to Doc and Gerda's for afternoon tea, she asked Doc what she should expect when having her baby. Doc told her she would get pains and when they got close together, she was to push her baby out. She waited for the next pains to come so she could tell when she should push. The pains when they came weren't yet close enough for her to push, she lay back against the rocks and waited.

Day turned to night, the full moon rose into the sky allowing Sarah to scan the area around her. She squinted to see what was lurking about. Feeling satisfied when she couldn't see anything, she looked up at the moon and saw how it cast a ribbon of silver across the river, a gentle breeze made the trees sway. A sudden pain surged through her, she gasped out loud and held both hands on the boulders either side of her. The pain seemed to last a long time this time. When the pain eased, she put her head back and looked up at the stars, just as another pain surged through her. She pulled her legs up and screamed out loud, her baby was on its way.

The sun had just gone down. Joe, Will, Garrett and Fergus were sitting around their camp fire. Having set up camp at the River Flats almost a month ago and filled their days with hunting, skins sat piled up beside each man's bedroll. Frank had built his shelter close to where they camped, but after a violent storm, Frank's shelter stood in ruins. After Sarah told the men to leave her alone, they weren't about to let her have her baby on her own. Joe worried about her being distraught over Frank's death. He knew Sarah and Frank loved each other deeply. How much Frank loved Sarah became evident at the place where they found Frank's body. He worried too Sarah wouldn't know what to do when her baby came, he needed to be there for the birth.

Joe stared into the fire. "Come on, it's time we went over to Sarah's camp and checked on her." He stood up and stretched. Having counted the days, by his reckoning Sarah was ready to give birth, he didn't want to waste another minute.

"Do you think she is ready to drop Joe?" Garrett picked up his rifle and stood alongside Joe.

"More than ready I'd say, it has been almost a month since Frank died and Sarah was bloody huge back then, I don't think she knows the exact day she will have her baby, so we better be around to help her when it comes."

"Come on then, what are we waitin' for?" Fergus started packing up his gear.

"What if she doesn't want us there?" Will added, worried Sarah would be mad at them all over again.

"Well she bloody well won't have anything to say about it, because we are staying whether she likes it or not!" Joe headed off at a rush, it was no use hanging about, he wanted to get going.

The men packed up hurriedly, lifting their rucksacks tied with their skins onto their backs and set off after Joe. It would take the men three hours to get to Sarah's camp from the River Flats and it was already dark. Joe was thankful the moon was full and they could see their way along the trail. They kept their rifles at the ready, in case wolves or anything else they thought, might like to attack them.

By the time the pains started coming close together, Sarah had been lying on the riverbank for several hours, she couldn't be bothered worrying about wolves and other wild animals, she just wanted the baby out of her. She lay back and whimpered "help me Joe," and looked up at the sky. "I can't do this by myself Frank." Tears flowed down her face as she sobbed with regret, wishing she had made Frank make a promise to stay away from the High Country so he would come back to her. If he had made a promise on the mountain, he would have had to keep it, but she hadn't, and now she was all alone. Her father's shirt was made of cotton, but she wasn't feeling cold, not yet, that would come later, if she was forced to stay outside all night. She was sweating from pushing, but still the baby wouldn't come. Sarah kept crying, the next pain was such, she put her head back and screamed at the top of her lungs and pushed really hard.

Joe and the men got to Sarah's cabin and found it in darkness. The front door stood wide open and the fire was out, Sarah was nowhere to be seen. Garrett lit a lantern and searched all the rooms. "The cabin is empty," he said, sounding worried when he came back outside.

Fergus and Will, each took lanterns and searched the lean-to and Calahan's old cabin, they even looked in the outhouse. Garrett stood out on the porch, held his lantern up, lifted the lid on the water-barrel and peered down into it, not too happy when he found it to be empty. He pursed his lips and put the lid back down. Joe walked over to the clearing. All four men were worried something bad had happened to Sarah.

"Shit!" Joe swore out aloud, worried something Sarah had no control over may have happened to her or, he dreaded the thought, she may have done something to harm herself. Will, Garrett and Fergus came back from searching the area and stood at the bottom of the steps leading up to the cabin.

All four men heard the ear-shattering scream echoing all around them. Will, Fergus and Garrett hurried over to where Joe was standing in the clearing. Joe felt the hairs on the back of his neck stand up. "What the fucking hell was that?" Garrett held the lantern high when he queried the sound. He had never heard such a scream before and hoped he never heard it ever again. They all heard another noise too, a small cry echoed up from the river.

Joe pushed past the men and took off running, down the incline toward the river, where he came to an abrupt halt at the water's edge. He searched across the water into the moonlight then down either side. Garrett and Fergus ran down behind him. Will came running along behind all of them.

There it was again, a small cry, Joe knew what the sound was, they all did, the sound of a new born baby crying broke the silence of the night. Joe turned one way then the other, listening for the direction of the noise.

"Joe." He heard his name being called softly, so soft he only just made it out. He turned away from the edge of the river and pushed past Garrett and Fergus.

What he saw when he turned toward the rocky outcrop brought tears to his eyes. Sarah was lying amongst the rocks, and she looked a mess.

"Sarah, are you alright?" Joe hurried over to her and kneeling down beside the rock, looked at the blood-soaked shirt Sarah was wearing and reached in. When he couldn't see the baby, he became worried he might be too late. Sarah opened the front of her shirt, revealing the tiny bundle she was holding near her breast.

"Say hello to Frank's son …Thomas." Tears streamed from Sarah's eyes as she introduced her new born son to the men. Joe cried tears, while Will, Garrett and Fergus, all trying their best not to cry, crowded around to see the tiny bundle.

Able to see the baby was still attached to his mother, Joe pulled Sarah's shirt over her to cover her and the tiny baby.

"We have to get you up to your cabin." Joe took charge as he always did. "Will, go get a fire going and boil lots of water, Garrett, you go and find a blanket for Sarah and..." Joe looked back at Sarah "...and Thomas." The two men raced off to do as he asked. Fergus asked what he could do to help.

Joe pulled a small knife out of his boot. His skinning knife was far too large for what he had to do. "I need to cut the cord, Sarah has more work to do yet." He cut two strips of fringing off his jacket then handed the knife up to Fergus. "We need to be sure the knife is clean, take it to the cabin and boil it ...don't touch the blade when you bring it back, and hurry it up, we don't have time to stay here." Fergus raced up the incline with the knife and charged into the cabin. Meanwhile Joe took off his coat and lay it over Sarah to keep her and her baby from being cold. Sarah watched Joe intently. "How do you know what to do Joe?"

"I was here at the cabin with your Ma and Pa when you were born." He ran his finger down the side of Sarah's face and felt a surge of love for her. She endured having her baby on her own and now he would see she was taken care of.

Garrett came racing down the incline carrying a blanket off Sarah's bed and a smaller blanket he found in a crib in the cabin.

Will got the fire going, then searched the cabin to find a bucket to get some water in and when he found one made several trips to the river to get more water to boil. Fergus raced inside and threw the knife into the pot of boiling water. A few minutes later Fergus was back on the riverbank with the sterile knife. Will got busy, he found a second bucket and running back and forth from the cabin to the river, filled the washstand in the washroom and the barrel on the porch. Tomorrow, he thought, he would fill the second barrel in the washroom.

Joe worked quickly, tying a strip of fringe around the umbilical cord close to Thomas's tiny body, he tied the second strip near the first. Holding the knife carefully, he cut the cord between them. Thomas was now free from his mother. Sarah held her baby in her arms and cried, she was happy and glad it was all over. "Give Thomas to Garrett Sarah so he can take him into the warm cabin, we have more work to do." Sarah looked puzzled at Joe saying they had more to do, she hoped once her baby was born everything was over and done with. He hooked the cord over his finger and held it up for her to see. "We have to get rid of this darlin, then you can go up to your cabin and be with your baby." Sarah handed Thomas to Joe and Joe passed him up to Garrett.

Garrett held out the small blanket and took the baby. "Don't you drop him Garrett!" Sarah said sternly as she watched Garrett wrap her baby in the blanket and hold him close to him. "I won't drop him." Garrett walked slowly up the incline carrying his precious cargo. Joe and Sarah finished what they had to do and Joe wrapped Sarah in the blanket Garrett brought down to them. "I'm a mess Joe," Sarah said as she pulled the blanket around herself. Joe lifted her to her feet. "Don't worry about that ...how do you feel?" Joe was concerned for Sarah. Most women had their babies in a bed, then they spent several weeks in that bed recuperating.

"I'm fine, I just want to get up to my cabin and hold Thomas." Joe picked Sarah up in his arms. Sarah wrapped her arms around Joe's neck as he carried her up the incline. "He's beautiful isn't he Joe?"

"He's beautiful Sarah."

"Did you see his little fingers and toes, and what about his black hair, he's just like Frank isn't he?" Sarah sobbed when mentioning Frank, she put her head against Joe's shoulder. "Frank would have loved him," she wept. Joe felt the lump in his throat getting bigger. "I'm sure he would have loved him." Joe carried Sarah into the cabin.

"I heated up a bath for Sarah ...if she wants it," Will said as they came through the door.

"Yes, I should clean up, there are some things in my top draw in my room, Fergus, would you get them and put them in the washroom please." Fergus got the items out of the drawer while Joe carried Sarah through to the washroom and sat her on a chair.

"Will you be alright in here?" Joe looked at the steaming water in the tub.

"I can manage Joe, I don't need you to bathe me." Sarah giggled, feeling euphoric after the birth.

"Well, if I don't hear any noise coming from this room, I'll come back in." Joe threatened as he pulled the door closed. Sarah hummed loudly so the men could hear her. She hurried with her bath and when she emerged from the room she was dressed in a nightdress and gown that Gerda provided for her with this moment in mind.

The four men crowded around the table. A blanket had been spread out over it and a dish of warm water was sitting in the centre. Garrett still cradled the tiny new born bundle in his arms. He wasn't about to put him down, and he was adamant he wasn't going to hand Thomas to one of the other men to hold, Thomas had been entrusted to him for safe keeping.

"You need to bathe him." Joe smiled at Sarah. After bathing herself, Sarah looked surprisingly well, considering what she had just been through. She moved to Garrett and took Thomas from him, then lay him on the table and unwrapped him from the blanket Garrett had wrapped him in. The men watched as she felt the water to see how hot it was. The water thankfully, was lukewarm. Sarah didn't put Thomas into the warm water, instead, she reached for a cloth and wiped him all over while the men watched on. Will felt a pang of love for Sarah as he watched her gently washing Thomas. Sarah cooed when she picked Thomas up and held him over the dish. She kept cooing gently while she poured a handful of water over his head and gently rubbed his head of fine dark hair with her hand. Thomas bellowed suddenly, making the men laugh.

Sarah lay the slippery bundle back down on the blanket and quickly dried him off. She put a cloth diaper Gerda gave her on him then wrapped him in a fresh blanket. Carrying him over to her bed, she pulled the crumpled bedclothes back and climbed in. The four men crowded in the room to watch. Sarah looked over at them. "You're not going to stand there and watch me feeding him ...are you? get out, go make coffee or get something to eat, all of you, go on ...get!" Joe smiled over at Sarah.

"Get out you lot." Joe said as he pushed the men out the door. Sarah undid the front of her nightdress and put Thomas to her breast, he wriggled around and with a little help from Sarah found her nipple. When he latched on and started to suckle Sarah leant back on the pillows and closed her eyes. She felt the tiny bundle that was her son gently suckling on her breast and a tear rolled from her eye as she remembered Frank's gentle touch. Joe snuck a look in and saw Sarah had her eyes closed, he saw her tears and felt a lump rise in his throat. He went back to the men and got himself something to eat. It seemed to Joe right then, everything that had been said in anger weeks ago, appeared to have been forgotten.

The men spent the following two weeks happily with Sarah before she finally told them to leave. Joe was sitting at the clearing and Fergus was chopping wood. Will and Garrett were over at the lean-to hammering timber boards up high to close it in against the weather. The lean-to's walls were open to all sorts of weather and her horses needed protection. It was a job Sarah had been meaning to ask them to do since the storm sent Frank running from his shelter into her arms. Sarah was grateful for that storm, she would never have been with Frank if the storm hadn't destroyed his shelter, and she would not have Thomas. The men didn't hesitate to do the work for her when she asked them.

Sarah walked over to the clearing with Thomas nestled in her arms. Joe stood next to her and cooed at Thomas. It came as a shock to Joe when Sarah suddenly told them to go, he thought she had forgotten the rift between them. "It is time for you men to leave Joe," Sarah blurted out. "You being here doesn't change what happened to Frank ...I want you to go …now." Sarah didn't wait for Joe to reply, she turned away from him and taking Thomas back to the cabin, went inside and closed the door behind her.

Joe stood rooted to the spot, he couldn't understand Sarah's sudden change of attitude toward him and the other three men. They had gone out of their way to help her, to see she didn't have to do anything for herself while she recuperated from Thomas's birth, now she was telling them she didn't want them around anymore, Joe was heartbroken.

He sat back down on the log and stared at the cabin, the front door remained closed. Fergus stopped chopping wood after seeing the look that had come over Joe and went over to where he was sitting.

"What's the matter Joe?" Fergus stood in front of him.

"Sarah just told me she doesn't want us here anymore, she wants us to leave." Joe started packing up by shoving things furiously into his rucksack.

"What!" Fergus was just as shocked as Joe at Sarah telling them to go, he looked up at the cabin.

"She is still angry at us for what happened to Frank." Joe called Will and Garrett over and told them to get their things. The two men equally disappointed in Sarah telling them to leave, hastily packed up their belongings.

Before leaving, Joe went to the cabin door. “We are leaving Sarah …you take care of Thomas now, you hear?” Joe waited for Sarah to come out to see them off. When she didn’t come out, he continued speaking angrily through the door. “And don’t you go blaming us for what happened to Frank, you have to realize it wasn’t our goddamn fault!” Joe stepped back when Sarah opened the door.

Joe was sorry for the way he spoke to Sarah immediately after she came out. Her face clearly showed signs she had been crying. It was far too soon for her to be over the loss of Frank. “I don’t blame you …Frank was a man, he knew what he was doing …thank you for fixing the lean-to, but I will not ask you for anything else, ever again, I release you from your promise!” Going back inside, Sarah closed the door, leant her back on it and wept softly, because she wanted to take back everything she said, but felt she couldn’t, it still hurt her that the men hadn’t kept Frank safe. “You can’t release us from the promise Sarah, it’s not your promise to release us from, it was a promise made between your Pa and us four men, and we won’t break our promise ...not ever!” Joe wasn’t mad at Sarah, he had never raised his voice to her before, not even after all the trouble she caused after she met Frank. When Sarah didn’t come back out, Joe and the other men went back to the High Ridge Camp, leaving Sarah to raise her son alone.

The only way the men knew Sarah was coping was whenever other trappers came across her out trapping or hunting. She was unable to venture too far from her cabin with her new born baby. Hunting and trapping fell by the wayside when she couldn’t cope with having to stop and feed Thomas as well as hunt and trap, her skins at the beginning of winter were few.

Sarah regretted what she said to Joe and the other men, but she wouldn’t take what she said back, she was alone now and had to cope the best way she could. During the day, it was easy for her to keep herself busy looking after Thomas, but at night she cried herself to sleep. This winter was to be Sarah’s first time she was to leave the mountain on her own.

Joe didn’t know how he could help Sarah without her getting angry at him. The four men didn’t return to Sarah’s cabin until winter when they had no choice but to travel the trail past her cabin on their way off the mountain.

Chapter Twenty-four

Winter was ferocious again this year. Snow came early and the pass was almost blocked. The trappers had already left the mountain passing by Sarah's cabin on their way to Cedar Creek. Sarah refused to leave with them. Joe and Sarah stood in the snow and argued back and forth while the rest of the trappers filed past. Joe gave up arguing with her. He could see it was futile to continue on with trying to reason with her. Sarah was stubborn just like her father had been, so he reluctantly went on without her.

Sarah didn't care that she didn't have many skins this year, giving birth to Thomas made it difficult to go out hunting, but she wouldn't change a thing, she loved Thomas and was grateful she had him to keep her occupied. Sarah spent most of the day packing her belongings onto one packhorse, her other packhorse she loaded with Frank's skins and the few skins she had collected. Sarah would have to lead two horses and carry a baby at the same time. It was going to be tough going.

By the time Sarah rode in to Cedar Creek, she was struggling. Thomas was two months old, a tiny bundle of white skin and black hair. Sarah carried him strapped to the front of her body where he was warm and safe, covered by the long, thick fur coat she wore. She stopped several times along the trail before making it to town so she could put Thomas to her breast. Stopping at the caves was a relief, allowing her to get in out of the weather where she was able to make a fire. She sat in front of the fire for warmth while she let Thomas suckle, waiting until after he was settled to eat her own meal. Being careful when she got to the bottom of the mountain, wanting to avoid the wolves gathered there as much as possible, she skirted around the trail leading straight to the wells, riding out wide into the open prairie where she had to make an extra night's camp. The next day she doubled back. Setting up her camp at the wells in the dead of night, she made her fire and settled down to feed Thomas. Their journey to town took Sarah a lot longer than usual, making Joe relieved when he saw her ride in.

Sarah was relieved too when she rode across the bridge in to town. Turning down the main street leading her two packhorses behind her, she ignored town folk staring at her and headed straight for the riverbank. Usually she would go with the men first to take her skins to the Trading Post. This winter and because of her baby she wanted to prepare her camp before doing anything else. Since her father died, she spent the winter months with the trappers in the Ferguson House, but this year was different, Frank had been killed, and she herself made it impossible for her to stay with the men.

When Sarah opened her coat in the warmth of the Trading Post, Fess became aware of a baby in the room. When she stood near Fess's warm fire, Fess heard Thomas whimpering. He was surprised to see Sarah had a baby. No-one mentioned Sarah was expecting when she left Cedar Creek last spring. Foley Andrews knew, but he kept it to himself, so did Doc Harris and Gerda, they didn't tell anyone, and none of the trappers had spoken of it either. As tears threatened to roll down her face, Sarah introduced Fess to Thomas and told him about Frank. Fess made Sarah a warm drink and sat her down on a chair in front of his fire while he counted her skins. Fess was a good man, one of only a few people in Cedar Creek that didn't involve themselves in gossip or trouble. Sarah used Frank's skins to supplement her bank balance, it meant she was disqualified from taking part in The Pot, but that didn't bother her, she wouldn't have won The Pot anyway with the few skins she had.

After leaving the Trading Post and Fess, Sarah went to Morley's bank to put her chit in so she could get paid for her skins, the money wasn't a lot this year but it would help her get fresh supplies. Morley was as surprised as Fess at Sarah having a child. Morley heard what happened at the shack but still, it surprised him to see the tiny bundle. He welcomed her and her baby then invited Sarah to visit with Esther saying it would cheer Esther up no end to see both Sarah and her little bub.

Sarah had her usual run in with Crawley at his store, and when he saw Thomas, he sneered at her, called her a whore and Thomas a trapper's bastard. Sarah hated Crawley even more after his comments and vowed she would never let him forget it. After leaving the store Sarah went and saw Doc Harris. She needed him to check Thomas to see if he was growing. Doc Harris delivered her into the world and had been her doctor ever since, and he kept records. Every year when Sarah returned to Cedar Creek, she went to Doc to make sure she was staying healthy, now she had Thomas, she would take him along too.

Doc said Thomas was thriving, he was a solid baby, well fed, clean and seemed content. That's what Doc Harris told her, he said she was doing a good job considering she had given birth on the riverbank not far from her cabin. Doc worried about her being on the mountain on her own when her baby was born. She told him she expected Frank would be back so she wouldn't be alone, but deep down inside she hadn't held out any hope that Frank would return to her. Doc tried to get Sarah to stay in Cedar Creek for the term of her pregnancy but the mountain was her home and she wanted to get back there. There were things that happened in town she wanted to leave behind. Doc had been clear when he explained what would happen when she gave birth, wanting to make it easier for her to cope when she went into labour. Gerda worried too but gave her baby clothes and items she needed for herself to take with her back to the mountain.

Doc Harris said how sorry he was when Sarah told him how Frank died. He checked Sarah over thoroughly and said she was doing well, her milk was plentiful and her weight was normal.

Word soon spread around town that 'Cole had a baby with her.' The news travelled fast and word was sent to Major Hardy that Frank was dead and that Sarah Cole had given birth to Frank's baby. Major Hardy was gutted to hear his son was dead, and livid. As far as he was concerned Sarah Cole was a murderer, his son would never have died only because of her. He hated Sarah more than ever. He didn't want to believe Sarah's baby was Frank's, instead convinced himself the baby belonged to one of the trappers. Even so, that was when Major Hardy and his so-called friends, Harold Finch and Roy Connell, whom both considered themselves good upstanding folk, decided Sarah Cole, wolf trapper, was not a fit person to take care of a baby, and that a baby shouldn't be living in a makeshift shelter on a riverbank in the cold. Major Hardy and his upstanding good folk friends, decided for themselves to take Thomas away from Sarah. They even planned when and how they would do it.

After being in town a few days, Sarah was invited to a tea party at Harold and Mary Finch's house. If Sarah had known they were friends of Major Hardy's she would not have gone. But too many things happened for her to be aware of all the goings on in town. Mary Finch asked if Sarah would like to bring her baby to show him off to the other ladies. Sarah took Thomas and went to the ponds to get herself bathed and dressed neatly. Thinking how nice it was for the ladies of the town wanting to befriend her and see her baby, she dressed Thomas in his finest baby outfit, then Sarah happily went along to the house and was welcomed inside where a group of ladies were gathered. In the living room a table was set with an assortment of cakes and cookies, there were teacups of fine china waiting to be used. When Sarah walked in, they oo'd and aar'd over Thomas and said how beautiful he was. Sarah felt happy and smiled back at the women. Mary Finch asked to hold Thomas and Sarah let her nurse him. The women took turns passing him around the room. Felicity Connell asked Sarah to help her in the kitchen, so she went, unknowing what was about to happen.

Sarah stepped through a door and found herself outside. The door slammed shut behind her and was locked. She pounded on the door and screamed at the women to let her back in. One of Major Hardy's men sat waiting on his horse outside the back of the house. Sarah didn't know this, she was too upset at being locked out while her baby was still inside. One of the women hastily took Thomas out the back and handed him to the man who rode away with him. Sarah screamed at the top of her lungs and ran along the front of the house, banging on windows and the front door. She made one hell of a racket and Sheriff Clementine along with a crowd of people came to see what all the noise was about. The men of the house threatened to shoot Sarah if she didn't leave well enough alone. Sarah became wild with rage and fired her pistol at the house, smashing several windows and scaring the people inside.

Sarah stumbled around town, furious at the people who tricked her into believing they wanted to be her friends. She didn't know where her baby had been taken, no-one would tell her. For almost two weeks she couldn't find him, they took him off her and gave him away to someone. Sarah screamed for her baby as loudly as she could and threw rocks and smashed windows, she fired her rifle in the air, shot at the awnings and anything that was hanging from them and demanded for whoever took Thomas to bring him back. Sheriff Clementine grappled with her outside the jailhouse, dragged her inside and locked her up. Having to lock her up for her own and the towns safety several times in those two weeks, then only letting her out when she calmed down, but Sarah continued to rant and go wild.

George Clementine or 'Clem' as the town folk liked to call him was the only lawman in town, he had no deputies to help in times of trouble. He tried talking to the women who took Sarah's baby, but it was no use, they weren't going to tell him where Thomas was or hand him over, they had been paid well to do the deed and sworn to secrecy. Sarah screamed for Thomas and cursed the people of Cedar Creek until her throat hurt. Clem hustled Sarah off to the jailhouse once again and locked her in a cell to calm her down. When Clem tried to give her a hot meal, she threw it through the bars at him. The mess was left spread all over the floor all night when Clem gave up and went home to his wife. Clem was at a loss to know how to handle the situation.

The trappers watched what was going on but stayed out of Sarah's way. Part of their promise was not to interfere in Sarah's life, she had to learn about life for herself, besides, Sarah told them to stay away from her and that was what they were doing. Even so, Joe was furious that Thomas had being taken. He watched what was happening, and waited. Clem finally got Sarah to calm down and the next day when she said she wouldn't do anything to harm anyone he let her out. Sarah did as Clem asked, for a time. She stayed at her camp and cried all the next day and night.

During the two weeks Thomas was gone Sarah stopped eating, she stopped bathing and became dirty, she became vicious and spat at anyone who looked in her direction. She continued to pace up and down the street late at night crying for her baby and firing her pistol in the air. Town folk and cowhands alike, when passing her in the street avoided her, running almost to get out of her way. Even though Joe couldn't interfere, he thought Thomas's disappearance was a cruel way for Sarah to learn about life and he wanted to do something about it, but didn't know how to go about it without Sarah knowing. His three friends were equally at a loss to know what to do. They huddled together to think of a plan to get Thomas back, but came up with nothing.

Sarah found herself all alone, so she went to the only person she thought might be able to help her, Doc Harris. He enquired around town and found out Thomas was out at Major Hardy's ranch. Major Hardy, Doc told Sarah, was Thomas's grandfather and he wouldn't do anything to hurt Thomas. Except Sarah knew Major Hardy hated her. She knew he would never give Thomas back.

It was one Sunday after Thomas's disappearance the good folk of Cedar Creek attended their church. The trappers didn't go to church, they didn't have religion on the mountain so they didn't have it there in town, but they didn't consider themselves ungodly men either. Sarah took a walk from her camp to try and clear her head and think what to do to get Thomas back. Heading along the riverbank she passed beneath the bridge, then walked along until she got beyond the corrals. She made her way up off the riverbank and walked through the trees that grew along the sides of the river and at the back of the cemetery. Sarah thought she might sit beside her father's grave for a while, maybe she would find some solace in being near him. Standing hidden in the shadows of the trees that grew dense around the church and cemetery, she watched as men, women and families filed into the church. Reverend Barnes welcomed each man by shaking their hands, he said hello to the women and put his hand on the top of the children's heads to welcome them to his Sunday Service. When everyone had arrived, the doors were closed behind them and they began their prayers and hymn singing. Everyone stayed inside for a long time. Sarah stayed where she was and watched until everyone filed out again. Along with their wives and children, the good men folk of Cedar Creek attended church every Sunday, and they didn't take their guns.

After two weeks of not eating much of anything and sleeping very little, Sarah began to form a plan. She got the idea when she returned to her camp after watching the church. She couldn't see any other way to get Thomas back. If the good folk of Cedar Creek thought they got away with taking her son, they had made a terrible mistake. Sarah was going to fix the mistake they made. If they weren't going to give her baby back willingly, she would force them to give him back. Sarah was going to punish them for what they did.

Waiting until dark, she made her way along the riverbank to the Livery. Star was taken out of his stall, saddled and a rucksack was tied to the saddle-horn. Frank's colt .44 was loaded and in the rucksack along with coffee and a small amount of food. Sarah tied her fur coat to her bedroll behind the saddle, she carried her pistol down the front of her trousers. The large hunting knife was in its sheath hanging from her hip and her rifle was loaded and stored in its holster. She would need these when she got to where she was going. Sarah rode Star quietly out of the Livery and over the bridge out of town in the dead of night. No-one saw her go, not even the trappers.

The trappers searched the town for her, they went to her camp and could see how she hadn't been taking care of herself. The camp was a mess, blankets and furs in the shelter were dirty and the shelter stank. What river rats hadn't eaten, maggots crawled over. Fruit and vegetables had gone rotten and the stench was overpowering. Joe was upset that Sarah had come to this. He ordered the men to get rid of the rotten food, then asked them to keep watch over her camp, while with Fergus, Garrett and Will, he rode out to Major Hardy's to beg him to give Sarah back her baby. When Joe accused Major Hardy of kidnapping Thomas, Major Hardy accused Sarah of killing Frank. He threatened Joe and the three trappers with him to get off his land or he would have them shot as trespassers. Joe and the other three men rode away in disgust.

Soon after Sarah left town, the town began to settle back to normal, everyone felt they were safe, Sarah Cole was no longer around to cause them trouble.

Riding all that night and all of the next day toward the mountain Sarah didn't stop until she got to the wells. Once there she got out her fur coat and put it on. It had begun to snow and the air was freezing. She made a small fire and brewed coffee to warm herself.

Wolves could be heard howling in the distance, so Sarah decided not to sleep at all during the night. The coffee worked to warm her and she was glad she brought her fur coat. Next morning as the day began to dawn, she moved on toward the mountain. Only she wasn't going up onto the mountain. She was going to the South Side Camp. The camp was a full day's ride south, away from the trail that led up to the caves and the pass that took the trappers onto the mountain and beyond her cabin.

Sarah rode on from the wells, making the trail to the mountain mid-afternoon. She thought how easy it would be for her to head straight up the trail and go home, but she knew if she tried to go there, she wouldn't make it. The pass would be blocked and the snow would be deep. She rode on past the trail.

Wolves followed Sarah as she drew closer to the South Side Camp, so far, they were keeping their distance. She spotted a wolf crouching in the stand of trees watching her closely. The grey of the wolf's coat stood out against the white of the snow and Sarah spotted it easily. As Sarah pulled her rifle from its holster the wolf came running from the forest making straight toward her. She kicked Star and made him move faster. Sarah looked over her shoulder as her horse galloped away from the pursuing wolf. The wolf was not alone, two more wolves were coming up on her fast. She raised her rifle and turning in her saddle, took aim at one of the wolves and fired. The wolf yelped and rolled over, going down with a bullet to its leg. Another ran wide then came back towards her. She kicked Star again and he picked up his pace, stretching himself forward and galloping harder. Sarah hung on tight to the reins as Star raced toward the camp. This wolf though, kept up with Star, running in close and trying to bite him on his back leg. Star kicked out, trying to ward off the wolf's snapping jaws as he ran, and it was all Sarah could do to hold on. Her rifle proved too big for her to fire with the wolf so close to Star. She pushed the rifle back into its holster and drew her pistol. Luck was on her side. When the wolf made a mistake and ran out wide, she took aim and fired. Her bullet struck the wolf in its rear leg, causing it to stumble in the snow, but as Sarah watched, the wolf got up and kept coming. One shot from Sarah's pistol wasn't enough to bring it down. She fired again, this time her bullet struck the wolf in the head. The wolf stumbled again, stopped rolling and didn't get up.

Star came up fast on the camp. Its timber walls loomed in front of them out of the quickly fading light. Sarah pulled Star up hard, but before he had time to stop completely, she jumped down and ran to the gate, hoping to get the gate open before the wolves could catch up to them. Their howling was getting louder as they came closer. Sarah got the gate open, then hit Star on his rump getting him to race into the compound. She quickly pulled the gate closed behind her, relieved both her and her horse were safe, for the time being.

The South Side Camp had been built by Sarah's father and Joe. The two men trapped there for a time and they built the fort like camp for protection from wolves and the elements. A high log wall had been built at the front to protect the camp on three sides, the rear of the camp sat against the high escarpment of the mountain. Inside the compound was a cabin and a shelter, where horses could be kept out of the weather. The camp was seldom used now, the trappers preferring to hunt further up the mountain.

An old pile of dry wood was stacked inside the shelter and Sarah was grateful for it. A fire was necessary at night and Sarah was going to stay in the compound just long enough to get back to Cedar Creek the following Sunday when the good folk were in church. She wanted the good folk of Cedar Creek to get a sense that she was gone for good. Sarah needed them to relax so what she was about to do would shock them into returning Thomas to her. She put Star in the shelter where she found a pile of hay and a half sack of grain that had shriveled with age. This grain, she felt, would be good enough for Star to feed on. She unsaddled him, then taking her rucksack and saddle, went inside where she set about lighting the fire. When she had the fire going, she took a look around. The cabin consisted of one large room. An old rusted steel frame that used to be a bed was pushed against the far wall. A small wooden table and two chairs sat in the middle of the room. A rough wooden bench with shelves sat along the wall next to the fire. Rusty tin mugs and plates covered in dust sat stacked on the shelves.

Sarah went out to the shelter and brought in enough wood to do her for the night. The fire soon warmed the inside of the cabin and she was able to take off her fur coat. Her food supply didn't consist of much. She had a small amount of flour, some salt, dried milk powder, four apples and her bag of coffee. Sarah cooked up an apple and made some hotcakes, she made coffee then wrapped the cooked apple in the hotcakes, it was the only food she allowed herself to eat for the week, but then she didn't feel very hungry, she hadn't been able to eat much at all since Thomas was taken.

Sarah lay down on the floor in front of the fire and thought about what she was about to do to the people of Cedar Creek. She decided on her plan before leaving town, all she had to do was put it into action. But if her plan failed because the wolves got her, at least she would die with the knowledge she died trying. Wolves weren't always this plentiful around the camp. Trappers stopped going there because they didn't think trapping at this camp was worth their trouble, wolves had not been seen there for years. Sarah was in luck, this year the wolves followed her back there. In three days when Sarah went back to Cedar Creek, she would be taking a wolf with her.

She didn't sleep much during the night, the sound of wolves howling close by kept her awake. 'Good,' she thought, she shouldn't have too much trouble getting one, it needed to be a fresh kill. Sarah cried some more, her breasts ached, her milk leaked, staining the front of her shirt. She tried squeezing the milk out of them, but it hurt like hell. When she shot herself in the shoulder it didn't hurt nearly as much as this. She continued to cry throughout the night.

The days dragged on, Sarah slept on and off and ate little, coffee was the only thing keeping her going. When the morning of the last day came Sarah was nervous. It was time to leave the camp and go back to town. Sarah could see it was snowing heavily. The wolves had gone quiet, but she knew they would be out there somewhere close by. She saddled Star and got her rifle ready. She carried bullets in a small pouch she tied to her knife belt where she could get at them quickly, enabling her to reload as fast as she could once the wolves started to attack. One bullet she placed in her shirt pocket, this she would use on herself if her plan failed. Sarah doused the fire in the cabin, then went outside. She was ready to head back to town.

Sarah opened the gate, took Star out to the front of the camp, then quickly closing the gate, climbed into her saddle. Star snorted and moved around agitated, knowing what was to come. With her rifle in her hand, she kicked Star in the flanks, he bucked and started to run. Star galloped fast but the snow had gotten deeper overnight and their getaway wasn't as fast as Sarah hoped. She looked around on all sides searching for wolves.

They travelled a good distance from the camp and Sarah thought she might get as far as the trail up the mountain without seeing a single wolf. She thought this wouldn't do, not if her plan was to work, she needed the wolves to come. She pulled Star up and turning him around, rode a little way back toward the camp. Suddenly spying wolves watching her from the forest, she turned Star back toward the mountain trail, and made a run for it. The wolf pack lay in wait knowing they had a chance of getting fresh meat. When Sarah drew level with them the wolves made their move, dashing out from the forest and circling her horse. Sarah let them get close before starting to shoot. The first wolf she took down came up on her fast. Racing for the trees, she jumped off Star and let him go. Star was running scared and galloped off into the forest. When a wolf came hurtling straight toward her, Sarah fired her rifle and dived behind a fallen tree for cover. Striking the wolf in the head with a straight shot, it barreled over the log where it fell dead. Another came at her from her left, she fired again, her bullet hit the wolf in the shoulder but this wolf kept coming. Sarah darted over the log and crouching on the other side, faced the wolf. The wolf leapt over the log, springing into the air, its underbelly exposed high above her. Sarah pulled out her pistol and fired. The wolf dropped beside her as her bullet pierced its heart. She didn't have time to dwell on her kills, another wolf was coming at her from behind. She fired her pistol but the wolf kept coming, she fired again, still the wolf kept coming. Sarah fired once more, the wolf charged toward her, giving her just enough time to jump sideways as it hurtled passed, tumbling over and over, before stopping dead in a bloody heap in the snow.

Sarah was breathing heavily, all around had gone quiet, nothing moved, there was no wind, no sound. Suddenly hearing a crashing sound coming from the trees, she wheeled around quickly, her pistol up and ready, surprised at seeing Star come hurtling out of the woods from where he ran to hide. 'Cowardly horse,' she thought as she laughed at him and shoved her gun back in her trousers. Star ran straight past Sarah with a wolf growling savagely at his heels. He kicked and bucked wildly trying to ward the wolf off. The wolf, on seeing Sarah, changed direction, charging at her with its teeth bared. Sarah put her arm up, protecting her face as the wolf's mouth went around her arm and clamped down hard on the sleeve of her coat. The thick fur the only thing protecting her from the wolf's bite. Sarah and the wolf tumbled together. She pulled out her knife as the wolf got up with her arm still in its mouth. Shaking its head furiously from side to side, she drove her knife hard at the wolf's throat, piercing through one side of its neck and out the other. Blood covered Sarah's coat, she checked herself quickly for bites, grateful when she could see it wasn't her blood. Sarah staggered to her feet and looked at the wolves lying dead all around her. What wolves Sarah didn't kill gave up and went slinking back into the forest to try again another day. When Star saw the wolves had gone, he came walking back to stand near Sarah.

Sarah dragged all of the wolves' carcasses together, then set about skinning them. Wolf skins were worth money no matter how bloody they were, she wasn't going to waste them, she needed the money to be able to buy supplies to feed herself, and Thomas when she got him back. Sarah skinned all of the wolves except one. This wolf was needed for her plan to work.

Star became agitated when the blood-soaked skins were tied to the back of Sarah's saddle. Sarah tethered him tightly to a tree to stop him from shying every time the skins touched his flank. When she tried to hoist the dead wolf up on Star, he snorted and moved away from her in disgust. Sarah calmed him down enough to get the wolf carcass up where it lay draped in front of her saddle. When she finished loading the skins and dead wolf onto Star, Sarah's clothes were saturated with blood, her hands and arms were bloody up to her elbows.

Sarah headed back toward Cedar Creek. Arriving at the wells on nightfall she would have stopped, but rode on through the night, wanting to be back in town by the time the good folk of Cedar Creek were in church.

A few days after Sarah went missing, Joe gathered the other three men and together rode back to Major Hardy's ranch to try once more to talk him into handing Thomas over, but Major Hardy again refused to give him back. "Cole took my son and now I've got hers, let her see what it is like to lose someone you love, besides, he is my grandson, he belongs with me!"

Joe argued with him. "Cole lost someone she loved Major, that was Frank, and Frank loved Sarah ...she is Thomas's mother for Chris' sake." Major Hardy became angry at Joe's comments. His plans for Frank were ruined because of Sarah Cole, he yelled back at Joe. "And I am Frank's father ...after Frank's whipping I was prepared to let it go, but because of her my son is dead …she killed my son and now she is going to pay for it!" he said seething with anger.

"Sarah didn't kill Frank, he killed himself ...the goddamn wolves surrounded him and he had no choice but to shoot himself! " Trying to make Major Hardy see reason, Joe yelled back. Major Hardy's men standing nearby listened to the exchange between the two men. They heard talk Frank shot himself because he was hunting alone. But they hadn't known Sarah was pregnant until she turned up back in town with a baby. They questioned if it was Frank's child and not one of the trappers. The men soon found out the baby was Frank's when the trappers angrily let them know it was Frank who made Cole his woman and they vehemently denied ever having been with her.

"It was because of that trapper bitch he was up there on that mountain instead of here with me, I warned you before Jones, my men will shoot you for trespass ...now get off my land!" Major Hardy was furious at Joe for even suggesting his son would take a coward's way out and take his own life. Major Hardy having been a loyal cavalry man would never do such a thing. He turned and stormed back inside his ranch house slamming the door behind him. Joe could hear Thomas crying somewhere in the house and was filled with anger as he stormed over to his horse. Will, Garrett and Fergus were just as angry when they followed him.

The four men rode past a fenced in yard where some of Major Hardy's men were corralling a huge animal. Ropes were tied to its legs and around its horns to stop it from getting loose and attacking them. Joe stopped and watched as one of the men accidently let go of a rope holding the biggest black bull with the biggest set of horns Joe had ever seen. Joe leant on his saddle-horn as he watched the bull charge around the corral. Some of the men dived quickly through the railings and others climbed up the fence and over it to get out of the bull's way. They waved their hats and yelled when they were safe, some even laughed at their near miss. "What kind of bull is that?" Joe asked one of the cowhands.

"He's what you call a Longhorn …on account of the size of its horns, he's worth a lot of money, the Major's plannin' to breed his herd up with this bull, goin' to make a hell of a lot more money." The cowhand seemed proud to be in charge of such an animal. "How much is he worth?" Joe wanted to know. "Well, the Major paid five thousand dollars for this here bull, what with getting him out here and all, goddamn if he ain't a beauty, the Major's onto something here I reckon." The cowhand was eager to tell Joe all about the Major's plans. Joe had never seen the likes of these bulls. He thought maybe he had spent far too long on the mountain to know what was happening in the rest of the country. He spurred his horse and the four men rode out the gate and away from the ranch.

Chapter Twenty-five

Sarah stopped only once on the trail back to town to relieve herself and take her coat off. The sky was getting lighter, and she would be back in town in a few hours. Star settled down becoming used to having the dead wolf and blood-stained skins draped over his back. Sarah didn't have time to clean the skins properly, fresh blood from the skins oozed over Star's rump and down his flanks. The wolf draped in front of her saddle lay near Star's neck. Blood from its wound where Sarah stabbed it with her knife, ran over Star's side, flowed down his front leg and onto the ground. Star, as was Sarah, was saturated in wolf's blood.

It was Sunday morning when Sarah rode over the bridge and headed straight to the church. All the good folk were inside when she arrived. A few trappers leant on a hitching rail talking on the opposite side of the street, Joe and Fergus amongst them. Will and Garrett were at the corrals looking over a couple of horses. When they saw Sarah, they left the horses and ran toward the church. As she came riding in over the bridge the men across the street straightened up and took particular notice to Star covered in blood, at Sarah's clothes and how she looked dead in her saddle. The wolf carcass lying in front of her was stained red. Sarah glanced across the street to where the men were. As the men started walking slowly towards her, she watched one of them run off to get Sheriff Clementine. Sarah had to hurry, she took her rifle out of its sheath and pointed it at the men to warn them off. Seeing her gun, the men stopped in their tracks, none daring to make a move toward her. Their faces told Sarah they were surprised to see her back in town and shocked by what she brought with her on her return. 'Good' she thought. 'Now to surprise the good folk in the church.'

Sarah could hear the good folk singing their hymns and was glad she made it in time. She could tell when she looked over at Joe just how angry he was with her. His brow was furrowed in a frown, his mouth curled as he silently cursed her. He placed his hands on his hips, keeping his .45 and hunting knife in full view. Keeping her rifle trained on the men, she got off Star, quickly tied him to the hitching rail and pulled the dead wolf off the front of her saddle. The men started inching slowly towards her again.

Sarah dragged the wolf up the steps and entered the church. Before the men could get any closer, she closed the doors behind her, put the bar across the doors locking the good folk in and the trappers outside. Standing in the dark letting her eyes adjust to the dull light she could see Preacher Barnes standing in the middle of the aisle singing along with the rest of the good folk. When he saw Sarah standing at the back of the church, his voice caught in his throat, causing him to gag and stop singing. The rest of the singing gradually stopped when everyone turned and took in Sarah, her blood-soaked clothes and the wolf lying at her feet.

Joe watched Sarah as she walked up the steps to the church, dragging the wolf along with her. He was upset by the sight of her but wasn't about to interfere with what she was about to do. He watched her push open the church doors and enter. He heard the organ stop playing and the worshippers stop singing. The screams that followed told Joe everyone turned to see what the disturbance was. Sarah looked like the devil had just entered their church.

Women screamed in fright and the men cursed, children began to cry. Preacher Barnes crossed himself. "For God's sake Cole, what are you doing?" Preacher Barnes started to walk toward her. Sarah held up her rifle to stop him. "Stay where you are preacher!" He did as she bid and stopped where he was. Sarah stood behind the good folk standing in the pews. She knew how she must look. Holding onto the dead wolf by the back of its neck, she dropped her rifle on the floor next to her then quickly pulled out her hunting knife and clutched it firmly in her hand. The men tried to push their women folk behind them to protect them but the pews were close together and they were unable to move. No-one was able to leave because Sarah blocked their only way out.

Sarah looked around the room. There were children of all ages and some couples holding babies. Martha Henderson was holding her new baby boy whom Sarah could see wasn't much older than Thomas. Martha looked frightened, Dave her husband was fearful for his precious family, he had one arm around his wife, the other across the front of his son trying to protect them.

The only ones Sarah wanted left in the church were the women whom had been at the tea party and their husbands. Six women that were present that fateful day Sarah could see were all present in the church. Sarah told Preacher Barnes to go but he wanted to stay, he would not desert his flock in their hour of need, so Sarah let him stay.

"All you children get out!" she ordered. The children had to walk around her to be able to get out. The older, more brave children led the smaller children by their hands. When they got level with Sarah, some of them were crying hysterically. Sarah stood to one side and let them pass, then quickly pulled the door closed and barred it before the trappers or Sheriff Clementine could get in. "You!" she said pointing her knife at the middle-aged man and woman. "Henderson, take your wife and baby and go." The Henderson's hadn't been involved in Thomas's disappearance, they were at home with their baby boy Billy when Thomas disappeared. Dave Henderson ushered his wife and baby outside.

Sarah picked more people that weren't involved. Ham and Patrice, the Livery Stable owners, they had a daughter Sissy, two years younger than Sarah with them, Patrice nursed her other young daughter Lilly in her arms. Ham looked after Sarah's horses and Patrice befriended her when she was small. Doc and Gerda Harris were there too, they faithfully attended church every Sunday. They were unable to have their own children and when Sarah's mother Elizabeth died, Gerda became the mother Sarah never had a chance to get to know. Both couples attended her father's burial, they were good people. Sarah considered these two couples her friends. Sarah ordered all of them to leave.

When everyone whom had nothing to do with Thomas' disappearance had gone, Sarah pulled the wooden bar down over the latch and locked the doors. The only people left inside the church now were those women that attended the Finch's tea party, their husbands and the preacher. Sarah believed it was the men that planned Thomas's disappearance, but their wives were going to pay equally for their crime.

The remaining women became frightened. They sat down and sobbed uncontrollably. The men kept their eyes on Sarah, waiting to see what she would do next. "Stand up all of you!" Sarah demanded of the women. The women stood back up on shaky legs and faced her. The men held on tight to their wives to stop them from collapsing.

Everyone in the church heard the pounding on the church doors. "Cole! open the goddamn doors! ...Cole, open up!" Sheriff Clementine stood outside trying to get in. The four trappers stayed back while he pounded his fists against the heavy wooden doors. Sarah ignored him and commenced to skin the wolf.

Laying the wolf on the floor she proceeded to remove its skin while every now and then lifted her eyes to look at the men. She cut along its belly, slicing from its back legs to the front, then down each leg, peeling the skin off as she went. When the skin came off clean, Sarah lay the skin to one side, even though it was blood-soaked, the skin was worth money, she was going to take it to Fess at the Trading Post along with the other skins she collected at the South Side Camp.

Next, Sarah set about gutting the wolf. Stabbing her knife into the carcass, cutting between the back legs and pulling the knife along its gut until coming to the breast-bone. Working quickly, Sarah forced her knife through the bone, opening the carcass further. The congregation watched in horror as Sarah, using her hand, reached inside the wolf's body. While Sarah was bent over, Roy Connell tried rushing her. Sarah saw him, and quickly pulling her bloodied hand out of the wolf, held up her knife, stopping Connell where he was. "My knife can cut through man's skin much easier than it can wolf skin!" Sarah threatened. Connell's stomach began to rise when he saw the bloodied entrails from inside the wolf lying in a heap at Sarah's feet. He swallowed and stepped back to stand beside his wife.

Sarah reached back inside the wolf while keeping an eye on the group of frightened men and women. Some of the women started to sob loudly. One vomited and another fainted, her husband tried in desperation to hold the big woman up but had to give in and let her go. She slid to the floor where she remained, oblivious to what was happening to the rest of them. Some of the men continued to curse, others were too frightened to speak.

Sarah finished pulling out the entrails and threw them at Harold Finch. It was the Finch's house where the tea party was held and she was going to make Harold Finch and his wife Mary pay dearly for their part in taking Thomas. Everyone watched the mess sail through the air toward Finch and hit him in the chest. Finch gasped and stepped back, his arms instinctively grabbing what was thrown at him. The bloody entrails slipped through his hands and dropped to the floor. Sarah pulled out the stomach and tossed it high. It caught Finch's wife Mary on top of her head where it landed with a squish, causing blood to run through her hair and down her face. Sarah watched where it landed and almost laughed. Mary screamed really loud and put her hands to her face trying to wipe the blood away but instead smeared it over her face, making it worse.

Sarah cut out the heart and the lungs and threw them at Roy Connell and his wife Felicity. Connell got the heart, and his wife, because she was the one that closed the door on Sarah at the tea party, locking her outside, got the lungs in her lap. The women fell back on the seats, the fronts of their Sunday best dresses saturated with blood and guts. Sarah didn't mind them sitting back down, it made it easier for them to catch what she threw at them.

Several men who were Finch and Connell's friends tried to stay out of the mess that Sarah was creating, but their turn was coming. Their wives weren't so lucky, they were blood soaked along with Mary Finch and Felicity Connell. Preacher Barnes begged Sarah to stop once more. "For God sake stop this fiendish madness Cole, or you will burn in hell!" he warned. Sarah glared at him. "You think I'm not already in hell preacher!" Her knife dripped with blood, it splashed her face and pieces of flesh clung to her hair, her clothes were soaked with more blood than before. Sarah reached her hand inside the wolf and pulled out the rest of its innards, then threw the pieces at the rest of the frightened women and men, sending it flying around the chapel, landing on the pews and the walls. Slimy entrails landed in the laps of the women that were already blood soaked and crying. Pieces of gut and pieces of flesh clung to their hair. They all tried to get away from the mess, but they had to stay, there was nowhere for them to go.

While the pounding on the church door continued, Sarah began to cut up the wolf's body. She cut off each of the wolf's legs and threw them one at a time at each man. The first she threw at Finch, he caught it squarely on his chest, stumbled backwards and swore. Sarah thought his wife was going to be sick, she watched Mary's face pale as she heaved. She threw the other legs hard at different ones, each cursing her to hell, but Sarah ignored their curses, she had gone to hell and now she was on her way back. Sarah was almost enjoying herself watching these so called good folk suffer her wrath. She would see this through until she got Thomas back or was dragged off to jail. She quickly sliced through the wolfs neck, cutting through the backbone taking off the wolf's head and held it up. "Who would like this?" she asked, blood running down her arm and dripping off her already soaked sleeve as she held the head up high and looked around the room. No-one volunteered to take the head. Sarah threw the head across to Finch, he stumbled back against the seats as he caught the head in his hands. Finch was getting the brunt of Sarah's hatred, he became hysterical, cursing Sarah to the devil.

"For god sake Cole, stop this insanity!" Preacher Barnes again tried pleading with Sarah. Sarah pointed her bloodied knife at him.

"I'll stop this preacher …when these so-called god-fearing people…" She waved her knife at everyone around the room. "… *Bring my baby back!*" she screamed at the top of her lungs. The men continued holding onto their wives trying to stop them from collapsing. The women moaned and sobbed uncontrollably.

"*Give me my son!*" Sarah yelled at everyone. "If you don't return him...." she said calmly, holding up her knife and moving it in an arc around the room, pointing it from one to the other as blood dripped from the end of the blade. Sarah was filled with hatred for these people. "...You better lock your doors …because nowhere will you be safe!" The pounding on the door stopped and inside the church grew silent, no one dared utter a word.

"I promise you..." Sarah calmed her voice more and continued. "I will punish you for what you have done." She looked from

Finch to Connell and back again. These two men, Sarah believed, were the main instigators of Thomas's disappearance and she focused her hatred on them. "Rest assured Finch, and you Connell ...neither of you will know how, or when, but you will pay for taking my son!"

The loud banging commenced again and a voice raised in anger called. "*Open up Cole! ...let me in goddamn it!*" Sarah heard Sheriff Clementine and had no doubt there would be a lot of angry people after what she did here today. Sarah had to hurry and finish what she started. She continued to speak calmly to the now bloodied hysterical group.

"Don't think this is over..." Sarah paused, "...because until I get Thomas back, it isn't finished!" Sarah put her rifle over her shoulder, picked up the wolf skin, and holding her knife in her hand, pushed open the church doors and walked out, leaving a bloody mess inside the church. The sun was shining brightly as she stepped out on the steps, causing her to squint in the bright light.

The person Sarah saw first when she stepped outside was Sheriff Clementine, standing on the steps nearest the door when she burst out. He stepped backwards and almost fell down the steps when he saw her. "Jesus Christ!" he muttered as Sarah, dragging the wolf skin with her, walked down the steps. Joe and the other three trappers moved out of her way. Sarah untied Star and he followed her down the street and back to her camp. None of the men tried to help Clem get the church doors open nor did they try to stop Sarah as she walked away from the church.

Sarah heard the shouts, and the cursing when Sheriff Clementine and the trappers entered the church. She wondered just what Joe and the other men had expected to find. Did they think she slaughtered the people in the church? Maybe they had wondered that! but she wasn't that crazy.

A crowd gathered outside the church to watch the goings on. When Sarah came out, they quickly stepped back to get away from her. Sarah kept holding her knife in her hand as she walked along the street. Joe came back out of the church and stood on the steps looking after her. Shocked into silence at what she had done, he could only watch her go.

When Sarah got to her camp, she was shaking so much she felt ill, she only hoped what she had done was enough and would work. She wanted Thomas desperately and did the only thing she knew how to do to get him back. She had been gone a week, except for the rotten food that had been taken away, her camp hadn't been touched. When Joe realized she had gone, he enlisted his three friends as well as some of the other trappers to keep watch to make sure no-one went near her shelter. Joe searched the trails leading out of town to see where Sarah had gone but couldn't follow her. Snow quickly covered her tracks and he couldn't find in which direction she had gone. Joe had a promise to keep, and he would try to keep it no matter what Sarah did, even though it was getting near impossible for him and the other men to do. Sarah continually made it that way.

Sarah unsaddled Star and led him into the river. Standing in water up to the tops of her legs she washed the blood off him. While he frolicked, relieved the wolf was no longer on his back, Sarah sat down and washed the blood out of her clothes. The water was freezing, flowing down from the mountain bringing ice with it. Sarah let the water wash over her, wetting her hair to try and remove blood and bits of flesh that clung to it. She rubbed her hands over her clothes until the water around her ran red. "Come on Star, time to get out." Star came to her when she called and nuzzled her as she sat in the water. Sarah took him by the reins and led him up to the grass near her shelter. She rubbed him down with his saddle blanket before giving him his feed, then set about making a huge fire.

Sarah sat in front of the blazing fire waiting for her clothes to dry. While wondering what was happening up in town, Joe came walking down the trail towards her, a determined look on his face. Sarah didn't get up, she was wet and cold so stayed where she was.

"What do you want Joe?" Sarah had her rifle lying on the ground next to her with her hand resting on top of it. "Just what the hell do you think you're doing cutting up that wolf in the goddamn church and scaring everyone?" It would take a long time to clean up the mess Sarah made in the church. Joe's eyes scanned the area around the firepit. Sarah looked up at Joe from behind the fire. "I'm getting my son back!" Joe looked at Sarah's wet matted hair and sodden but filthy clothes. She looked pale and drawn, her face was still dirty, her eyes had dark circles around them, Joe could tell she hadn't been sleeping. "You won't get him back by doing crazy things like that, goddamn it!" Joe kept looking down at her. Sarah kept her eyes cast down at the fire, she didn't need Joe telling her she wasn't getting Thomas back.

Joe saw her rifle sitting on the ground beside her and kept a good distance between them, he didn't want Sarah taking any shots at him. He opened his coat and kept his hand near his gun. He wouldn't shoot her to kill her, but in her state of mind, he would have to do something to defend himself if she tried anything, he would just try to wound her, but only if he had to. "What you did just now isn't going to help you get Thomas back, you ought to know that."

"I did what I had to Joe." Sarah noticed how Joe was standing, keeping his hand close to his gun. She had never seen Joe take that sort of stance when he was around her. Joe would never hurt her, she knew that, he didn't promise her father to take care of her only to shoot her, that would be breaking his promise and Joe would never break his promise. 'That's good' she thought. 'I have Joe worried.'

"That was a stupid thing to do, frightening all those people like that, it isn't winning you any friends." Sarah looked up at Joe suddenly and snapped. "I don't need friends! I need my son! you won't help me, will you Joe? you won't interfere, will you? because of a stupid promise you made to my father, you could do something, if you really wanted to!" Sarah felt like crying, she loved Joe, he was the closest person to being a father to her since her father died, but she wouldn't cry, crying was a sign of weakness and she had to stay strong. "What can I do that I haven't already done Sarah? I've been out to talk to the Major and he won't budge, the boy is his grandson for Christ sake."

"Yes, he is his grandson, but that doesn't give him the right to take him from me." Sarah put her head down when suddenly remembering Frank followed her to the mountain, and how it must seem to everyone, the same as having taken him from his father. Major Hardy warned her he would make her pay for being with his son, and now he was punishing her by taking Thomas. Sarah kept her eyes focused on the fire as tears welled in her eyes. She swallowed them back and neither she nor Joe spoke for a long time. Joe stood there looking over the fire at Sarah. He felt sorry for her, and wanted to help her, but felt there was nothing he could do. He loved her like she was his daughter, even though he shouldn't, because of a stupid promise he made. Joe made to walk away and had taken a few steps back along the trail when Sarah spoke.

"I'm not asking you to do it for me Joe, you know I would never ask you for anything …do it for Frank ...and Thomas ...that way you wouldn't be breaking Pa's promise!" Sarah's eyes overflowed. "Do something for Frank ...and his son!" she sobbed, swiping her face with her hand. Joe turned and looked at her, she looked small, frail and ill. He wanted to take her in his arms and comfort her, to tell her everything would be alright, but he could never forget what she said to him on the mountain, remembering her saying she would never ask him for help, ever, and he had been devastated by her bitterness toward him. Joe walked back up the trail without saying a word.

Chapter Twenty-six

As he walked back up the trail his heart was heavy. After seeing Sarah come from the church, he went to her camp and there she was, sitting beside her fire, her face dirty and her clothes filthy, her once beautiful waist long hair now short and tangled. He could see she tried to wash the blood and pieces of flesh out of her hair but still it looked like it hadn't been washed properly or combed for the whole time Thomas had been gone. Joe kept his distance as Sarah requested the men do after Frank died, but he hated having to stay away from her, and now she had come to this. When he stood on the other side of her firepit he felt at a loss as to why Sarah would let herself get to this point in her life when so much had already happened. Major Hardy, the Finch's and the Connell's hadn't helped Sarah's situation either. By taking Thomas, it only made matters worse. He wanted to help her, if only she would swallow her damn pride and ask him. Joe spoke with Sarah across her fire, her voice was low, almost inaudible, but he heard what she said before he left her.

Joe hurried away from Sarah and stormed into the Ferguson House. He went straight to Garrett and Fergus who were sitting at the table drinking coffee and talking about what happened in the church. He felt he had to do something, the four of them sat on their hands long enough. Sarah was suffering and he had to help end her pain, he desperately wanted to help get Thomas back where he belonged. On his way back from Sarah's camp, he came up with a plan.

"Listen, I just spoke with Sarah." Garrett and Fergus put down their mugs and listened as Joe began to tell them what he wanted them to do. "Where's Will?" he looked around for Will but couldn't see him anywhere.

"He's over at the saloon, want me to go get him?" Fergus volunteered.

"Yeah, and hurry will you, I may have a plan to get Thomas back." Joe got up and poured himself a mug of coffee while Fergus rushed off to the saloon.

Will didn't like what happened at the church, but thought Sarah was within her rights to do what she did. No-one had a right to take her child from her. He laughed to himself at seeing the good folk covered in wolf blood when they came staggering out of the church. He knew what it was like to have blood and guts spread all over him after skinning wolves for a living. There was nothing he could do to help Sarah, so he left Garrett and Fergus and went off to the saloon for a drink and a game of Poker.

Fergus pushed his way into the saloon through the crowd of drinkers standing three-deep at the bar. The bar-room was packed with men all talking about what happened at the church. He spotted Will sitting at a card table toward the back of the room, a glass of whiskey in front of him and a hand of cards in his hand, four men sat around the table with him. Fergus rushed over and bent over Will's shoulder, bringing his head close to Will's ear. The four men sat back and watched as Fergus said something into Will's ear they couldn't hear. After hearing what Fergus had to say, Will threw down his hand of cards. "Sorry gentlemen, I've got something much more important to do right now." He leapt to his feet and followed Fergus back to the Ferguson House. One of the men sitting next to where Will had been sitting picked up Will's cards and looked at them. Will had four Ace's and would have won the game, he would have taken a thousand dollars off the table. Will folded, so the men shrugged and continued on to finish the game.

Joe waited until Fergus returned with Will. The four men huddled together at the table and Joe filled them in on his plan.

"It won't work Joe," Garrett said shaking his head.

"How we goin' to get near the bloody thing?" Fergus wanted to know.

"Any of you got any better ideas?" Joe looked at each man in turn. They were quiet while they digested what Joe suggested they do.

"We aren't interfering are we Joe? we won't be breaking the promise will we?" Will sounded worried as he thought about what they promised on the mountain fifteen years ago. They promised not to interfere with Sarah's life and here they were going to interfere in a big way. Even though Sarah was desperate, Will thought resorting to slaughtering a wolf in the church in desperation to get Thomas back wasn't going to work. It only served to scare all the town folk. He got the impression the town folk didn't trust any of the trappers anyway, especially Sarah. Harold Finch and Roy Connell had already been out to Major Hardy's several times to see if they could get Thomas back, but were unable to persuade the Major into handing him over, nor could the four of them persuade him. They practically begged him to give Thomas back and they weren't the kind of men to stoop to begging for anything, most times they would just take what they wanted and be damned about the consequences. But Sarah was becoming desperate, she needed their help and Will would do anything to help get Thomas back to her.

"We won't be breaking the promise Will, because we are doing this for Frank and Thomas, not Sarah." Joe got up and stood in front of the fire. Sarah put the idea in his head and this way he could help her without her asking, he thought her smarter than he gave her credit for.

"We should give it a try, maybe it will work, maybe it won't, at any rate it will scare the b'Jesus out of the Major." Fergus laughed quietly and the other men nodded in agreement.

"When do we do this Joe?" Garrett asked.

"Tonight."

The plan was set. All they had to do was wait until it was dark, then wait a little longer until the other trappers had gone to bed, then they would carry out their plan.

At midnight, while the town folk slept, the four men rode out. Heading west toward Major Hardy's ranch, they came to a gully where they tied their horses up to brush not far from the corral where they had seen the big bull being held. Creeping along the fence line, the men peered into the corral, but the bull was nowhere to be seen. Joe and Fergus went one way and Will and Garrett another. They searched several corral's before meeting up again back at the first corral where the bull should have been.

"Damn!" Joe whispered. The men huddled together inside the corral with their heads together discussing what to do next.

"Where the fuck is it Joe?" Will asked sounding disappointed.

"I don't fucking know!" Joe said angrily. "It was supposed to be here!"

"Jesus, this ain't going to work, not if we can't find the fuckin' bull!" Garrett's face was nearly up against Joe's. Joe pushed him back away from him.

"Get the fuck out of my face, he's got to be around here somewhere!" Joe crouched over and held onto the rail so he could peer through the fence, hoping to see where the bull was.

"Well it ain't fuckin' here!" Fergus said. "And keep your fuckin' voices down, someone might..." he was cut off before he could finish speaking.

"You men couldn't catch a fuckin' wolf if it jumped up and bit you on the fuckin' arse! you make a hell of a lot of noise creeping about," came a voice out of the dark. The four trappers jumped in surprise at being caught out. Four wild looking men in fur coats leant forward and peered through the fence.

Foley Andrews was leaning back against the fence, he put his cheroot in his mouth and struck a match. Joe and the other three men melted back into the dark as the match lit up the night around them.

Joe let go of the rail and stood upright. "Foley what the fuck?" Joe was disappointed they had been caught.

"What are you doing out here Joe?" Foley pushed his hat back on his head, kept his back to the fence, and one foot resting back against the post.

"We're tryin' to help Cole, that's what we're doin'...how about you Foley?" Joe knew Foley liked Sarah, he told him so the night he brought Sarah back from the shack, the night Frank had been whipped and he got the scar on his face.

"Now how the hell you trying to help Cole by being out here?" Foley turned his head to the men and whispered quite loudly. Joe didn't answer, he couldn't find anything to justify why they were there, they had been caught red handed on the Major's land. Foley thought he had a pretty good idea what the men were there for.

"You wouldn't happen to be trying to find a big black ...bull ...now! ...are you Joe?" Foley glanced around the yard making sure no-one else was around.

"What! no! hell ...no! we're just lookin' around ...that's all." Joe sort of sniggered when he answered, thinking he might as well make light of the reason they were there, they were caught anyway, he reasoned his plan was ruined before it had even started.

Foley wriggled his finger to indicate for the men to come closer. All together, the three men leant in close to Foley on the other side of the fence.

"If you happen to be creeping around ...quietly! ...over there near that big barn ...you just might come across what you are looking for." Foley threw his cheroot on the ground, pulled his hat back down to cover his eyes and walked off.

After watching Foley disappear out of sight, the four men crept over to the barn he pointed out to them. The trappers looked at each other, then trying their hardest to be quiet, made their way around to the back of the barn.

Joe thought Foley was going to put them in to the Major, but instead helped them. Joe was grateful for what Foley did for Sarah the night Frank had been whipped and here he was helping them again. Joe was sure Foley was more a friend than a foe. He was satisfied Foley wouldn't breath a word about them being there.

Locating the small side door leading into the barn, Joe stuck his hunting knife behind the steel bar holding the padlock to the door then, forcing his knife down hard, broke the bar off the wall. The men waited in case someone heard the noise. When no-one came to investigate, Joe pushed his big frame through the small door. Three, equally as big men, followed him inside. Lanterns lining the walls allowed the men a clear view of what they were looking for. They walked stealthily, trying to keep their boots from making a noise on the floorboards as they made their way along rows of stalls until they found the one they were looking for. Four men stood with their mouths agape in front of the biggest bull they had ever seen in their entire lives. Its long horns stuck out between the railings on either side of its stall. Will closed his mouth and swallowed. All four men seemed mesmerized by the enormous size of the beast.

"Holy jumpin' coyote, look at the size of it! it's even bigger when you're up close!" Wills voice boomed out in the empty barn.

"Shut up Will!" Joe cursed him quietly. The men suddenly became serious, this was serious business, what they were about to do could get them in a whole mess of trouble with the law, so they had better not get caught. Joe pulled out his knife, Garrett and Fergus followed suit.

"We have to do this quick, if that bull gets loose, he's going to kill us!" Joe did the talking and the men followed his instructions. Will pulled out his knife. 'The Major's cowhand was right,' Joe thought. 'The Major would make a fortune out of breeding animals like this.'

"Alright Will, Garrett, you get on either side, Fergus, you and I will be at the head." The men moved into position. Standing outside the stall they held their hunting knives up so each man could see the other man had his knife ready. For Joe's plan to work it came down to each man acting at the same time as the other.

"I don't want any mistakes, we have to do this right." Joe nodded to the men, then each man got into position, sticking their arms through the railings into the stall with their knife blades pointing toward the bull but not touching it. The bull stood motionless, not having any room to move inside the tight stall, its nose touched the front, it's rump almost touched the back wall. The four men stood ready.

"When I say three, we do it, Will, you right?" Joe couldn't see Will standing on the opposite side toward the middle of the bull.

"Yeah Joe, I'm ready," he whispered.

"Garrett?" Joe looked to his side and saw Garrett in position.

"Ready."

Joe peered over at Fergus standing opposite him and Fergus nodded.

"One," perspiration broke out on Joe's forehead.

"Two," the men moved their knives closer.

"Three!"

As all four knives plunged deep into the bull, the bull looked up in surprise. It tried to raise its head but its horns were stuck between the railings and it couldn't move. Joe stuck his knife in the side of the bull's neck, keeping himself clear of the horn's and pulled his knife down hard, tearing through the bull's hide and flesh and opening up a gaping hole. At the exact moment Joe's knife entered the bull, Fergus's knife was driven into the other side of its neck. Fergus and Joe pulled their knives down together and their cut met up under the bull's head. The bull reared for an instant, its eyes bulged then suddenly glazed over. At the same time Joe and Fergus slit the bull's throat, Will and Garrett drove their knives low into the beast's sides and sliced quickly from the front legs all the way to the back. The bull's sides split open and its innards fell out onto the floor of the stall. Its almost severed head stayed up, its long horns stuck fast, stopping it from falling. The bull was dead before the rest of its body hit the floor.

The men pulled their knives swiftly back and stepped away from the stall as a pool of blood and guts spread out and soaked the straw and the floorboards. The bull never made a sound. The men stood watching for a moment surprised at how easy it had been. Joe stepped back from the spreading pool of blood.

"Come on, let's get out of here!" He raced for the door and scurried out into the dark. Keeping himself low, he ran fast across the clearing until he was in the corral. Adrenalin pumped through his body making his heart race as he ran along the inside of the corral fence. Staying hidden in the dark, Fergus, Will and Garrett followed. Making their way to the gully and their horses without being challenged they spurred their horses hard and galloped through the dark back to town.

Foley waited in the dark and watched while Joe and his three friends were in the barn. He knew what they were doing. Feeling glad Joe had done what he did, he waited while they scrambled back to their horses. He didn't go anywhere near the barn, he would let someone else find the Majors expensive bull. He went back to the bunkhouse and reported that everything was as it should be. His guard duty was over for the night, he lay on his bunk and smiled up at the ceiling before going to sleep.

Chapter Twenty-seven

Dawn couldn't come quick enough for Sarah. She lay in her shelter under her furs and blankets wondering when someone would bring Thomas back to her. She did everything she thought possible to get him back, now all she could do was wait. She slept fitfully, keeping her knife alongside her in case anyone tried to jump her.

"Cole! hello Cole! ...you in there?" The day had not yet dawned when Sarah heard the voice. She swiftly jumped to her feet and gripped her knife firmly in her hand. Her pistol lay on the blanket beside her. She picked it up, shoved it down the front of her trousers, then staying inside, peered through the opening to see Sheriff Clementine standing outside.

"What do you want Clem?" Sarah called him Clem, the same as everyone in town that knew him did. He never minded when town folk called him Clem instead of Sheriff, it served to make him appear friendly.

"I need to talk to you Cole, come out of your shelter." Clem was in his late forties, his hair was greying and he had a limp from being shot while arresting a drunk, his leg played havoc with him, especially in cold weather. Sarah came out of her shelter and watched him rub his hand nervously up and down his thigh.

"I rode out to the Major's and tried talking him in to bringing the baby back." Clem was nervous, Sarah looked like she hadn't had much sleep and he wasn't sure after what she did in the church if she would do something to harm him when he told her what Major Hardy said. "What did he say?" Sarah asked him quickly.

"He said he wouldn't be bringing the baby back." Clem saw Sarah grip her knife firmly and went on. "Now don't you go doin' anything to folk like you did in the church, that won't get the baby back, Finch and Connell went out to the Major's with me and begged the Major to let them bring the baby back to you but they couldn't change his mind either, they did everything they could Cole."

"The baby has a name Clem!" Sarah said through clenched teeth. "His name is Thomas …Connell and Finch didn't do enough, if Thomas isn't back here by tomorrow *…they are going to pay!*" Sarah spat the threat loudly. Clem took a step back when Sarah raised her voice.

"You do anything Cole and I'm going to have to arrest you, you want another spell in the jailhouse?" Clem put his hand on the butt of his gun to show he meant business. "I don't want to arrest you, but I will if I have to, to protect the town folk …I know what you're going through," he added more thoughtfully.

"*You don't know anything!*" Sarah yelled suddenly. Clem was taken aback by her outburst. He had children, even though they had left home and were living in Moreton, he still cared about them and wouldn't like any of them to be taken from him. He didn't know what to say to appease Sarah, so he warned her once more not to do anything she would regret and returned to the jailhouse.

Sarah stayed awake the rest of the night, sitting at the firepit and loading it with wood to keep it burning. Instead of holding her knife or her pistol, she gripped her rifle, determined she would shoot anyone that came near her or her camp.

When the Finch's and the Connell's settled in for the night they nailed all their windows shut and bolted their doors. After what happened in the church and the threats Sarah made, no-one in town felt safe, they could no longer leave their windows and doors open like they used to. They weren't taking any chances Sarah would enter their houses and do something to harm their families. What Sarah did in the church succeeded in scaring more than just the Finch's and the Connell's.

Sarah waited all that day, sitting in front of her fire and kept her rifle in her hands, she trusted no-one. As the hours went slowly by, she kept waiting. Sheriff Clem came back to her camp once more and let her know more men had gone to the Major's begging him to give her Thomas. Connell and Finch had gone back too but failed to sway the Major. "He won't give up the ...er ...Thomas, I don't know what else to do for you Cole." Clem was beginning to find it all too hard to handle. He begged Sarah not to do anything. "Please, don't take this out on the town."

"They started it and I'm going to finish it." Sarah said without feeling. Clem walked away feeling defeated. Sarah had nineteen trappers that could back her, but if she started something it would fall on him to try to finish it, Clem was at a loss at what to do next.

Major Hardy wasn't swayed by any of the men that came out to his ranch asking him to give Sarah her baby. They rode away wondering what else Sarah could do to them when she learnt she wasn't getting her baby back. From now on they would have to lock their windows and doors and sleep with their rifles close to their beds to protect their families.

Major Hardy was furious when told what happened to his bull. He raced to the barn to find his expensive bull slaughtered and was determined to find out who did the deed. He wanted to punish the person who killed his precious bull and cause him to lose five thousand dollars. He questioned Foley endlessly. He had been on guard duty when the bull had been slaughtered and should have seen whoever it was skulking about. Foley swore he didn't see or hear a thing and he told Major Hardy he watched diligently all night. Major Hardy's prize bull almost had its head severed from its body, its sides were split open and its intestines scattered across the floor, the bull never stood a chance. Major Hardy knew, or at least thought he knew who was to blame.

He lost his son to Sarah Cole and now he lost to her again, but he had no real proof Sarah killed his bull, she wouldn't have been able to do it on her own, she had to have had help. She had a lot of friends around her and he thought any one or more of those men could have been involved in slaughtering his valuable bull.

The baby boy called Thomas was supposed to be his grandson. If he was, he figured, Sarah Cole would have been pregnant that awful stormy night he caught Frank and her at the shack where he whipped Frank by accident. Frank never said anything to him about her being pregnant. Major Hardy thought the reason Frank didn't tell him was because Frank knew he despised her. It became obvious to him Frank loved Sarah and she loved Frank in return. He knew Sarah would never let a trapper touch her, but she let Frank, and while living together on the mountain he made her pregnant. After giving everything that happened serious consideration, Major Hardy was beginning to regret his actions.

Major Hardy and his housekeeper couldn't get Thomas to stop crying. They did everything they thought possible for him. He didn't take too kindly to drinking full strength cow's milk, bringing it up each time he was fed, so they watered it down. Thomas drank greedily but then commenced crying again. He screamed when he was bathed and cried when they tried rocking him. Major Hardy wasn't getting any sleep. He had no choice but to take Thomas back to his mother where he belonged. This way he hoped, his grandson would be taken care of and perhaps he would occasionally get to see the boy. He regretted having lost his son and a valuable animal that was going to make him a lot of money, but he would arrange to take Thomas back to his mother the next day.

Sarah stayed awake another night, sitting by her fire and watching as the sky grew light. The morning dawned on a clear blue sky. She hadn't any sleep at all for several nights and found herself struggling, but she had to keep going, she wouldn't dare stop, not until she got Thomas back, or died trying. She went to the river and washed her face, fed Star his grain and made some coffee, then sat and waited. The day dragged slowly on, it reached noon and nobody had been to see her.

Sarah was beginning to wonder what else she could do to get Thomas back when a tall man came striding down the snow-covered trail toward her camp. She watched his demeanour as he approached. Sarah knew this man, he was one of Major Hardy's hired gun-hands. Even though he had a scar from his forehead to his chin Sarah thought him a good-looking man. He wore his coat open, his hat low on his head, his chaps hit his legs as he walked, the gun on his hip shone when the sun hit the metal, and he came striding toward Sarah with purpose.

Sarah didn't get up when Foley came to a stop in front of the firepit, choosing to remain sitting on the opposite side of the fire with her pistol down the front of her pants, her knife on her hip and her rifle on the ground beside her. Two full days passed since the wolf had been cut up and she had no knowledge of what was happening up in town. She picked up her rifle, lay it across her leg then holding her finger on the trigger, aimed it furtively at Foley.

"Cole," he said looking out from under his hat. Sarah felt sorry for Foley when he was whipped the same time as Frank, because he and his brother came back to the shack for her that night, making her grateful for their help. She liked both men, but Foley was still Major Hardy's gun-hand.

Foley stopped when he reached the firepit and looking down at her furrowed his brow. 'Damn,' he thought. 'She looks ill.'

"Hello Foley," Sarah managed to say. Her voice cracked and she was tired, she didn't know how much longer she could keep going.

"Hello Cole," he answered warily.

"What are you doing here?" she asked, keeping her rifle pointed at him.

Foley held his hand away from his holster when he saw Sarah holding her rifle aimed in his direction, hoping she wouldn't try to shoot him. He didn't want to have to shoot her. "Major Hardy is bringing Thomas back, you better get yourself up town, he will be here any time." Foley kept his eyes fixed on Sarah, waiting for any sudden move she might make with her rifle.

Sarah's ears pricked. Had she heard Foley right or was he just lying to try and get back at her for scaring everyone? "Are you telling me the truth, you wouldn't be lying to me, would you?" Sarah's eyes narrowed suspiciously, she didn't trust anyone, not even Foley.

"I'm not lying, someone slaughtered the Major's prize bull, he's had enough, he said you can have the kid back, come on, get yourself up to the street, the Major sent me on ahead to let you know he is on his way, now if you want your son back, you'll get yourself up there!" Foley's face remained stern when he told her about the Major's prize bull being slaughtered, he helped, albeit in a small way and was glad he done it. He stared down sadly at Sarah when he told her the good news about Thomas.

"I've been sent here to tell you, so you better get yourself up town ...now Cole!" Foley put his hands on his hips, feeling sickened when he looked around the camp. The camp was a mess, nothing had been cleaned up, this wasn't like Sarah at all, she was meticulous when it came to cleanliness. Sarah's horse was tethered to a tree and was feeding. 'Typical' he thought. 'Sarah would always feed her horse before she would feed herself.'

"Tell me again why I need to go up there?" Not believing what she heard, Sarah held her hand tighter on her rifle. Foley saw the action but kept his hands on his hips.

"Major Hardy is bringing Thomas back." He looked back down at Sarah, her face didn't change expression when he repeated the good news. Foley frowned, Sarah had lost her spark, she was always one for smiling and laughing with the men, that was one of the reasons a lot of men were in love with her, she was always happy when hanging around them, but not now, not now she had lost her reason for living.

Sarah had to be certain what Foley said was true. Her heart skipped a beat when she heard him repeat what he first told her, her back straightened and she became more alert.

She put the rifle down and stood up, her legs felt weak and she staggered. Foley let his hands drop by his side as Sarah wavered. "You alright?" he asked her softly. He felt sorry for her, she was the cause of the scar on his face but he didn't hold it against her. Even though she had been with Frank and had his baby, he still loved her. He was surprised at just how much he loved her and every now and then he let his feelings for her betray him.

"I'm fine, don't you go worrying about me none," she smiled sadly at him.

"I better get back, the Major is on his way ...just get yourself up town Cole." Foley turned on his heel and walked quickly back up the trail.

Sarah pushed her pistol further down the front of her trousers. She grabbed her rifle, and checking that it was loaded, found it to be empty. She laughed at herself for being so stupid. Foley could have shot her and she would have been too slow to have retaliated. Reloading her rifle, she now felt she was as ready as she ever would be to confront Major Hardy.

There was nothing Sarah needed to do at her camp. She quickly followed Foley up the trail, bringing herself to a stop in front of

Doc Harris's practice. Foley got on his horse and headed back along the road leading to Major Hardy's ranch.

While Sarah waited, a crowd started to gather on both sides of the street. Standing on the boardwalks under the shade of the awnings, staring and whispering amongst themselves and wondering what Sarah was doing standing in the middle of the street, her rifle at the ready.

Sheriff Clementine was standing on the boardwalk on the opposite side of the street to Doc Harris's practice and stepped off the boardwalk when he saw Sarah. Sarah didn't move, she stood stock still and stared up the street the way Major Hardy would come to town. Horse riders and wagons had to go around her to get past her.

Clem walked over to her. "What are you doing standing here like this Cole?" Sarah didn't look at him, she thought if she took her eyes off the road, she would miss seeing Thomas come back to her. Her gaze remained fixed on the end of the street when she answered. "I'm waiting for the Major, he's bringing Thomas back to me." Clem was shocked at Sarah's sudden revelation. "Are you sure of that?" he looked surprised and wondered if what happened at the church had made the Major change his mind. "I'm sure," was all she answered, her gaze remaining on the way the Major would enter town. Clem looked at the gathering crowd as people stopped to stare at Sarah.

Word travelled up and down the street that the Major was 'bringing Cole's baby back.' Doc Harris and Gerda came out of his practice to watch. Down the end of the street behind Sarah, Joe and the trappers, waiting for the Major's horses to come in to the corrals, came out of the Ferguson House and stood in a group and watched. Horses were quickly hitched to hitching rails, wagons stopped moving along the street, people moved out of the way. The street became deserted except for Sarah standing in the middle holding her rifle. Clem walked away from Sarah and stood to one side, ready for any trouble.

Joe walked up to where Sarah was and stood next to her. He looked towards the end of town where she was looking. Sarah told him the same as she told Sheriff Clem, that Major Hardy was bringing Thomas back to her. "Is that a fact? …I wonder what made him decide to bring him back?" Joe looked at Sarah, a hint of a smile on his face. Sarah glanced fleetingly at Joe then turned her gaze back along the street. Joe walked over to another group of trappers standing on the boardwalk outside the saloon and stood in front of them and watched. Joe, everyone knew, always watched.

The sound of horses and a wagon approaching made everyone turn their eyes to the end of the street where a buckboard came into view. Two men holding rifles rode along each side of it. Major Hardy sat up straight in his seat, a wicker basket lay at his feet, a tiny bundle could be heard crying as the wagon bumped along the dirt road.

Major Hardy's buckboard came rumbling toward Sarah. Foley sat tall in his saddle as he rode along on one side, Brady his brother, rode on the other. The two men had their rifles raised with the rifle-butts resting on their legs. Sarah raised her rifle and aimed it at the man in the buckboard. Foley and Brady sat on their horses and kept their eyes on Sarah. Sarah could hear Thomas crying, she wanted to run to him but held her ground, even so she could feel her legs threatening to give out on her.

A dozen trappers stepped out from where they were standing, and grouping together, stood a short distance behind Sarah. The three men coming down the street looked beyond Sarah and saw the men gathering. Foley and Brady could see they were outnumbered and hoped the handover would go without a hitch.

Major Hardy stopped his buckboard when he saw Sarah standing in the middle of the street pointing her rifle in his direction. He stared wide eyed at her. "Put down your rifle Cole, or I will turn around and go back the way I came." He spoke harshly, not at all fazed when he saw the trappers standing behind her. None of them would work anywhere in the county if any of them tried to interfere. Sarah didn't know the men were standing behind her in support of her.

Sarah lowered her gun and Major Hardy got down from the buckboard. She watched him reach back in and pick up a small bundle wrapped in a blanket. The crowd of onlookers remained silent. Joe and the trappers stood their ground, each man opening their coats to show they were armed.

Major Hardy walked toward Sarah carrying Thomas in his arms. She let him come close enough so that she could almost reach out and touch him. He stopped walking when he got close to Sarah and moved out from in front of her, letting Foley have a clear shot if Sarah tried to shoot him. Sarah raised her rifle again and pointed it at the Major's chest. Foley lowered his rifle and pointed it at Sarah, hoping she wouldn't do anything stupid. Brady left his rifle pointing up in the air. A dozen trapper's hands moved to hold the butt of their guns. "Put Thomas on the ground Major and step back!" Sarah's voice quavered when she spoke. Snow had turned to sludge from wagons and horses moving along the street.

"Well isn't that typical of you Cole …you want me to lay him in the mud! ...you don't mind a bit of mud, now, do you?" Major Hardy sneered at Sarah.

"Put him down Major" Sarah said, ignoring his snide remark, this time her voice firm.

Major Hardy bent down and lay Thomas on the muddy frozen ground, then straightened back up. "Once a dirty stinking trapper, always a dirty stinking trapper, you'll never change."

Sarah no longer cared what Major Hardy thought of her. "You can go Major." She kept her rifle aimed at him. But Major Hardy hadn't finished. "Be warned Cole ...I don't want you or your bastard son anywhere near my land." Sarah wavered, shocked when Major Hardy called Thomas a bastard. "Thomas is Frank's son …you would call your own grandson a bastard?" Sarah's eyes filled with tears, she still didn't understand why Major Hardy hated her so much, she hadn't hurt Frank in any way.

Major Hardy swallowed before answering. Looking at Sarah's tear-filled eyes, almost convinced him Thomas was his grandson, but wanting to believe otherwise, wouldn't back down, he couldn't, not in front of all these people, it would make him appear weak. "I don't believe that child is my grandson, as far as I am concerned …he's a trapper's bastard." Major Hardy inclined his head in the direction of the trappers. "Any one of those men could be his father." Joe, hearing the Major's remark, tightened his mouth in anger and gripped his gun until his knuckles went white. A lot of other men did the same.

Sarah almost lost control at the Major's insinuation she had been with one or more of the trappers. Her legs felt numb, she hadn't had much sleep in the last three weeks and could feel herself beginning to weaken.

Major Hardy could see Sarah wavering. She had suffered badly for the loss of her son, more so he thought than he suffered when Frank had been taken away from him as a small boy by his mother. But he wouldn't concede defeat, he had been a Major in the cavalry and was known for his tough exterior, he couldn't back down now, so went on with his charade. "You ever set foot on my land Cole, I will have my men shoot you on sight, that goes for your …son too!" Major Hardy stopped himself from calling Thomas a bastard again. He wheeled around and climbed back in his buckboard. Sarah stood fast and watched as Major Hardy turned his buckboard and headed up the street.

Foley took his time going, lifting his rifle and looking at Sarah, he nodded, a small hint of a smile on his face. Foley was relieved she hadn't tried to shoot the Major, there would be no bloodshed in Cedar Creek today. He looked over Sarah's head to where Joe and the trappers stood and nodded to Joe, Joe nodded back. Brady waited for Foley. The two men turned their horses and rode off after the Major.

Sarah waited until they were gone, then dropping her rifle on the ground, scooped up Thomas. Joe and the trappers raced up to her and crowded around. Will picked up her rifle. Thomas was crying loudly.

"I guess he needs a feed," Joe said above the noise of the men all talking at once. Sarah didn't speak, she couldn't, the lump in her throat threatened to burst, she knew if she cried, she would crumple to the ground and she didn't want to collapse in front of everyone. Sarah pushed her way through the crowd and went to Doc Harris. Doc put his arm around her and opened his door, then while pushing the men crowding around back, ushered her inside. "We'll take care of her Joe," Doc said and closed the door. "Gerda!" he called for his wife. "Heat up some water and make a bath for Sarah."

"I don't need a bath Doc, I just need to hold my son." Sarah knew how filthy she must look and how bad she smelt. "He needs a feed Sarah and you need to be clean for him to suckle at your breast, when was the last time you bathed?" Doc took her into their washroom and sat her on a chair. Gerda made Doc leave them alone while she tended to Sarah and her baby.

While Gerda poured the bath, Sarah continued to hold Thomas tight, letting her tears flow as she looked down at her tiny son lying in her arms. She vowed then never to let him out of her sight. But Sarah trusted Doc and Gerda with her life, she willingly handed Thomas to Gerda while she climbed into the tub. As she sank down into the warm water, she felt her body giving in to its warmth. Gerda bathed Thomas while Sarah quickly washed her hair and scrubbed her body until it was raw. Before dressing, Sarah let Doc check both of them over. Thomas was a little raw on his bottom but other than that he looked healthy. Sarah had lost weight but otherwise still in good health, going hungry hadn't hurt her, walking the mountain to trap and hunt had kept her fit. All Sarah needed now was some food and a good night's sleep. Gerda wrapped Thomas in a fresh blanket, she dressed Sarah in clean nightwear and put her to bed, then handed Thomas to her. Sarah wept softly while she watched him sucking hungrily on her breast. She held him close to her until he had his fill. After Sarah finished feeding Thomas, Gerda brought her in a bowl of vegetable broth and some bread, her appetite returned and she ate the food hungrily. That night, Thomas slept cradled in Sarah's arms in a warm bed.

Over the following days, Sarah heard about Major Hardy's bull being slaughtered, but she didn't hear who did it. It seemed no-one knew, or if they did, no-one would say. It was something Joe said that made her figure it was her four guardians. She couldn't get Thomas back by scaring the town folk with slaughtering a wolf. The trappers couldn't get Thomas back with their talk either. Knowing the bull cost a lot of money, Sarah figured they resorted to using other means. The Major, all Sarah was told, planned to breed up his cattle and make a fortune. But right there, the Major's plan had failed. Sarah also thought Foley may have played a big part in the bull's demise too. He seemed rather pleased when she got Thomas back, his smile when he left her in the street convinced her he had something to do with it. The Major needed to be punished for what he did to Frank and what he did to her, she was glad all of the men had done what they did.

As Foley rode back to the ranch with Major Hardy and Brady, he was happy. Sarah got Thomas back, he was in love with her and hoped she would realize he didn't mean her any harm. Maybe now Frank was gone he would stand a chance with her. He didn't mind that she had a child out of wedlock. Foley reckoned he could be a father to the boy and a loving husband to Sarah, if she wanted it. He just had to get the courage up to ask her to marry him. First, he had to give her time to mourn the loss of Frank and let her settle down to raise her son, then he would ask her.

Joe was happy their plan worked, it cost the Major dearly for what he did to Sarah. After what Sarah did at the church and what she said to him afterwards at her camp, he couldn't see any reason why he couldn't do something the same. The Major needed a lesson in that he couldn't mess with trappers, and the trappers had given him an expensive one.

Major Hardy was in deep thought as he steered his buckboard back to his ranch. He saw the state Sarah was in when he left Thomas with her. It was his fault the way she looked, and he felt he had done her an injustice by taking her son from her. Frank would never have forgiven him if he were alive. He missed his son growing up and missed him terribly right then but he didn't hold a grudge against Sarah, his son had been in love with her and he could see why.

Seeing Sarah standing in the street, he could have sworn he was looking at her mother Elizabeth, except Sarah was suffering, and all because of him. He made up his mind while riding along in his buckboard that Sarah would have been good for Frank. By the time he got back to his ranch, he was regretting the things he had done in the past and vowed he would try to make amends for them in the future.

While Sarah stayed at Doc and Gerda's for several days to recuperate from her ordeal, she vowed Major Hardy would never know his grandson.

Chapter Twenty-eight

Cedar Creek settled down after Sarah got Thomas back, although Harold Finch and Roy Connell still locked their doors and windows at night while Sarah was in town. The rest of the town folk relaxed, convinced she wouldn't do them any harm. During the day, Sarah avoided the Finch and the Connell's like they had the plague. Sarah remembered Frank saying he would avoid Millicent Crawley like she had the plague. Sarah hoped the Finch's and the Connell's would catch it. Although, Finch and Connell had small children, Sarah didn't wish the plague on them. After dark, she walked the streets carrying Thomas in her arms and humming a tune to soothe him, making sure never to pass by the Finch and Connell houses. Thomas settled down, happy to be in his mother's arms. Sarah continued to cause trouble with Crawley every time she entered his store for supplies and Sheriff Clementine continued to warn her, he would lock her up if she didn't behave herself. Sarah however, would never let Crawley forget what he had done to her and her Pa.

Joe talked to Sarah at length about going back to the mountain with them, and Sarah finally agreed it would be safer for Thomas if she rode with the men. The trappers, along with Sarah and Thomas, returned to the mountain each spring to keep hunting wolf for their skins.

Returning to Cedar Creek every winter, Sarah continued to make her camp on the riverbank below the Ferguson House. Joe kept trying to get her to move back in with them, arguing it would be much better for Thomas if she used the house as her own. But this Sarah refused, she was adamant she would keep camping on the riverbank, she wanted to remain independent and didn't want to inconvenience the trappers with her small child.

Thomas was three years old when Sarah had her first marriage proposal. Thomas sat in front of her on her saddle as she rode out of town to snare rabbits. While he leant back against her, she held her arms tight along both sides of him to keep him from falling off Star. Sarah liked to catch rabbits for their dinner and thought maybe today she could snare a few extra to give to the people in town whom she considered her friends. She set her snares out on the prairie and now all she had to do was wait for the rabbits to be caught. She lifted Thomas up on Star and climbed into the saddle. They rode a little way away from her snares to a stand of shade trees that grew along the riverbank not far from the ponds. Sarah made a fire and put her coffee pot on to boil, keeping her eyes on Thomas while he ran around playing. She laughed at his funny little antics as he picked up sticks and threw them, then watched as he ran and picked them up and threw them away again. Thomas was getting further away from Sarah when she spotted a rider coming out of the trees from across the river. The rider was heading straight toward them.

Sarah rushed over and picking Thomas up, carried him back to her fire. It didn't take her long to recognize Foley before he got to her, his horse being a tall black stallion. Foley sat straight in his saddle, his long legs rested comfortably down the side of his horse. His black hat had a silver studded band around it, and the sun glinted off his gun on his hip. Foley got off his horse, tethered it beside Star and came striding over to Sarah's fire. Standing on the opposite side of the fire he greeted her. "Hello Cole," he said looking at Thomas hiding behind her.

"Hello Foley." Sarah greeted him cheerfully, while Thomas held on tight to one of her legs, trying his best to hide from the tall man.

"What are you doing out here?" Foley dug around in his coat pocket but kept looking at both Sarah and Thomas.

"I'm trying to catch dinner, what are you doing here? why aren't you at Major Hardy's minding his precious cattle?" It hadn't taken Major Hardy long to find another five thousand dollars to buy himself a new bull and now his Longhorn herd was starting to pay off. Sarah didn't mind talking to Foley, but because he worked for Major Hardy, she kept him at a distance.

"Got a bit of time to myself so I thought I'd go for a ride that's all, didn't expect to see you out here," Foley lied. Like every other winter since Thomas was born, when he left the Major's ranch for a break, he hoped he would run into Sarah. He had something important he wanted to ask her. He knew she bathed at the ponds so he rode by there every day hoping she would be there. His heart skipped a beat when he came over the river today and saw her. He walked over to a tree opposite Sarah's fire and squatting, pushed his hat up on his head, got out his tobacco pouch and papers and started to roll a smoke. Every now and then he glanced over at Sarah, unable to get what he wanted to ask her off his mind.

"You're looking well Cole, you been keeping yourself healthy? …staying away from the Major's land?" he added while continuing to roll his smoke. Whether Foley meant to or not Sarah heard a note of sarcasm in his voice.

"I don't go anywhere near the Major's land, you know that!" Sarah didn't know what he meant about keeping healthy. If he meant keeping alive by staying off the Major's land then yes, she was keeping healthy.

"Yeah, I know, but I've seen you riding near the boundary sometimes, well, you know we got orders." He went quiet while he put his smoke in his mouth and lit it. Sarah was well aware of his and the other men's orders to shoot her on sight if she stepped foot on the Major's land. She tried not to go anywhere near his land, but it was hard to tell sometimes where his boundaries ended and the open range began, and she had never been back to the shack. For the past three years when she rode out to the ponds, she met up with Foley and it seemed to her he was looking for her. Foley liked meeting up so they could talk and have coffee together. Those days he rode away from her feeling happy they were getting along. Sarah was equally glad of his friendship and wondered if the Major ordered him to shoot her, would he go through with it. Sarah had a pretty good idea it had been Foley that spied on her when she was bathing with Thomas at the pond's when Thomas was a little over a year old.

Desperate to bathe and wash her hair, she rode out to the ponds with Thomas strapped to her chest. She tethered Star to the trees and set up her fire along with her coffee pot and mug ready for when she was finished. She carried Thomas down to the pond's, spread a blanket out on the ground and undressed him. After checking she was on her own, she undressed, then carrying Thomas, the cake of soap and her hunting knife out into the shallow pools, she sat down in front of a small waterfall. Thomas sat between her legs while she wet her hair and washed it, then she soaped herself up and splashed water over her body. Thomas waved his hands up and down in the water and splashed water everywhere, giggling loudly when the water splashed him. Sarah washed his curly hair and soaped him all over then washed him off. He laughed up at her when she tickled him with the cold water. When she picked him up and held him high in the air above her, he pulled his little legs up and put his fists in his mouth. He giggled really hard at his Ma holding him up high. It was at that moment Sarah felt someone watching them from across the river. She put Thomas under her arm, picked up her knife from out of the water and hurried back to the boulders where her clothes were. She grabbed her drying towel and wrapped it around her body, then stood up and looked across the ponds. Whoever it was that had been watching her was gone.

Thomas came out from behind Sarah's legs when Foley squatted down to make his smoke and was twirling around in circles in front of him. "You want coffee Foley? ...there's enough in the pot for two!" Sarah was leaning against a tree near her fire watching Thomas as he got closer to Foley.

"Sure, I'll get my mug." Foley stood up quickly and went to his horse. Foley was a solidly built man with broad shoulders and he carried himself straight when he walked. Sarah reckoned he was around twenty-five or twenty-six years old. She watched him as he got his mug and came striding back over to her at the fire. Foley held out his mug and while Sarah poured the coffee, he kept his eyes on her.

"Thanks," he said softly when she finished. Sarah smiled up at him and his heart quickened as he walked back to the tree and squatted back down with his smoke in one hand and the mug of coffee in the other. Thomas continued to twirl in front of him. Foley and Sarah watched as he squealed with laughter as he twirled, Foley laughed at Thomas's antics. "Say hello to Foley Thomas,"

Sarah said to Thomas. "Lo Foleee!" Thomas said cheekily. "Hello Thomas," Foley returned. "He's growing fast Cole," he said looking over at Sarah. "How are you getting on trapping now he's running around?" Foley was starting to ask questions about Thomas and Sarah wondered why.

"Yeah …it's alright, I don't do nearly as much as I would like, when he gets older it will be better, I'll teach him to hunt and he'll be able to help with my trapping." Sarah reflected on the fact her name was still on the bottom of the board at the Trading Post where it has remained since trapping on her own. She told Foley Thomas was a handful on most occasions and that he tired easily, finding she had to stop a lot to let him rest.

Foley finished his coffee and smoke and sat his mug on the ground. Thomas ran over to him and tried to get between his legs, nearly knocking Foley off his feet. Foley put his hand on the ground to balance himself and Thomas pushed his way right in against Foley's body. Unsure what to do, Foley put his arms around Thomas and Thomas lifted his tiny hands up to Foley's face, placing them on Foley's neatly trimmed beard and holding them there. "Lo Foleee," he said in his baby voice. "Hello again Thomas," Foley said while looking seriously down at him. Sarah watched the exchange between man and boy. Foley's face was close to Thomas's. Sarah's eyes opened wide when Thomas suddenly put his face to Foley's scarred cheek and kissed it, then before Foley could do anything, he darted out from between Foley's legs and ran back to Sarah. Thomas threw his arms around her legs and hugged her. Sarah didn't know who was the most surprised, her or Foley. Foley got to his feet quickly.

"Goddamn!" he drawled, as he paced back and forth in front of Sarah. Thomas peeked out from behind Sarah's legs and giggled. "I thought Thomas would be scared of me."

"Why would he be scared of you?" Sarah didn't see any reason why Thomas should be scared of Foley. Just because he had a scar didn't make him a man to be afraid of. Foley kept pacing back and forth in front of the fire, making Sarah believe there was something else on his mind. Since Thomas was born, she often ran into Foley out on the prairie. They shared her coffee and talked on friendly terms but today he seemed different, like he had something important he wanted to get off his chest. After Frank's whipping, although seriously hurt himself, Foley got her safely back with the trappers. It had been him that returned Star, and him, who came and told her the Major, after losing his bull, was giving Thomas back to her. It didn't matter he was hired to give the Major protection. At Thomas's handover he smiled at her and she knew then a bond had formed between them. Sarah is sure he helped whoever it was killed the Major's bull, but he has never divulged anything about that night. She would never forget what he did for her and was glad of his friendship.

"Why would Thomas be scared of you Foley?" Sarah asked him again.

Foley stopped pacing and faced her. "Look at me!" he said savagely, pointing his finger at his face. "If you didn't know me, wouldn't you be scared of me?"

"But Thomas knows you," Sarah reassured him.

"I'm damn ugly Cole, this scar on my face makes me goddamn ugly!" Foley said angrily.

"No it doesn't, you only think it does," Sarah said softly. Foley went quiet for a few minutes while he digested what Sarah was saying to him. "You don't think I'm ugly?" he asked after a time.

"No …I don't think you're ugly." It was the truth, Sarah never thought of Foley as being ugly, he was a handsome man. Gerda stitched his face up the night he had been whipped and she did a good job, the scar was visible but didn't overpower his features.

"Thanks Cole." Foley was relieved with Sarah thinking he wasn't ugly, he thought no woman in her right mind would want an ugly man like him as their husband. He needed Sarah especially not to think he was ugly. He went quiet again, while thinking about the day he was out riding the boundaries on the Major's land. Riding from the dry gulch along the river and coming down the opposite side to the ponds, he could see someone sitting in one of the pools near a small waterfall and so tethered his horse to a tree to take a look. Then, after making his way through the stand of trees to a spot hidden by thick undergrowth, stood behind a tree and recognized Sarah.

Foley watched Sarah sitting in the shallow pool of water right in front of the small waterfall, her naked body in full view. When she leant back under the waterfall to rinse her hair her breasts lifted further into the open. That was when he got a clear view of her, the water was cold making her nipples stand up like beacons. He felt a ripple of wanting course through him as he watched her soaping her body, running her hands over her breasts and down her stomach, finishing with washing between her legs. After Sarah washed Thomas, she picked him up and held him in the air, he heard the little boy squealing with laughter along with Sarah. They looked happy and he felt his heart start to race. He thought Sarah a beautiful woman, even if she did have a child, it didn't make one bit of difference to the way he felt about her. When Sarah suddenly looked up to where he was standing, he had to duck quickly back behind the tree and wait. Taking a chance to look back across the ponds he saw Sarah had picked Thomas up. He watched her hand go into the water and when it came out, she was holding her hunting knife. He smiled to himself, glad she was being cautious. If someone tried to attack her, she could get to her knife quickly and that person would be caught off guard. No-one would stand a chance against Sarah's sharp skinning knife. He wanted Sarah desperately, but would never try taking her without her wanting him, that wouldn't be right. He didn't mean to spy on her, but was glad it was him that came across her in the ponds and not someone else. A lesser man might have tried taking advantage of her sitting in the water completely naked. He watched her walk out of the water, her wet body shimmering in the sunlight as she walked across the flat rocks. He left Sarah at the ponds and rode back to the Major's ranch, keeping what he witnessed to himself.

"I want to ask you something Cole." Foley looked at the ground. He was nervous and found it difficult to come straight out and say what he wanted to ask her. Sarah folded her arms, waited for a moment then coaxed him to get him to say what he wanted to ask her. "Come on Foley ...what do you want to ask me?" she smiled, but the answer she got was not what she expected, taking her completely by surprise.

Foley started to pace back and forth, then swallowing said what was on his mind. "I want a family ...if I could marry someone like you,

I would be satisfied with my life." The image of Sarah sitting naked in the ponds was still fresh in his mind. He stopped pacing and went and stood in front of her. Thomas was sitting at her feet playing in the dirt. Foley was shy where Sarah was concerned, he squinted in the sun and looked at the brush around them, then reaching down pulled a piece of grass out and twisted it in his fingers then went on. "What I mean is …I don't want to marry someone '*like*' you Cole …I want *you* …marry me and let me take care of you and Thomas." Foley stepped in closer to Sarah, waiting for her answer.

Sarah unfolded her arms and looked up into his face, for a moment taken aback by him asking her to marry him and so didn't quite know what to say. "Foley! what did you want to go and say that for …goddamn it!" She was feeling completely overwhelmed and more than a little shocked, even confused to know why Foley would ask her to marry him. He paid a terrible price for helping her and she had never thought of him as anything more than a friend.

"I would be good to you and Thomas." Foley wanting desperately to kiss Sarah, but because her hand was resting on her knife hanging from her waist he knew to stay where he was.

"Foley don't …I …I …can't!" Sarah looked pleadingly up at him. She didn't want to hurt his feelings, she liked him, a lot, but she wasn't in love with him, or any other man.

"Why not …are you afraid of me?" Foley walked away and stood out in the open while he waited for Sarah to answer. His hat shaded his face, his body stood erect and his gun hung low making him appear to be a man not to be reckoned with. Sarah studied him for a moment, he was very tall, standing a good head and shoulders above her. She thought seriously about Foley's proposal. Could she take Foley as her husband even though she didn't love him? She thought not, it wouldn't be fair to him, he should have a woman that could love him in return, besides, she belonged on the mountain and would never stay in Cedar Creek, not for any man.

"I'm not afraid of you, it's just…" Foley interrupted her before she finished. "Well, what is it then? don't you want someone to take care of you? I'd be good to you, you know I would never hurt you, or Thomas." He stopped speaking and looking away for a moment, thought about what to say next, then out of the blue he shocked Sarah even more. "I love you Sarah!"

Foley finally declared his love for her, he looked down at his feet then looked up at her, relieved his feelings for her were finally off his chest. "I've loved you for a long time ...I think you know that already ...I can't see any reason for us not to be married." He kept looking at her, hoping she would say she loved him too. Sarah blushed, Foley was serious and she didn't know what to say. She studied his face while his light blue eyes stared back into her dark blue eyes, looking for some sort of acknowledgement.

"I like you Foley, but don't you see, I was very much in love with Frank, I won't ever love anyone like I did Frank ...you and me, we are friends, we will always be friends ...won't we?" Sarah waited while Foley digested what she was saying, hoping when she refused him, their friendship would remain intact.

"Yeah! well!" he said after a time, looking away then back again. "If you ever change your mind." To Sarah, Foley looked disappointed and sounded dejected. "Let's forget it for now." Foley didn't want to hang around after being rejected, so going to his horse, threw his mug into his saddlebag and climbed up into the saddle. Before riding away, he looked down at her. "I'll ask you again next winter Sarah, and I'll keep asking you every winter, maybe, one day, you might change your mind." He didn't smile, instead tipped his hat, prodded his horse with his heels, then rode away. Sarah watched him go. Picking Thomas up in her arms she sighed. "There goes a really nice man Thomas," then smiled. Thomas hung on tight to Sarah and watched the tall man on the big black horse as he rode off into the distance.

As far as Foley was concerned, asking Sarah to marry him just now wasn't going to be the end of it. He was determined he would ask her again next year and the year after that if he had to. He would keep on asking her until she gave in to him. He was very much in love with her and was sure given time, she would learn to love him. Right now, Foley figured, Sarah was too busy raising Thomas, she needed to be left alone to do it. When Sarah gets lonely, Foley vowed, he would be there for her.

Chapter Twenty-nine

As time went on, it got easier for Sarah to camp on the riverbank. Thomas had now turned four and they had been camping there every winter since he was born. But Joe wouldn't give up on getting her back in the fold. He argued with her again, insisting her room in the Ferguson House was still hers if she wanted it, and that she and Thomas needn't stay on the riverbank in the cold. Joe worried Sarah or Thomas, or both, may catch fever if they continued to camp out in the open. Sarah remained stubborn, refusing point blank to enter the house.

Even though the trappers helped get Thomas back, she wouldn't give in to Joe's demands. The trappers let her down when Frank died so she continued to keep the men at a distance. Sarah knew the four men would always be watching out for her, but still, she could never bring herself to forgive them for not stopping Frank from going to the High Country.

Sarah made do with what little she had, her camp was reasonably comfortable, sometimes it was cold, especially when it snowed, but all in all she liked being on her own. Thomas slept next to her under a blanket and thick wolf furs and Sarah made sure he was never cold. He sat with her at the fire and ate his meals, they went riding and hunting together. Thomas was never out of Sarah's sight and she always filled their days with fun. She loved Thomas with all her heart. When she looked at him, he reminded her so much of Frank, causing her heart to ache for what she had lost.

As Thomas grew, she saw Frank in him more and more, his dark curly hair, his cute button nose, even his walk mimicked Frank's. At night Sarah still cried herself to sleep whenever her thoughts turned to Frank, she was lonely, all she wanted was to be held and made love to.

There are a lot of men on the mountain and in town Sarah is friends with, and there are those that thought they were in love with her. Some had even begun to tell her how they felt. Foley Andrews proposed marriage to her last winter and again this year. She turned him down once more and he said he would ask her again next year and they both laughed about it. Foley rode away from her with a disappointed look on his face. He wanted her badly but would never take advantage of her. He respected Sarah for who she was and how she lived. But there were some men who thought they had the right to take what they wanted without asking.

Sarah put Thomas to bed, then sat in front of the fire until the late hours. Her thought's as she sat in front of her fire were mostly about Frank and what little time they spent together. She thought about her mountain too, and it was her mountain, she was born to it, she loved her cabin and being her own woman. She hated leaving the mountain each winter, letting her feelings for leaving show when she stomped around in the snow cursing to herself while angrily loading her packhorse.

She stood up and went to check on Thomas. The little boy was sleeping on his side, tufts of curly hair could be seen protruding out from under the furs. Sarah crept on her knees to his side and brushed his hair away from his face, then bent down and kissed him on his cheek. It was still too early for her to go to sleep, so she went back to her firepit and poured herself another mug of coffee. The night air was brisk, snow was not far off falling in Cedar Creek. Snow would mean she would have to build the fire up much more if she was to keep Thomas from getting cold. It also meant it was time to build another firepit closer to the shelter. The firepit would need to be built so the heat from the fire would radiate outwards, warming the inside of her shelter. First thing tomorrow she would take Thomas and collect firewood from along the riverbank, then get the new firepit sorted.

After finishing her coffee, she made her way back to her shelter. While undressing carefully next to Thomas and watching the little boy in case he stirred, she wondered when it would be time for her to separate where she and Thomas slept, thinking maybe next winter or the winter after that would be soon enough. Before removing her trousers quietly so as not to disturb Thomas, she removed one of her boots and promptly dropped it. Sarah grabbed the boot quickly and held it, waiting to see if the noise would wake him. When Thomas didn't stir, she removed her other boot, then finished undressing. The night air felt cool on her bare skin, by morning it would be a lot colder in their shelter, so she covered herself with a blanket then pulled the furs over her shoulders and fell asleep.

The first Sarah knew of the man was when his hand came in under the blanket touching her on her bare leg, his hand then slid up over her knee. She came wide awake and began fighting to stop the man from touching her, but the man's weight crashed down on her, pinning her down. She clung to the blanket keeping it between her and the man while she fought him off. The blanket the only thing keeping him from forcing himself against her bare body, but he was heavy and Sarah struggled. She didn't need to see his face, she could smell him. She knew it was Logan, the worst trapper that ever trapped on the mountain. Although he was only one of many men who thought they were in love with her, she managed to keep avoiding him because, while he thought he was being nice when saying rude things to her, she constantly had to ward off his advances. Now though his hands pulled at the furs trying to expose her. "*Get the hell off me Logan, you son-of-a-bitch, goddamn it, so help me, I will kill you!*" she screamed. "I'm goin' to fuck you Cole, and bitch…you're goin' to like it," he slurred drunkenly, his face close to Sarah's. Holding the blanket to keep herself covered, Sarah hit out with her fist, kicked her legs, and screamed while trying to get him off her. The strong whiskey smell on his breath overpowered Sarah as he tried to kiss her.

Logan had been drinking in the saloon and as the night wore on started to become boisterous. He and his partner Reeves had their heads together, laughing and making rude gestures. The four trappers, were sitting around a table with other men, drinking and minding their own business when Will thought he heard Logan mention Sarah's name. He leant over to Joe and told him what he thought he heard. Joe glared over at Logan and Reeves. He watched the two men closely to see if they mentioned Sarah again. Logan and Reeves had their arms around each other and were heavily intoxicated. Joe couldn't miss the rude gesture Logan made with his hand nor Reeves laughing at him. When the two men staggered out of the saloon Joe gave them a minute while he finished his drink, then stood up from the table and followed them outside. Logan and Reeves quickly disappeared into the dark. The four men stood on the boardwalk for a moment allowing Joe to check up and down the street to see which way Logan and Reeves may have gone. Stepping off the boardwalk, Joe headed down the street to the Ferguson House, walking fast, with Fergus, Garrett and Will following him. When they made the trail to the riverbank and Sarah's camp, they could hear Sarah's cries coming from her shelter. Garrett and Will grabbed Reeves when they saw him standing outside the shelter waiting for Logan. Reeves was quickly knocked to the ground with a sharp blow to his jaw from Garrett. Meanwhile Joe and Fergus reached into Sarah's shelter and took hold of Logan.

Logan's weight suddenly shifted as he was dragged backwards out of the shelter. Sarah heard the commotion outside. The dull thud of fists slamming into a body echoed along the river and into her shelter. Several more trappers came to the riverbank after Joe to see what was happening. The raised voices of four trappers in particular could be heard as they dealt with Logan. Sarah tucked the blanket around her body and held it tight. Fergus stuck his head into the shelter. "Are you alright Sarah lass?" The noise outside was becoming sickening, Logan didn't stand a chance of getting away from the four trappers. "Yes, I'm alright," Sarah answered. She quickly checked Thomas was still sleeping before she stepped out of the shelter to see Joe beating Logan to a pulp. Logan was a nasty trapper, even the other men tried to avoid him, he cursed every second word and said vile things about everyone, he liked to pick fights and fought with anyone that he thought was in his way, his partner Reeves wasn't much better.

Logan was taking punishing blows to his head and body. He kept falling to the ground and Joe kept pulling him to his feet. "*Get up you son-of-a-bitch!*" Joe's fist connected with Logan's mouth that was already bloodied, knocking him to the ground again. Sarah watched Joe pick him up again and prepare to take another swing. "*Joe!*" Sarah screamed. Joe's arm stopped in mid-air when he looked over at Sarah. "Did this bastard touch you Sarah?" Joe kept a firm grip on Logan. Logan swayed as he tried to keep his balance, his eyes were already swollen and almost shut.

"He tried, but he didn't get far, let him go Joe." Sarah was sickened to see the beating Logan was taking and she wouldn't be the cause of a man's death. "Did he touch you in any way?" Joe said more sternly. Garrett, holding onto Joe, tried to get him to let Logan go. Sarah knew what Joe was asking her. If she said Logan put his hands on her in any way inappropriately, Joe would keep hitting him until he killed him. Joe was a huge man, the power behind his fist a force to be reckoned with, he could fight any man young or old and come out the winner, and Joe was of the belief he was Sarah's sole protector.

"No Joe, he didn't touch me." When the voices of the men grew louder, Thomas woke up and started to cry. Sarah turned away, leaving the men with Logan and hurried back into the shelter. "Shush honey, everything is alright, mommies here, shush baby," she soothed cradling Thomas in her arms and rocking him. Joe let Logan go and he fell in a heap on the ground.

"Get him out of my fucking sight!" Joe said to the men. Will and Garrett hauled Logan to his feet and began to take him with them. Before they got very far, Joe threatened Logan. "You ever lay a hand on Sarah again, I will kill you, you hear me, you fucking snake, don't you ever try that again!" He angrily pointed his finger at Logan. Will and Garrett dragged Logan away. Reeves staggered after the men as they took Logan along to Doc Harris's practice to get his badly battered head and body seen to.

Still furious when he went to Sarah in the shelter, Joe pointed his finger at her. "You listen to me!" seeing Thomas was cradled in her arms Joe quietened his voice down. He was angry at Sarah but didn't want to frighten Thomas. "You don't go sleeping like you do out here in the open, you get some goddamn clothes on!" Sarah rocked Thomas to try and get him back to sleep, she didn't look at or answer Joe. Joe went back to the firepit to wait until Sarah got Thomas to sleep. Fergus and Joe were sitting in front of the blazing fire when Sarah came out with her blanket wrapped tightly around her. "I should be able to sleep how I want without those goddamn barbarians coming here thinking they can get into bed..." Sarah didn't get to finish speaking before Joe started to admonish her. "Those barbarians are men, Sarah, they have needs, they have wants and they are well aware of how you sleep and of you being on your own!" Joe looked up at her.

"You think you can sleep like that and not have men want a piece of you, goddamn it Sarah, wake up and look at what you are doing!"

"What am I doing Joe? I've always slept like this." Sarah stood defiantly in front of Joe and Fergus. Fergus kept his eyes averted.

Joe, seeing the blanket wrapped tightly around her and secured under her bare arms, stared at her. Sarah isn't the child they had taken in when her Pa died, she is an attractive woman and now she has a child, men are noticing her a lot more. It hasn't escaped Joe how all the men look at her. Sometimes he is confused by his own feelings toward Sarah, he loves her, but his feelings for her are different to other men. He harbours a secret concerning Sarah that no-one, only he and Calahan, Sarah's now dead father knows about. Joe is glad he has feelings for Kathleen, the owner of the saloon, she keeps him satisfied every winter, and trapping keeps him occupied on the mountain.

"I damn near killed him goddamn it, you want to be the cause of a man's death for a fuck is that it? is that what you want?" Joe's voice rose, not in anger but in dismay.

"No!" Sarah pulled the blanket around her more tightly and looked at the ground. A shiver suddenly ran through her body.

Joe stood up. "I can't always protect you," he said softly.

"I'm not asking you to protect me Joe!" she suddenly snapped back at him.

"Goddamn it! Sarah, if I hadn't been here tonight what do you think would have happened, huh! what?" Joe held out his arms in bewilderment when he questioned her. Sarah looked away from him. "Alright Joe, from now on I'll protect myself." Joe looked over the river then back at Sarah. "How the fucking hell will you protect yourself from men like Logan?"

Sarah was trying hard to ignore Joe's lurid words, she knew he cursed when he was with the men but he rarely uttered the words around her. "I'll sleep with my knife next to me."

Joe stared at Sarah in amazement. "I thought you already slept with your knife!" Sarah just stared back at Joe and didn't answer. Joe decided then he had had enough trouble for one night, he turned and made his way around the firepit, Fergus stood up to go.

"You keep it handy for next time Cole." Joe yelled over his shoulder as he walked off. "Because there will be a next time! come on Fergus," he said to Fergus walking beside him. "Let's get out of here."

It was a week before Sarah saw Logan again. He was standing outside the saloon with a group of other men. Sarah walked along the opposite side of the street passing the group on her way to visit Patrice at Ham's Livery. She looked up under her hat at Logan. His face was battered and bruised, he had two black swollen eyes and a split lip, Joe had broken his nose. As Sarah got level with the men her right hand went instinctively to her knife. She carried Thomas on her hip and her arm tightened around him. Logan turned when he saw Sarah and pushed his way angrily past the men and went back inside the saloon. The friendship Sarah once thought she had with Logan had been destroyed, she could no longer trust him.

Over the next eight years, a lot of men proposed to Sarah, some serious about their proposals, others not so serious, and Sarah was getting tired of them all. Whenever she went walking, cowhands and farmhands alike thought it funny to yell their proposals from where ever they happened to be. "Hey Cole! how about you marry me!" they would call out, some hoping she would say yes, others just laughing. To warn them off, Sarah would pull out her gun and put a shot above their heads, making the men duck for cover. If she happened to be outside the saloon or standing close by, her warning worked best if she took out her hunting knife and held it pointed towards them. They soon shut up if they thought she would cut them. But if either Joe, or one of his three friends, or all of them, heard any of the men making fun or rude gestures to her, they would be taken aside and warned to shut up. That man or men, usually ended up with a black eye or a busted lip for their trouble.

Chapter Thirty

As another winter drew to a close on the mountain and in Cedar Creek, spring arrived in all its glory and passed by just as quickly. All of the trappers made a safe journey back to the mountain and were in the middle of the wolf trapping season. The hot summer sun bore down on the mountain and the trappers discarded their heavy winter coats. Thomas was growing up fast. Occasionally when Sarah and he were out checking Sarah's traps or hunting, they came across the four trappers. The men greeted her and Thomas happily and shared their coffee with them. Those times Garrett liked to help Thomas learn about the many different plants and animals that habitat the mountain. Thomas loved learning all about the mountain too. While in Cedar Creek after Thomas had become old enough to attend school, Sarah made him go so he could learn to read and write. It was the only time Thomas was ever out of her sight. She didn't want him growing up being as ignorant about the world as she. Sarah had never been taught to read, or write, and felt it was too late for her to learn, but she wouldn't stop Thomas from learning. At first, Thomas didn't like school. Most of the other children didn't like him either, simply because he was the son of Sarah Cole. They reckoned she was the meanest trapper that ever came off the mountain, because she scared their parents by cutting up a wolf in their church and throwing bits and pieces of it at them. Although the other children didn't like him, Thomas put up with their torments and took to learning with a passion, becoming adept at reading and writing. But he was always happiest when it came time to go back to the mountain with his Ma and the trappers.

Summer passed and autumn arrived, cooler days and cold nights were upon them. The trees were losing their leaves, it would not be long before winter returned, bringing heavy snowfalls with it. Sarah was busy preparing to leave the mountain. She had a good many grey skins to take to the Trading Post but still wasn't satisfied. When she passed several trappers hunting along the trails, their horses loaded with skins, it was obvious she would have no chance at winning The Pot with the men outdoing her with their kills again this year.

One night not long before it was time to leave, Sarah and Thomas were sitting at their table having dinner. Dinner was always a noisy affair with Thomas chatting constantly about whatever he and his Ma did that day, but this particular night Thomas was unusually quiet.

"What's wrong Thomas?" Sarah looked across the table at Thomas sitting with his head down concentrating on his meal.

"Nothing's wrong Ma." He didn't lift his head and Sarah didn't press him to tell her what was on his mind, but he continued to eat without his usual banter.

Once dinner was over, Sarah cleared the table while Thomas was in the washroom getting ready for bed. When he came out and headed straight for his room without saying goodnight to her, she folded her arms in front of her and stopped him before he could disappear into his room. "Thomas, before you go to bed you need to tell me what's wrong." Sarah watched him closely, her instinct was sharp, she knew something was bothering him, the tension in the cabin was overpowering. Thomas looked at his Ma with her arms folded and knew by her stance that she knew he was bothered by something. "It's nothing Ma, honest!"

"Thomas!" Sarah said almost too sternly. She had never raised her voice to him and she would not start now, even so, she kept her arms folded because she wasn't going to let him go to bed with something on his chest. "Say it Thomas, let it out!" Thomas walked over to Sarah. He had to say what was on his mind whether it hurt his Ma or not, she wasn't going to let him go to bed and he was tired. "Ma ...when is my birthday?" Sarah was taken aback by his question, she unfolded her arms and looked into Thomas's eyes. "I don't rightly know what day it is …all I remember was, the leaves were falling from the trees and the nights were starting to get cold."

Sarah's eyes became distant. Thomas could see he made his Ma sad by asking her to remember the day he was born. Thomas knew the story about how his Pa died and how his Ma gave birth to him on the riverbank.

Sarah thought about the day Thomas was born. It had been about this time of year. Frank hadn't long died up in the High Country. She remembered she couldn't have cared less about the mountain right then, she had lost her reason for living and slept most of the time. The night she gave birth to Thomas she was alone on the riverbank until Joe came along. Fergus, Will and Garrett were there too. The four men stayed several weeks with her, helping out with chores and making the lean-to more secure, keeping her horses out of the weather, staying until she was on her feet and able to do things for herself. Then she became nasty and made them leave. "Maybe you should ask Joe or Fergus, they would remember the day, or ask Will or Garrett ...I remember they buried your Pa not long before you were born." Sarah felt like crying at the memory but managed to hold back her tears. "Why do you want to know that?" Thomas put his arms around Sarah's waist and hugged her. "It doesn't matter Ma." He looked up into her face. "It was just something I was thinking about." Sarah embraced Thomas, holding him close to her, then just as suddenly pushed him away. Thomas watched her go to the wooden chest in the alcove and get out the little black bible that once belonged to Frank. She got her pencil and brought them both back to the table. "Sit down Thomas." Sarah sat down and opened the book to the back cover. Thomas sat opposite his Ma and watched what she was doing.

"These crosses are for every year you have been born, I don't know how to read or write, you know that, but Frank showed me how to mark off the days, well, these are your years ...one cross for each year." Sarah drew another cross in the book for this year and turned the book around to Thomas for him to see the crosses she so proudly marked each autumn.

"How many are there?" Sarah asked him.

Thomas counted the crosses. "There are eleven!" he announced proudly.

"Well!" Sarah sighed. "You are eleven years old today, or yesterday, or maybe tomorrow." Thomas got up and going around to Sarah, put his arms around her shoulders and hugged her. "I love you Ma, now I know I'm eleven years old." Thomas let her go. "Ma ...some of the kids at school well, some of them had birthdays last winter, and some of them got gifts, like Billy Henderson, he got a new pair of boots and Lilly Hammond, she got a new dress, but it doesn't matter, I just wanted to know how old I was, that's all." Thomas moved to his bedroom door. "I'm glad I know ...goodnight Ma." He went into his room and closed the door. "Goodnight Thomas." Sarah was left sitting at the table holding Frank's little black bible.

She turned the bible over to the front and opened the cover to where Frank wrote his last words to her. She couldn't read the words but knew what they said. Joe read them to her that first time when he handed her the book after they came to tell her Frank had died. Thomas read them to her too, now that he was attending school in Cedar Creek. Sarah tried to keep her tears back, she swallowed then wept silently. She cried this time every year when she put a cross in the little bible. She put the book back in the wooden chest then lifted out the silver timepiece that once belonged to Frank. Sarah remembered Frank taking his timepiece out of his pocket and announcing to her it was time for lunch or dinner or bedtime. She remembered hitting him on his arm and laughing at him, he would laugh back at her for laughing at him. She didn't need a timepiece to tell her when it was time to eat or sleep, she didn't need it to tell her when it was time to make love to Frank. She ate when she was hungry, slept when she felt tired and made love to Frank when the urge took hold of her, and that was often.

Sarah smiled through her tears and cried some more at her memories. Thomas heard his Ma crying. He didn't mean to make her cry, he loved his Ma dearly, she was good to him and he would never do anything to hurt her. He rolled over and pulled the blankets over his head, then cried softly until he fell asleep.

Sarah rummaged around in the chest until she found a faded piece of brown paper she saved from the Christmas gifts Frank had once given her. The paper was old and some of it was faded and brittle, she tore a piece off and went to the pantry. She found the roll of twine and cut a length, then gathered the ingredients to make a cake. While Thomas slept, Sarah baked.

The cinnamon cake came out of the oven and onto the plate perfectly. When it cooled, Sarah wrapped the cake in a cloth, placed it in a large pot with a lid then stored it in the pantry. She found a long candle and with a sharp knife cut it down to size, then went to bed.

The next day went along as usual. Sarah rose at dawn and got the fire going, she made hotcakes for their breakfast while Thomas got himself washed and dressed. After eating and tidying up the cabin, Sarah and Thomas went out to check Sarah's traps. Sarah carried the small rifle under her arm. A rucksack on her back held freshly baked bread, and a tin of beans for their lunch. It also held Thomas's drawing book, some pencils and a box of bullets for the rifle. Sarah wore her hunting knife around her waist. Thomas carried a small hunting knife strapped around his waist and two canteens of water over his shoulder.

They came up on Sarah's traps after two hours trudging through the forest and on up the mountain behind their cabin. A lone wolf was caught by its front leg in one of Sarah's traps. Standing off to one side looking at the wolf, Sarah readied her rifle to shoot it when she suddenly held the rifle out to Thomas.

Thomas's eyes went wide with surprise. "Go ahead Thomas, you shoot it!" Sarah looked seriously at him. He stared at his Ma, she couldn't be serious he thought. "I ...I don't know Ma!" he stammered. This was too much for Thomas to suddenly have the rifle thrust at him. "You are eleven Thomas, I was about your age when I learnt to shoot, it is time for you to learn." Thomas's eyes welled. "I can't shoot it Ma!" he said, bursting into tears and heading back the way they came. Seeing Thomas upset, Sarah shot the wolf herself. She didn't question why he was afraid to shoot the wolf, she knew he would learn in time. Thomas stopped when he heard the shot and came back. Sarah proceeded to skin the wolf while Thomas wiped his eyes and watched her. "Thomas, one day you are going to have to do this, we will start you off with learning to shoot at trees and ...thing's!" Sarah took the wolf skin off clean. Thomas didn't want to kill living things, not even wolves, he much preferred to draw them in his drawing book. But he went along with his Ma because she knew living on the mountain was dangerous and knowing how to shoot could save his life.

Sarah started Thomas off shooting at the empty bean can. She sat the can on a fallen tree and told Thomas to shoot at it. At first his bullets didn't hit anything, then he shot the fallen tree several times. "Don't pull the trigger, squeeze it gently." Sarah kept her voice calm while telling Thomas what she wanted him to do. Sarah helped him aim the rifle straight and on his next try he sent the can flying off the log. Finding the rifle easy to hold, Thomas was pleased with himself, and so shot the can twice more. Sarah was pleased with Thomas too, he only needed a few guiding remarks before he picked up how to hold and aim the rifle properly as she had done when she was his age. The next thing she would have to teach him, was how to shoot a wolf and skin it.

At dinner that night Sarah was the one that was quiet. Thomas talked incessantly about his shooting the can. He hadn't hurt anything by learning to shoot the rifle at a can and he was pleased about that. Thomas saw the small rifle leaning against the dinner table next to his Ma. He knew his Ma never left her rifles lying about, she always made sure they were safely stored where she could get at them. Her Pa's long rifle was hanging over the fireplace and the small rifle was always left by the front door if it was needed in a hurry, but tonight the small rifle was by his Ma's side. Thomas didn't say anything about the rifle, his Ma knew best what she was doing.

When dinner was nearly over Sarah got up from the table and went to the pantry. She got the cake out of the tin and pushed the thin candle into the centre of it. She lit the candle and came out of the pantry carrying the cake. Thomas's eyes lit up, his face broke into a wide grin. He was so much like Frank when he smiled Sarah thought. As she proceeded to walk carefully to the table so as not to let the candle go out, the flame flickered, but stayed burning. Sarah put the cake on the table in front of Thomas and sat down opposite him. "Happy Birthday Thomas," she smiled. Thomas's eyes began to water, Sarah could see a tear threatening to fall. Thomas blinked and wiped his eyes with his fingers as the tear ran down his cheek. Sarah felt a lump forming in her throat. "Make a wish, then blow out the candle so your wish can come true." Thomas closed his eyes and took a moment to think. Sarah watched him closely. Sometimes when she watched him, she could see little things that reminded her of Frank. His hair was a thick mass of black curls, just like Frank's had been. Sarah loved Thomas, he was a gift from Frank to her. Sarah could almost feel herself losing control of her emotions and struggled to hold them at bay. To get her mind off thinking about Frank, she watched candle wax run down the side of the candle and pool on top of the cake.

Thomas made his wish. But his wish wasn't for himself. It was for his Ma to find someone just like his Pa. He wanted a man that would love his Ma as much as his Pa had. He wanted that man to make his Ma happy again, just like she had been with his Pa. He opened his eyes and blew out the candle, then Sarah let him cut the cake. He cut a large piece for himself and a smaller piece for Sarah.

Thomas was licking his fingers when Sarah reached for the small rifle. "Thomas, I want you to have this." She lay the rifle on top of the table and slid the gun towards him. "But Ma, what will you do for shooting wolves?" he picked up the rifle and held it. "I will use Pa's rifle, I have used it before, it's a good rifle." She wiped a tear from her own eyes while Thomas studied the rifle that was now his. "Thanks Ma."

Sarah had one more surprise for Thomas. She reached into her pocket and brought out a small brown paper wrapped parcel tied with twine, a bow of twine festooned the little gift. Sarah held onto the parcel and studied it for a moment before sliding the parcel across the table to Thomas. He leant the rifle against the table next to him and eyed the small gift. "Happy Birthday Thomas," Sarah said again as a tear ran down her face. Thomas pulled on the twine and undid the bow, then tearing the brown paper away, was left holding the silver timepiece that once belonged to his Pa in the palm of his hand. He was never allowed to touch the timepiece, he could only look at it if his Ma was holding it. "You don't have to give me this Ma, the rifle is enough." Thomas could see how upset his Ma had become when she gave him the timepiece, fresh tears rolled down her face.

"I want you to take care of it for me," she said as she drew back a sob and wiped her eyes with her sleeve. "You have to promise me you will take care of it, a promise made here on the mountain isn't to be taken lightly Thomas ...once the promise is made you can't break it, it is forever ...besides, your Pa would want you to have it ...take care of it Thomas."

Sarah waited for a moment before finally speaking. "Can you make the promise?" Sarah's voice was low, almost a whisper. She remembered her Pa telling her Joe, Fergus, Will and Garrett promised him they would each teach her to hunt and to ride, they promised too they would take care of her. They made their promise on the mountain and the four men had tried their best not to break it, but sometimes it was hard for them. Sarah knew she made it difficult for the men to keep their promise. When Frank died, she tried to release the men from their promise but Joe told her it wasn't her promise to break. The four men were still keeping their promise to her Pa.

Thomas wanted to keep his Pa's timepiece, he thought it a wonderful gift. "I promise." Thomas went around the table and hugged Sarah tight. "I love you Ma, I promise you I will take care of it." Sarah held him to her. "Can you tell the time Ma?" he asked while keeping his head resting on her shoulder.

"No, I can't, I don't need a timepiece telling me when to eat or sleep, maybe you could get Will or Garrett to teach you next time we see them."

Thomas went to bed happy, he had his very first birthday cake and his Ma gave him two gifts. He thought the timepiece was the best. It was his Pa's and now it was his. He lay in bed and opened the silver cover. When the timepiece chimed, he smiled, studied the numbers on the dial and the hands that pointed to them, then held the timepiece to his ear and listened to it ticking. Thomas read the inscription on the inside of the silver cover softly to himself. 'Frank Happy 16th Birthday Love Mother.' His Pa had been given the timepiece for his birthday, and now, his Ma had given it to him for his birthday. Thomas whispered, "I promise to take care of it for you Pa." He made a promise to his Ma that he would take care of her precious timepiece, and he made a second, solemn promise to his Pa.

Thomas carried his very own rifle when they went out trapping and was feeling more responsible and grown up now after receiving such treasured gift's. Sarah was surprised when they came up on her traps and found four wolves caught in them, it was a good days trapping, but Sarah was worried. Four wolves meant there could be a wolf pack on the hunt. She told Thomas to keep watch while she skinned her kill. Thomas scanned the forest in front of him from where he sat on a fallen log. Sarah had her head down, her hands were bloody, her knife moved swiftly through the wolf's skin. While Thomas watched his mother intently as she peeled the skin loose, he became oblivious to the wolf lurking behind him. Sarah stopped her knife in mid cut when she sensed something nearby and glanced over at Thomas sitting on the log. As she removed the skin, she saw the wolf lurking about but still some distance off. Sarah looked over to where her rifle rested against the trunk of a tree. Having moved away from it after skinning the first three wolves, her rifle she could see, was too far away from her to reach. If she made a sudden move now, it wouldn't take long before the wolf attacked Thomas.

"Thomas." She said keeping her voice low and steady as she instructed Thomas on what to do. "Get up slowly and walk toward me ...don't run, just walk ...and cock your rifle." Thomas stood up. "Why Ma?" he laughed.

"Don't be scared honey ...but there is a wolf behind you." The smile disappeared off Thomas's face. Sarah held up her hands to keep Thomas calm. "It's still a good way off, but you need to move slowly ...now!" Sarah stood up, her bloodied knife held up in her hand. She would run as fast as she could to get to Thomas if he were to come under attack, but she thought she may not get to him in time. Thomas stepped away from the log and cocked his rifle, then started to walk slowly toward Sarah. The wolf sensed the two-legged animal start to move away from it and moved closer. Thomas was taking furtive steps when his foot suddenly slipped on damp ground, causing him to stumble over thick grass and loose earth. Sarah saw him stumble, the wolf did too and became more alert. Sarah's eyes darted quickly to the wolf.

When the wolf saw Thomas stumble, its head went down, its bristles stood up along its back and it bared its teeth. The wolf growled long and low then made its quick decision to attack and raced towards him. "*Thomas turn around and shoot!*" Sarah screamed at the same time she raced toward Thomas, her bloodied hunting knife held ready to strike. A look of sheer terror crossed Thomas's face. There was no time to question his mother, he turned as he stumbled to see the wolf come charging toward him. He didn't have time to take aim. He lifted the rifle and fired, hoping to scare the wolf off. His bullet hit the wolf in the chest, its head hit the ground. The wolf skidded along the grass and stopped dead in front of Thomas. Sarah got to Thomas but wasn't needed. Thomas stumbled backwards toward Sarah. Sarah grabbed hold of Thomas and held him.

"Ma, I killed it! I killed the wolf!" Thomas's heart was pounding in his chest.

"If you hadn't killed it, it would have killed you …how does it make you feel?" Thomas stepped up to the dead wolf and kicked it, Sarah followed him. "It's not as bad as I thought."

Sarah was pleased with his answer. "You want to skin it?" she smiled and held her bloodied knife out for Thomas to take.

Thomas looked horrified at her. "No Ma! ...you can do it!" Sarah laughed.

That day Sarah made Thomas her partner. Thomas killed his first wolf and it was a good skin. Sarah couldn't put a skin in to the Trading Post that wasn't her own kill, but if she had a partner she could. Thomas had to be included if she wanted to take part in winning The Pot.

A month passed since Thomas shot his first wolf. While out hunting once again they met up with the four trappers. Sarah sat at their fire and they let her share their coffee while Thomas sat with Garrett. Although Sarah and the four men were getting along fine, she still kept them at a distance but never stopped Thomas from having a friendship with the men, just like she had when growing up on the mountain. After all, it wasn't Thomas's fault what happened to Frank.

Thomas told the men it had been his birthday and that his Ma gave him her rifle and his Pa's timepiece. Garrett took out his own timepiece and taught Thomas how to tell the time. Joe looked at Sarah when Thomas told them about his birthday and getting the gifts. Sarah shrugged her shoulders at Joe. "They are his Pa's things and he should have them ...I've still got Frank's bible." Joe noticed how Sarah became sad, her eyes were downcast whenever she spoke of Frank. Joe let the moment pass after Thomas told them about him shooting the wolf. The four men were pleased when Thomas told them about his kill and that now he was his Ma's partner. After spending several hours together relaxing and talking the men headed back up the mountain to the High Ridge Camp and Sarah and Thomas headed back to their cabin on the Low Ridge.

Thomas didn't like to take the timepiece with him when they went out trapping and hunting, he worried he might lose it or it would get broken, although he liked to carry it in his pocket when he was home at the cabin.

Sarah sent Thomas out to bring in an armload of firewood for the fire. He picked up several blocks of wood and remembered he had his timepiece in his shirt pocket. He was afraid carrying the armload of wood against his chest would break the timepiece so he took it out of his pocket, reached up and sat it on the floorboards of the porch, then went back to get his load of wood. He carried the wood inside and packed it in the wood-box next to the fire making several trips back to the woodpile. After finishing his chore, he was lying on his bed with his drawing book and pencils scattered around him when he suddenly remembered he left the timepiece out on the porch. He raced out to the porch but couldn't find the timepiece anywhere. Hurrying down the steps he searched the ground around the bottom of the porch where he thought he sat the timepiece for safe keeping. When he couldn't find it, his heart began to race. He knew he sat the timepiece up on the porch so it wouldn't get broken but now it was gone.

Thomas was devastated, he made a promise to take care of his Pa's timepiece and now he had lost it. He went to his room, sat on his bed and went over in his mind what he had been doing to have misplaced it. He knew he sat it on the porch. "So, where is it?" he asked himself. "Maybe it fell through the floorboards and is under the porch." Thomas raced outside and down the steps where he loosened a few boards under the porch, clambered in and searched around, but it wasn't there. He didn't know what he was going to do or how he was going to tell his Ma he lost the timepiece she had entrusted to him. His Ma was going to be upset and madder than a trapped wolf. Knowing Sarah would be upset, Thomas didn't want to have to face her. He scurried out from under the porch and ran to the lean-to to hide. Sitting in a dark corner in front of Star, he pulled his legs up in front of him, wrapped his arms around his legs and bent his head down on his knees, his sobs becoming loud gasps.

It was almost dark and dinner was ready. Sarah called for Thomas but he didn't answer. She called him again but still there was no sign of him. Sarah had been busy getting dinner when Thomas ran out of the cabin behind her. She shrugged her shoulders and went back to preparing their meal. Thomas always ran whenever he was excited and Sarah took no notice until she called him and he didn't answer. Looking for him was a chore in itself, there were so many places he could be. Sarah walked down to the river first. Thomas sometimes played along the riverbank, even when she told him to be on the lookout for wolves. He wasn't anywhere down there. She searched the old cabin in case he was hiding from her, he wasn't there either. Next, she checked the outhouse, Sarah called out, but there was no sign of him. The last place to search was the lean-to, she thought maybe he would be in with the horses as he sometimes liked to sit and talk to Star. Sarah often thought Star may have understood every word Thomas said to him, horse and boy seemed to have an affinity with each other. When she came to the door of the lean-to, she heard him sobbing. She opened the door and found him sitting in the dark. "Thomas whatever is the matter?"

Thomas didn't answer, instead he sprang to his feet and ran past her back to the cabin. He raced to his room and threw himself face down on his bed. Sarah came in behind him, sat on the edge of the bed and waited a few minutes while he continued to sob. "Thomas, did you lose something?" Thomas sat up and threw his arms around her, he had no choice but to tell her he lost the timepiece. "I'm sorry Ma, I was sure I put it on the porch." Sarah pushed him away and dug in her pocket. "Is this what you lost?" Sarah held up the timepiece for him to see. Thomas was relieved when he saw it, he looked at Sarah in confusion with red swollen eyes. "I didn't lose it Ma ...you took it ...didn't you?" His eyes brimmed with fresh tears, afraid his Ma would take the timepiece back because he had broken his promise.

"I picked it up and brought it inside to teach you not to leave it lying about." Sarah handed the timepiece back to Thomas. "Now, why don't you keep it in your box of treasures instead of carrying it about, it will be safe there and we won't mention it again." Sarah didn't console Thomas, she felt he needed to learn a valuable lesson in that making a promise on the mountain was not to be taken lightly.

Thomas never carried the timepiece on him again, when he wanted to know the time, he got it out of his box of treasures, looked at it then put it back where he knew it was safe and he couldn't break his promise.

Chapter Thirty-one

The day for leaving the mountain arrived too soon. The journey down the mountain was made a little easier now Thomas was able to ride one of their horses by himself. Leading one of their packhorses, Thomas rode down the trail behind Joe. Sarah pulled along the packhorse carrying her skins and rode along behind him. Fergus, Garrett and Will along with the rest of the trappers that came by Sarah's cabin made their way through the pass to the caves without too much difficulty. This year, the heavy drifts of snow blanketing the pass seemed to have built up more along the sides of the trail. Joe commented on how easy the trail was after they made their camp in the caves. He only hoped when they reached the bottom of the trail, getting past the wolves that congregated around the base of the mountain would be just as easy.

Joe was disappointed, the wolves were as bad as they had always been, coming out from the forest in packs to chase their horses. The trappers bunched up as they made their horses race away from the pursuing wolves. Keeping Thomas in the middle of the bunch for his protection, Sarah rode on the outside where her horse could have his head and carry her along steadily. Her packhorse raced along behind Star, it's long tether tied to Sarah's saddle-horn so she could keep her hands free to shoot at wolves that ran in close beside them. When the rest of the wolves gave up the hunt and disappeared back into the forest, the trappers were able to stop and skin their kill. Sarah skinned several wolves herself, adding to her final tally of skins for taking part in The Pot.

Sarah had a good lot of skins this time round, outside the Trading Post her name was written halfway up the board. Some of the trappers hung around afterwards to congratulate her and

Thomas. Sarah laughed and joked with the men and thanked them. After going to Morley's bank to put their chits in their accounts and get some money, Sarah and Thomas went to Crawley's store to get their supplies. Crawley and Sarah had another argument with Sarah storming out but not before taking hold of a vegetable stand just inside the door and tipping it over, causing a mess on the floor. It would take Crawley hours to clean up, what with potatoes and onions rolling all over the floor and disappearing under shelves. Sarah was pleased with herself. Sheriff Clem gave her a stern warning, he didn't abide trouble in town, telling Sarah she would spend a night in one of his jail cells if she didn't stop causing trouble. Although, now he was getting used to having trouble with Sarah and Crawley going head to head with yelling vile remarks back and forth every time Sarah went to the store to get supplies, Sarah couldn't help herself, she ignored Clem's advice. Sarah and Thomas made their usual camp down on the riverbank and the next time Sarah and Thomas went to Crawley's store, Sarah sniggered when she noticed the vegetable stand had been moved away from the door.

Samuels, one of the men that hung back at the Trading Post to congratulate Sarah for beating a lot of the other trappers was standing next to Sarah at the corral fence. They peered through the railings together as they watched Garrett working a horse. The mood was a happy one, everyone was in high spirits. They all got off the mountain and past the wolves without any incidents and they all had been paid well for their skins. Samuels and Sarah were talking about Garrett and the horse he was breaking when Samuels suddenly changed the talk between them to marriage. "I've been meaning to ask you something Cole, since you came to live with the trappers all those years ago ...I've been wondering if …well …if you were ready to get married ...I mean now that Frank..." Before he could go on, Sarah raised her eyebrows and interrupted him. "I haven't given it any thought Samuels, Thomas has taken up all of my time." Sarah looked up at Thomas sitting on top of the fence to see if he overheard her and Samuels talking. Thomas appeared to be taking more interest in the trappers breaking in the horses than listening to them. But Thomas was listening. Thomas was just like his father, stubborn and very strong willed. He had his own personality, and was adamant when telling Sarah he didn't like shooting or trapping wolves, saying he would rather draw them in his drawing book and write about them in his journal rather than kill them. Sarah tried her best to get him to change, but he insisted he didn't like to kill living things so she gave in and let it go. Thomas was a good listener, even though he appeared not to be paying attention to what was going on around him, he was paying careful attention, because he didn't like to miss anything. Samuels asking Sarah about marriage just now made her think of Frank. Sometimes she still missed him, but she hadn't wanted any other man to take Frank's place, resigning herself to raising Thomas on her own.

'Why Samuels, why would you be asking me that?" she turned to face Samuels when he addressed her. "I just thought I might um…you know …I'd like it if you would marry me." He smiled at her. "I'm not such a bad catch and I would take care of you and Thomas." Hearing Samuels ask his Ma to marry him, Thomas peered over the fence at Samuels. Thomas didn't mind Samuels. Out of all the trappers baring his four uncles, the rest of the trappers didn't know how to stop cursing and fighting, but Samuels, Thomas hardly ever heard him curse, and he never saw him get into fights. Thomas thought his Ma could do worse, but he also knew his Ma would not marry anyone from the mountain, and another thing, Foley Andrews asked her to marry him every year. He was from Cedar Creek and she wouldn't marry him, so he couldn't see his Ma marrying Samuels.

"I'm not ...I don't ...I mean!" Samuels wasn't the first trapper to propose to her but she was having trouble putting how to let Samuels down gently into words. She didn't mind Samuels, he was a pretty decent man, he didn't curse much, at least not when Thomas was around, and he had a nice smile. But as far as being a trapper, he was just like the rest of them, he didn't wash very often and he got involved in fights. Sarah decided she wasn't interested in marrying him or anyone else. She just wished the men would stop asking her to marry them all of the time. At that moment Sarah made up her mind to ask Joe to have a word with the men to try and stop them from proposing to her, it was becoming monotonous. "No, Samuels, I don't want to get married, I'm fine the way things are." Samuels was disappointed, but accepting what Sarah said, tipped his hat and walked away. As Sarah watched Samuels go, she thought him not a bad sort of man. She looked up at Thomas. Thomas was looking down at her. They both shrugged their shoulders, then laughed.

Planning on taking Thomas to the Blackberry Patch to pick Blackberries to make a pie and some spread for her and Thomas's hotcakes, Sarah left Thomas still up at the corrals with Garrett and Will, while she went back to their camp to get a bag to put the Blackberries in. She also felt it time to take Star for a run.

Doyle and Reece were sitting on the steps of the Ferguson House when Sarah came walking up from the riverbank. Both Doyle and Reece were aware Sarah had a lot of suitors. Everyone in town knew Foley Andrews proposed to her every winter. They often laughed about it over a drink at the saloon. But that didn't deter Doyle or Reece. While Sarah was back at her camp getting the bag for the blackberries, their partner Samuels came back from the corrals and informed his friends he had proposed to Sarah in the hope she was ready to choose someone to marry her and become a father to Thomas, only to tell the two men she rejected him. Still feeling dejected Samuels went off to the saloon with some of the other trappers to drink his fill and try to forget about Sarah for this winter. He thought he might not ask her ever again, unlike Foley whom would never give up asking.

Doyle stood up when Sarah drew closer to the two of them. "Howdy Cole," Doyle said with a smile. "Howdy Doyle." Sarah looked over at the two men and gave them a smile, unprepared for what followed. "How about you marry me Cole ...look at me, I'm as good a man as you'll ever get!" Doyle grinned stupidly at Sarah and held his arms out wide for her to see all of him. Doyle was a big man, his gut stuck out over his trousers, he had unruly hair and a really wild looking bushy beard covered his face. Reece, sitting on the steps listening, jumped up suddenly and shoved his partner out of the way. "He ain't what you are looking for Cole, I'm the better man!" Reece was the complete opposite to Doyle, a tall thin man with no hair growth whatsoever on his head. The two men started to argue and spar with each other over who Sarah should marry while Sarah dropped the smile from her face and gripping the handle of her knife, glared at them. Joe when he heard the two men's loud voices, came out of the Ferguson House and stood on the porch. "What's going on Sarah?' Joe looked questioning down at the two men. Doyle and Reece stopped their fooling about as soon as they saw Joe. Both men held a fear they would be in serious trouble with Joe for making fun in front of Sarah. They looked at Sarah expectantly, and waited to see what she would say to Joe. “Nothing Joe.” When Sarah looked up at Joe her face was serious. “They were just …foolin.” Joe leant on the railing and looked up the street. “Well, you two men ought to get on up to the corrals, they could use you up there.” Joe slapped his hand on the railing, nodded to Sarah and went back inside.

Sarah started to walk away from Doyle and Reece and head up the street. Both men ran along and caught up to her. “Thanks Cole,” Doyle said. “Yeah, thanks Cole,” Reece echoed. They both knew if Sarah wanted too, she could have Joe give them both a black eye or worse some broken bones. All three walked up to the Livery together where Sarah stopped outside. “Just don’t go proposing to me anymore, I wouldn’t want Joe hurting you two.” Sarah looked sternly at each man when she warned them off. Doyle and Reece dropped the smiles off their faces. Sarah laughed suddenly at the serious looks they were giving back to her. She liked both men and knew they were only funning with her. When they realized Sarah was only joshing, the two men’s faces broke out in wide grins. They slapped each other on the arm and raced on up to the corrals.

To Sarah there is only one man that comes near to what Frank had been like, but Foley has nothing to offer her, they are friends, nothing more. She used to hate leaving the mountain each winter, but these last few years she looked forward to coming to town. She likes it when they meet up out at the ponds. She likes it when he asks her to marry him. So far, he has managed to propose every year since Thomas was three years old. Even though she keeps telling him no and he rides away feeling rejected, they still remain friends. She can have a decent conversation with him without feeling he is just after her for what he can get. She isn’t naïve, she is certain other men propose to her in the hope they can bed her. Like Logan, he hasn’t proposed to her since Joe beat him up after he thought he could take what he wanted. But he still hangs around slyly in the off chance she may change her feelings toward him.

Each year when Foley and she meet out on the prairie where she is rabbit snaring, they share her coffee, and every year she takes longer to refuse his proposal, making him think she is slowly falling in love with him.

The last time Foley asked Sarah to marry him was this winter when Thomas was eleven years old. The school teacher got herself married and left town with her new husband. School has been suspended until the town can get a replacement, so this day Sarah and Thomas went out snaring rabbits together.

Foley rode up to where Sarah built her fire. Her pot of coffee was steaming but there was no sign of her. He tethered his horse next to Sarah's horse Star and another horse that made him frown. It looked to him as though Sarah wasn't alone. He walked through the trees and down the track leading to the ponds, glancing around as he went. He got quite a shock when he came across Thomas standing on the track with his rifle in his hands aiming at him.

"Stay where you are Foley, Ma's bathing, if you try to get past me, I'll have to shoot you!" Thomas gripped the rifle tight as he made his threat.

"Sorry Thomas ...I'll …just ...wait up here." Foley pointed over his shoulder back the way he came. He looked at Thomas standing poised with a look of determination on his face that told him Thomas was serious. Foley walked back up to the fire and waited. Thomas wouldn't shoot Foley, he didn't like to shoot wolves and certainly would never shoot a person, but he had to keep Foley from seeing his Ma bathing in the ponds. He was relieved when seeing Foley disappear back to where they had their fire going.

A few minutes passed before Thomas, with Sarah following closely behind came walking up the track. Sarah's wet hair hung down her back, her shirt was still unbuttoned past her breasts, causing Foley's heart to quicken when he looked at her. Sarah quickly did up her buttons and looked up at him as she came to the fire. "You want some coffee Foley? …there's enough in the pot for ...three!" she laughed because each time they met she usually said there was enough in the pot for two, but Thomas was with her today. "Yeah, thanks Cole." Foley went back to his horse to get his mug.

Thomas put down his rifle and held out his mug along with Foley letting Sarah fill them. Foley studied Sarah while she concentrated on pouring their coffee. Her hair was drying nicely in the warm sunlight. Being sheltered amongst the trees from the cool winter wind blowing across the prairie, Sarah's hair looked soft, like silk and Foley had a sudden urge to reach out and run his fingers through the glistening strands. But he thought it best not to try, Sarah had her hunting knife strapped around her waist, besides that, Thomas was with her. Thomas sat down on a log and watched Sarah and Foley as they stood beside each other talking. Foley asked Sarah about trapping and Sarah asked Foley about cattle drives and horse breaking. Thomas watched them smiling at each other as they talked. Sarah told him she and Foley were just friends, but he could see they liked each other, a whole lot more than they were letting on. There was something happening between them, Thomas could see it.

Foley asked Thomas how his trapping was coming along too. Thomas told Foley he left trapping to his Ma, telling him he would rather write in his journal or draw in his drawing book.

Sarah shrugged her shoulders "What can I do ...Frank liked to draw." Foley said writing and drawing wasn't going to feed them but he said it in a lighthearted way. They continued to talk until Thomas packed up his and Sarah's rucksacks and carried them to their horses. Foley knew this was the moment for him to ask Sarah to marry him.

Foley put his hand on the trunk of the tree Sarah was leaning back on and leaning in close, looked into her dark blue eyes. Sarah noticed how Foley kept his beard neatly trimmed close to his face. His scar had faded to a thin line running from his forehead, down his cheek, then disappeared into his lightly greying cropped beard on his jaw. A long strand of dark hair hung over his forehead almost in his eyes. Sarah thought at that moment when her heart suddenly gave off a quick flutter, she could possibly marry him.

"Well Cole ...will you marry me?" Asking Sarah to marry him each year when they met on the prairie was getting easier for him. He would ask her to marry him and she, he already knew, would say no. He expected the same answer every year, nothing he said would sway her to change her mind.

Sarah was a good deal shorter than Foley, causing her to tilt her head back to look up into his face. She looked into his eyes while he leant toward her. He was standing so close, if they moved just a fraction, they would be able to kiss each other, but it didn't happen. Foley would never take liberties where Sarah was concerned, he wouldn't touch her, not unless she invited him to. Foley took his hand off the trunk of the tree and straightened up when Sarah didn't answer him right away. Sarah was deep in thought, she liked Foley a whole lot and over the years they had become closer, able to talk easily with each other. Foley wasn't hard to look at either, she liked looking at him. Sarah liked him more than she cared to admit, but something held her back from saying yes to his proposal.

Foley still didn't have anything to offer her except maybe himself, and he worked for Major Hardy, a man she despised. Foley didn't have anywhere to live except with the other cowhands in the bunkhouse at Major Hardy's ranch, and Brady, his mute brother, would always be there alongside Foley wherever he went.

"I'm sorry Foley," she said looking sadly into his eyes. She didn't like to turn him down again, but she couldn't picture them being married. "My answer is no."

Foley thought when Sarah hesitated there may have been a chance she was going to say yes. Although he felt disappointed, he wasn't surprised by her answer. He looked away from her for a moment to gather himself.

"Well," he started, looking back down at her, disappointment visible on his face. "I guess I'll just have to ask you again next year." He put his hat on his head, walked over to his horse and shoved his mug into his saddlebag. He put his foot in the stirrup and swung his leg over the saddle. Thomas moved away from the horses and went back to where Sarah was standing as Foley tipped his hat and rode off.

Foley rode away feeling sorry for himself, he loved Sarah a whole lot more than she knew. But he wasn't a man who would dwell on her refusal either. He was going to head straight to the saloon and get drunk, then he would go see Maria, a woman he began seeing last year. After Sarah turned him down and went back to the mountain last spring, he felt he couldn't wait forever for her to say yes, he had feelings he needed taking care of and Maria, everyone believed, was a nice woman. She was a hard worker, working around the county doing housework for families that couldn't manage on their own. Maria didn't mind when Foley had more than his fill of whiskey under his belt when he visited her.

"Why does he keep asking you to marry him Ma?" Thomas watched Foley ride away. "I don't know Thomas." Sarah kept her eyes on Foley as he got further away from them. She had a pretty good idea why Foley kept asking her to marry him. She thought he must be in love with her. He told her once before he loved her when he first proposed but she hadn't believed him. He has never said those three words to her again, but he keeps on proposing.

Of all the men she had proposals from over the years since her Pa and Frank died, Foley was the most persistent, and of all the men she knew, she liked Foley the best. Sarah questioned her own feelings toward him, feeling there was a definite spark between them. Sometimes she wondered if she could love Foley enough to marry him, once even imagining being married to him. She also imagined they would live in Cedar Creek. There was no way she would ask him to go to the mountain to live with her in her cabin like Frank had done, and there was no man she would leave the mountain for to live in Cedar Creek.

For that reason, she brushed the idea of being married to Foley off. She felt she couldn't commit herself to marriage, not to Samuels, not to Foley, not to anyone ...not yet!

Epilogue

This winter after Thomas turned twelve, proved to be a turning point in Sarah's life. This year Sarah and Thomas crossed the wooden bridge and rode into town on their own. Her horse Star, was getting on in years, but was still pushing along at a steady pace. Sarah held on tight to the reins of her packhorse that carried her load of skins. Thomas was a fair distance back, leading the second packhorse carrying all of their belongings that would get them through the bleak winter camped on the riverbank.

Spending yet another winter in Cedar Creek wasn't going to be nearly as bad as being stuck on the mountain, cut off from civilization by deep drifts of snow. No-one, not even a wolf would get through the pass once it was blocked completely. There was a time when two men got caught out after heavy snow blanketed the mountain. When Sarah's father, Calahan and his friend Joseph Beauford Jones first came to the mountain to trap wolves, they didn't know of any other way off the mountain except through the pass. The two men were forced to sit winter out, barely able to survive the icy blasts coming off the snow. As soon as winter passed, they built their cabins, but they didn't hang about the following winter, making sure they were off the mountain when the first snow began to fall. The two men never took things for granted after that first year. Sarah and Thomas never took things for granted on the mountain either. They always left the mountain well before the snow got too deep.

This winter however, they had good reason not to leave straight away. Sarah knew the mountain better than most what it could do to them. Sarah was aware they could both perish locked up inside their cabin if they stayed too long. Not being able to get outside to trap or hunt, their food would eventually run out, leaving them to starve or freeze to death. But still, she waited until the very last moment before the pass was completely blocked to take Thomas and head for town.

Sarah reckoned the trappers would have left the mountain already. None of the men would ever contemplate venturing back to the mountain, not until the snow melted sufficiently, allowing them easy passage back through the pass.

Sarah was right, Joe and the other trappers had left. Making the journey more than two weeks before her and Thomas. The ground was only lightly covered with a dusting of snow when the men made their way through the pass. Sarah didn't think it necessary to leave as soon as snow started to fall. She and Thomas could still get around easily, but Joe was getting old and didn't believe in taking chances. Sarah was pleased they stayed that extra two weeks. It paid off with two beautiful white skins that were going to fetch them good money from the Fur Trading Company.

The young female wolf was by herself at first, then a few days later the male turned up. Their skins were pure white and their eyes the palest blue. Sarah had been watching the two wolves for several days. The female was in her sights the very first day she saw her.

After being out hunting and having killed and skinned four grey wolves, Sarah and Thomas were on their way back to their cabin. Two nights, she kept Thomas away from the cabin and the nights had begun to grow colder. It was on their way back she spotted the young female wolf. She was magnificent, her fur was thick and in excellent condition.

Sarah lay on the cold snow-covered ground holding her rifle steady with the wolf lined up in her sights. Thomas lay beside her, both as still as they could be, neither daring to breathe and neither of them speaking a word as they watched the wolf. Sarah was ready to pull the trigger when the wolf suddenly turned her head and looked in her direction, making Sarah hesitate.

Having hesitated once before a long time ago, something told her to wait. It had been before Thomas was born and her hesitation almost cost her, her life. The day she accidently shot herself while hunting a grey wolf was always in the back of her mind. Badly wounded from her own rifle, she and the wolf faced each other on a ridge above the river. When the wolf charged, she plunged her knife into its belly before both of them plummeted off the ridge and into the icy river flowing across the River Flats where Frank had his camp. She would have drowned only for Frank seeing her fall and pulling her out of the river. Sarah vowed then never to hesitate again, but what she was faced with here now was different to back then.

The wolf walked off behind the trees and Sarah lost sight of her. Knowing the value of the white skin, Thomas jumped up and yelled that she was getting away. He hated having to kill the beautiful wolves but they meant money and that meant food on their table. Sarah stood up and let the wolf go. Thomas felt disappointed they hadn't got the wolf that day.

Sarah and Thomas walked along a well-worn trail through dense forest and headed back to their cabin. The trail being one of a dozen that were easy to follow after the many treks they had taken to go out hunting.

They weren't far from home when Sarah spotted the female wolf again. The wolf tracked them almost all the way back to their cabin. Sarah lifted her rifle off her shoulder and took aim. This time she was determined she would shoot her.

Sarah's aim was good, the wolf stood stock still, listening, waiting. Did it sense what Sarah was about to do? Sarah hesitated again and took her finger off the trigger. She could see the female had company, a male wolf, her mate, had shown up.

The male was as white as the female, his fur looked just as thick as hers. Sarah reckoned he was worth as much as the female if not more. If Sarah fired at the female now, she would scare off the male and she could lose them both. All Sarah had to do was trap the pair of them and her and Thomas could leave the mountain.

Sarah set six traps around in an arc a short distance from their cabin. She tied bright red rope around the trees so she knew where her traps were. Once the snow got heavier, the snow would cover the traps in a matter of minutes and she would have to dig the traps out. Sarah couldn't risk having Thomas or herself stepping into one of them.

It was one of those days Sarah and Thomas were away from their cabin checking their traps, that the four trappers passed by her cabin. Joe Jones, Brent Garrett, Will Sloan and James Fergus all stopped to let Sarah know they were leaving for Cedar Creek.

The snow was heaviest up at the High Ridge Camp so most of the trappers moved to lower hunting grounds. Some going to the River Flats, while others ventured as far south as the South Side Camp. Since Sarah ventured there to kill a wolf to take back to Cedar Creek to scare the town folk into giving Thomas back, the South Side Camp once again has come into its own as a good place for hunting.

Joe's group of four, along with a few other trappers were always the first to leave the mountain. When word got around that Joe had gone, it was the signal for other trappers to prepare to leave.

When Joe got to the cabin he called out to Sarah, but when he got no answer he went inside. Sarah's fire was still smouldering, almost out of wood. Joe knew both Sarah and Thomas would be together and weren't far away, so he built the fire up with more wood and put the grate in front to stop any wood or ash falling onto the floor. Then he closed the front door and he and the other trappers headed for their first stop at the caves. From there they headed down the trail and rode another two days toward Cedar Creek.

Sarah and Thomas came back to their cabin that evening and found it nice and warm. Sarah knew Joe had been and that he had left the mountain. He would have tried to talk her into leaving then too but she still had traps set. She had two wolves she wanted to catch. Sarah wouldn't leave and Joe would be angry. She was glad she and Thomas hadn't been there when the men came past.

Every day over the next two weeks, Sarah and Thomas went out to check her traps and each day found the traps empty. Sarah dug around in the snow with a stick, setting the traps off each time, then reset them.

The trappers had been gone quite a while when Sarah and Thomas went out for the last time. Snow banked up around the cabin making it difficult to get in and out. Thomas struggled more than Sarah when they walked through the snow. Sarah told Thomas if they didn't have anything in their traps this day they would pack up and leave the mountain.

Sarah was thankful when they came upon the first trap and found the red rope marker was still visible tied around the tree. Sarah poked about in the snow underneath the marker with a long stick until the stick hit the trap setting it off. The stick snapped in two and Sarah silently cursed it. She took the trap and slung it over her shoulder and moved on to the next, only to find the second and third traps were the same as the first.

When they came upon the fourth trap the red marker was still intact just like the others but the mound of snow seemed different, it looked much deeper around the base of the tree. Sarah poked around with a long thin tree branch until it hit something, but it wasn't the trap. Whatever was under the snow was soft, and big. She started digging with the branch when the male wolf leapt out of the snow snapping its jaws and growling savagely making Sarah jump back in fright. The only thing holding the wolf back from attacking Sarah was the trap gripping the wolf firmly by its hind leg. Sarah crawled backwards on her hands and feet until she was out of its reach.

Thomas grabbed Sarah under the arms and dragged her back further. Sarah watched the wolf as it growled and bared its sharp teeth. The vicious snapping continued until Sarah picked up her rifle and standing just out of its reach, shot the wolf in the head.

That was her first white skin. After skinning the wolf Sarah and Thomas moved on to the next trap, finding it empty just like the first three. After setting them all off and gathering them up, she told Thomas if they didn't have anything in the last trap it didn't matter, they had one good skin to take down to the Trading Post this year. One white skin would make up for all the grey skins they had collected since last winter.

Sarah's last trap proved to be the best. The white female wolf was caught by her front leg. She was whimpering for her mate when they came upon her. Sarah's bullet ended her life as it had her mates. Sarah and Thomas could now leave the mountain.

The journey down the mountain to Cedar Creek took them four days. They had to get through the pass first to get to the caves and they needed to get there well before nightfall on the first day or be caught out in the dark in the freezing snow. It was tough going, the snow was deeper than Sarah first thought it would be. She had to get off her horse and lead the way on foot, watching for the markers Joe left for others to follow.

Every year the trappers lagging behind relied on markers Joe left in the trees. No trapper ever became lost while traversing the pass off the mountain thanks to Joe's markers. Sarah carefully picked out the snow-covered markers as she went and was thankful for Joe having the foresight to place them along the trail. The blizzard howled through the pass making the trip all the more difficult. Freezing wind swirled around Sarah making it difficult for her to see. Thomas stayed on his horse and could just make out Sarah's horses ahead of him.

The trek out took them much longer than Sarah anticipated. Star kept getting bogged down in the snow and the snow was over Sarah's knees making her push herself harder. Thomas pushed his horse and his packhorse along, keeping both horses in Sarah's tracks.

They made it through the pass to the caves just as night began to fall. Grateful the caves were large enough to allow them to take their horses inside out of the cold, they quickly tethered their horses to a makeshift hitching rail and left them packed.

There was plenty of firewood stored in the caves, the trappers having stocked them well before winter for the purpose of leaving the mountain. There were blankets, and pots and pans for cooking, and cans of food stored for anyone who came out late, it proved a godsend for Sarah and Thomas. Sarah was exhausted after trudging through the snow and didn't feel like unpacking their belongings just for one night. Thomas opened a can of food and heated it up in one of the pots. They wrapped themselves in blankets and sat in front of a blazing fire to eat. Sarah warmed herself with a mug of coffee as well. It didn't take long before an exhausted Sarah and Thomas fell asleep.

They set off at daybreak the next day stopping only for short breaks before getting to the bottom of the mountain trail. Their next camp would be at the wells. The two deep wells were sheltered on either side by tall stands of trees and there were grassed areas that made good places to camp. Sarah would be relieved when they arrived at the wells, it was a sign the worst part of their trek was over.

Sarah and Thomas only just got on the trail at the bottom of the mountain when she spotted two grey wolves following them. She told Thomas to get his rifle ready and pulled her shotgun out of its holster. Sarah anticipated this sort of thing would happen, she was used to wolves coming down the mountain before the snow became too deep and the pass was blocked. She yelled at Thomas to pick up his pace and keep up with her as he was starting to lag behind. Sarah quickly tied the lead from her packhorse to her saddle-horn, stretching the rope between her horse and the packhorse, then yelled at Thomas to do the same with his. Thomas, heeding his mother's advice, set up his two horses in the same manner, allowing his hands to be free to use his gun.

The wolves came on them fast, running along on either side of their horses. Thomas yelled there were two more coming behind him. Sarah looked over her shoulder at the wolves as they urged their horses on. When Sarah had a wolf run in close to Star, she fired off a shot. The bullet struck the wolf in the side above its front leg, causing the wolf to stumble before it staggered away and dropped dead.

Thomas fired his rifle. Sarah heard the shot and looked back to see a wolf trying to nip Thomas's horse on its hind leg. His horse kicked out its back legs and bucked as it tried to fend off the wolf. Thomas hung on tight to his reins and couldn't get off another shot. Sarah tried to shoot but didn't have a clear shot either. She didn't want to hit Thomas's horse, that would put both of them in danger.

The wolf suddenly swung out, running away from behind Thomas's horse. Thomas turned and fired again. His bullet struck the wolf in the head and it rolled head first in the snow until it came to a stop.

The other two wolves slowed, Sarah looked back and watched as the wolves stopped at the dead or now dying wolves. Sarah and Thomas kept their horses galloping away from the wolves and the mountain, not slowing down for quite a time, putting as much distance between them and the wolves as they could.

When they finally stopped, they hopped down from their horses and walked around to stretch their legs and catch their breath. They hugged each other and laughed at how lucky they had been.

Sarah congratulated Thomas on his kill. Even though he never liked that he had to kill the wolves, he was relieved he and his Ma got away safely. Sarah wasn't worried about getting these skins, they had to keep moving to make their next camp. She reloaded her rifle and after a short break, they set off again, leaving the snow and the wolves behind. The next leg of their journey took them until nightfall to make it to the wells.

A huge bonfire blazed that night, Sarah knew wolves could travel great distances and could just about catch up with them if they wanted to. She could hear the sound of wolves howling far off in the distance and didn't sleep at all, preferring to keep watch while Thomas slept. They still had one more night's camp out on the open prairie to go, but Sarah wasn't worried, the land was open and she would keep watch. Although her eyesight at night wasn't nearly as sharp as she liked, she could spot any animals moving about close to their camp. By late afternoon the next day they would be in Cedar Creek.

As Sarah neared the bridge into Cedar Creek, she saw a board nailed to a post. It had red lettering on it, but she couldn't make out what it meant. When she got close to the board she frowned and slowed her horse down to a walk, then moved slowly across the bridge into town.

Thomas caught up to her and was now right behind Sarah's packhorse. As they passed the corral's, Sarah glanced over at the cemetery. She was deep in thought as she turned her horses past the church and the schoolhouse. Her Pa was buried in the cemetery and she would have to visit him sometime while she was in town. She would pick foliage from the forest growing along the riverbank and place it on her father's grave, something she did every year since his death. Even though a full-grown woman, she still missed her Pa. She missed Frank too, but he was buried somewhere up in the High Country on top of the mountain and she had never been up there to visit his grave, it was far too dangerous. A person was at the mercy of wolf packs in the High Country. Frank had learnt that lesson with his life. A person would be a fool to venture up there.

Their horses were almost in the main street. Their plan was to head straight to the Trading Post so they could get their skins unloaded and get paid. Sarah was thinking about the money they would get for her skins when they approached the bend not far from the Livery and Stables. They would need the money for supplies and Thomas would get new clothes to wear to school, he was growing at a fast rate and his pants didn't cover his boots anymore, his shirts weren't much better, they were threadbare and the sleeves were getting short.

They just turned the corner near Ham's Livery when a bell suddenly started to peal, it was loud and shattered the silence. Star became frightened, the packhorses shied too, they bucked wildly and tried to get away. Thomas was having trouble holding his horse steady, his packhorse tried to make a break for it. Sarah looked back at him and yelled. "*Let it go Thomas ...let go of the goddamn horse!*" She let go of her packhorse and seeing her, Thomas let go of his. Finding themselves free, the two horses bolted down the street.

As the bell continued to ring, Sarah held on to Star with one hand and grabbed her rifle with the other. She suddenly let the reins go, swung her leg over her saddle-horn and slid to the ground, landing on both feet. Star bolted down the street and raced along behind the two packhorses.

Sarah stormed towards the school house, her rifle held up in her hands. She aimed her rifle at the bell-ringer, wanting to put a bullet in him for scaring her horses, then changed her mind and aimed it at the bell. The bell kept swinging as the bell-ringer kept pulling on the rope. Sarah took aim at the rope and fired. The rope shattered where it joined the top of the bell, slithered to the ground and coiled around the feet of the bell-ringer, that was when she aimed her rifle at him.

Sarah stood in the middle of the street and cursed him. "*Don't you move, you slimy maggot!*" She yelled at the top of her lungs. "*You almost killed me and Thomas with that god-awful noise, what the hell did you want to ring that goddamn bell for anyhow, scared my horse's half to death, I should put a bullet through your goddamn empty head!*" She stared at the man holding on tight to the end of the bell-rope. Sarah never laid eyes on him before, he hadn't been in town when she left last spring.

Sarah's hat was pulled down over her eyes, shading her face from the afternoon sun. Jonathon O'Rourke, the new school teacher and bell-ringer, looked horrified when he couldn't see Sarah's face. Sarah wore an oversized fur coat that hid her body and the rifle she held, making her a frightening sight. O'Rourke had been present when all the trappers rode in from the mountain and most of them made him feel afraid for his family, but right now with this wild looking trapper standing in front of him and pointing a double barrel shotgun at him, he almost fainted dead away. O'Rourke had never been confronted by anyone like this before, he was scared he was going to be shot, right then he wished he never brought his family to Cedar Creek and he froze where he stood.

Sarah could hear town folk starting to gather around, but she didn't move, she kept her gun aimed squarely at the stranger holding the rope. She also heard the noise of a gun being cocked and felt the muzzle slide in under her hat, coming close to her ear. She thought right then it best not to move.

A man's deep voice ordered her to put down her gun. It wasn't a voice she was familiar with, she knew Sheriff Clementine's voice, Sarah knew it wasn't him. She grew up with Clem being Sheriff. He locked her in the jailhouse more than once after she shot up the town, scaring the town folk with her cursing and threats to kill them if they didn't return Thomas. He was always threatening he would lock her up for arguing with Crawley when she went to his store for supplies. Sarah knew Sheriff Clem well, so who did this man think he was telling her to put down her gun?

She told the man in no uncertain words she wasn't about to let this bell ringing mangy Coyote get away with scaring her horses, and she scared the bell-ringer even more when she threatened him by saying she was going to send him off to Mexico after them. Sarah thought she sounded kind of funny saying she would send him to Mexico. Everyone knew Mexico was a hell of a long way from Cedar Creek.

When some of the trappers began to call out to her, letting her know her horses were down at the Trading Post, Sarah knew the voices of each trapper without having to lift her gaze from the bell-ringer.

After one of the men said her horses knew where they were going, she almost laughed out loud, because her horses did know where they were going, she trained them to follow her and they had been to the Trading Post enough times to know the way. Loud guffaws could be heard coming from the crowd.

Sarah cursed the men for laughing from under her hat and told them to go get her horses heads out of the trough before they keeled over with guts ache. She knew horses shouldn't fill their bellies with too much water after a hot run, they could keel over and die.

She didn't have to look around at the next voice that called out to her either, she recognized Joe straight away as the person who spoke.

He told her, her horses had been caught and that Will tied them to the hitching rail outside the Trading Post and that they were doing just fine. Sarah knew her horses were in good hands with Will looking after them, she just hoped he had the good sense not to try to unload any of her skins, if he did, that would mean she couldn't take part in The Pot.

Joe was angry with her for taking too long to get off the mountain, he cursed her and she cursed right back at him, ignoring the man holding a gun on her.

Sarah reckoned Joe was just trying to find out the reason why she had taken so long to leave and she wasn't about to tell him. She wanted to see the look on all their faces when they saw her two white skins.

Sarah told Joe she had things to take care of and left it at that, she was well aware Joe didn't take chances anymore. Joe reckoned she cut leaving the mountain a bit too fine, and Sarah knew she had. He also reckoned the pass was already blocked when he left, and Sarah admitted to herself it was close to being blocked, and she did struggle to bring Thomas out safely. She vowed she would never wait so long to come off the mountain again, but she wouldn't let Joe know that either. She could tell he was angry, he was always angry with her these days. What happened next took Sarah completely by surprise.

The man holding the gun near her ear grabbed her rifle by the barrel, right in front of the stock. He pulled her rifle upwards while she still had her finger on the trigger causing her to squeeze it, making the rifle go off. Sarah heard the crowd yelling and screaming as they ducked for cover. She didn't know where the bullet went, it seemed to go up in the air, but the man pulled the rifle back towards him and she went with it.

When she slammed into the man's body, she let the rifle go and her arms went around him and her chest pressed against his. She got a quick glimpse of what looked like a badge pinned to his shirt. Her pelvis hit him in his lower body and her pistol dug into her. This being the reason she always carried her gun sideways in her trousers, so it didn't dig into her when she was walking or riding. She was sure her gun dug into the man's groin too. The man was strong, managing to stay upright as she bounced off him. But Sarah wasn't going down without trying to defend herself. She reached into her coat as she started to fall backwards.

It was Garrett and Will who taught her if she ever got in a fight and was knocked to the ground to get her knife out of its sheath before she hit the ground. "Count to five Sarah," Garrett said and he and Will demonstrated how it was done. Will pushed Garrett over and as he fell, he counted. By the time Garrett got to five he had his knife in his hand. Will taught her to count rabbits on her fingers and she practiced until she could count to ten without using her fingers.

Now as Sarah fell, she counted to five in her head. She reached inside her coat and grabbed her knife, pulling it clear of its sheath. That was what she did when she bounced off the man and started to fall.

One... she put her hand inside her coat.

Two... she reached for the knife.

Three... her hand was on the handle.

Four... the knife was out of its sheath.

Five... she hit the dirt with her knife held firmly in her hand.

Her body hit the ground with a thud and her hat fell off and rolled away. As her head went back, she felt her long braid land in the dirt. Her arms went wide and her legs spread out. She looked up at the man just as he stepped on her arm pinning it down with his foot, then in a booming voice demanded she drop her knife.

Sarah wouldn't let go of her knife, not until she felt the man press his foot firmly down on her arm, then she let it go. When the knife lay on the ground near her hand, she looked up at the man standing over her, but the sun was behind him and she couldn't get a good look at his face. All Sarah could see was the muzzle of his gun pointing straight at her nose. When she dropped her knife the man relaxed, un-cocked his gun and lifted his foot off her arm. That was her cue.

She twisted her body in her fur coat and brought her legs around behind the ankle of the man's left foot. His right foot was already in the air and when he took his weight off her arm, she swept her legs through and knocked his legs out from under him. The man had no chance of staying upright. When he hit the ground hard on his back his legs spread out, his gun hand went out away from his body.

Will and Fergus taught her how to get the better of someone when she was on the ground. "Listen and watch, and if the person who is attacking you loses concentration, that's when you move," Will informed her. Fergus knocked Will to the ground then moved up and stood alongside of Will's body so his legs were near Will's arm.

Garrett, watching all the proceedings while resting under a tree alongside Joe, yelled out unexpectedly. "Hey Fergus!" Fergus looked over at Garrett, making him lose concentration for a split second. Will brought his legs around fast behind Fergus's legs, twisting his body to the side, carrying on through with his legs and knocking Fergus right off his feet. Fergus went up in the air and landed on his back with a thump. "Goddamn son-of-a-bitch!" Fergus cursed. Sarah burst out laughing when she saw Fergus hit the ground. "Now you try Sarah," Will said. Sarah stopped laughing "I can't, you are too big." She grew serious when Joe suggested she try it. "No-one is too big, not if you take them by surprise ...have a go Sarah." Joe watched patiently as Will and Fergus taught her a few tricks that might help her if she ever needed to protect herself. Sarah tried knocking Will over. At first, she didn't have the strength in her legs but gradually with practice she got Will on his back. That first day she had bruises all up and down her shins, but they kept her practicing until she could knock each of them off their feet without hurting her legs.

Sarah saw the man's gun wasn't cocked, and that gave her more time. She grabbed her knife and scurrying up onto her knees, crawled along his body between his legs. She was poised over him, her thick coat draped over his legs and her knife blade pointed at his face. But the man was quick, he cocked his gun and brought it around in front of her nose almost before she had time to lean forward over his chest. Sarah looked right into his face as he threatened to shoot her, giving her a chance to size the man up. What she could see in the bright afternoon sunlight, told her he was quite handsome, his eyes appeared to be dark blue like hers and she looked straight into them. His nose was straight, his mouth and jaw looked firm, Sarah already knew he had a hard body.

When he told her to drop her knife, Sarah didn't put her knife on the ground, instead she put her knife back in its sheath then held her hands up to show him the knife was gone. Holding his gun on her, he told her to get up. Sarah backed out from between his legs and picked up her hat. While he was getting up, she took her time belting her hat against her leg to get the dust off it, her braid was dusty too, but she pulled her hat back onto her head, leaving it pushed back a little so she could see the man better. Sarah's ears pricked when she heard what one of the trappers sang out to the man. "Hey Sheriff! I think Cole may have won that round!" There was a lot of laughing and Sarah smiled too. Now she knew there was a new Sheriff in Cedar Creek and that was why this man was the one trying to take control of the situation and not Sheriff Clem. This man clearly wore a badge, but she couldn't read what was on the badge so hadn't known he was Sheriff. She asked him where Clem was and he told her Clem was still in Cedar Creek, but he didn't elaborate on much more than that.

The new Sheriff turned his face to the crowd, giving Sarah a chance to study him while he was busy telling them to go about their business to notice her looking at him. Sarah knew some of them wouldn't go. The four trappers would hang about to see what was going to happen next.

Sarah moved her eyes over the Sheriff from head to foot and back again, making her eyes travel slowly over his body so she could see all of him. The Sheriff wasn't much taller than her, the top of her head coming up about as far as his chin. His hair was light brown and neatly cut, he looked strong and his shoulders were broad. His arms were muscled and strained against his sleeves. Sarah already knew his chest was hard from bumping into him. She noticed too how he wore his gun low and how the holster rested against his thigh. The thin leather cord holding the holster to his leg, he had tied just above his knee. She knew wearing his gun low would make him fast on the draw.

Sheriff Christian Morgan was standing on the boardwalk outside the Sheriff's Office when three horses went galloping past him. He heard the gunshot that took the bell-rope off the bell. He stepped off the boardwalk into the street and hurried to the schoolhouse where he could see a crowd had gathered. Pushing his way through the crowd, he pulled his gun from its holster. Stepping up to stand beside the raggedy hat and fur coat wearing trapper aiming a rifle at Jonathon O'Rourke, he demanded the trapper give him the rifle. What happened next left Christian stunned.

When the trapper refused to give him the rifle, he made a grab for it, only to have the trapper crash into him, then fall flat on its backside at his feet. Looking down, his heart skipped a beat. In all his days chasing outlaws around the country, he never came across the likes of who was laying sprawled on the ground in front of him. His heart thumped wildly in his chest when he caught Sarah looking up at him.

He was even more shocked at getting knocked off his feet, and ending up laying on his back with Sarah hovering between his legs. Gathering himself and getting to his feet, he turned to face her.

Sarah got herself up off the ground, and looking into his eyes, felt her heartbeat quicken. After studying each other, they both decided, right then, they liked what they were looking at...

...To be continued

Sarah and Christian's story continues in Book Two - Cedar Creek

Part Two of the Trappers Promise

About the Author – Bronwyn Trotter

Being a new author, my inspiration for writing comes from a lifetime of growing up in a family that enjoyed western movies and reading a variety of novels. My father especially loved westerns and whenever I and my three brothers visited, I could guarantee dad would be watching a western or reading a western novel. I loved to sit and watch them with him, enjoying the posse chasing the baddies, the hero saving the little ranchers from the big. Forget about superheroes, modern romance stories, robots fighting robots or fighting monsters. Don't get me wrong, I like those stories (and movies) and I love to read a variety of different genres - Dan Brown, Jeffrey Archer, Jack Higgins, John Grisham, Markus Zusak, Stephen King, Nora Roberts, Di Morrisey, J R R Tolkien to name a few. As you can see, they are varied but not westerns. My collection of books is extensive, consisting of the above authors and others. My writing is new, The Trappers Promise is my first attempt at telling a story. My writing stems from my own personal memories and love of a good western. When I sat down to write, my story just came to me, so I put pen to paper, yes literally. After filling an exercise book with what I wanted to say I decided using a computer was much easier. My brain just ticked over with recollection after recollection of those days watching movies and dad getting to the exciting part in a western book. (I could always tell when the action started, dad had a way of making a noise with his teeth that sounded like a horse galloping and when it was really galloping the noise got faster. We children laughed because we knew the posse was on the chase).